Few scholars match Stephen Krasner in incisive analysis of central issues of world politics. These essays make strong arguments without following any party line, and even those who have read them before will benefit from seeing how they fit together.

Robert Jervis, Adlai E. Stevenson Professor of
International Affairs, Columbia University

Stephen Krasner is one of the most widely acclaimed scholars of international relations of the past century. This collection features in a single volume his most important and enduring works, along with an integrative introductory essay and a conclusion that reflects on his time in government service. *Power, the State, and Sovereignty* is a "must have" book for any serious student of international politics.

David Lake, Professor of Political Science,
University of California, San Diego

Krasner has been for several decades a leading theorist of international relations, and was so long before he joined the Bush administration. Whether one agrees with him or not, he is always worth reading and arguing with!!

Peter Gourevitch, Professor of Political Science,
University of California, San Diego

Power, the State, and Sovereignty

Stephen D. Krasner has been one of the most influential theorists within international relations and international political economy over the past few decades. *Power, the State, and Sovereignty* is a collection of his key scholarly works. The book includes both a framing introduction written for this volume, and a concluding essay examining the relationship between academic research and the actual making of foreign policy.

Drawing on both his extensive academic work and his experiences during his recent role within the Bush administration (as Director for Policy Planning at the US State Department) Krasner has revised and updated all of the essays in the collection to provide a coherent discussion of the importance of power, ideas, and domestic structures in world politics.

Progressing through a carefully structured evaluation of US domestic politics and foreign policy, international politics and finally sovereignty, this volume is essential reading for all serious scholars of international politics.

Stephen D. Krasner is the Graham H. Stuart Professor of International Relations at Stanford and a Senior Fellow at the Freeman Spogli Institute and the Hoover Institution. He has served as Director of Policy Planning at the US State Department and on the National Security Council staff. He has written on US foreign policy, north–south relations and sovereignty and is a Fellow of the American Academy of Arts and Sciences.

Power, the State, and Sovereignty

Essays on international relations

Stephen D. Krasner

Routledge
Taylor & Francis Group

LONDON AND NEW YORK

First published 2009
by Routledge
2 Park Square, Milton Park, Abingdon, Oxon OX14 4RN

Simultaneously published in the USA and Canada
by Routledge
711 Third Avenue, New York, NY 10017

Routledge is an imprint of the Taylor & Francis Group, an informa business

© 2009 Stephen D. Krasner.

Typeset in Times New Roman
by Taylor & Francis Books

British Library Cataloguing in Publication Data
A catalogue record for this book is available from the British Library

Library of Congress Cataloging in Publication Data
Krasner, Stephen D., 1942–
   Power, the state and sovereignty : essays on international relations /
Stephen D. Krasner.
     p. cm.
   1. United States–Foreign policy. 2. Hegemony–United States. 3.
International relations. I. Title.
   JZ1480.K725 2009
   327–dc22

                                             2008035319

ISBN13: 978-0-415-77482-6 (hbk)
ISBN13: 978-0-415-77483-3 (pbk)
ISBN13: 978-0-203-88213-9 (ebk)

For Patricia with love

Contents

List of illustrations   xi
Preface and acknowledgements   xii

Introduction: actors and institutions in the study of
international politics   1

PART I
Domestic politics and foreign policy   23

1   Defending the national interest   25

2   US commercial and monetary policy: unraveling the paradox
    of external strength and internal weakness   36

3   Approaches to the state: alternative conceptions and
    historical dynamics   66

4   Sovereignty: an institutional perspective   89

PART II
International politics   111

5   Structural causes and regime consequences: regimes as
    intervening variables   113

6   State power and the structure of international trade   129

7   Global communications and national power: life on the
    Pareto frontier   151

PART III
Sovereignty   177

8   Sovereignty and its discontents   179

9   Organized hypocrisy in nineteenth-century East Asia   211

10 Sharing sovereignty: new institutions for collapsed and
    failing states   232

    Conclusion: garbage cans and policy streams: how academic
    research might affect foreign policy   254

    Bibliography   275
    Index   297

Illustrations

Tables

2.1	Some indicators of United States potential external power	41
2.2	Executive departments involved in international economic policy	47
2.3	US sectoral trade balances	49
2.4	US foreign direct investment	51
2.5	Foreign activities of US banks	51
4.1	Dimensions of institutionalization	98
4.2	Consequences of increasing returns	105
6.1	Probability of an open trading structure with different distributions of potential economic power	134
6.2	Regional trading patterns	140
6.3	Indicators of British potential power	142
6.4	Indicators of US potential power	143

Figures

0.1	Three realms of international relations: foreign policy, international politics, state-building	22
5.1	Regimes as intervening variables	116
5.2	Regimes as causal variables	117
5.3	Regimes as autonomous variables	118
6.1	Ratio of trade to aggregate economic activity, nineteenth century to 1960, at current prices	137
6.2	Ratio of trade to gross domestic product 1950–1972, at current prices	138
7.1	Simple coordination problem	153
7.2	Battle of the Sexes	154
7.3	Battle of the Sexes with tactical linkage	155

Preface and acknowledgements

It was very flattering to be asked to put together a collection of my essays. The timing was propitious. I had just served two years in Washington and I thought that my return to Stanford would give me time to reflect. This positive glow lasted until I actually started to reflect. What to make of more than thirty years of work? Would it all actually hang together in any coherent way? Would I, like Molière's M. Jourdain, discover that I had been speaking prose my whole life, or would I find a jumble of unrelated themes and ideas? Would I have to appeal to Ralph Waldo Emerson's observation that a "foolish consistency is the hobgoblin of little minds, adored by little statesmen and philosophers and divines," a statement that never made much sense to me?

Although nothing that I have written about international politics has ignored the importance of power, much of my work has also been attentive to the importance of ideas, particularly the role that Lockean liberal values have played in American foreign policy, and to institutions, especially domestic structures, international regimes and sovereignty. My initial work dealt primarily with issues associated with international political economy, a field that did not exist when I began my academic career. In the 1970s and 1980s I wrote about American raw materials policy, international trade, and relations between industrializing and developing countries. More recently I have focused on sovereignty, how it should be understood and how it has actually functioned.

The analytic frameworks deployed by political scientists have also changed dramatically over the last thirty years. Economistic thinking, most notably the idea of self-enforcing institutions as a key to understanding politics, has become much more prominent. Sociological analyses of decoupling between logics of appropriateness and logics of consequences have influenced much of my recent work. I have had the very good fortune to be at institutions where some of these key ideas were developed and expanded, and my own thinking has changed over time as a result of these influences.

I have organized this volume into three sections. The first deals with domestic structure and foreign policy. Within polities, at least reasonably well-developed polities, institutionalization matters. Structures are deeply embedded. Values motivate political leaders and organize their supporters.

Legal provisions define the authorities of public officials. These values and institutions vary across countries. The world is not composed of billiard balls differentiated only by their volume; different states with different historical trajectories and different institutions act in different ways even if their relative capacities are more or less the same. Traditional realism provides a more accurate description of international relations than neo-realism, but offers a less compelling analytic framework.

The second section on international politics discusses outcomes in the international system. Here, power dominates. Institutions reflect the preferences of the strong. If power or interests change, institutions will change as well. Institutions can be consequential, they can move states closer to their most preferred outcomes, but institutionalization is weak.

The final section deals with sovereignty, for almost all international relations scholars the master variable of the international system. For realists and liberal institutionalists, sovereign statehood is taken for granted. States are the actors in the international system. For constructivists states are constituted by international society. When I began thinking about sovereignty in the late 1980s I approached the topic as barefoot empiricist. What I discovered was that there were clear rules and norms associated with sovereignty but that these rules and norms were often violated. This was not a finding that sat well with conventional analytic frameworks. Most rationalist approaches would predict that if rules were violated they would change. Most sociological approaches would predict that if rules and norms were violated they would wither away. But the rules of sovereignty persisted even though they were violated. My colleague John Meyer rescued me from the intellectual morass in which I was sinking by pointing me to the idea of organized hypocrisy. In the international system, which is characterized by power asymmetries, complexity, and the absence of any final authority, rules are necessary but they will not always be honored. For instance, in most situations political leaders in powerful states can pursue their interests most effectively by trying to change the foreign policies of their counterparts in weaker states, but in some situations it may be more attractive to try to change their domestic authority structures. Inevitably one of the core norms of sovereignty, non-interference in the internal affairs of other states, will be recognized but violated. Even states with relatively equal power may compromise their own autonomy because sovereignty norms are trumped by other material interests and normative conceptualizations. German political leaders, for instance, embraced the semi-sovereign status of their country after the Second World War. To understand sovereignty it was necessary to pay attention to ideas, institutions and power. I have elaborated on the distinctions between these three different spheres—domestic structures and foreign policy, international politics, and sovereignty—in the introductory essay for this volume.

The concluding essay, written for this volume, attempts to make sense of the relationship between academic research and the actual making of foreign policy. Between 2001 and 2007, I spent three and a half years in the State

Department, first as a staff member and then as the Director of the Policy Planning Bureau, and at the National Security Council. Making policy, or at least suggesting what policy might be, poses very different challenges than writing about it. Policy makers must look to the future with imperfect information. Academics write about past events where they can find good information. OOB and COB, opening of business and close of business, define deadlines in the policy world which are often hours or at best a week or two away. And missing a deadline means missing the boat. In academia deadlines are often fluid and if you miss one boat another usually comes along. Academics are paid to think and reflect; they have lots of choice about how they will use their time. Policy makers, especially those in cabinet and sub-cabinet positions, have to make decisions about problems that are exogenously generated; they have very limited discretionary time. Even if more academic work were policy oriented, research findings would not flow smoothly into the policy world. The relationship between academia and policy is best conceptualized by garbage can or policy streams models of decision making which emphasize chance and the differing incentives of players in the policy game.

The essays in this volume have been slightly revised from the original either to bring them up to date or because my thinking changed over the years. Essay 1 is a revised version of the concluding chapter of *Defending the National Interest* (Princeton: Princeton University Press, 1978), reprinted with permission. Essay 2, "US Commercial and Monetary Policy," first appeared in *International Organization* 31 (1977), © Cambridge University Press, reprinted with permission. Essay 3, "Approaches to the State," was published in *Comparative Politics* 16 (1984), reprinted with permission. Essay 4, "Sovereignty: An Institutional Perspective," first appeared in *Comparative Political Studies* 21 (1988), reprinted with permission. Essay 5, "Structural Causes and Regime Consequences," was the introduction to the special issue of *International Organization* on regimes that appeared in 1982, © Cambridge University Press, reprinted with permission. Essay 6, "State Power and the Structure of International Trade," was published in *World Politics* 28 (1976) and Essay 7, "Global Communications: Life on the Pareto Frontier," in *World Politics* 43 (1991), both reprinted with permission. Essay 8 appeared as the first chapter of my book *Sovereignty: Organized Hypocrisy* (Princeton: Princeton University Press, 1999), reprinted with permission. Essay 9, "Organized Hypocrisy in East Asia," was published in *International Relations of the Asia-Pacific* 1 (2001) and Essay 10, "Sharing Sovereignty," originally appeared in *International Security* 29 (Fall 2004), both reprinted with permission.

Every effort has been made to contact copyright holders for their permission to reprint material in this book. The publishers would be grateful to hear from any copyright holder who is not here acknowledged and will undertake to rectify any errors or omissions in future editions of this book.

The opinions and characterizations in this book are those of the author, and do not necessarily represent official positions of the United States Government.

Introduction
Actors and institutions in the study of international politics

Introduction

Of all the many areas of political science international relations may be the most challenging. The only thing that circumscribes the field is that the phenomena that it tries to explain or the factors used in these explanations, its explanatory and dependent variables, are not confined to only one state. International relations scholars have tried to understand among other things war and peace, international trading patterns, international regimes, foreign assistance, transnational terrorism, transnational norms, sovereign lending, the logic of nuclear weapons, the impact of domestic political structures on foreign policy, the consequences for cooperation of organizational and bureaucratic structures, cognitive failure, and the role of international norms. The analytic approaches used to explain these and other phenomena have come not only from political science but from economics, sociology, and psychology as well. Most, perhaps all, of us that have been involved in this endeavor have felt, if not always explicitly recognized, how difficult it is to reach conclusions that are informed by theory and substantiated by conclusive empirical evidence. If we were backed against the wall and pressed to describe only those findings about which we are deeply confident, my guess is that almost all of us would only endorse the proposition that democracies do not fight with each other, although we would have different explanations for why this is so.

My own work has examined a number of different issues, most notably American foreign economic policy, the nature of the state, the impact of the international distribution of power on patterns of trade and international regimes, the behavior of developing countries, and the nature of sovereignty. My approach to these issues has been informed by the major theoretical perspectives that have roiled the field over the last several decades. The most prominent perspectives have been realism, liberalism, and constructivism, and at an earlier point in time, Marxism. What distinguishes these different approaches is not just the analytic reasoning which they use to explain outcomes but more important their understanding of the exemplary problem that needs to be understood. As I argued in "International Political

Economy: Abiding Discord," published in the *Review of International Political Economy* in 1994,

> Each of these approaches assumes a different exemplary problem, a different puzzle that is the focus of the theory's analytic explications. For realism the exemplary problem is to explain how either zero sum or distributional conflicts are resolved given the power and interests of states. For liberalism the exemplary problem is to show how market failure problems in which rational individually self-interested action fails to result in pareto optimal outcomes are resolved through the creation of appropriate institutions. For Marxism the exemplary problem is to illuminate how the exploitative mechanisms of capitalism operate through either the process of production or exchange. And for international society (or constructivist) approaches the exemplary problem is to demonstrate how structures constitute specific actors with regard to both their interests and their capabilities.
>
> (Krasner 1994: 3)

Less well recognized has been an even more encompassing distinction between actor-oriented and institutional-structural approaches, realism and liberalism being examples of the former and some aspects of constructivism and Marxism of the latter. These approaches are not necessarily in conflict with each other because actor-oriented perspectives may be nested within a larger institutional context. Constructivists like Alexander Wendt and Hedley Bull understand states to be constructed by international society, which constitutes their interests and capabilities. Once constituted the actions of these states might be interpreted from a liberal or realist perspective depending on whether an analyst understands them to be dealing with market failure or zero sum or relative power situations. For realists and liberals, in contrast, the actors in the system are unproblematic. The nature of these actors, their preferences, and their capabilities do not need to be explained. These actors may, especially for liberals, create institutions that enhance their utility, but the actors are not constituted by the institutions.

Institutional-structural and actor-oriented approaches

I explored the distinction between actor-oriented and institutional-structural approaches in "Sovereignty: An Institutional Perspective," published in *Comparative Political Studies* in 1988. Institutional-structural approaches do not take actors as given but rather as a product of the institutional structures within which they are embedded. Structures constitute actors: that is, they define their capabilities and their interests. Institutionalization could, I argued, be understood in terms of both vertical depth and horizontal breadth. Vertical depth reflected the extent to which the interests of actors and their capacities are constituted by a particular institutional structure.

Horizontal breadth reflects the extent to which different kinds of activities are inherently linked to each other. For instance, modern industrialized democracies, and many other states in the contemporary international system are highly institutionalized. The domestic institutional structures of states constitute many of the actors within them including bureaucrats, legislators, chief executives, citizens, corporations, civic groups, property owners, stockbrokers, prisoners, parolees, judges, police, and generals. The parts of the states are also bound to each other; changing one element of the state, the authority of the military, the rights associated with property ownership, the mechanisms for dispute resolution often involve changing other elements as well. Contrast the modern state with an isolated religious sect like the Pennsylvania Dutch which is characterized by very high vertical but low horizontal institutionalization: the lives of individuals within the group, their values, beliefs, and authority, are constituted by membership within the group; but the group has limited impact on other elements of society. A modern urban traffic system, in contrast, has high breadth: an accident on one major artery can snarl traffic on many others with ripple effects beyond the transportation system; but shallow depth: not many drivers within a particular system will see this activity as part of their basic identity.

For institutional-structural approaches, structures persist over a long period. They do not necessarily adapt in a smooth and seamless fashion to changing environmental conditions. This persistence can be explained using both economic and sociological logics. Economists have pointed to the importance of path dependence. An initial choice, possibly random, can be reinforced over time through increasing returns to scale, network externalities, agglomerating externalities, and increasing returns to adoption. Once set in place a particular institutional arrangement precludes other, possibly more efficient, structures. Many of us trapped by Microsoft Word would prefer to be using WordPerfect, but as file transfers over the internet became more and more common the dominant program won out because individual users found that the advantages of easy communication (a network externality) outweighed the disadvantages of a less elegant word-processing utility. Path dependence produces a Nash equilibrium outcome. Individual actors have no incentive to change their behavior even if another path could have led to a more efficient equilibrium.

A sociological logic can also explain persistence over time: once constituted by an institutional structure, actors and structures become mutually reinforcing. The capacities of actors and the rewards accruing to them are a function of their position within a given structure. The identities of actors are constituted by the structures within which they are operating. No professors without universities; no generals without a military organization; no bureaucrats without bureaus.

Nothing, however, lasts forever and I suggested in both "Approaches to the State: Alternative Conceptions and Historical Dynamics" and "Sovereignty:

An Institutional Perspective," that the idea of punctuated equilibrium developed by Eldredge and Gould in the field of evolution offered a useful metaphor for thinking about political institutions. Evolutionary biologists contrast punctuated equilibrium with gradualism. The standard Darwinian model holds that species gradually adapt to changing circumstances, a position analogous to functional arguments in the social sciences. Environmental change, for instance, could alter the beaks of Darwin's finches over a few generations. In contrast, punctuated equilibrium suggests that long periods of stasis followed by relatively short periods of change characterize evolution. Species can tolerate variation in environmental conditions; they can persist even if the environment changes. Only if there is a dramatic change are some characteristics disadvantaged relative to others, leading to the emergence of new species. Species existing in localized environments can experience spectacular success if the larger environment shifts in favorable ways. The now familiar story of a meteor strike opening opportunities for small mammals and closing them for dinosaurs is one dramatic example of punctuated equilibrium. An obvious political analogy would be the impact of Western imperialism on political structures in other areas of the world, some of which were destroyed, for instance the Incas, others of which were radically transformed, such as that of China, and still others of which adapted by making significant changes in extant institutions, for instance Meiji Japan.

In contrast to institutional perspectives, actor-oriented approaches take actors, whether individuals, groups, corporations, or states, as the starting point of the analyses. The basic nature of these actors, including their interests, are taken as a given; they are not explained by some larger structure. For realists, for instance, states are the basic actors in the international system. All states are unified rational actors. And all states must be alert to relative power. Some realists, notably Waltz, understand states to be defensive positionalists; their basic goal is survival. Others, such as Mearsheimer, see states as offensive realists striving for hegemony (Waltz 1979; Mearsheimer 2001). Liberal institutionalists also understand states to be unified rational actors. States are utility maximizers and some of the goals which they seek are absolute rather than relative. States may create institutions that allow them to enhance their utility by overcoming market failure problems (Keohane 1984).

In my own work I have deployed both institutional structural and actor-oriented orientations. Explicitly, and I confess sometimes implicitly, I have used institutional-structural arguments when looking at the impact of domestic structures on foreign policy. When looking strictly at interactions among states in the international system I have relied primarily on actor-oriented approaches, more specifically some variant of realism. When examining questions of sovereignty, the meta-structure, of the contemporary international environment, I have argued that institutional-structural approaches are deeply flawed and that the basic rules for the contemporary, or any other, international system are most appropriately understood through the lens of organized hypocrisy. Despite appearances, the depth of institutionalization at the international level is shallow and the breadth is limited. Some states have more attributes of sovereignty, as it is conventionally understood, than others. The rules of the game for the international system are not self-enforcing equilibria. Some actors have both the interest and capacity to violate the rules. The rules persist over time but their impact on behavior is imperfect. In the international system it is the power and interests of states that matters most.

Domestic structures

The institutional structures of states—the ways in which they are organized including the relationship among the different components of the executive and between the executive and the legislature, the extent of centralization, the scope of government authority and control, the autonomy of the private sector, and the values that infuse political discourse—are, in all states, institutionalized to one extent or another. All states in the international system that have significant capacity have highly institutionalized structures. This includes all of the modern industrialized democracies, major regional and sometimes global players such as India, South Africa, Brazil, and China, and other smaller but competently governed states. There are, though, states in the contemporary international system, for instance big man states in Africa or post-conflict states emerging from international transitional authority, where institutionalization may be much more modest. Various studies of failed and fragile states, essentially states with weak institutionalization, place their number at between 37 and 73 countries depending on the source used (*Foreign Policy* 2007; Weinstein *et al.* 2004; Kaufmann *et al.* 2005; United Kingdom, Department for International Development 2004).

In trying to understand the impact of state structures on foreign policy, and through foreign policy on the nature of the international system, I have argued that a perspective that focuses on the key role of central decision-makers, what I called a statist perspective, is most useful. I elaborated this argument in *Defending the National Interest* and in "US Commercial and Monetary Policy: Unraveling the Paradox of External Strength and Internal Weakness." These central decision-makers are embedded in a larger institutional structure which defines their authorities often by constitutional provisions that are difficult to change. They are relatively insulated from specific societal pressures. In a well-governed democracy with a presidential system, for instance, the president must appeal to wide swaths of the electorate. In the United States the two officials that most obviously embody, and have an incentive to act on, the general or national interest are the president and the secretary of state. Some elements of the national interest will be the same for all states, such as security from external attack and economic well-being.

Other aspects of the national interest, especially those associated with values and ideological commitments, will vary from one state to another. The national interest is not, I argued in *Defending the National Interest*, a vacuous construct or simply the sum of particularistic interests as would be suggested by interest group pluralism. Rather, it is a set of objectives designed to enhance the material utility and ideational values of the polity as a whole.

The ability of central decision-makers to pursue the national interest depends on both the resources within the polity and the ability of political leaders to extract these resources for public purposes. States can, I noted in "US Commercial and Monetary Policy," be makers, breakers, or takers of international regimes and the international system more generally. The United States, for instance, has been a maker or breaker of the international system since the First World War. The kind of international regimes that leaders want to make is a function of the state's material interests, both economic and security, and its ideational beliefs. When the United States moved to a global leadership role after the Second World War it sought to create liberal international regimes, regimes that reflected not only American interests but also American values. The core of American identity is not ethnicity or race, but rather a belief in Lockean liberal values, which understand the individual as the basic building block of the society. In politics this means democracy; in economics a market economy.

For American leaders the lesson of the 1930s was that economic closure and protectionism led to war and instability. They were determined to follow a different course from the one that the country had chosen after the First World War. In monetary and financial affairs, American political leaders were very successful in getting what they wanted, at least once they had overcome domestic constraints by identifying these goals with national security.

In trade, American political leaders were more challenged. Here they suffered from what I termed the weakness of the American state, by which I meant the fragmentation of power and authority within the United States. The American Constitution was designed to divide power among the different parts of the of the government; hence the creation of the two houses of Congress, the separation between the legislature and the executive, the independent status of the Supreme Court with its lifetime appointments, and the delineation of powers between the federal government and the states.

Trade is an area in which there are often diffuse winners and concentrated losers. The Congress, many of whose members represented constituents with clear interests, constrained the freedom of action of the executive. The effort to create the International Trade Organization, a sister institution to the Fund and the Bank, failed; a charter was agreed to at Havana in 1948 but never ratified by the United States. Instead, the United States settled for the General Agreement of Tariffs and Trade (GATT), which could be implemented through an executive agreement rather than requiring approval from

Congress. The GATT proved to be an effective organization over time, although negotiations were always lengthy and painful. By the time that the World Trade Organization superseded the GATT in the mid-1990s trade had been dramatically liberalized. In the late 1970s I did not predict this development, arguing that the relative decline of American power would mean a turn toward greater closure. I failed to see both how robust the American economy would be and how the collapse of the Soviet Union would greatly enhance the international position of the United States.

American foreign policy, I argued in the concluding chapter of *Defending the National Interest*, was driven by ideational not just material concerns. A statist perspective that emphasized the role of central decision-makers who were embedded in a larger institutional structure could be used to explain American security policy, not just policies related to trade, monetary affairs, and raw materials investments. The one common factor in every instance of the use of force by the United States, covert or overt, from the end of the Second World War to the collapse of the Soviet Union (with the exception of Panama) was anxiety about the spread of communism. In some cases, such as the Cuban missile crisis or even the Bay of Pigs, security issues and anti-communism were indistinguishable. In other cases, such as intervention in the Dominican Republic in 1965, the United States misperceived the threat of communism. In the most important cases, Korea and Vietnam, the United States committed very substantial resources to a cause whose direct relationship to American national interest was attenuated. The costs of Vietnam were particularly high: growing distrust of the state at home; alienation of allies abroad; loss of American lives (not to speak of Vietnamese ones); and treasure. The most frequently articulated rationale for the war (although there were many), the domino theory, proved to be incorrect, as many at the time predicted. Neither structural Marxism, with its emphasis on the state as the rationalizing agent for the long-term preservation of capitalism, nor interest group pluralism, with its focus on the preferences of domestic political actors, can explain decisions by the United States to use overt or covert force.

This pattern of intervention, I argued, could only be understood from a statist perspective, which emphasized the importance of ideology for American central decision-makers. Communism was in all of its aspects antithetical to a belief system that focused on individual freedom, democracy, and a market economy. Usually decision-makers do not have the luxury of pursuing ideological objectives that are not disciplined by rational calculations of material gains and losses. A hegemonic power is an exception, however. Hegemons have slack resources. They have the luxury of making not illogical but non-logical choices, that is, choices in which costs and benefits do not have to be carefully calculated because the level of slack resources is so high. Their leaders are not disciplined by external constraints. Only a very powerful state could have pursued the war in Vietnam, a war that weakened rather than strengthened American national security and material well-being.

Vietnam and Korea are not the only example of this phenomenon. After the attacks on 9/11 an invasion of Afghanistan that would deny to al-Qaeda the safe haven where it had trained its operatives and planned its attacks was a foregone conclusion. The war to overthrow the Taliban regime was a stunning success, accomplishing in a matter of weeks what the Soviet army had failed to do in years. The war against Iraq, in contrast, was not a foregone conclusion and engendered tremendous controversy both globally and domestically. The United States was not able to secure explicit Security Council authorization for the invasion. The Turkish parliament denied transit rights, complicating the invasion plans at the last minute. The number of countries and their contributions to the American effort in Iraq were relatively smaller than the contributions made in Afghanistan. Nevertheless, the military operation itself was, again, a stunning success.

The aftermath was much more problematic. The most prominent justification for the invasion, Saddam's weapons of mass destruction, proved to be erroneous. It is, however, important to note that we do not know what a counter-factual history would have been. Saddam wanted weapons of mass destruction. His regime was successfully circumventing UN authorized sanctions and collecting billions of dollars in revenue. That Saddam did not have WMD in 2003 does not mean that he would not have had them in 2005 had his regime not been destroyed. Over time the idea of bringing democracy to the Iraq and to the broader Middle East, which had always been part of the administration's rationale, came to play a much more prominent role. The 2006 National Security Strategy begins with the following paragraph:

> It is the policy of the United States to seek and support democratic movements and institutions in every nation and culture, with the ultimate goal of ending tyranny in our world. In the world today, the fundamental character of regimes matters as much as the distribution of power among them. The goal of our statecraft is to help create a world of democratic, well-governed states that can meet the needs of their citizens and conduct themselves responsibly in the international system. This is the best way to provide enduring security for the American people.
>
> (United States, Office of the President 2006: 1)

In the *National Security Strategy* and elsewhere, the administration argued not only that Iraq could become a democratic state but also that success in this endeavor would serve as an example to the entire Middle East. The administration's basic framing device, its grand strategy, was that transnational terrorism, which posed an existential security threat to the United States, could only be addressed if the root causes of terrorism were confronted. These root causes were the failure of freedom and democracy in the Middle East, a failure that created political frustration that had been galvanized by leaders using a radical Islamic ideology that justified terrorist attacks against the West.

The beliefs that emboldened the Bush administration were not pulled out of thin air. They had deep resonance among the American electorate and in the highest echelons of the government. American leaders have not always acted on these beliefs, primarily because of external constraints, but as the unrivaled global hegemon in 2003 it could. The United States was awash in slack resources, its military budget greater than the next twenty, or by some measures all other, countries combined. The initiation of war is one area where the institutional structure of the American state gives key decision-makers, notably the president, exceptional authority. By acting on his authority as commander-in-chief, the president has been able to free himself of internal constraints despite the fragmentation of authority within the American government, at least at the initial stages of a conflict. The president has also been able to initially rely on rally-round-the-flag support from the electorate.

If a policy fails, however, the president will pay a cost. Both Vietnam and Iraq imperiled the ability of sitting presidents to govern. Lyndon Johnson resigned. George W. Bush's popularity ratings fell into the low thirties by the spring of 2006.

In the United States the behavior of critical leaders cannot be explained in terms of some effort to promote the interests of specific groups. They are better understood from a statist perspective: key decision-makers can pursue the national interest, both material and ideational, within constraints imposed by domestic institutional structures and the power of other states.

The United States is hardly the most telling example of the way in which domestic structures and values can constrain the foreign policy behavior of states, sometimes with fatal results. In the eighteenth century, Poland's neighbors were able to extinguish its independence at least in part because the Polish parliament's requirement for unanimity made it impossible to respond effectively to challenges from Russia, Austria, and Prussia. I suggested in "Organized Hypocrisy in 19th Century East Asia" that at the end of the nineteenth century, Korea's leaders were not able to forestall Japanese colonization in part because their internal legitimacy depended on adhering to Confucian practices which precluded seeking support from Western actors. At the beginning of the twentieth century the Balinese nobility essentially committed suicide for themselves and their society by marching into the machine guns of the Dutch because traditional norms could not incorporate subordination to an external actor (Geertz 1980).

Thus, foreign policy is determined by key decision-makers operating, with the exception of failed and fragile states, in an institutionalized environment. Domestic structures define the authority of key players within the polity and determine the level and kind of resources that leaders are able to extract from their own society. Widely held societal beliefs are a part of this structure because they inform the objectives of leaders, provide shared understandings of legitimate behavior, and can be deployed to bolster societal support. These structures are embedded both by path-dependent and sociological processes, and change only slowly over time.

The international system

The international system, in contrast to domestic structures, is weakly institutionalized. I have argued in a number of books and articles that the outcomes of interactions among states is the result of power and interests. Actor-oriented theories, realism and neo-liberal institutionalism, provide more compelling explanations of outcomes in the international system than institutional-structural arguments such as some Marxist and constructivist approaches.

Marxism

Of all of the approaches that have informed the literature on international relations, Marxism is the most encompassing. Structural Marxists offered a theory that purported to explain both domestic and international politics. Capitalist systems were fundamentally unstable. In the long run prices were determined by the amount of labor embodied in any product. In an effort to increase profits, capitalists introduce new technology, which reduces the amount of labor embodied in any product. Innovators benefit in the short run, because average prices still reflect pre-innovation labor inputs, but profits fall over time as other capitalists adopt the new technology. By generating pressure for ever higher capital labor ratios, capitalism ineluctably presses down the rate of profit. Imperialism offered one way in which the capitalist state could stave off inevitable collapse by providing new sources of cheaper labor to exploit and more attractive investment opportunities than were available in the home country.

   Marxist analysis wrapped domestic and international politics into one very elegant package, but it was fatally flawed. The labor theory of value on which the argument about labor exploitation rests is incorrect. Value does not derive from the labor content of goods. Empirically profit rates have not fallen over time (Cohen 1973). The empirical cases presented in *Defending the National Interest* showed that for the United States, the most capitalist of capitalist countries, foreign policy was driven by ideology and security, not economic interests.

Constructivism and international society

Some constructivist arguments about the international system offer another example of institutional-structural analysis. The basic claim of this variant of constructivism is that there exists a set of norms and values that define an international society; these norms and values constitute the actors in the system, delineate their authorities, and define their capacities. In the modern world sovereignty norms constitute autonomous, mutually recognized, formally equal states. Classic Sinocentric norms stipulated a world comprising China as the imperial center and tributary states that were subordinate to China. For constructivism, these norms and values have a taken-for-granted quality which precludes the consideration of alternative institutional arrangements.

In my work on the international system as opposed to foreign policy, I have sought to demonstrate that constructivism, like structural Marxism, is not persuasive. First there is no set of norms and values shared by all significant actors in the international system. Sovereignty norms, which contructivists such as Hedley Bull and Alexander Wendt see as constitutive of the system as a whole, have been contested explicitly and implicitly (Bull 1977; Wendt 1999). Osama bin Laden's vision for the international system would not comport with that of any political leader in Western Europe, North America, or East Asia, but it has resonance with many millions of individuals throughout the Islamic world. For Western Europe the most important development of the last fifty years has been the creation and success of the European Union (EU). The member states of the EU have used their international legal sovereignty, their right to voluntarily enter into any agreement they choose, to gut their domestic autonomy by creating supranational institutions such as the European Court of Justice and the European Central Bank. They have accepted qualified majority voting in many issue areas, meaning that a member state can be bound by a decision with which it does not agree. In doing so, they have defied the conventional norms of sovereignty one of which, perhaps the most important, is that the state is not subject to any external authority.

Constructivists have obviously viewed some norms, although not constitutive ones, as contested. Consistent with constructivist arguments they have sometimes been able to demonstrate that these differences have been resolved through normative discourse. More often, however, disagreements about norms are determined by power and interest, not discourse. Developing countries preferred the GATT to the WTO but they accepted the latter, with its expanded scope such as the protection of intellectual property rights, because advanced countries had taken adherence to the GATT alone off the table. In the 1980s developing countries supported the idea that deep seabed nodules should be part of the common heritage of humankind; most industrialized countries rejected this idea and the United Nations Law of the Seas Treaty was not accepted until this concept was expunged. The United States disagreed with many other countries about the appropriate response to Saddam Hussein's defiance of the international community; it went to war citing previous Security Council resolutions and relying on a coalition of the willing. That what constructivists point to as the constitutive norm of the system, sovereignty, is not constraining, and that disagreements among states are only sometimes resolved through normative discourse, underlines the fact that in the international system actors differ on their understanding of appropriate norms and that because there is no authoritative structure for adjudicating these differences power and material interests are the most important determinants of outcomes.

Norms and values are imperfectly institutionalized in the international system as opposed to domestic systems because socialization is weaker. Political leaders experience many different socializing pressures, but the most salient will be domestic, not international. For almost all leaders (perhaps the only exception would be those in post-conflict states that are highly dependent on international assistance) success depends on conforming with domestic, not international or transnational, concepts of identity and appropriate behavior. And these understandings vary, often dramatically, across states; think only of the United States, Venezuela, Italy, the Sudan, Zimbabwe, Iran, Saudi Arabia, Turkmenistan, China, and North Korea in the contemporary system.

As I will note in the concluding section of this essay, I do not believe that norms are irrelevant in the international system, but an adequate understanding of their impact must recognize that logics of appropriateness (norms and values) and logics of consequences (actions to realize material interests) can be decoupled. Norms may persist, as I argue they have with regard to sovereignty, but their impact on actual behavior is attenuated. Constructivism has provided valuable insights, especially with regard to the way in which different domestic normative structures have influenced the foreign policies of different states and the way in which they have responded to external challenges, but it has not adequately explained outcomes in the international system as a whole (Katzenstein 1985, 2005). Here actor-oriented arguments, realism and liberal institutionalism, provide the most powerful insights.

State power and international regimes

My introductory essay for *International Regimes* defined regimes as "sets of implicit or explicit principles, norms, rules, and decision-making procedures around which actors' expectations converge in a given area of international relations" (Krasner 1983: 186). The definition was jointly agreed to by the authors contributing to the volume. John Ruggie's thinking was particularly consequential. It is strongly constructivist. If I were to re-write the essay now, I would argue that it is impossible to have a theoretically neutral definition of regimes. For realism, regimes should be understood as principles, norms, rules, and decision-making procedures that reflect the interests of the most powerful states in the system. For liberal institutionalism, regimes should be defined as principles, norms, rules, and decision-making procedures that mitigate market failures.

In understanding the international system, my own work has focused on power. In "State Power and the Structure of International Trade," I argued that open international trade was most likely in an international system with a single dominant state, one that was larger and more technologically advanced than others. Such a state would benefit economically from an open system, could potentially use economic exchange as a source of political leverage, could more easily adjust to the disruptive impact of trade on domestic factors, and would find it rational to provide collective goods that the system might need. In contrast, a multipolar system comprised of large but relatively underdeveloped states would favor a closed trading system: the economic benefits of trade would be limited; the dangers of being subject to political pressure could be high; the social disruption could be significant. In making these arguments I drew heavily not only on conventional trade theory but also on Albert Hirschman's first book *National Power and the Structure of Foreign Trade*, which explored the way in levels of development and trade dependence affected the ability of states to make credible threats, and Charles Kindleberger's *The World in Depression, 1929–1939*, which emphasized the need for a hegemon to provide collective goods.

When I wrote "State Power," liberal institutionalism was hardly a glimmer in the eye of Robert Keohane and other exponents of this approach. Fifteen years later, when I wrote *Global Communications and National Power: Life on the Pareto Frontier*, it had become the dominant approach in the field of international political economy. Liberal institutionalism was a revelation. It demonstrated that international institutions could emerge as Pareto-improving self-enforcing equilibria by facilitating the flow of information, creating focal points, opening opportunities for issue linkages, establishing reputations, increasing iterations, and defining rule violations. No serious scholar could ignore this line of argument because of both the power of its logic and its ability to explain a wide range of outcomes in the international system. In "Global Communications and National Power" I pointed out, however, that the possibility of reaching the Pareto frontier did not mean that distributional conflicts were irrelevant. Every move along the Pareto frontier makes one actor better off and another worse off. The point that is chosen along the frontier, or the vector that is chosen in moving toward it, is not just a matter of clever institutional design, but rather a question of the bargaining power of states. In global communications, for example the development of new satellite technology gave the United States bargaining leverage, which allowed it to dramatically change the extant regime. That regime, based in the International Telecommunications Union, where each state had one vote, gave countries at the terminus of transnational cables the right to regulate traffic. To govern satellite communications the United States successfully pressed for the establishment of a new international organization, INTELSAT. Voting within INTELSAT was weighted according to usage, giving the US a dominant role. INTELSAT was privatized in 2001, again largely reflecting the preferences and power of the United States. The way in which market failure problems are resolved in the international system depends upon the power as well as the interests of states.

Looking at the various elements of the regime for global communications, which included radio and TV transmissions as well as telecommunications, convinced me not only that power mattered even for market failure issues in the international system, but also that institutionalization as opposed to institutions did not. The idea of punctuated equilibrium did not hold for international communications. Power and interests changed and institutions changed along with them.

This conclusion applied not only to global communications but to other international institutions as well. Socialization is always relatively weak in the international system because political leaders are responding to national values and norms rather than international ones. Path dependence and lock-in is possible in international regimes, but unlikely. Powerful states are able to determine who plays in the game. They are able to set the rules. They may be able to change opportunity sets by moving unilaterally (Gruber 2000; Drezner 2007). In trade, for instance, the United States and other major industrialized countries incorporated the GATT into a new and more encompassing organization, the World Trade Organization, because they wanted to expand the scope of liberal market-oriented rules to new issue areas. Developing countries, many of which were uncomfortable with this change, had no choice but to go along. Had they refused, they would have been denied Most Favored Nation (MFN) access to the largest markets in the world. In 1971, faced with a growing trade deficit, the United States unilaterally transformed the international monetary system by refusing to exchange dollars for gold, a step that led to the end of the postwar fixed rate exchange system. When the preferences over strategies of powerful states change, they will change institutions provided that the transactions costs of creating new structures does not exceed the anticipated benefits.

Sovereignty

Concluding that institutionalization was essential to understanding the foreign policies of states, since with the exception of failed and fragile states their leaders were embedded in well-institutionalized structures that defined their authorities and interests, but not important for understanding the interaction among states in the international system where power and interests are the master explanatory variables, failed to explain what appeared to be a persistent constitutive structure in the international environment, sovereignty. Students of both foreign policy and international politics have taken sovereignty for granted. They have assumed that the object of their study is sovereign states. In fact, sovereignty is more problematic than conventional approaches to international politics suggest.

Sovereignty, I have argued, has three core elements. The first is international legal sovereignty. States mutually recognize each other. Recognition carries with it the right to voluntarily enter into international agreements or treaties. Membership in international organizations is usually limited to states. Embassies enjoy extra-territorial status. Diplomatic representatives enjoy immunity. For the conventional legalist view in international law states are analogous to individuals in the state of nature. Each is free and equal (Vattel 1852: Preliminaries, 3).

The second element of sovereignty is what has conventionally been referred to as Westphalian sovereignty, although it should more appropriately be designated as Westphalian/Vattelian sovereignty. The principle of Westphalian/Vattelian sovereignty is that states are juridically independent, autonomous, not subject to any external authority. The corollary rule is that one state does not have the right to intervene in the internal affairs of another state.

The third element is domestic sovereignty, which refers both to the legitimated authority structure within a state and to its effectiveness, its ability to actually control activities both within and across its borders. The formally legitimated authority structures of states vary. They may be democratic or autocratic, federal or unitary, parliamentary or presidential. The effectiveness, the actual ability to govern, also varies across states, with failed states having no ability to govern even if they do have formally legitimated authority structures. In *Sovereignty: Organized Hypocrisy*, I identified four aspects of sovereignty by differentiating the ability to control activities within the states from the ability to control transborder activities. Here I incorporate interdependence sovereignty into domestic sovereignty.

The beginning of the sovereign state system has been conventionally associated with the Peace of Westphalia, concluded in 1648, which brought the Thirty Years War to a close. Scholars have pointed to the fact that the two treaties that comprised the Peace, Osnabrück and Münster, endorsed the principle that the prince could set the religion of his territory, *cuius regio eius religio*, first articulated in the Peace of Augsburg of 1555, and the right of the princes of the Holy Roman Empire to make treaties. Leo Gross described the Peace as the "majestic portal which leads from the old into the new world" (Gross 1948: 28).

In fact, the Treaties of Münster and Osnabrück were not a clear break with the medieval past or even an obvious portal to the sovereign state future. The princes of the Holy Roman Empire had always had the right to sign treaties, a right that was given to them in the founding document of the Empire, the Golden Bull of 1356. The Treaty of Osnabrück confirmed this right but also stipulated that such alliances must not be "against the Emperor or the Empire" (Treaty of Osnabrück 1648: VIII. 1).

In the Peace of Westphalia, the principle of *cuius regio eius religio* was endorsed but then compromised by specific provisions of the treaties. The Peace recognized the right of private worship. Public churches that were in place in 1624 could not be closed. Eight imperial cities, that had mixed religious populations, were officially designated as bi-confessional. If the religion of the ruler changed from Calvinist to Lutheran or vice versa, existing practices had to remain in place, although the prince could practice his own religion. Most important, within the Holy Roman Empire questions of religion had to be decided by a majority of Catholics and Protestants voting separately in the imperial courts and Diet. The Peace is better understood as the beginning of consociational political structures in Europe than as an opening to modern state sovereignty (Lehmbruch 1997).

With regard to religious practice the Peace of Westphalia is an example of organized hypocrisy. *Cuius regio eius religio* reflected a logic of appropriateness for seventeenth-century Europeans who were loath to accept religious toleration. At the same time, to maintain peace rulers had to find a way to accommodate religious diversity, which they did by constraining the arbitrary exercise of authority over religious matters. The Peace of Westphalia, a basic constitutional document for the Holy Roman Empire, was part of a settlement that involved virtually all of the major powers of Europe with the exception of Russia and Britain.

The principle of non-intervention in the internal affairs of other states for which *cuius regio eius religio* is seen as a stand-in was not explicitly articulated until 1758 by Emmerich de Vattel, a Swiss jurist, in his *The Law of Nations or the Principles of Natural Law Applied to the Conduct and to the Affairs of Nations and of Sovereign.* Vattel argued that:

> But, though a nation be obliged to promote, as far as lies in its power, the perfection of others, it is not entitled forcibly to obtrude these good offices on them. Such an attempt would be a violation of their natural liberty. In order to compel any one to receive a kindness, we must have an authority over him; but nations are absolutely free and independent.
>
> (Vattel 1852: prelim. 4)

The three aspects of sovereignty—international legal sovereignty, Westphalian/Vattelian sovereignty, and domestic sovereignty—are much better understood as part of a long historic process stretching back to the late Middle Ages and extending into the nineteenth and even early twentieth centuries. Sovereignty did ultimately come to be accepted as the only legitimate way to organize political life, not only in Europe but around the globe. How could the persistence and durability of sovereignty be consistent with the view that while institutionalization may be strong within states it is weak in the international system?

Addressing this problem required recognizing that the conventional approaches to understanding institutions was inadequate. These approaches assume that if there are persistent institutional structures with associated principals and norms, then behavior conforms to them. For rational choice, economistic approaches institutions, designed to facilitate movement toward the Pareto frontier, must be self-enforcing equilibria. If actors stop playing by the rules, institutions crumble. For conventional sociological arguments, socialization leads to rule-conforming behavior. If actors are not socialized, behavior fails to conform with accepted norms and institutions atrophy and become irrelevant.

In looking at how the principles of sovereignty have actually functioned over the last several hundred years, I found that there were many examples of inconsistent behavior; nevertheless, sovereignty persisted. Logics of appropriateness were decoupled from logics of consequences.

I was initially befuddled by these observations. Conventional theoretical approaches, not only in international relations but also more generally, at least the ones I was familiar with, provided no guidance. When I described my puzzle—persistent rules and norms that were frequently violated—to my colleague John Meyer, actually sitting under a palm tree in the Stanford quad, he immediately pointed me to the sociological literature on decoupling and to the book which provided me with the title for my own work on sovereignty, *The Organization of Hypocrisy* by Nils Brunsson (Brunsson 1989).

Logics of appropriateness, the rules and norms associated with a specific institution, may be inconsistent with logics of consequences, what actors must do to maximize what they understand to be their utility. Actors do not associate decoupling with sin or crime, nor does decoupling necessarily lead to a quest for new institutions. There may be no better alternatives. When sovereignty rules are violated, these violations are always justified by an appeal to other principles and norms, although not necessarily ones associated with sovereignty, such as the right to protect or the need to further freedom.

The three aspects of sovereignty, international legal sovereignty, Westphalian/Vattelian sovereignty, and domestic sovereignty are neither logically nor empirically joined. States can have one aspect of sovereignty without having others. For instance, in the contemporary international order, failed and fragile states have international legal sovereignty; they may have Westphalian/Vattelian sovereignty: they do not have domestic sovereignty. The member states of the European Union have international legal sovereignty and domestic sovereignty, but not Westphalian/Vattelian sovereignty because they have used their international legal sovereignty to create supranational institutions that supersede national authority. Taiwan has Westphalian/Vattelian sovereignty and domestic sovereignty, but only limited international legal sovereignty. It is recognized only by a small number of states, and it is denied membership in most international organizations.

Some violations of conventional sovereignty are the result of contracting among states in which they use their international legal sovereignty to compromise their Westphalian/Vattelian sovereignty, the EU being one example. Others are the result of coercion where the target state has no option but to accept the proposal offered by more powerful states. There are, for example, many cases where the major powers have conditioned their recognition of new states on the acceptance by these states of minority rights. This was true for all of the successor states of the Ottoman Empire in the nineteenth and early twentieth centuries: Greece, Romania, Bulgaria, Serbia, Montenegro, Albania, and Turkey. It was true for more than thirty states after the First World War, both newly created states like Czechoslovakia and Poland, and already established although altered ones such as Hungary. And it was true in the Balkans during the 1990s when the member states of the EU insisted that the successor states of Yugoslavia accept the Copenhagen human rights principles before being recognized. In all of these cases bargaining power was highly asymmetrical. The offer of the major powers essentially was: if you want to have life as a sovereign state, to enjoy international legal sovereignty, you will have to compromise your autonomy and accept domestic authority structures that you might otherwise not choose.

However, once recognition was offered it could not easily be withdrawn. The time inconsistency problem associated with these kinds of arrangements has meant that most of them have unraveled. Only if countries were committed to minority rights, such as Czechoslovakia in the interwar period, were the terms of the original agreement honored.

There are also examples of outright imposition in which one state has conquered another and imposed its preferred domestic structure. This was true for the United States in Germany and Japan after the Second World War, and for the Soviet Union in Central Europe.

That efforts to change domestic authority structures in other states have been part of the foreign policy repertoire of the powerful ought not to be surprising. The international system is anarchical; there is no authoritative body that can resolve differences. In most instances it has been more efficient for political leaders to try to change the foreign policies of other states rather than their domestic authority structures, but this has not always been the case. The domestic authority structure of another state may be so threatening that targeting that structure is the best policy option. After the Second World War, the Allies were not about to allow a Nazi regime to continue to exist in Germany. The Soviet Union was committed to the preservation of communist regimes once they were established, hence the invasions of Hungary, Czechoslovakia, and Afghanistan, because the collapse of a communist regime would bring into question the teleological vision which legitimated the Soviet regime itself. The Austro-Hungarian Empire made a series of demands on Serbia for domestic regime change after the assassination of Archduke Ferdinand because it saw Serbian nationalism as an existential threat to the Empire's security. The United States overthrew the Taliban regime in Afghanistan because it harbored a terrorist organization that had perpetrated 9/11. The Holy Alliance sought to suppress the spread of liberal regimes after the Napoleonic wars because such regimes were seen as a threat to the conservative monarchical order. John Owen has identified 198 cases of forcible regime change since the seventeenth century, most of which have occurred after major wars (Owen 2002: 375).

We have, however, little understanding of when such practices have worked and why. Scholars have been trapped or blinded by the assumption that sovereignty as an ideal type has conformed with actual practices. International relations scholars have looked almost exclusively at state-to-state relations. Students of comparative politics have focused on autochthonous developments within states except in glaring cases where external influence was impossible to ignore, such as Central Europe when it was part of the Soviet Empire. The extent to which political decision-makers in one state have been able to influence domestic authority structures in another has only recently, in the literature on state-building, become a focus of concern.

The organized hypocrisy that has characterized the modern sovereign state system has also characterized other international systems. I argued in "Organized Hypocrisy in 19th Century East Asia" that the Sinocentric system also experienced decoupling of logics of appropriateness from logics of consequences. In the Sinocentric system there was no conception of sovereign equality: China was the center; other political entities were tributary states. Ritual was centrally important for legitimating the Chinese regime; tributary states sent tribute missions to Beijing, which were also opportunities for trade, and China send investiture missions to tributary states.

China, however, did interact with political entities that did not recognize its superior position. In treating with the English expedition to Beijing in 1793–94, whose purpose was to open China to trade and establish a permanent embassy based on sovereign equality in Beijing, both the Chinese and the British accommodated their respective logics of appropriateness by forging documents and misreporting events. The Chinese officially recorded that Macartney, the leader of the British expedition, had kowtowed to the Emperor. He had not. The British mistranslated documents from the court in Beijing to the king of England to obfuscate the fact that the Emperor could not even conceive of the English king as a brother, an equal (Peyrefitte 1993). The establishment of the treaty port system after the Opium Wars was a clear violation of the rules of sovereignty since these were essentially exterritorial entities within China. The Europeans recognized, however, that China was too big to be formally colonized, and the treaty ports offered a mechanism for facilitating trade and protecting European nationals. Rules and norms were not taken for granted. Logics of consequences trumped logics of appropriateness.

Organized hypocrisy, a disjunction between logics of appropriateness and logics of consequences, is not surprising in an environment as complex as the international system. There is probably no single set of rules that could align interests, power, and principles; no set of rules that would create a self-enforcing equilibrium from which actors never had incentives to deviate. But what is, perhaps, surprising is the durability of this decoupling. Every major peace treaty from the Peace of Westphalia to the United Nations Charter enunciated principles that were inconsistent with accepted sovereign norms. Despite these inconsistencies, no enduring alternative construct has arisen to replace or even complement sovereignty.

Sovereignty has endured because the interests of key players in the system could be accommodated by deviations from its rules and practices. For the rules to change, key actors—those with an ability to change the system—would have to support some alternative set of constructs, something that they would only do if such alternatives could provide better outcomes. When sovereignty rules have manifestly failed to provide desirable outcomes, states have been able to cobble together alternatives. In Bosnia, for instance, governance has been provided under the auspices of the Contact Group and the European Union. When the United States and other countries moved from recognizing the government on Taiwan as the government of China to recognizing the government in Beijing, they established quasi-diplomatic arrangements for conducting business with Taiwan. The American Institute in Taiwan operates what is, in effect, a diplomatic mission. Hong Kong, formally a part of China, has a separate visa regime from that of China and is a member of some international organizations where China is also a member. When China assumed control of Hong Kong in 1997 it was anxious to reassure both the Hong Kong and international business communities that the Hong Kong economy could operate under different rules from China itself. The rest of the world was happy to accommodate China's desires even though this meant violating conventional sovereignty norms.

Sovereignty is not a self-enforcing equilibrium. There are circumstances where states are better off following alternative principles and norms. This does not mean that these norms are irrelevant. They may be embodied in the highly institutionalized domestic structures of states. While some states may want to violate norms, others may want to defend them, and this defense will be easier because the norms are so widely understood. The complexity of the international system, the variety of challenges with which political leaders must deal, means that even if sovereignty principles are violated there may be no alternative construct which is ideationally or materially more attractive. Organized hypocrisy persists because there is nothing better to take its place.

Conclusion

International relations scholars have focused their attention on the foreign policies of states and the interaction among states. Foreign policy examines the way in which the domestic political institutions, interests, and values of a state affect the objectives that it pursues and the level of resources that it can deploy to achieve those objectives. International politics looks at the way in which interactions among states determine outcomes in the international system including everything from war to the creation of exclusive economic zones in the oceans. Scholars have investigated the second image reversed: the way in which the international system can affect the domestic structures of states, for instance the way in which external threats led Japan to radically change its domestic authority structures at the end of the nineteenth century (Gourevitch 1978). What international scholars have not paid as much attention to is state-building, situations in which one state has tried to influence the domestic authority structures of another, not just its specific policies. State-building, which violates the precept of non-intervention in the internal affairs of other states, is one example of organized hypocrisy.

Foreign policy is, in all but fragile and failed states, strongly influenced by domestic institutional structures that define the authorities of officials and their ability to extract resources from their own society. In international politics, institutionalization is weak. Power is what matters. The strong do what they will, the weak what they must, as Thucydides famously wrote in the Melian dialogue.

The realm of state-building in which one state intervenes in the internal affairs of another is much less well understood. It is not surprising that scholars have failed to come to grips with this issue. Addressing it requires altering basic ontological categories such as the state as the key actor in the international system. If a state is not autonomous, conventional analytic approaches, whether realist or liberal, are of little value. Poland, during the Cold War, was not choosing between bandwagonning and balancing. Its secret police reported to Moscow, not to officials in Warsaw. After the Prague Spring of 1968, the Soviet Union configured Czech military forces, and those of other satellite states in Eastern Europe, so that they could not operate independent of Warsaw Pact units commanded by Soviet officers.

In the realm of organized hypocrisy the principles of sovereignty, especially non-intervention, are decoupled from actual behavior. The principles have blinded scholars more than they have policy makers. Policy makers have to solve specific problems. They are concerned about outcomes. Principles are not irrelevant, but they are not dispositive either. They may, for instance, create a focal point that allows political leaders in target states to organize resistance to external efforts to alter domestic authority structures. Or they may provide would-be interveners with a rallying point, such as the need to stop genocide. Policy makers do not take these principles and norms for granted. The principles are one policy tool among many others, such as military force and economic sanctions, that can be deployed to achieve specific objectives. The challenges that will confront the United States and other major powers in the decades to come will be associated not with the better-understood worlds of foreign policy or international politics, but rather with the challenges of state-building. For scholars, more than practitioners, this will require abandoning or stretching conventional analytic frameworks (see Figure 0.1).

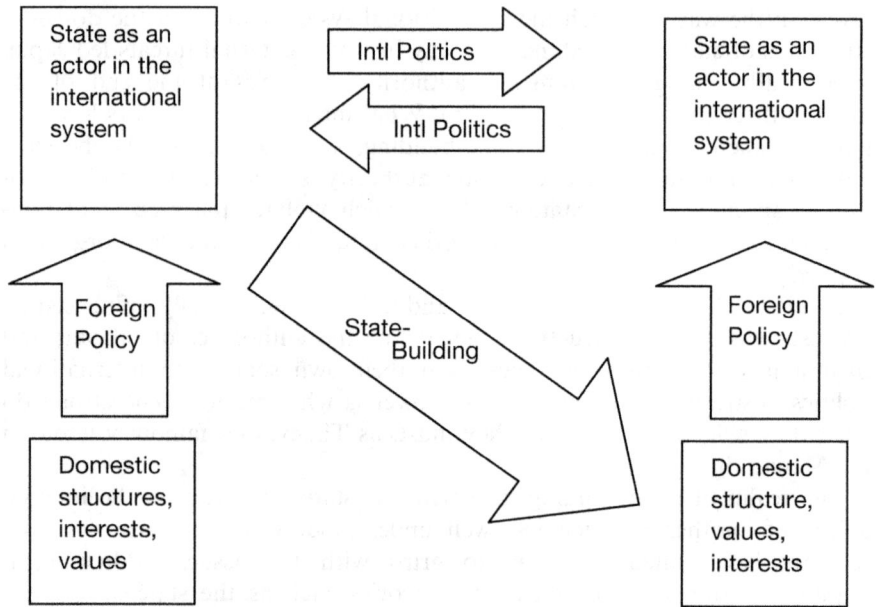

Figure 0.1 Three realms of international relations: foreign policy, international politics, state-building.

Part I

Domestic politics and foreign policy

1 Defending the national interest

For at least a decade students of foreign policy have had to deal with a dis-
comforting problem: most used a conceptual approach that treated the state
as a unified rational actor, yet many felt uncomfortable with its assumptions.
While the conventional model yielded many interesting findings, its analytic
categories did not appear to represent actual institutions faithfully. The
notion of the state seemed merely a shorthand for a complex set of bureaucratic institutions and roles. No modern country is run by a prince. Officials
in Washington, who spend a good part of their time at interdepartmental
meetings, play bureaucratic politics even if they do not know the proper
label, just as Molière's Monsieur Jourdan spoke prose. It has become commonplace to think of the American government as a large blundering
bureaucratic mass incapable of sustained action and rational behavior. The
greatest problems of public policy are described not in terms of goals but
in terms of management skills. Decision making is seen as a morass of
conflicting interests extending from the society through the ostensibly
hierarchically ordered central bureaucracy of the state.

In addition, the state-centric model used in international relations has
seemed at odds with the most prevalent approaches to domestic politics. At
least in the United States, a pluralist image has dominated the analysis of
politics. The behavior of the state is seen as a product of societal pressures. A
liberal perspective may grant that the state is one interest among many
(indeed, the bureaucratic politics model extends interest-group politics into
the bureaucracy), but it rejects the notion of a national interest that is
not a product of the aggregation of particularistic societal goals. Interest-
group analysis has not been applied to high politics because it could be
assumed that all groups in the society would support the preservation of
territorial and political integrity; but in the area of international economic
relations there is, *a priori*, no such clear societal consensus. Tariff levels,
exchange rates, and foreign investment all benefit some groups and harm
others.

Marxist theories have offered a clear alternative to the realist model. This
approach has an integrated view of domestic and international politics. In
both spheres state behavior is seen as a product of societal needs. For

instrumental Marxists, government officials are the handmaiden of particular societal groups.

There is a more sophisticated version of the Marxist position, structural Marxism, which views the state as an autonomous institution whose task is to preserve the coherence of capitalist society as a whole. This may mean acting against the preferences voiced by particular capitalist groups. For both liberals and Marxists, however, the state is, in the final analysis, an epiphenomenon: its behavior reflects disaggregated societal needs, either directly for interest group and instrumental Marxist analyses or more circumspectly for structural Marxist ones. The concept of the national interest has no meaning except as a summation of particularistic preferences.

This study has tried to demonstrate that neither a liberal nor a Marxist conception is adequate. Its micro-theoretic task has been to elaborate a statist approach by inductively investigating the national interest and policy-making processes in the United States. This investigation has shown that the state has purposes of its own. The national interest does have empirical reality if it is defined as a consistent set of objectives sought by central decision makers. The cases analyzed in this book suggest that there has been a clear rank ordering of goals for American policy related to foreign raw material investments. In order of increasing importance the ranking has been: (1) maximize the competitive structure of the market and thereby reduce prices; (2) increase security of supply; (3) secure general foreign policy objectives.

This is not to say that the policies actually implemented by the United States have been coherent. Looking at what the American government actually did, as opposed to what central decision makers preferred, presents a complicated picture. The fragmentation of power in the political system has allowed powerful private groups to block many state initiatives. This has been most evident when achieving state aims required positive action from private firms. This situation existed in all of the cases involving the promotion of foreign investment. To get oil investment in Iraq in the 1920s and Iran in the 1950s, central decision makers had to compromise their desire for greater competition by sanctioning the Red Line Agreement and downgrading the oil antitrust suit from a criminal to a civil action. While government officials were successful in getting Firestone into Liberia during the 1920s, other US rubber firms were not responsive to the government's call for new investments in non-British areas. Private actors were also able to block public initiatives when decisions could not be held within the executive branch. During the 1940s, efforts to buy Aramco, construct an oil pipeline, and sign an agreement with the United Kingdom were frustrated because they needed Congressional approval.

In contrast, cases requiring positive action by the state rather than the private sector present a different picture of power relationships. This category includes almost all issues concerning the protection of foreign investment. Companies usually wanted more support than central decision makers were willing to give. Even the largest and most powerful private corporations were not able to turn instruments of state power to private purposes when this would violate the national interest, the aims sought by central decision makers. Such instruments, particularly the use of force, were controlled by public institutions that have been well insulated from private pressures. The White House and the State Department were concerned with broader foreign policy goals.

The cases are not equally useful in contributing to the macro-theoretic aim of this study—distinguishing among statist, Marxist, and liberal interpretations of foreign policy. Some are more or less compatible with all three theories. These include all of the examples of investments actively promoted by the state—rubber in Liberia, oil in the Middle East and the Dutch East Indies during the 1920s, and oil in Iran in the 1950s. In these instances public and private preferences were fairly closely aligned and were associated with general societal goals. Although the assertive role played by the state here cannot be as readily understood from a pluralist or instrumental Marxist position, nevertheless the evidence these cases provide for preferring one competing interpretation over another is not very decisive.

Cases that show a clear divergence between corporate and state preferences are more analytically useful; they support statist and structural Marxist positions over interest group and instrumental Marxist ones. Such divergences arose most frequently from disputes involving the takeover of US firms. In 1919, Woodrow Wilson rejected private appeals that troops be used to protect American interests in Mexico. Before World War II American central decision makers turned a deaf ear to oil company entreaties for more vigorous official backing in Peru and Mexico. In 1966 Assistant Secretary of State Lincoln Gordon relaxed economic sanctions against Peru while Exxon officials continued to prefer strong pressure. At the Teheran negotiations in January 1971, US policy makers undermined oil company bargaining strategy by endorsing separate negotiations for the Persian Gulf, the procedure favored by Saudi Arabia and Iran. Examples such as these weigh heavily against any interpretation that views state behavior as a function of direct private pressure. The strongest conclusion that emerges from the evidence presented in the case studies is that instrumental Marxist and liberal arguments are inadequate.

The two approaches whose relative merits are most difficult to assess are structural Marxism and statism. Both see the state as an autonomous actor concerned with long-term objectives. The difference lies in the type of aims that are sought. For a statist paradigm, the state has its own needs and goals, which cannot be reduced to specific societal interests. For a structural Marxist paradigm, state behavior is ultimately related to preserving a set of exploitative economic relationships that benefit a particular class. It is not easy to find empirical evidence that can separate the two. Here the argument that a statist paradigm is more powerful rests upon two examples. The first is the effort of the American government to buy Aramco during the Second World War. A violation of the basic norm of capitalism—private property—in a situation in which there was neither immediate pressure from the working class nor a clearly demonstrable long-term need cannot fit easily with a structural Marxist interpretation. Nevertheless, the state failed, and this case could be explained away, albeit with some sacrifice of elegance, as an aberration based upon individual peculiarities. The second set of empirical cases that support a statist perspective are drawn from instances where the United States was prepared to use either covert or overt force. After 1945 all of these were clearly associated with the goal of preventing communist regimes from assuming or holding power. This aim can be comprehended from a structural Marxist perspective: communism does not enhance capitalism's long-term prospects. It can also be understood from a statist perspective: the United States wanted to remake the world in its own Lockean liberal image. However, the nonlogical manner in which American leaders pursued their anticommunism is not compatible with a structural Marxist position. The absence of means–ends calculations, coupled with misperception, led to policies that undermined the coherence of American domestic society, particularly in Vietnam. This is the very opposite result from the one predicted by a structural Marxist argument, but it is compatible with a statist view that sees the state as capable of defining its own autonomous goals.

Interest and ideology in US foreign policy

The final piece of the puzzle that must be fit into place is to relate more precisely the broad foreign policy goals pursued by US leaders to a statist interpretation of American foreign policy. It is all well and good to create a catchall category for any apparently noneconomic objective sought by policy makers, but this is hardly a convincing defense of a statist interpretation of American behavior. If these aims changed from one day to the next, or even from one year to the next, because of bureaucratic battles, or private pressures, or the transitory moods of presidents, then a statist approach would not be adequate. This study has not tried to identify the national interest with some divinely or logically ordained goal for the state, nor has it viewed it as an analytic assumption that can be used to derive propositions about the international system. Instead, this has been an inductive enterprise. What this study demonstrates is that the general aims of American policy have moved from a concern with territorial and political integrity and with security of supply before World War II (with the exception of Woodrow Wilson's presidency) to an emphasis on ideological goals after 1945.

In *The Logic of World Power* Franz Schurmann posits a fundamental distinction between interests and ideology, between expansionism on the one hand and imperialism on the other. Interests involve *material* aims and the social and physical quality of life. Ideology is concerned with order, security, and justice. Imperialism is a manifestation of ideology, a vision of how the world should be ordered on a global basis. It has a "total world-wide quality," whereas expansionism is incremental and concerned with material interests (Schurmann 1974: 6).

The broad foreign policy aims implicit in US policy toward foreign raw materials investments must be seen as both expansionist and imperialist. The division between the two is largely chronological. Before the Second World War the United States was an expansionist but not an imperialist nation. With the exception of Wilson's policies in Mexico, American behavior can be understood in terms of interests—that is, specific economic aims or the preservation of territorial and political integrity (the core goals of any state). US policy after the Second World War must be understood in terms of ideology: leaders were driven by a vision of what the global order should be like. Covert or overt force was used only when policy makers saw their vision threatened. This politics of vision had been foreshadowed by Woodrow Wilson's actions toward Mexico. The vision itself was a manifestation of American liberalism, what Louis Hartz has called the totalitarian hold of a Lockean worldview on American life (Hartz 1955).

The use of force by the American government cannot be explained without reference to America's ideological commitments. After the Second World War the one thing that all of the cases associated with the use of force shared was that policy makers feared a communist takeover. Vietnam and even Korea make it clear that American policy makers were willing to bear heavy costs to prevent communist regimes from coming to power. It is not possible to explain this behavior in terms of strategic interests, that is, protecting the territorial and political integrity of the United States. It is not possible to explain it in terms of the goal of strengthening ties with major allies, the Western European states and Japan, with the possible exception of the relationship between Japanese concerns and Korea. It is not possible to explain these interventions in terms of economic interests. One must look to the realm of ideology, of vision, for a persuasive explanation of American policy.

As Louis Hartz has argued, the intensity of this reaction is best understood as a result of the exclusive dominance of Lockean liberalism within the United States. In the United States this political vision has never been effectively challenged from either the left or the right. The application of America's worldview to the Third World has been most fully articulated by Robert Packenham. Packenham argues that the attitudes of American policy makers were dominated by four basic assumptions: change and development are easy, all good things go together, radicalism and revolution are bad, and distributing power is more important than accumulating power. All of these assumptions reflect liberal commitments to individualism and democracy, or the American historical experience of rapid growth without revolutionary upheaval (Packenham 1973: Ch. 3).

Communism was antithetical to this set of beliefs. It had grown out of a socialist perspective that had never taken root in the United States. It emphasized basic disharmonies within society. It advocated violent change. It rejected individualism. In practice, communist societies had given the state great power. Communism was more threatening to US leaders than any other ideology they encountered.

I do not mean to argue that American policy makers were immaculate liberals who sought nothing but Lockean ideals. In the period after the Second World War the United States supported many authoritarian regimes of the right. In part this practice resulted from constrained choice. US leaders in the 1950s and 1960s were not quite as naive as Woodrow Wilson about the prospects for instant democracy; to paraphrase President Kennedy, the United States preferred democratic regimes, but when this alternative was unrealistic, they favored right-wing over left-wing dictatorships. This choice is consistent with a Lockean belief structure. First, right-wing regimes were more prone to recognize the legitimacy of a private sphere of action; they rarely made the same totalitarian, that is total, state claims on the society that were typical of the left. In addition, the right was less of a threat because it lacked the external support that a communist regime might be able to draw from the Soviet bloc. Soviet assistance could bolster such regimes, making it less likely that they could be transformed along lines that more closely followed the contours of America's vision.

But why has ideology only become important at a certain period in the nation's history? Basic beliefs are not variable: they are constant over time. Why do they affect policy during some periods but not others? The answer is basically found in the international distribution of power among states. Ideological goals can be pursued only by the very powerful and perhaps also the very weak, by those who can make things happen and those who cannot change what happens. For most states it must be interests, and not visions, that count. A state whose core objectives are threatened can rarely engage in creating a global order. Political culture or ideology will affect perceptions and therefore policy, but the objectives of policy will be in the realm of interests. Even when core objectives are not at stake, most states are likely to seek identifiable, usually material, objectives. Small and medium-size states do not have the resources to change domestic regimes in other countries or create new international structures. Even quite large states are likely to be expansionist rather than imperialist, to impose their will on others to secure specific goals, to act in terms of a calculus in which costs are weighed against benefits. Only states whose resources are very large, both absolutely and relatively, can engage in imperial policies, can attempt to impose their vision on other countries and the global system. And it is only here that ideology becomes a critical determinant of the objectives of foreign policy. Great power removes the usual restraints on central decision makers. Very powerful states escape some of the consequences of the inherently anarchic nature of the international system. For them it is not a Hobbesian world because there is no opponent that can threaten their core interests. Policy makers have at their disposal resources that are not committed to preserving identifiable economic aims or territorial and political integrity. They can enter the realm of vision (although it has rarely turned out to be the kingdom of God).

Perhaps two analogies will make this argument clearer. The association of an ideological foreign policy with a hegemonic state is based implicitly upon an assumption of a hierarchy of goals. The state can only move on to higher things (structuring foreign regimes and the international system in its own image) if more fundamental aims (protecting territorial and political integrity) have been satisfied. In *Sociobiology* Edward O. Wilson offers a similar explanation for the diversity of human cultures. He argues that humans display an extremely wide set of cultural variations. The behavioral range of other animals is much narrower. Humans are able to establish more diverse social habits only because they have so thoroughly dominated their environment. Basic needs are no longer the determinant of social organization. "No species of ant or termite enjoys such freedom. ... In short, animal species tend to be tightly packed in the ecosystem with little room for experimentation or play. Man has temporarily escaped the constraint of interspecies competition" (Wilson 1975: 550). Just as man in the biosphere can engage in many activities not directly related to the survival of the species, hegemonic states can pursue ideological goals because more basic needs are not threatened.

A second analogy is offered in the work of the psychologist Abraham Maslow, who makes an argument explicitly based on a hierarchy of needs. When more basic individual needs are satisfied, he sees new ones emerging to motivate human activity. Physiological necessities are the most fundamental. If food, clothing, and shelter are available, then safety, love and affection, esteem (including freedom, competence, prestige, recognition, and dominance), and finally self-actualization become, in that order, the most important driving forces. An individual only moves on to a higher need when more basic ones are satisfied. Maslow summarizes his argument in the following terms:

> We have seen that the chief principle of organization in human motivational life is the arrangement of needs in a hierarchy of lesser or greater priority or potency. The chief dynamic principle animating this organization is the emergence of less potent needs upon the gratification of more potent ones.
>
> (Maslow 1954: 107)

Just as the human species in the biosphere, and individual men in their quest for fulfillment, can move on to less pressing goals only after more basic ones (the survival of the species or the individual) have been satisfied, so hegemonic states can indulge in ideological foreign policies because their core objectives are not in jeopardy.

The historical evolution of US policy

Writers who have emphasized the importance of ideology have generally argued that there has been a cyclical tendency in American foreign policy.

Periods of external expansion have alternated with periods of insularity. Americans move in one generation to remake the outside world, encounter failure and frustration, and turn away from external involvement in the next generation. The argument here suggests that there has been a more linear development in American foreign policy. The basic determinant of the goals sought by American central decision makers has not been generational experience but America's place in the international political system—that is, its power in relation to other states.

Until the last decade of the nineteenth century the country was insular and isolationist. The Monroe Doctrine was a symbol, not a guide to action. The resources of the nation were devoted to internal development. The United States still relied on European capital. It was British naval power that limited European incursions into the Western hemisphere. American leaders did voice support for various bourgeois revolutions in Europe, but the resources they were willing to expend on such activities were quite small. Lockean liberalism did have an impact, but the distribution of power in the international system, and America's place in it, precluded ideological goals from dominating American actions.

With the exception of Wilson's tenure, the United States moved to expansionist but not ideological policies between 1896 and 1941. It translated its power resources derived from its size and technological capabilities into a more aggressive foreign policy. But its actions were directed to material goals, strategic or economic. This kind of behavior was first manifest in the Caribbean and the Pacific. No longer were US central decision makers content to rely on Britain to limit European penetration of the Western hemisphere. In Cuba, the Dominican Republic, Haiti, Venezuela, Nicaragua, and elsewhere, American policy makers intervened both diplomatically and militarily. Regardless of whether American expansionism is viewed as aimed at economic exploitation or limiting strategic vulnerability, it can still be seen as a manifestation of a politics of interest: specific, identifiable goals related to material or political well-being were at stake.

During the interwar years the United States remained expansionist but non-imperial. America turned against Wilson's attempt to create a new international order after the First World War. Decisions taken by American policy makers in the late 1920s and early 1930s helped precipitate and exacerbate the Great Depression, because Hoover and. Roosevelt paid most attention to domestic economic problems and failed to perceive the relationship between American welfare and the health of the global system. In the area of raw materials American policy makers were primarily concerned with security of supply. They actively promoted rubber investment in Liberia and oil investment in the Middle East and Dutch East Indies. They opposed efforts to establish cartels in natural rubber, coffee, and other materials. They supported new raw materials investments in Latin America.

All of these activities can be understood in terms of a calculus of interests. There was a direct pay-off, usually economic, in the concentration on domestic economic problems, opposition to cartels, and new raw materials investments. In retrospect some of these actions appear shortsighted. American leadership might have mitigated the Depression of the 1930s, but only by adopting policies that broke radically with past behavior. Moreover, it is not clear that during the interwar years the United States had the power to construct a new global order. London was still the world's financial center. The British pound remained the world's leading international currency. Until the Second World War the United States was an expansionist, not an imperial, state.

Only after 1945 did American leaders move consistently to a politics of ideology, although such behavior had been foreshadowed by Woodrow Wilson. Wilson was a man whose time had not come. By 1914 the United States was, in economic strength, the most powerful nation on earth. But it had near rivals in Russia, Germany, and Britain. The beliefs of its citizens and many of its institutions were still attuned to the insularity of the nineteenth century, or at best the expansionism of McKinley and Roosevelt. Wilson had at his disposal substantial resources, but these were not sufficient to implement and carry through a politics of vision, although a visionary he certainly was. Probably no American leader has ever so clearly articulated the ideals of liberalism. His policy toward the Mexican Revolution was but one manifestation of his more general attitudes. He eschewed acting for the sake of interests. He castigated American corporations. He helped bring down Huerta, the Mexican leader most favorably disposed toward American investors during the first decade of the revolution. For Wilson, democracy was more important than oil, silver, or copper, especially if it triumphed through his efforts.

Although Wilson failed in his more global goals, they were resurrected after World War II. The United States emerged from the war in an extraordinarily powerful position. The economies of all of the other major industrial states had been shattered. Great Britain, a rival of the United States in the interwar years, was starving and freezing by the winter of 1946–47. The United States controlled almost all of the world's gold reserves. Its economy was several times larger than that of its nearest rival. It was the only possible source of capital and equipment for postwar reconstruction. Although the United States had disbanded most of its army, it did have a monopoly of atomic weapons until 1949.

In this setting American leaders were not content to pursue only interests: they wanted to impose their vision on the world. This imperative was all the stronger because of the experience of the previous fifteen years: the Depression and the Second World War had almost shattered capitalist societies. The vision American leaders drew on, Lockean liberalism; was their own; it was particularly intense because of its totalitarian hold on the American psyche. The greatest challenge to that vision came from communism, a challenge all the more severe because it had the support of another powerful state, the Soviet Union.

The ideological goals pursued by US central decision makers cannot be relegated to the realm of interests, as Marxist analysts are wont to do. For Marxism, ideology is a mask or a weapon used to further underlying class interests. Ideas do not have a life of their own. They do not play an independent part in organizing social and political behavior. In the American interventions after the Second World War, however, economic goals and the stability of the social system in general were, ultimately in Vietnam, sacrificed to an ideological vision. American behavior lacked the central hallmark of a politics of interest—rational calculation. Relationships between means and ends were unclear. There was a persistent tendency to misperceive. A belief in how society ought to be ordered was more powerful than material concerns. In Pareto's terminology, American policy was nonlogical.

It is not surprising that an imperial country's foreign policy should assume an ideological cast in which objectives are associated with basic social values and behavior is nonlogical. Clifford Geertz has argued that ideologies become important when the existing body of tradition or belief that guides political action breaks down. "It is a loss of orientation that most directly gives rise to ideological activity" (Geertz 1964). In international relations the functional equivalent for the state of traditional guides to action are the imperatives imposed by the anarchy of the international system. Normal states cannot follow policies that endanger their territorial and political integrity. However, such constraints do not exist for an imperial state. Like the society that has lost its bearings, it is in a world that lacks clear markers. It has power that can be used for objectives that are not associated with clearly definable needs. It can try to remake the world. World-makers are not guided by prudence, for they see their objectives as consummatory goals that are worth virtually any sacrifice. Although the form of expansionism varies, depending upon the dominant ideology of the state, countries with enough power to ignore specific foreign policy goals have virtually always become imperialists.

Ideology and the statist paradigm

An ideological foreign policy is best understood from a statist perspective for two reasons. First, the central characteristic of such a policy is that it does not offer benefits for any specific societal groups. Neither interest group nor instrumental Marxist approaches can offer a very satisfactory explanation for such behavior: for both, government action is understood to result from particular societal pressures. A structural Marxist approach also fails to give an adequate understanding of American behavior after the Second World War. It would be possible for this paradigm to deal with the pursuit of ideological ends if this were necessary to preserve the coherence of capitalist society. However, in a number of cases, particularly Vietnam, efforts to remake political and economic structures in other countries weakened the social fabric of the United States itself. Central decision makers did not act in the prudential and calculating way that one would expect from a structural Marxist approach. Ideological goals became an end in themselves. Only the state, viewed as an autonomous institution, can make such goals the primary objectives of policy, for the state is the only institution that can formulate aims that either have very diffuse benefits or impose costs on specific societal groups or the society as a whole. Such behavior can be understood from a statist perspective whose basic assumption is that the state is autonomous. The independence of central decision makers from particular pressures allows them to formulate objectives that could not be effectively articulated by any nonstate actors. The state is not one interest group among many, or the servant of general societal needs; it is an institution with purposes and powers of its own.

The second aspect of an ideological foreign policy that suggests the power of a statist approach is that the ability to carry out such a policy is intimately related to a nation's place in the international system. To understand an ideological foreign policy, it is necessary to begin at the basic starting point for a realist approach to international politics: the distribution of power among states. An ideological foreign policy can be associated with a hegemonic state, because such a state can ignore interests. A state acting in an imperial role, as an orderer of the global system, is not sensitized to material limitations.

Neither a liberal nor a Marxist perspective can deal with the importance of the international distribution of power in explaining American foreign policy. Both of these perspectives begin with internal pressures on the state emanating from either particular or general societal needs. Policy comes from the bottom up. A statist or realist perspective begins with the distribution of power among states. Policy comes from the top down. Under normal circumstances states will act on the basis of interests. However, a state that is so powerful that it no longer need be concerned with its territorial and political integrity, and all of the ancillary policies that follow from these basic goals, such as preserving the security of raw materials supplies, can make ideological goals the most important aspect of its foreign policy. For two and a half decades after the Second World War Lockean liberalism was the key to American foreign policy; it was the desire to create a world order in America's image that led to the use of force.

2   US commercial and monetary policy
Unraveling the paradox of external strength and internal weakness

There are makers, breakers, and takers of international economic regimes. Economic transactions do not take place in a political vacuum. Political power is needed to establish a system or regime—a pattern of rules, norms, and practices. In international affairs that power can only come from a state or group of states. Historically, a stable international economic regime has been associated with a hegemonic maker of the system. Medium-size states can be breakers of the system. They do not have the power to establish a regime, but by changing their policies they may be able to undermine an ongoing pattern of rules and behavior: they can move international economic relations from the pole of order toward the pole of chaos. Small states are takers of the system. They can adjust their own policies to try to maximize their particular objectives, but, for them, the general nature of the regime is a given.

In the period after the Second World War, the United States was the maker of the system. Its power and policies shaped the international economic regime. An exposition of American foreign economic policy must examine its external consequences in terms of establishing, maintaining, and undermining the international economic regime, as well as the domestic determinants of US policy.

The fundamental objective of American central decision makers was to create a liberal international economic regime. This meant that barriers to the movement of goods, services, capital, and technology would be minimized. It also meant that these transactions would be carried out by private, as opposed to state-owned, firms. American leaders sought this objective not only because it was initially in the economic interest of the US, but also because America's liberal ideology led them to believe that such a regime would promote prosperity and peace around the world.

In pursuing this goal American central decision makers confronted external and internal constraints—resistance from other international actors and from particular domestic interest groups. This dual challenge of external and internal resistance must be faced by any state leader.

The US was more constrained by internal than by external factors, at least from 1948 until the last ten years. The US emerged from the Second World

War in a position of unprecedented international power. The economies of all of the other major industrial states had been severely strained or destroyed by the global conflagration. It was not until the late 1960s or the 1970s that the decline in America's relative international position began to impose limits on the ability of the US to maintain a liberal global order.

However, US central decision makers were persistently confronted by challenges from domestic groups. This endemic problem was a product of the structure of the American political system. The key characteristic of that structure is that power is fragmented and decentralized. The American state—those institutions and roles that are relatively insulated from particularistic pressures and concerned with general goals (primarily the White House and the State Department and to a lesser extent the Treasury and Defense Departments)—is weak in relation to its own society. In comparison with their counterparts in other industrial countries, US central decision makers have difficulty extracting the domestic resources that they need to implement state policies. The potential international power of the state—the ability of central decision makers to change the behavior of other international actors and to provide collective goods for the international system if *all* of the society's resources could be used for state purposes (that is, if there are no domestic constraints)—is great. But the actual power of the state— the power resulting from the resources that central decision makers can actually extract from their own society—is much less.

The problems presented by domestic political weakness were more manifest for commercial policy than for monetary policy. American monetary policy and the orderliness of the international monetary regime very closely paralleled the rise of American external power through the early 1960s and the decline that followed. But commercial policy, where Congress was a relatively more important decision arena, always presented American central decision makers with domestic constraints: it was necessary to buy off some import-competing industries that were being hurt by the pursuit of a liberal global order. However, even here, the pervasiveness of ideology, the vision of peace and prosperity flowing from a free and open international economic system, offered US leaders a lever of power that dampened, even if it did not entirely suppress, demands for protectionism.

America's foreign economic policy has moved through four stages during the postwar years, distinguished by changes in specific international economic policies. Each of these shifts reflected changes in the international position of the United States and in the constraints imposed by domestic pressure groups.

1945–47, a false start: Initial efforts to create a liberal order failed because US leaders were unable to extract from their domestic society the resources necessary for postwar reconstruction. By 1948, the international institutions which they had envisioned as the centerpieces of the new order were either inactive, such as the International Monetary Fund

(IMF) or the World Bank (IBRD), or nonexistent, like the International Trade Organization (ITO).

1947–62, an opening wedge: In 1947 American central decision makers broke with the amorphous Wilsonianism that had animated their previous activities and redefined international economic issues in terms of a global struggle with communism. They moved from the World Bank and the IMF to the Marshall Plan. By changing the nature of the debate, US political leaders were able to extract much higher levels of resources from their own society. These resources facilitated the creation of a liberal economic order by promoting European and Japanese economic growth. International liquidity for higher levels of world trade was provided by the American balance of payments deficit. However, commercial policy was still trammeled by domestic resistance.

1962–71, apogee and decline: In the early 1960s, the United States still enjoyed an extraordinary international position. During the 1950s, growing international trade and investment made the benefits of a liberal order a reality or an immediate promise for American business rather than a long-term and uncertain vision. Both international and domestic constraints were low. This made possible the passage of the Trade Expansion Act in 1962 and the Kennedy Round. However, during the 1960s the relative economic position of the US declined. Balance of payments difficulties became more apparent. More domestic industries faced stiff foreign competition. Protectionist demands increased and policy became less coherent.

1970s, growing strains, international and domestic: The problems for domestic groups, which first developed in the 1960s, became more severe during the 1970s, and the decline in America's *potential* international power continued. In August 1971, the US broke the Bretton Woods system. The 1974 Trade Act was more protectionist than the 1962 Act. During the early 1970s, the world monetary system became more disorderly and little progress was made in multilateral trade negotiations.

The goals of American central decision makers

The most important and consistently pursued policy of American central decision makers since the Second World War has been the creation and maintenance of a liberal international economic regime. Such a system has two basic characteristics. The first is the minimization or elimination of barriers to the movements of goods, services, technology, and capital across international boundaries. The second is the control of such movements by private, as opposed to state-owned, corporations.

The desire to construct a liberal regime stemmed from three different sources. The first was the historical experience of American decision makers. The Depression had been accompanied by a sharp increase in economic nationalism as countries moved to protect themselves from the ravages of a malevolent global economy. The economic crisis was also associated with Hitler's rise to power. Nazi Germany had not only caused the Second World War. It had also followed international policies that were highly discriminatory and nationalistic and which were heavily influenced by the state. One lesson that American leaders drew from this experience was that economic nationalism was a threat to both peace and prosperity (J.M. Jones 1955: 92; R.N. Gardner 1969: 19–20; Wilkins 1974: 289).

The second source of America's commitment to a liberal international order was more closely related to definable American interests stemming from America's international structural position. America emerged from the war as a hegemonic power; it was much larger and more technologically advanced than any of its rivals. Such a state is likely to prefer an open international economic regime. Such a regime will increase its static economic well-being and help to promote its economic growth. It will also further its political power by locking other countries into economic relationships that they cannot break without greater cost to themselves than to the hegemonic state (Krasner 1976: 318–21).

The third reason for the commitment to a liberal international economic regime was ideological. A new world economic order was one aspect of the general vision animating US leaders after World War II. It was a vision that had its roots in America's own historical experience. As Louis Hartz has argued, that experience has been heavily colored by Lockian liberalism, by a worldview that has emphasized individual liberty and the minimization of state interference in the society. This ideology has had a "fixed, dogmatic" hold on Americans' view of the social and political order (Hartz 1955).

Liberalism has not always been manifest in American foreign policy in general or foreign economic policy in particular. During the nineteenth century, the costs of openness, in terms of stifling America's own industrialization, were too great. It was not until Woodrow Wilson's presidency that Lockian ideas strongly affected international economic policy. Although Wilson did not succeed, those leaders who came after him held the same beliefs. Ideology became so important after the Second World War because American power was so great. Unlike in the nineteenth century, the US was not concerned about foreign competition. It could seek not just to protect its own narrow objectives but also to create an international system in its own image: a system that reflected the virtues of liberalism (R.N. Gardner 1969: 8–12; Schurmann 1974: Part I).

Of the three factors affecting the objectives of American central decision makers since the Second World War, ideology has turned out to be the most important. Historical memories have faded. The structural position of the United States has changed; it is no longer clear that American interests are furthered by a laissez-faire system (Gilpin 1975: Ch. 8). Nevertheless, American leaders have continued to pursue this policy, although the explicit rationale has changed from Wilsonianism to anti-Communism to building democracy to interdependence, all of which are facets of America's liberalism. While American leaders have been concerned with specific objectives ranging from balance-of-payments equilibrium to the import of instant coffee, they have not seriously entertained any alternative to a liberal order. Furthermore, central decision makers have not adopted policies that they perceived as being antithetical to such an international regime. While more and more groups within the United States have advocated protectionism, none has been able to offer a worldview that can replace liberalism, not only in terms of specific American economic interests, but also in terms of preserving world peace and prosperity.

The international structure

With the exception of the United States, the Second World War devastated the economies of all major industrial states. While the US had become the world's largest producer of manufactures in the 1880s and the most important source of international credit after the First World War, the impact of the Second World War elevated America to a position of potential power unprecedented in the modern era (Krasner 1976: 333–34). Once the Soviet Union and its allies had withdrawn into their own international order, the relationship of the US to other states with which it carried on active economic interchange was even more asymmetrical.

The extraordinarily powerful position of the United States with respect to the rest of the non-communist world is brought out by Table 2.1.

These aggregate indicators alone do not show America's potential international power—its ability to influence the behavior of other states and provide collective goods for the international system, if *all* of these resources could be utilized by central decision makers. Such an evaluation would require a detailed study of the vulnerabilities of other countries relative to those of the US (Hirschman 1945), but Table 2.1 does give a picture that is indicative of general trends. The US emerged from the Second World War in an unchallenged position. Its economy was much larger and more prosperous than that of any other country. Furthermore, it enjoyed a dominant position in virtually every economic issue-area ranging from capital to manufacturing to raw materials.

During the 1960s America's potential international economic power began to decline. In some areas, such as wheat and energy consumption, there is not much change from the 1950s to the 1970s. But in others, such as iron ore, steel, and petroleum, the relative position of the US in the world was much different in 1973 than it was in the late 1940s. This is not to say that America has become a second-rate power, but it is to say that America has become more like a normal nation-state. No longer does American power dominate in virtually every issue-area. No longer can the US simply impose its will on others.

Table 2.1 Some indicators of United States potential external power

	A National income		B Per capita income	C Crude petroleum production		D Crude steel	
	Ratio of US to total market economies	Ratio of US to next largest	Ratio of US to next highest	Ratio of US to total world production	Ratio of US to next largest producer (excl. E. Bloc)	Ratio of US to total world production	Ratio of US to next largest producer (excl. E. Bloc)
1937							
1945					3.81 (Ven.)	.64	6.02 (UK)
1948							
1949							
1950						.45	5.31 (UK)
1953		6.43 (UK)	1.58 (Switz.)	.51	3.33 (Ven.)		
1955						.39	4.98 (W. Ger.)
1958		6.33 (UK)	1.52 (Switz.)	.43	2.91 (Ven.)		
1960	.45	6.96 (UK)	1.78 (Sweden)	.33	2.33 (Ven.)	.26	2.64 (W. Ger.)
1965		6.59 (W. Ger.)	1.51 (Switz.)			.26	3.23 (W. Ger.)
1966				.25	3.42 (Saudi Arabia)		
1970	.39	5.23 (W. Ger.)	1.14 (Sweden)	.21	2.48 (Iran)	.20	1.27 (Japan)
1973		3.27 (Japan)	0.98 (Sweden)	.16	1.25 (Saudi Arabia)	.20	1.15 (Japan)

Sources: United Nations, *Statistical Yearbook* and *Yearbook of National Account Statistics*, various years

Domestic constraints

The potential or maximum international power of the state, the power that could be derived from all the resources controlled by its citizens relative to those of other societies, establishes only the outer boundaries of state power. Central decision makers cannot utilize resources that are beyond their sovereign control, but they may not even be able to mobilize all of the capabilities nominally within their jurisdiction. While political leaders must look outward toward external dangers and opportunities, they must also look inward toward their own domestic societies. In the extreme, a regime may be threatened by civil disorder and dissolution. Short of that, however, political leaders may find that they are unable to mobilize the resources that are needed to achieve the state's international goals because of resistance from domestic groups.

The ability of political leaders to mobilize domestic resources is a function of (1) the structure of the domestic political system, and (2) the convergence between private and public interests. In the following section we will consider the former; in the succeeding section, we will turn to the question of private and public interests.

The domestic weakness of the American state

The defining characteristic of a political system is the power of the state in relation to its own society. I realize that this hardly conforms with conventional notions. Liberal analysts treat the state, at worst, as an epiphenomenon whose behavior is explained by societal pressures and, at best, as another interest group or as an arbitrator among competing interests. Marxists regard the state as a servant of particular economic interests or as an agency preserving the general structure of capitalist society. Both liberals and Marxists deny the assumption of this paper that the state is an independent, autonomous entity with powers and objectives that are distinct from any particular societal groups (Lowi 1967: 5–24).

This power can be envisioned along a continuum ranging from weak to strong. The weakest kind of state is one which is completely permeated by pressure groups. Central government institutions serve specific interests within the country, rather than the collective aims of the citizenry as a whole. Lebanon even before the civil war of 1975–76 can be thought of as such a state. Public functions and positions were divided between Moslems and Christians. There was little or no general agreement on what constituted the general good or the collective interest of the country. The situation was exacerbated during the early 1970s, when the Palestinians were able to establish de facto control over some areas. At the other extreme from a state which is completely permeated by political pressure groups is one which is able to remake the society and culture in which it exists: that is, to change economic institutions, values, and patterns of interaction among private groups. Such extraordinarily powerful states only exist immediately after major revolutions. It is not that the state is so strong during such periods, but that the society is weak because existing patterns of behavior have been shattered. The clearest examples are the Soviet Union after 1921 and China after 1948. Both countries had suffered many years of war. In China, the old regime had been disintegrating for a century, unable to cope with pressure from the West. In Russia, the First World War had devastated the country and demonstrated the incompetence of the tsarist government. The communist regimes which were able to seize power made fundamental changes in economic, cultural, and even familial relationships.

Obviously, most states are neither as weak as Lebanon nor as domestically strong as post-revolutionary communist regimes. All advanced market economy countries fall someplace in between. The domestic strength of the state can be indicated by the answer to three questions:

1 Can the state formulate policy goals independent of particular groups within its own society?
2 Can the state change the behavior of specific groups?
3 Can the state directly change the structure of the society in which it operates? With regard to the economy, structure can be defined in terms of the nature of ownership (public versus private), the degree of concentration within an industrial sector, and the importance of particular sectors in the economy as a whole.

Obviously, the answer to any of these questions may vary with the issue-area that is being considered. But if the answers to all three are generally positive, then one is dealing with a relatively strong state. Of the countries examined in this volume, Japan comes closest to the pole of strength, at least for the period before 1976. Japanese leaders have been able to pursue a coherent set of objectives. They have not been confronted with serious domestic resistance. They have been able not only to influence the behavior of specific groups but also to change the structure of the Japanese economy. This power has reflected several characteristics of Japanese polity and society. Until the 1976 elections, Japan essentially had a one-party state minimizing the problems presented by executive-legislative clashes. Japanese interest groups accepted the legitimacy of state intervention in the economy. The state controlled a wide range of policy instruments, most importantly the dispensation of credit, which allowed it to influence private behavior and to change economic structures.

With the exception of the control of the Liberal Democratic Party, all of these factors are integral products of Japan's historical experience. As a late industrializer, the Japanese state played a decisive role in bringing modernity to Japan. The pattern of intervention established during the Meiji restoration has persisted to the present day, although the external forms have changed dramatically (Gerschenkron 1962: Ch. 1). Furthermore, Japan has always been confronted with scarce resources. It could not avoid involvement in the world economy without seriously sacrificing economic prosperity and growth, and this involvement has been accompanied by a high degree of state intervention.

The United States is closer to the pole of weakness. American policy makers have had a clear objective, the creation and maintenance of a liberal international economic order. Indeed, if the state cannot formulate a set of coherent goals, it is difficult to defend the concept of the state at all. But implementation in the face of domestic political opposition has been another matter. It has been very difficult for American central decision makers to change the behavior of non-state domestic actors. Political leaders have relatively little command of material resources, such as the control of credit, that can be used to offer incentives or to make threats. The most important mechanism through which American leaders have affected private actors and the Congress has been ideology: they have been able to appeal to a liberal vision of the world order to change the perceptions of interest held by non-state actors. Furthermore, the US political system offers its leaders few opportunities directly to change the structure of the economy. Some macro-economic policies, such as the determination of the money supply, do have an *indirect* impact over time, but central decision makers have rarely been able to act *directly* at the level of the industrial sector or the firm. When such intervention has occurred, as in the case of regulatory agencies or particular tax laws, the initiative has come from the private sector more often than from the state.

The central feature of American politics is the fragmentation and disper-sion of power and authority. This has been recognized by pluralists such as Polsby and Truman, who tend to emphasize the system's virtues, as well as by writers such as Huntington and Burnham, who see the American polity as basically flawed. Polsby argues that the different branches of the Amer-ican government were designed so that they "would be captured by different interests" (Polsby 1971: 140–41). Truman notes that the "diffusion of lea-dership and disintegration of policy are not hallucinations" (Truman 1971: 529). Huntington summarizes the situation as one in which there is a "fusion of functions and division of power" (Huntington 1968: 110). Burnham argues that the political system has been "in domestic matters at any rate—dispersive and fragmented ... dedicated to the defeat, except temporarily and under the direct pressure of overwhelming crisis, of any attempt to generate domestic sovereignty" (Burnham 1970: 176).

The Constitution is a document more concerned with limiting than enhancing the power of the state. The founding fathers were wary of power. They sought to deal with its temptations by limiting legal authority, dividing power within the government, and dividing power among groups in the society. This is reflected by their preserving the states, giving Con-gress and the president specific, not unlimited, legal powers, denying some power to Congress, establishing a bicameral legislature, and creating an independent judiciary. While the concept of dividing power among societal groups is not explicitly reflected in the Constitution, it was voiced by Madison at the Convention and clearly explicated in Federal Paper Number 10 (Dahl 1967: 39).

Within the executive branch it is unclear whether the president or the Congress controls particular bureaus. Permanent bureaucracies have their own interests. Some have their own independent ties with particular societal groups and Congressional committees (Neustadt 1960; Allison 1971: Halperin 1974; Krasner 1972: 159–79; Art 1973: 467–90).

The dispersion of power is even more striking in the American legislature. Bills can be blocked at any one of a number of decision-making nodes. In the House, these include subcommittees, full committees, the Rules Committee, the full House, the Rules Committee again for a bill going to a conference committee, and the conference committee. The situation is similar in the Senate, except that there is no direct parallel with the Rules Committee. The jurisdictional authority of individual committees is often not clearly differentiated. The Appropriations and Government Operations Committees, the House Rules Committee, and the Joint Economic Committee all have virtually universal scope in the matters they can consider. There is usually little cooperation between committees with the same jurisdiction in the two Houses (Fenno 1973: 63–90; Huitt 1973: 91–117).

There are several reasons for the fragmentation of power and authority, and thus the weakness, of the American political system. First, this situation is as integral a part of America's historical experience as Japan's strength is of its. American society was born modern; it was not necessary to have a strong state to destroy a traditional society. Early Americans were favorably disposed to change and to social status based on achievement rather than birth. Commitment to social classes was weak. There were neither feudal institutions nor an aristocracy that blocked social and economic development. America was an early industrializer. Economic change took place slowly and with relatively little state direction. In comparing Europe with America, Huntington argues that "[i]n Europe the opposition to modernization within society forced the modernization of the political system. In America, the ease of modernization within society precluded the modernization of political institutions" (Huntington 1968: 110).

A second reason for the persistence of a weak political structure is that America has not, until recently, confronted a serious external threat to its territorial and political integrity. On the European continent, the great impetus to the centralization of political authority during the sixteenth and seventeenth centuries was the constant threat of war. Fledgling states could not defend themselves without a standing army. To raise and maintain such forces, it was necessary to strengthen the political system (Huntington 1968: 122ff). The United States, on the other hand, enjoyed the protection of Britain's maritime dominance during the nineteenth century. By the time America was thrown upon the world scene in the twentieth century, its size and mastery of technology made it possible to create the world's most formidable military force. Curiously, the very weapons that have, for the first time, made the territorial integrity of the United States vulnerable may also, because of their capital intensity, allow the state to maintain its defenses with a weak political structure. The burdens imposed upon the domestic population by hardened missile sites and nuclear submarines are less than those resulting from large armies and extensive reserve corps.

A third reason for the persistence of a political system with diffused power has been material abundance and high levels of social equality. Tocqueville was struck by America's egalitarianism. He found a high level of literacy and relatively little social deference outside the cities of the eastern seaboard (Dahl 1967: 58–61). This social equality is intimately related to the abundance of American society. America has been rich from its beginnings. In terms of per capita income, it surpassed Britain in the middle of the nineteenth century. It then fell back as a result of immigration and other factors but regained its lead by the outbreak of the First World War. Abundance and rapid growth facilitated more equal opportunity and the belief that things would always improve. Social problems were often solved by technological and economic changes rather than political initiatives. The country was well endowed with natural resources. All of this reinforced the myth of social equality and mobility. It was possible to believe that things would always get better because they usually did for most people. The pressures brought upon the political system were usually modest because the level of social dissatisfaction was mitigated by economic growth. A weak political system could exist because politics was less necessary for a citizenry that perceived itself dividing an expanding rather than stagnant national product. In the words of David Potter, "Economic abundance is conducive to political democracy" (Potter 1954: 112) and, one might add, a democratic system that diffused rather than concentrated power and authority.

The laws and practices affecting America's foreign commercial policy illustrate the fragmentation and diffusion of power that can exist for particular issue-areas in the American political system. The problem has been much less acute for monetary policy.

The number of institutions involved in US trade policy is very large. The power to impose countervailing duties against foreign goods, which are receiving a "bounty or grant" from their own government, is vested in the Treasury Department by the Tariff Act of 1897. The 1921 Anti-Dumping Law also gives the Treasury the responsibility for protecting the American market from goods that are unfairly exported (Pastor 1976: 17). Under the 1974 Trade Act, the Commerce Department is charged with judging applications for adjustment assistance from businesses and communities, and the Labor Department with applications from labor. The Office of the Special Trade Representative (STR) was established by the 1962 Trade Expansion Act because Congress felt that the State Department, which had carried the main responsibility for multilateral negotiations to that date, was not sufficiently responsive to domestic needs. The 1974 Act makes the STR a cabinet-level post subject to Senatorial approval (M.J. Marks and Malmgren 1975: 348). The agricultural advisory committees established by the 1974 Act are chaired by the Agriculture Department, the industry committees by Commerce. A former administration official, writing for the Peterson Commission in 1971, outlined the involvement of administrative agencies in the area of international trade and investment as depicted in Table 2.2.

The decision-making structure for foreign economic, and particularly commercial, policy also gives representatives of the private sector more than ample access. The most significant point of entrance is the Congress. Congressmen may try to put off constituency entreaties, but they cannot ignore them. Various laws have given domestic groups formal standing with regard

Table 2.2 Executive departments involved in international economic policy

Issue-area	Agencies
Revenue and expenditure	Treasury and office of management and budget
Injury	Commerce, labor, council of economic advisors, special trade representative
Negotiability	State, STR, Treasury, Commerce
International trade effect	Commerce, State, STR, Agriculture
Foreign policy effect	State, National Security Council

Source: US Commission on International Trade and Investment Policy (1971): 424

to some trade issues. The 1951 Trade Act provided that the Tariff Commission could investigate a motion under the escape clause (the provision that the US could withdraw a trade concession if a domestic industry were seriously injured) instigated by the president, a resolution of either House, a resolution of the Senate Finance or House Ways and Means Committees, or by the application *of any interested party* (J.W. Evans 1971: 17–18; Weil 1975: 37–38). Although the Executive had always consulted with private groups before entering trade negotiations, the 1974 Act mandates the establishment of a system of advisory committees. The Executive has established a 45-member advisory Committee for Trade Negotiations with representatives drawn from industry, agriculture, and labor. It has also established separate committees for industry, labor, and agriculture. As of January 1976, 27 industry sectoral committees, eight agricultural sector committees, and six labor sectoral committees had been created (National Journal Reports 1975, 18 January: 77–78; United States, Congress, Senate, Committee on Finance 1974: 19).

Private groups can also affect foreign economic policy through the judicial system. Rulings of the International Trade Commission can be appealed to the US Customs Court, then to the Court of Customs and Patent Appeals, and ultimately to the Supreme Court. Recently, consumer groups have brought legal suits against trade controls. They have challenged the president's authority to conclude voluntary export agreements on the grounds that they violate US antitrust and due process laws (National Journal Reports 1975, 10 May: 696). In sum, the laws give Congress, the president, Treasury, Commerce, Labor, Agriculture, state, the special trade representative, the courts, and private groups access to US commercial policy making.

In contrast, there is less diffusion of power with respect to international monetary policy making. Only during the period from 1945 through 1947 was domestic restraint a significant factor for central decision makers. At other times, it was America's position in the structure of international power that primarily determined US policy and its impact on the global monetary regime. Decisions about monetary policy have been taken in the White House, the Treasury Department, and the Federal Reserve Board, arenas that are well insulated from particular societal pressures. Once the system of stable exchange rates, based more on the US dollar than on Bretton Woods, was established, there were not many issues that came before the Congress. Private actors rarely saw how monetary decisions related to their specific interests and therefore did not press for greater access to the decision-making machinery. In fact, until the late 1960s, virtually all sectors of the American elite regarded both the value of the dollar and fixed exchange rates as graven in stone and beyond the tampering of mere mortals.

In summary, the American political system is relatively weaker than that of most other industrial countries. Central decision makers in Japan and France can more easily manipulate their own domestic societies. In the US, private groups can penetrate the decision-making process more easily. There are many decision-making nodes where state initiatives can be vetoed. US leaders have relatively few policy instruments for intervening in the economy. This is not to say that American central decision makers are hapless victims of societal pressure groups. They are not. US leaders have been able to formulate clear policy objectives. They have been able to sway private groups through appeals to a widely shared ideological vision. In international monetary issues, they have had a relatively free hand because of the arenas in which decisions have been made. For the US, monetary policy is unusual in that it is decided in a small number of arenas that are insulated from societal pressures. Other aspects of foreign economic policy, including investment and aid as well as commercial policies, are fought over in a larger number of arenas (Schattschneider 1960: Ch. 1). However, the structural characteristics of the American polity allow domestic groups to impose more constraints on the state than in most other advanced countries.

The changing nature of domestic interests

The structure of the political system is only one variable determining the ability of central decision makers to carry out their preferences without regard to domestic societal pressures. The other is the extent of convergence between the policy goals of public and private actors. More specifically, the issue for this paper is the extent to which private preferences have converged with the desire of American leaders to create a liberal international economic system. If there is complete agreement between private and public actors, then the weakness of the political structure will not create many difficulties for central decision makers.

In the United States, private support for a liberal international economic order reached its peak around 1960. At that time, few import-competing industries were seriously threatened by foreign competition, and export industries and multinational firms saw many opportunities for foreign activities. Before 1960, support for a liberal order was lower because the involvement of the American economy in world trade and investment was still modest. After the early 1960s, the consensus for an open global economic regime began to decline because more sectors of the American economy were negatively affected by imports.

Table 2.3 gives some indication of the changing pattern of domestic interests with respect to foreign economic activities. Obviously, this table does not show the policies followed by particular domestic groups. But it does give some indication of the impact of international economic activities on different groups within the US. This impact is suggested by patterns of trade, direct investment, and banking.

Table 2.3 shows American trade balances for single-digit Standard International Trade Classification (SITC) numbers as well as five specific industries that have been the subject of controversy and demands for protection. These five are crude and partly refined petroleum, textiles and clothing, iron and steel, road motor vehicles, and footwear.

Table 2.3 US sectoral trade balances

UTC number	Clcrw of goods	1949 Balance	1960 Balance	1970 Balance
0	Food	119	−336	−923
1	Beverages & tobacco	154	85	−139
2	Crude materials inedible, except fuels	−513	−381	1,357
3	Minerals ruel, lubricants, related material	388	−740	−1,379
312 or 331	Petrol crude & partly refined	−232	−943	−1,448
4	Animal & vegetable oil and fats	62	211	336
5	Chemicals	629	1,298	2,390
6	Basic manufactured goods	539	−676	−3,360
	Textiles & clothing	861	−248	−1,603
681 or 67	Iron & steel	563	96	−1,708
7	Machines, transport equipment	3,386	5,527	6,847
732	Road motor vehicles	715	598	−1,907
8	Misc. manufac. goods	438	246	−2,154
851	Footwear	15	−141	−629
9	Goods not classified by kind	137	57	199
Total		5,287	5,292	3,273

Source: United Nations, *Yearbook of International Trade Statistics*, various years; and US, Census Bureau, *Statistical Abstract of the United States*, various years for textiles and clothing.

The first postwar year for which statistics are available from the United Nations is 1949. It is more indicative of the situation immediately following the Second World War than is 1950, by which time American trade was already affected by the Korean War. The most striking aspect of the 1949 data is not just that the US was running a heavy overall surplus, but that it had a positive trade balance for every major (single-digit) category of commodities. For the other items shown on the table, only crude and partly refined petroleum shows a negative balance, but this was a trivial percentage of total American oil consumption. Europe and Japan had hardly begun their postwar recoveries. The only economy capable of generating a wide variety of goods for export was that of the United States.

By 1960, the situation had changed. The US had a negative trade balance for food, crude materials, fuels, and basic manufactures (SITC numbers 0, 2, 3, and 6). However, except for fuels, none of these deficits was very large relative to exports. There were positive trade balances for beverages and tobacco, animal and vegetable oils, chemicals, miscellaneous manufactured goods, and machines and transport equipment (SITC numbers, 1, 4, 5, 7 and 8). SITC number 7, machines and transport equipment, includes the most technologically sophisticated group of products. However, some of the technologically older sectors of the American economy were suffering from foreign competition even in 1960. American shoe manufacturers had ceased exporting altogether, and imports were nine times greater in 1960 than 1955. Textiles and clothing went from a positive balance in 1955 to a negative one in 1960. While iron and steel still showed a positive balance, the ratio of exports to imports had fallen from 3.27 to 1.17. Road motor vehicles, a more technologically sophisticated product, continued to show a strong surplus. American dependence on foreign petroleum continued to grow and had reached about 20 per cent of consumption. In sum, by 1960, technologically older industries, such as textiles and footwear, were already showing trade deficits. Goods utilizing advanced and intermediate technologies had positive balances.

By 1970, the US economy was still more exposed to foreign competition. There were strong negative balances not only for unprocessed goods but also for basic manufactures. Textiles and iron and steel showed negative balances even though both were protected by "voluntary" export agreements negotiated during the 1960s. The value of imported road motor vehicles now significantly exceeded exports. Industries with intermediate levels of technology were confronting significant foreign competition. SITC number 7, machines and transportation equipment, continued to show the largest positive balance. Hence, by 1970, many sectors of the American economy faced significant foreign competition, while others had become very heavily involved in export markets. The convergence of interests in an open system among advanced, intermediate, and even some technologically older industries, which had existed as late as 1960, had disappeared. At least through 1973, the devaluations of the early 1970s had not changed this pattern.

Trade figures alone are a misleading indicator of the way in which America's changing place in the world economy has affected different societal actors. Trade balances do suggest the interests of labor, but not necessarily those of industry. Accompanying the growth of world trade since the Second World War has been a massive increase in foreign investment. While some sectors of the American economy, such as shoes, were unable or unwilling to try to end-run foreign competition by buying foreign plants, others were far from reluctant. In some areas, such as raw material exploitation, US firms were already well established. While SITC number 2, crude materials excluding fuels, has consistently shown a negative trade balance, until 1970 almost all imports involved the flow of goods within vertically integrated companies, mostly American. With the exception of Shell, and later British Petroleum, virtually all American imports of fuels (SITC number 3) were controlled by US companies. In other areas, particularly manufacturing, many firms have significantly increased their overseas activities during the last three decades. Table 2.4 shows the net capital outflows, value, and earnings of US direct investment.

American banks rapidly began to expand their foreign activity after major European currencies became convertible in 1958. This is shown in Table 2.5.

Table 2.4 US foreign direct investment (millions of dollars)

Period	Average annual net capital outflow	Year	Value of US direct investment	Earnings of US direct investment
1950–54	676	1950	11,788	1,766
1955–59	1,553	1955	19,395	2,878
1960–64	1,823	1960	32,765	3,546
1965–69	3,227	1965	49,217	5,431
1970–74	5,034	1970	75,456	8,023
		1975	133,168	17,433

Source: US Department of Commerce, *Survey of Current Business*, various issues.

Table 2.5 Foreign activities of US banks

Year	Number of banks with overseas branches	Number of overseas branches	Assets of overseas branches ($ billions)	Total assets of commercial banks in the US ($ billions)	Assets of foreign branches as a percentage of total assets of all commercial banks in the US
1960	8	131	3.5	255.7	1.3
1965	13	211	9.1	374.1	2.4
1970	79	536	52.6	576.2	9.1
1973	125	699	118.0	827.1	14.2
1974 (Sept.)	129	737	155.0	872.0 (June)	

Source: Brimmer and Dahl 1975: 345.

These tables suggest why the private consensus for a liberal international economic order was greatest around 1960. In the early 1950s, the international involvement of American corporations, and particularly American banks, was still relatively small. But by 1960, it was substantial for corporations, and banks were on the verge of a great foreign expansion. Once these institutions became involved in foreign direct investment, their stake in a liberal international regime became increasingly apparent. During the 1950s, virtually all US industries enjoyed a positive trade balance. However, during the 1960s, the number and variety of industries that had to deal with foreign competition increased sharply. In cases where US manufacturers had established foreign subsidiaries, this created an ambiguous set of interests. An open international order was beneficial for their international activities, but more protectionism would help their domestic ones. For American labor, the situation was clearer. Whether imports came from foreign-owned firms or American multinational corporations (MNCs) was immaterial. Jobs were being lost. As more and more sectors of the American economy confronted a negative trade balance during the 1960s, the attractions of protectionism became greater for the American labor movement. Hence, in 1960, US economic groups, with the exception of a few technologically older industries, found a liberal order attractive. During earlier periods many firms, including banks, were not heavily involved in foreign activities. Later, more sectors of the US economy faced foreign competition.

In sum, three basic factors bear on the analysis of American foreign economic policy after the Second World War:

1   The state (group of central decision makers) wants to create and maintain a liberal international economic regime.
2   These central decision makers have at their command potential international power that is overwhelming immediately after the war, but erodes thereafter. This erosion becomes apparent during the 1960s.
3   US central decision makers must act in a weak domestic political system that limits their ability to extract resources from their own society when their goals conflict with private ones. Such conflicts are least apparent around 1960.

The historical evolution of American policy

The interplay of state objectives, international economic power, and domestic political constraints is revealed by an examination of four periods of American foreign economic policy. Each of these periods is defined by some decisive policy choice: Bretton Woods in 1944, the Marshall Plan in 1947, the Trade Expansion Act of 1962, and the new economic policy of August 1971. The first, from the war years to the Marshall Plan, was an unsuccessful attempt to construct a new international economic order. The second period, from the Marshall Plan through the 1950s, saw the re-establishment of economic stability in Europe and Japan, at least in part because of American assistance. During these same years, the external power of the United States almost automatically led to a well-functioning international monetary system. However, domestic support for a decisively open commercial policy did not yet exist. The third period, the 1960s, saw the apogee and decline of support for a liberal order. At the beginning of the decade, there was a very strong domestic consensus for freer trade, which led to the passage of the Trade Expansion Act. By the end of the decade, increasing protectionist pressures were coming from American labor and from US industries that were suffering from foreign competition. While a number of ad hoc measures were used to deal with international monetary problems, they were not fully successful. The last period, ushered in by the proclamations of August 1971, has been one of growing tensions. The relative decline of America's power has been translated into international monetary disorder almost as automatically as its preponderant power had been translated into stability during the 1950s and early 1960s. In commercial policy, internal cleavages were reflected in the Trade Reform Act of 1974, which moved to protect specific economic sectors without abandoning a general commitment to freer trade.

A false start: the war years to the Marshall Plan

During the Second World War, American central decision makers developed an unambiguous commitment to a more liberal international economic order. They wanted to lower trade barriers, eliminate discrimination, and establish currency convertibility. Their strong belief in this set of goals stemmed from US interests, the immediate experience of the Depression and World War II, and, most important, a Lockean view of political and social life.

Planning for postwar economic arrangements reflected the desire to create a liberal order. The Atlantic Charter, signed in 1941 by Roosevelt and Churchill, called for equal access for trade and raw materials and full cooperation in "the economic field." Article 7 of the 1942 Mutual Aid Pact between Britain and the United States, which governed the dispensation of Lend-Lease, committed Britain to working toward an end to discriminatory trade practices, a phrase directed at the Imperial Preference system (R.N. Gardner 1969: 65–67). By the middle of 1942, Treasury Department officials had drawn up plans for an international bank and an international monetary fund designed to prevent the disruption of exchange systems and the collapse of credit, and to provide capital for reconstruction (Eckes 1975: Ch. 2). The charters of the World Bank and the IMF were approved at an international meeting held at Bretton Woods, New Hampshire, in 1944. Work on an organization to deal with trade began in 1943. The differences between the US and Great Britain were more manifest here than elsewhere, and a charter for an International Trade Organization was not concluded until 1948. The General Agreement on Tariffs and Trade (GATT), which was expected to be an interim arrangement, had been signed in early 1948.

These efforts to construct a new international economic order were a nearly complete failure. The International Bank for Reconstruction and Development, as the World Bank was officially known, was funded only at the very modest level of $10 billion. Its resources were completely unequal to the task of postwar reconstruction. By the middle of 1947, its funds were nearly exhausted. After an initial burst of activity in 1947 and 1948, IMF activities sank to very low levels until the Suez crisis nearly a decade later. Britain did establish convertibility on 15 July 1947, in accordance with the terms of a $3.75 billion loan received from the United States. But convertibility was suspended on 20 August because of a tremendous outflow of dollars from London. The International Trade Organization was never brought to a vote in the American Congress, much less ratified. The GATT, an institution with few resources, in which American participation was based on an executive agreement rather than a treaty or a Congressional–Executive agreement, became the most important postwar institution dealing with commercial practices (R.N. Gardner 1969: xxx–xxxxi, 118, 312ff; Eckes 1975: 220–22).

Why were America's first steps to create a liberal global economic order so unsuccessful? Part of the answer involves a failure of perception. As late as 1946, US officials were far more optimistic about the resources that would be needed for their plans than was warranted. They felt that the Fund and the Bank, with an additional $3–4 billion from the Export–Import (EXIM) Bank, would take care of the world's dollar needs. They also believed that the extra $3.75 billion for Britain would be enough to establish convertibility and promote reconstruction (J.M. Jones 1955: 95; R.N. Gardner 1969: 288–93; Acheson 1969: 230–71). They were wrong. The dislocations caused by the war were far more serious than American leaders had anticipated.

However, there is a second reason for American failure, one more relevant to the analysis in this paper: domestic opposition prevented US leaders from extracting the resources needed to create a liberal global regime. The period before 1948 is the only one examined in this paper in which monetary as well as commercial policy was constrained by domestic political considerations. These constraints reflected the active role played by Congress and Congress' sensitivity to the values of its members and to particularistic pressures. While central decision makers were committed to an open international system, many societal groups were not. A liberal order could not be established without the appropriation of funds. These funds were necessary to try to restore convertibility in international exchange markets, to coerce or entice European colonial powers to give up their systems of Imperial Preferences as well as to enable reconstruction. The appropriation of funds required the approval of Congress. And many Congressmen did not share the goals and visions of central decision makers.

In 1945, as the previous section of this paper suggests, the actual stake of American business and labor in foreign economic activities was small. The war had not interrupted a healthy and growing world economy but rather one that had not moved out of the Depression. US businesses were leery of overseas investment (Wilkins 1974: 300–1). Their primary concern was the domestic market and adjustment to a peacetime economy.

Furthermore, American leaders encountered difficulties because their international efforts became embroiled in domestic political struggles. The Fund and the Bank were philosophically related to the Roosevelt administration's domestic programs. Both involved greater state management of the economic order. Groups opposing the New Deal were also suspicious of the new international arrangements. Large private bankers in New York feared that the Fund and the Bank would encroach on their activities. From the outset, American officials rejected British efforts to create an international monetary fund with very liberal credit provisions (the Keynes Plan) because they felt it would never pass the Congress. US economic interests opposed the ITO because of provisions calling for full employment, host-country control of foreign investments, international commodity agreements, and foreign aid (R.N. Gardner 1969: 77, 87 ff; Eckes 1975: 220–22; Wilkins 1974: 288).

Midwest isolationists also opposed the administration. This became an acute problem when the Republicans won control of the Congress in 1946, and a number of powerful committee chairmanships, including that of the Senate Finance Committee, passed into the hands of men unsympathetic to efforts to create a liberal global order (R.N. Gardner 1969: 194, 349).

US leaders were not completely unsuccessful in extracting resources from their domestic society. Bretton Woods did pass the Congress. EXIM Bank authorizations were increased. A $3.75 billion loan was made to Great Britain in 1946. However, given the devastation of the war, this was not enough. What was involved in the late 1940s was the establishment of a new international economic regime, not simply the maintenance of an ongoing pattern of rules and behavior. Before other advanced states could lower trade barriers and make their currencies convertible, they needed to reconstruct their own societies. And for that, a very high level of resources was needed from the US. Hence, despite the enormous potential external power of the US in the period immediately after World War II, the actual resources at the disposal of central decision makers were not adequate for the establishment of a liberal economic regime because of misperception of central decision makers and the resistance of domestic groups.

An opening wedge: the Marshall Plan and the 1950s

The vague Wilsonianism that had informed the Bretton Woods agreements was not sufficiently compelling to enable American central decision makers to extract the resources necessary for European reconstruction. They had to transform the basic way in which international economic relations were perceived. It was necessary to move from the Wilsonianism of the Fund and the Bank to the hard-headed anti-communism of the Truman Doctrine and (despite the disclaimers of its progenitors) the Marshall Plan. Only by picturing American aid as part of a global struggle against communism were American central decision makers able to get the resources necessary to create a prosperous economic order in Western Europe.

The events that precipitated the Truman Doctrine and the Marshall Plan, in what J.M. Jones has immortalized as the *Fifteen Weeks*, 21 February to 5 June 1947 (J.M. Jones 1955) were closely associated with the danger of communist takeovers in Europe. On 21 February 1947, Britain informed the US that it could no longer carry the burden of aid to Greece and Turkey. Intelligence data suggested that Greece could "go communist" in a matter of weeks. There were already communists in the Italian cabinet. The first government appointed by the French Fourth Republic included four communists. American leaders became starkly aware of the inadequacy of existing levels of aid to Europe and of the weakness of Britain, a country which only two years before they had treated as a proto-rival (J.M. Jones 1955: 5–11, 96; Acheson 1969: 226).

In 1947, the external world presented great dangers for US leaders, but they feared that domestic constraints would prevent them from responding. Roosevelt's death, not popular votes, had brought Truman to power. The Republicans had won control of the Congress in the 1946 elections. A majority of them had voted against the Reciprocal Trade Agreements Act and its renewals, Bretton Woods, the 1945 increase in Export–Import Bank credits, and the 1946 loan to Great Britain. American leaders were not naive anti-communists. Many had a grasp of the realist view of international politics. But they felt that only by shocking the American people could they get the resources that they needed. The only sentiment strong enough to give such a jolt was anti-communism. Truman harped on the theme in his presentation of the Truman Doctrine to Congress. The Marshall Plan was also explicated in terms of a global struggle with an implacable and malevolent enemy. In his memoirs, Dean Acheson writes:

> I have probably made as many speeches and answered as many questions about the Marshall Plan as any man alive, except possibly Paul Hoffman, and what citizens and the representatives in Congress alike always wanted to learn in the last analysis was how Marshall aid operated to block the extension of Soviet power and the acceptance of Communist economic and political organization and alignment.
>
> (Acheson 1969: 233)

The weakness of the American political system, the inability of the president to secure domestic resources for reconstruction without painting the world situation in lurid colors, inevitably led to what Theodore Lowi has termed the tendency to "oversell" policies to the American public (Lowi 1969: 174–75).

Nevertheless, the result was the transfer of enormous sums to Europe. By 1953, the World Bank had made $1.2 billion in disbursements, while the US had transferred $41.3 billion. Marshall Plan aid amounted to about 33 per cent of Europe's imports (Eckes 1975: 224–75; Yeager 1976: 385–86). Most of these funds were given as outright grants. At the same time, American leaders also toned down their expectations. Rather than constructing a global open order, they were now willing to settle for one that included only their European and Asian allies. In the Marshall Plan, the US explicitly pushed European integration rather than globalism. Thus, in the issue-area of reconstruction, US policy was a success.

In the monetary issue-area, American policy makers were also fairly successful during this period. By the end of 1958, convertibility had been restored for all major currencies. The US supported European arrangements for multilateral clearings that began in 1947, most importantly the European Payments Union. During the 1940s, Marshall Plan funds were used not only to cover payment deficits with the Western hemisphere, but also to facilitate the extension of credit among European countries. In 1950, the US granted $350 million to the European Payments Union to facilitate its multilateral clearings. Furthermore, by 1949 the US had forced substantial devaluations of all major European currencies. This contributed to a persistent American balance-of-payment deficit that began in 1950 and continued for the next two decades. One product of this deficit was an increase in world liquidity because of the excess dollars being held by foreign central banks (Yeager 1976: 410–13; Rolfe and Burtle 1973: 67–68). Hence, the critical developments for monetary affairs during the 1950s were the devaluations of foreign currencies, the dispensation of Marshall Plan aid, and the dollar's central role as an international reserve currency. The first two were policy decisions taken largely within the Executive branch and the third was an almost automatic consequence of the strength of the American economy. Domestic political groups did not constrain US central decision makers in this issue-area.

In the area of commercial policy, US leaders were less successful. The Trade Agreements Act was renewed in 1948, 1949, 1951, 1954, 1955, and 1958. Virtually every instance touched off a political struggle. While the president was given some additional tariff-cutting authority during the 1950s, other protectionist elements were introduced into the legislation. In 1947, there was the escape clause which allowed the US to rescind a concession if it resulted in injury to a domestic industry. There was the peril point in 1948 which provided that the Tariff Commission establish a rate prior to trade negotiations below which a domestic industry would be injured. In 1951, Congressional action forced the president to impose quotas on some agricultural exports in violation of GATT rules (J.W. Evans 1971: 72).

The continued conservatism of American trade legislation reflected isolationism in Congress, pressure from industries that were being threatened by imports, and the inaction of groups that would benefit from greater openness. In 1953, domestic coal and oil producers began asking for quotas on oil imports. This eventually led to the establishment of quotas in the late 1950s. In 1955, Southern textile manufacturers began to put heavy pressure on their

Congressmen. With a technology that was widely dispersed, textile manufacturers were among the first to feel foreign competition. Both the coal and textile campaigns were industry-wide, supported by corporations and labor unions alike (R.A. Bauer *et al.* 1967: 60–61, 363–72). In addition, there were still strong isolationist sentiments in the Republican Party. In 1953 and 1954, both the Finance and Ways and Means Committees were controlled by legislators who had no sympathy for a more expansionary trade policy.

The support for a more liberal order was weak. Large American companies and banks with growing exports or investments were reluctant to take a strong stand. In part, this was because such enterprises are prone to follow risk-avoiding policies and taking very explicit public stands can be a risky business. Perhaps more important, as Table 2.4 and, especially, Table 2.5 indicate, the benefits of an open order became apparent gradually. Only as the prospects for foreign trade and investment became clearer, by 1960, did large American businesses take a more decisive positive stand on commercial legislation. Politics has few laws, but one of them is that people are willing to fight harder to avoid giving up what they have than they are to get new benefits in the future. During the 1950s, this meant that those who wanted to avoid foreign competition were willing to fight more fiercely than those who had not yet tasted the full fruits of foreign activity.

In sum, American foreign economic policy during the 1950s did promote a liberal international economic system. The precondition for this success was America's unchallenged international position in the non-communist world. Still, US leaders had to deal with their own society. Funds for reconstruction were secured by defining US aims in Manichean terms. Monetary policy was successful because decisions were taken by the Executive, and because the size of the US economy led to the dollar's role as a reserve currency without an explicit policy choice. In commercial policy, progress was slow because the influence of import-competing industries was felt through the Congress.

Apogee and decline: 1960–71

The most unambiguous support for a liberal world order came during the early 1960s. This was a reflection both of America's still prodigious potential international economic power and of wide domestic support for state goals. However, by the mid-1960s, America's potential international economic strength was clearly waning. In addition, as the decade progressed, more and more domestic groups were negatively affected by imports and by foreign direct investment. Protectionist sentiments grew.

The central development of the early 1960s was the enactment of the Trade Expansion Act of 1962. It set the stage for the Kennedy Round of multilateral trade negotiations, the most successful ever held. The Act empowered the president to make 50 per cent tariff cuts and to eliminate duties entirely on goods where the US and the EEC provided 80 per cent of world trade. Because Great Britain did not enter the Common Market in the mid-1960s, this provision had little practical effect. It introduced adjustment assistance for domestic groups that were adversely affected by tariff cuts. It eliminated the peril point. It tightened the conditions under which the escape clause could be invoked. And, finally, it allowed negotiations on the basis of broad categories rather than item by item (J.W. Evans 1971: 142–43).

A number of factors prompted the Kennedy administration to press for more liberal trade legislation. The first was the fear that the EEC and the European Free Trade Association (EFTA) would limit American sales in Europe. Second, there was a need both to find a solution to the persistent American balance-of-payments deficit and to spur the domestic economy. Finally, and more generally, the commitment to a liberal regime continued to exist (Preeg 1970: 31–32; J.W. Evans 1971: 139–44).

However, the desires of central decision makers are not a sufficient explanation for the passage of the Trade Expansion Act and the success of the Kennedy Round. The aims of foreign economic policy were not much different in 1962 than they had been in earlier years when commercial policy had faltered.

What was different in the early 1960s was the structure of interests in the American economy. The expansion of trade and foreign investments during the 1950s had extended the benefits of a liberal international economic order more widely and deeply. At the same time, as Table 2.3 shows, only a few industries were experiencing serious foreign competition. Manufacturing sectors with intermediate levels of technology, like steel and automobiles, still enjoyed a trade surplus. Many corporations and banks were increasing their foreign investments. The 1962 Act enjoyed very broad support, including the endorsement of organized labor.

Even with this backing, the Kennedy administration was not able to formulate an unambiguously liberal trade policy. The fragmentation of the political structure, which gives powerful domestic groups the ability to block the initiatives of central decision makers, made it necessary to implement selective protectionist measures. The oil industry had already gotten a mandatory import quota program. The 1962 Act prohibited any concessions in this area. The fears of the textile industry were assuaged in a number of ways. The Long-Term Cotton Textiles Agreement of 1962 limited import increases to 6 per cent per year. In March 1962, Kennedy used the escape clause to levy higher tariffs on carpets. There was also a ban on eight varieties of cotton imports from Hong Kong and an 8.5 cent a pound subsidy to cotton growers (J.W. Evans 1971: 167, 201–2, 230–31; Pastor 1976: 28). Still, these were rather modest concessions. The 1962 Act did open the way for the Kennedy Round, which resulted in tariff cuts averaging 35 per cent.

However, even before the Kennedy Round was concluded, protectionist sentiment in the US was becoming more evident. The increasing openness of the international economy was subjecting more domestic sectors to international competition. By the mid-1960s, some industries with intermediate levels of technology began encountering serious competition from imports. For instance, the trade balance for iron and steel shifted from a small surplus in 1960 to a substantial deficit in 1965. The Congress failed to approve agreements involving American Selling Price (ASP) valuations and an anti-dumping code that had been concluded at the Kennedy Round. The Tariff Commission relaxed its definition of injury in anti-dumping cases of 1967. The number of judgments of injury increased from a total of three for the years 1965 through 1967 to a total of twelve for the years 1968 through 1970 (M.J. Marks and Malmgren 1975: 375). A number of new sectoral trade restrictions were put in effect after 1966. In 1967, quotas were imposed on some dairy products. In early 1969, a "voluntary" steel export agreement was concluded with major exporters from Japan and Europe. It provided that their sales to the US would be limited to increases of 5 per cent a year from 1969 through 1971. On 24 February 1970, the president suspended tariff reductions on pianos under the escape clause. This was the first positive escape clause recommendation from the Tariff Commission since 1962 (International Monetary Fund, *Annual Report on Exchange Restrictions*, various years).

During the 1960s, America's international monetary policy also showed signs of strain. The establishment of convertibility for major currencies in 1958 quickly revealed that the dollar shortage of the early 1950s had been replaced by a dollar glut; the US balance of payments deficit was excessive. To deal with the growing deficit, American policy makers implemented several programs during the 1960s. The most important were an Interest Equalization Tax which denied Europeans access to the New York capital market; voluntary, and later mandatory, controls on direct foreign investments; and controls on banks. In addition, a number of new devices including the Gold Pool, swaps, and Roosa bonds were concocted to aid in supporting the existing regime.

Domestic political constraints were less important for monetary than for commercial policy. It was external, not internal, factors that caused monetary problems. The issues were decided in very different decision-making arenas. While the Congress played a major role in commercial policy, monetary policy was set by the White House, the Treasury, and the Federal Reserve Board. Controls on direct investment were imposed by presidential proclamation. Controls on banking activity were set by the Federal Reserve Board. The secretary of the Treasury announced that the US would suspend the purchase and sale of gold from private sources in 1968. The only two monetary decisions that involved Congressional action were the Interest Equalization Tax and the creation of Special Drawing Rights (SDRs). The most careful empirical study of US monetary policy during this period concludes that it was very much in the hands of the president and his close advisors (Odell 1976).

A second reason why domestic fragmentation did not constrain monetary policy was that the groups that could have been adversely affected by capital export controls, multinational corporations and banks, were able to adjust to most of the new regulations. Constraints on the export of dollars from the US quickly led to the development of the Eurodollar market. Banks in Europe, many of them branches of US financial institutions, rapidly increased their dollar deposits. US companies could obtain their capital from this market rather than from New York. MNCs did protest the mandatory Foreign Direct Investment Program in 1968; but, since the program was established by an Executive Order, they could not stop it. By 1973, when a Federal Court in Washington ruled the program illegal, controls were being dismantled (Conybeare 1976: Ch. 5, 231–37).

In sum, the 1960s saw a transition of American foreign economic policy. During the first part of the decade, American central decision makers were able to take advantage of a domestic consensus for a more liberal trading order to secure passage of the Trade Expansion Act and conclude the Kennedy Round negotiations. By the end of the decade, more and more sectors of the American economy were facing foreign competition. To prevent Congressional action, the Executive was compelled to implement a number of measures that protected certain domestic groups. In the monetary area, policy was free of domestic constraints, but ultimately unsuccessful in dealing with balance-of-payments problems. The American economy could not sustain both the Vietnam War and high domestic expenditures, and still maintain balance-of-payments equilibrium or an acceptable deficit, without, at the least, exchange rate adjustment.

The 1970s: growing strains, international and domestic

During the 1970s, the fundamental objective of foreign economic policy for American central decision makers remained the maintenance of a liberal international economic regime. This goal was most frequently explained in terms of interdependence, the notion that at least all non-communist countries were locked into a complex network of relationships whose rupture would be extremely costly for everyone. While this rationale was different from the anti-communism of the late 1940s and 1950s, the policy implications were identical. However, American leaders found it increasingly difficult to implement their preferences because, as Table 2.1 indicates, America's potential economic power had declined. Simultaneously, as Table 2.3 indicates, the number of groups within American society that would benefit from protection had increased.

By the middle of 1971, a realignment of exchange rates was long overdue. In 1971, the US merchandise balance showed a deficit for the first time since 1894, although the overall balance had been in deficit almost continuously after 1949 (Kindleberger 1977: 413). On 15 August, President Nixon officially brought the Bretton Woods system to an end. He announced that the US would no longer buy and sell gold. He imposed a temporary 10 per cent surcharge on American imports. American leaders were not interested in moving away from a liberal order, but they did want a change in exchange rates and an improvement in America's balance-of-payments situation. They did not foresee the violent foreign reaction that developed against the import surcharge. Most members of the administration saw the surcharge as a device that would not only jolt America's trading partners, but that would also stave off protectionist legislation in Congress (Graebner 1975: 160–61).

The crisis precipitated by these announcements was temporarily resolved by a realignment of exchange rates in December 1971 known as the Smithsonian Agreement. But it was short-lived. By the end of 1973, international exchange rates were related by snakes, worms, and dirty floats. In addition, the quadrupling of oil prices in the fall and winter of 1973–74 led to very large deficits for almost all non-oil Third World countries, as well as some industrial ones. Some oil-exporting states recorded enormous surplus revenues which entered the international monetary system as a new and volatile source of liquidity, petrodollars. At Jamaica in early 1976, the IMF Articles of Agreement were amended to recognize actual practices, but no serious effort was made to construct a new order (Vries 1976: 577–605).

American commercial policy during the 1970s was also less successful in maintaining a liberal international order. As in earlier periods, the primary constraints on American central decision makers were domestic. However, these domestic constraints reflected a change in America's international economic position. As Table 2.3 indicates, the number of sectors of the American economy threatened by foreign competition has increased over time. Foreign countries, including some in the Third World, have been able to master more sophisticated levels of technology. Innovations developed in the US quickly spread to other countries. The technological lead that the US enjoyed in the 1940s and 1950s and which gave America a strong balance of trade surplus eroded.

More groups within the US demanded protection. Most of the American labor movement became protectionist, giving up a long history of support for free trade. Labor also advocated measures to cut foreign direct investment. However, labor did not always have the support of management in sectors of the economy that were threatened by imports. In a number of industries, there were large foreign investments by US corporations. These companies were torn between their domestic and foreign interests. Often there were differences within specific industries. For example, Sylvania supported quotas to protect the US color television industry, while RCA, which earned considerable sums from licensing fees in Japan, opposed them (*Wall Street Journal*: 1976, 16 December: 21.3). Furthermore, there were many sectors of the US economy, including agriculture, aircraft, and sophisticated machinery, which continued to run a heavy trade surplus. They wanted an open system.

Given the weakness of the American domestic political system, it is not surprising that, during the 1970s, US commercial policy has become more confused and less coherent (Katzenstein 1976: 1–46). The divisions within the society have been mirrored in official policy. Explicit efforts at protectionism such as the Mills Bill and the Burke–Hartke Bill were defeated. However, the 1974 Trade Act reflected societal cross-pressures and was less liberal than the Trade Expansion Act of 1962. First, the 1974 Act increased the decision-making role of the Congress for the first time since 1934, when the Reciprocal Trade Agreements Act gave the president real power to negotiate tariff levels. The Congress rejected a presidential proposal that would have implied consent for changes in non-tariff barriers negotiated by the president if they were not explicitly rejected within 90 days. Instead, the 1974 Act required Congress' acceptance or rejection within 60 days. For the first time, the law states that members of Congress (ten) must be fully accredited members of the US trade delegation at Geneva. The Congress may override a presidential rejection of a recommendation of the International Trade Commission (formerly the Tariff Commission). A majority of one House of the Congress can override a Treasury decision not to retaliate against foreign dumping (Weil 1975: 53–56).

Congress is not the mere handmaiden of particular interest groups. In fact, one of the reasons that Congress gave more power to the president in 1934 was that it wanted to free itself from the naked exposure to interest group pressure and the petty and time-consuming wrangling that had been a part of tariff legislation (W.B. Kelly 1963: 15; R.A. Bauer *et al.* 1967: 27, 37). Nevertheless, Congress is bound to be more sensitive to particularistic societal pressures than the president or the secretary of state. The geographical system of representation guarantees that this will be the case.

Aside from procedural changes, the Trade Act of 1974 included a number of measures that were less liberal than those of the 1962 legislation. The Act made it easier for a domestic group to claim injury under the escape clause. The Trade Expansion Act of 1962 required that imports be the result of trade concessions and be "the major cause" of injury. The 1974 Act required only that imports be a "substantial cause" of injury and did not require that imports be related to tariff concessions. The new legislation stiffened the procedures for imposing countervailing duties against exports that receive some form of subsidy by compelling the Treasury to make a judgment within twelve months. Previously, the Treasury had sat on some cases for years. The Trade Act also tightened US anti-dumping provisions (National Journal Reports 1976: 502–4).

However, it would be an error to regard the 1974 Act as an unambiguously protectionist measure. It authorized the president to reduce tariffs up to 60 per cent for rates above 5 per cent and to eliminate imposts altogether for rates below 5 per cent. The Act also made it easier for companies and workers to get adjustment assistance. During periods of economic prosperity, adjustment assistance can blunt protectionist sentiments by providing businesses and workers with funds to retrain or retool.

The incoherence that is inherent in the 1974 Trade Act was also reflected in a number of actual policy decisions. In June 1976, the specialty steel industry forced President Ford to accept an International Trade Commission recommendation for quotas because the administration thought that the industry had enough votes in Congress to override a presidential rejection of this recommendation. This was the culmination of an escape clause case brought by the United States Steel Workers and nineteen companies. A small but united industry (specialty steel imports), with Congressional support, could prevail against the preferences of central decision makers (*Wall Street Journal* 1976, 1 January: 4:2; *Wall Street Journal* 1976, 12 March: 24:3; *Wall Street Journal* 1976, 17 March: 2:2; *New York Times* 1976, 12 June: 29:5). However, an anti-dumping case brought by the United Auto Workers (UAW) against automobile companies in Belgium, Britain, Canada, France, Italy, Japan, Sweden, and West Germany resulted in an extremely ambiguous Treasury ruling against eight companies. They agreed to raise prices; countervailing duties were not imposed. The auto union was not supported by the four big US automobile companies, all of which had substantial foreign investments (*Wall Street Journal* 1976, 5 May: 3:1; *Wall Street Journal* 1976, 6 May: 5:2; *Wall Street Journal* 1976, 6 July: 9:1; *Wall Street Journal* 1976, 11 August: 2:2).

The 1970s witnessed strain on American efforts to create and maintain a liberal international economic regime. Constraints on US central decision makers came both from the international system and from domestic groups. The declining international power of the US was reflected in monetary relations which became fragile and disorderly. Domestic dissatisfaction with foreign competition was reflected in the 1974 Trade Act and in the success some import-competing groups had in forcing the Executive to accede to their demands.

Conclusions

A liberal international economic system could not have been established after the Second World War were it not for the power and policies of the US. The dollar has been the world's key currency. At the most important multilateral trade talks, which were held in 1947 and during the 1960s (the Kennedy Round), the US was able to take the lead in negotiations that led to very dramatic reductions in tariff levels. During the postwar period, world trade grew rapidly.

During the 1970s serious strains developed in the international economic system. The most obvious was the quadrupling of oil prices. This action contributed to inflation and to the creation of unmanageable debt for many Third World countries. It led to lower rates of growth and to a more volatile international monetary system. The Third World has become a more significant actor on the world scene; most of its members rejected the vision and specific policies that animated American leaders. At least 75 per cent of the holdings of US raw materials corporations located in Third World countries were nationalized by the 1970s.

In the years since this paper was originally written the dynamics that it describes have continued to hold. The 1980s were a rocky period for the international economy but, with the collapse of the Soviet Union, the United States was able to take effective leadership in the creation of the World Trade Organization in the mid-1990s. The WTO expanded liberal rules to a number of new issue areas. To secure this agreement the United States had to tie its own hands by accepting mandatory dispute settlement procedures. The Doha Round of trade negotiations, however, stalled and the George W. Bush administration's efforts to conclude a free trade area for the Americas was frustrated by both domestic and international resistance. The commitment of the major industrialized powers, the United States, Europe, Japan to economic openness provides a firm foundation for a liberal economic order but the integration of emerging economies—Brazil, India, and especially China—will continue to pose challenges and domestic interest groups in the United States will continue to influence the decisions that are taken by Congress.

3   Approaches to the state
Alternative conceptions and historical dynamics

From the late 1950s until the mid-1970s the term "state" virtually disappeared from the professional academic lexicon. Political scientists wrote about government, political development, interest groups, voting, legislative behavior, leadership, and bureaucratic politics, almost everything but "the state." However, beginning with the mid-1970s "the state" has reappeared in the literature. Marxist scholars made a self-conscious, theoretically grounded effort to develop a theory of the capitalist state. In *Between Power and Plenty*, an edited volume about the foreign economic policies of advanced industrial countries, Peter Katzenstein developed a typology of weak and strong states. Theda Skocpol's *States and Social Revolution* examined the political conditions, both international and domestic, associated with major social revolutions. Alfred Stepan's *The State and Society in Peru* investigated both the organic statist intellectual tradition and corporatist political structures that gave "the state" a major initiative role in the Peruvian and other Latin American political systems (Katzenstein 1977; Skocpol 1979; Stepan 1978; Krasner 1978). Several additional books added to this growing body of literature.

However, to note that terms have changed, that certain scholars self-consciously adopted a new vocabulary (or readopted an old one), does not necessarily imply that there was a change in substance. The purpose of this essay is to examine the ways in which several books explicitly concerned with "the state" differed from and challenged prevailing intellectual approaches that emerged out of the behavioral revolution of the 1950s. The following are discussed at length in this essay: Eric Nordlinger's *On the Autonomy of the Democratic State* (1981), Clifford Geertz's *Negara: The Theatre State in Nineteenth Century Bali* (1980), Stephen Skowronek's *Building a New American State: The Expansion of National Administrative Capacities, 1877–1920* (1982), Charles Tilly's edited volume *The Formation of National States in Western Europe* (1975), Raymond Grew's edited volume *Crises of Political Development in Europe and the United States* (1978), and Ellen Kay Trimberger's *Revolution from Above: Military Bureaucrats and Development in Japan, Turkey, Egypt, and Peru* (1978).

These studies were concerned with two central issues: the extent of state autonomy and the degree of congruity between the state and its environment.

The issue of autonomy has generally been cast in a temporarily static frame-work in which the state is viewed as an exogenous variable. The central issue is: can the state formulate and implement its preferences? The issue of congruity was placed in a temporally dynamic framework in which the state is viewed as an intervening variable. The central issue is: how do institutional structures change in response to alterations in domestic and international environments and then in subsequent time periods influence these environments?

Cutting across both of these analytic concerns is the prior question of how the state should be defined. Roger Benjamin and Raymond Duvall argue that the following conceptualizations have appeared in the literature.

1 The state as government, "by which is meant the collective set of personnel who occupy positions of decisional authority in the polity."
2 The state as "public bureaucracy or administrative apparatus as a coherent totality" and as an institutionalized legal order.
3 The state as ruling class.
4 The state as normative order.

(Benjamin and Duvall 1985)

The state as ruling class is, in one variant or another, the Marxist definition, and it will not be further considered here. The dominant conceptualization in the non-Marxist literature is the state as a bureaucratic apparatus and institutionalized legal order in its totality. The final phrase is critical, for it distinguishes statist orientations from the bureaucratic politics approaches which have parceled the state into little pieces, pieces that can be individually analyzed (where you stand depends on where you sit) and that float in a permissive environment (policies are a product of bargaining and compro-mise among bureaus) (Allison 1971). Statist arguments have emphasized the overall structure of the bureaucratic apparatus, in particular the degree of centralization of power at the national level and the extent of state power vis-à-vis the society. Among the books reviewed in this essay, the two excep-tions to the generalization that the state is seen as a bureaucratic apparatus and institutionalized legal order taken as a totality are Eric Nordlinger's *On the Autonomy of the Democratic State*, which adopts the state as gov-ernment conceptualization, and Clifford Geertz's *Negara*, which views the state as a normative order.

There are five characteristics of the statist literature that distinguish it from orientations associated with the behavioral revolution. First, statist approaches see politics more as a problem of rule and control than as one of allocation; they are more concerned with issues associated with preserving order against internal and external threats than with the distribution of utiles to political actors. Politics is not just about "who gets what, when, how;" it is a struggle of us against them (Poggi 1978; Lasswell 1958).

Second, statist approaches emphasize that the state can be treated as an actor in its own right as either an exogenous or an intervening variable.

Whether in its institutional form or in terms of specific policies, the state cannot be understood as a reflection of societal characteristics or preferences.

Third, statist orientations place greater emphasis on institutional constraints, both formal and informal, on individual behavior. This is especially true for authors who view the state as the bureaucratic apparatus and legal order taken as a totality or as the normative political order. Actors in the political system, whether individuals or groups, are bound within these structures, which limit, even determine, their conceptions of their own interest and their political resources. Political outcomes cannot be adequately understood as simply the resolution of a vector of forces emanating from a variety of different groups.

Fourth, statist analyses have been more anxious to take what Gabriel Almond has called the "historical cure" (Almond 1973: 22–24). It is necessary to understand both how institutions reproduce themselves through time and what historical conditions gave rise to them in the first place. Current institutional structures may be a product of some peculiar historical conjuncture rather than contemporaneous factors. Moreover, once an historical choice is made, it both precludes and facilitates alternative future choices. Political change follows a branching model. Once a particular fork is chosen, it is very difficult to get back on a rejected path. Thus, the kinds of causal arguments appropriate for periods of crises when institutions are first created may not be appropriate for other periods.

Fifth, statist arguments are more inclined to see disjunctures and stress within any given political system. Systems are not composed of interrelated and compatible components. Structures do not exist because they perform certain functions, and functions do not necessarily give rise to corresponding structures. Rather, political life is fraught with tensions and conflicts, especially for the state. For instance, international pressures frequently lead the state to attempt to increase the level of resource extraction from its own society. But these efforts can engender negative reactions from social groups who see their economic utility, and even their sense of justice, undermined by new state policies. Political life is characterized, not simply by a struggle over the allocation of resources, but also periodically by strife and uncertainty about the rules of the game within which this allocative process is carried out.

These five characteristics do not constitute a coherent theory of the state. Only structural Marxists could credibly make such a claim, and even they are plagued by deep and probably insoluble difficulties related to the degree of autonomy that can be accorded to the state before fundamental tenets concerning the determining character of economic structures are compromised. The studies under review here do not set out to present a general theory of the state. Eric Nordlinger's basic objective is to demonstrate that even in democratic polities public officials can autonomously determine public policy. Clifford Geertz is concerned with the symbolic attributes of the state as a unifying element for the entire social community. Stephen Skowronek investigates the ways in which the functional political challenges posed by nineteenth-century industrialization were met, or not met, in the context of the fragmented and localized political system that existed in the United States. Tilly, Trimberger, and some of the authors in Grew emphasize the impact of external threats on state-building.

Despite their diversity these studies do pose a challenge to the analytic traditions that have dominated political science in the United States. They see a different political universe, ask different questions, investigate different empirical phenomena, and offer different kinds of answers.

The second section of this essay reviews Robert Dahl's theory of leadership in his seminal study, *Who Governs*, to provide a clearer contrast between pluralist and statist orientations (Dahl 1961). The third section deals with problems of public policy in which the central issue has been the degree of autonomy of the state. The fourth section deals with problems of state-building in which the central issue has been the degree of conformity or congruence of the state with its environment.

The concluding section suggests that a model taken from evolutionary theory, punctuated equilibrium, can serve as an appropriate metaphor for understanding changes in the relationship between states and their environments.

A contrast with pluralist theories of leadership

One way to illuminate the distinctive characteristics of statist approaches is to contrast them with the pluralist approach. This is not only because pluralism is the prevailing model for the study of politics in the United States, but also because some major authors identified with the pluralist school have been explicitly concerned with the role of public actors. By examining how their studies, in particular, differ from the books reviewed here, one can clarify the distinct features of a statist orientation.

The more obvious general differences can be noted first. Pluralism emphasizes problems of allocation rather than ones of rule and control. Nordlinger points out that as "portrayed by pluralism, civil society is made up of a plethora of diverse, fluctuating, competing groups of individuals with shared interests. Many effective political resources are available to them" (Nordlinger 1981: 51). These groups struggle to maximize their own, autonomously defined self-interests. Cross-cutting cleavages and broad consensus on the rules of the game guarantee moderate political behavior.

Within the literature on American politics the central debate has not been about the relative power of societal and state actors, but rather about which societal actors most influence public policy. Conventional pluralists see a very wide array of interest groups, virtually all of which have some political resources. Neo-pluralists such as McConnell, Lowi, and especially Lindblom see a more constricted universe. Only a limited range of groups, among which business is particularly prominent, possess significant political

resources (Nordlinger 1981: 44). But this debate takes place within the confines of an intellectual universe that understands politics to be a problem,
both analytically and normatively, of allocation. Pure interest group ver-
sions of pluralism virtually ignore public actors and institutions. The government is seen as a cash register that totals up and then averages the
preferences and political power of societal actors. Government may also
be seen as an arena within which societal actors struggle to ensure the success of their own particular preferences. The major function of public
officials is to make sure that the game is played fairly. If public institutions
are viewed as figurative cash registers or as literal referees, there is no
room for anything that could be designated as a state as actor with autonomous preferences capable of manipulating and even restructuring its own
society.

However, most pluralist models are much more explicitly concerned
with the role of political leaders and public officials. Robert Dahl's *Who
Governs* offers an example. The simple answer to the question "Who Governs?" is that everyone does, including political leaders. If there is a hero in
Dahl's book it is Richard Lee, a working-class boy without a college education who made good not only as an official of Yale University but also as a
dynamic and active mayor of New Haven. Dahl argues that Lee's preferences were critical especially for urban renewal, a program that came to
dominate the city's public life. Lee was motivated initially by his own concern with conditions in New Haven, not by pressure from any particular
societal group. In fact, there were no groups particularly interested in urban
renewal one way or the other. The concluding sentence of *Who Governs*
says that there are "complex processes of symbiosis and change that constitute the relations of leaders and citizens in a pluralistic democracy" (Dahl
1961: 325).

What distinguishes Dahl's treatment, a seminal study of pluralist politics,
from the more explicitly and self-consciously state-oriented works of the
kind under consideration in this essay? The most critical difference is that
Dahl views the state as a collection of individuals occupying particular
roles, not as an administrative apparatus or legal order. Benjamin and
Duvall have referred to this formulation as "the state as the government."
They note that this "concept of the state is compatible with extreme liberal tenets of the behavioral revolution, in treating the state as merely a collection of individuals who occupy role positions (those of governing
authority) and who act as a group to govern" (Benjamin and Duvall 1985:
4). Institutional imperatives and constraints, including general political
beliefs, do not play a significant role in Dahl's formulation. The pluralist
universe is atomistic. Different societal groups and political leaders have
different objectives and political resources. Public policy is the outcome of
the resolution of vectors resulting from interests and resources. Formal,
authoritative institutions are of little importance. There is no detailed discussion in *Who Governs* of New Haven's governmental structure or of state

and national institutions. The defining characteristics of New Haven's political system are, for Dahl,

> universal suffrage, a moderately high participation in elections, a highly competitive two-party system, opportunity to criticize the conduct and policies of officials, freedom to seek support for one's views among officials and citizens, and surprisingly frequent alternations in office from one party to the other.
>
> (Dahl 1961: 311)

Dahl points out that at the very moment when Lee was being re-elected by an unprecedented majority the same voters were rejecting proposed revisions of the city charter that would have invested the office of the mayor with more power.

Dahl also disputes Tocqueville's proposition that American republican beliefs embodied in the legal structure are an important factor in American political behavior (Dahl 1961: 311–12). While there is widespread endorsement of general democratic values by the citizenry and the political stratum, these values are too vague, Dahl argues, to have much impact on actual political affairs. There is only limited agreement on the specific application of general principles. Even general consensus is only maintained by a complex and difficult process involving childhood socialization, particularly by the schools, and a

> recurring *process* of interchange among political professionals, the political stratum, and the great bulk of the population. The process generates enough agreement on rules and norms so as to permit the system to operate, but agreement tends to be incomplete, and typically it decays.
>
> (Dahl 1961: 180–88)

Statist orientations take institutions and political beliefs more seriously. The political universe is not atomistic. Atoms are bound within stable molecules and compounds. The preferences of public officials are constrained by the administrative apparatus, legal order, and enduring beliefs. There are only a limited number of ways in which political actors can combine their resources. The nature of political resources is itself defined by institutional structures. The ability of a political leader to carry out a policy is critically determined by the authoritative institutional resources and arrangements existing within a given political system. Industrial policy can be orchestrated in Japan through the ministry of international trade and industry. There is no American institutional structure that would allow a political leader, regardless of the resources he or she commanded, to implement a similar set of policies. Moreover, at least some statist arguments have emphasized the importance of ideology, not simply as an instrument of governance, but as an end in itself. Ideology may not only coordinate expectations and delineate legitimate modes of interaction between state institutions and societal actors, but it may also serve as a basic source of identity, and its preservation may be a consummatory function of the state. One of the critical purposes of the state is to represent symbolically the existence and unity of the political community.

A second distinction between sophisticated pluralist and statist views is that pluralism does not sharply differentiate public actors from their own society. Dahl's unit of analysis most closely related to the state is the political stratum, composed of subleaders and leaders. Members of the political stratum possess more political resources than ordinary citizens. Some of these resources are drawn from the public arena, including legality, but most derive from the society, including control over jobs and information. Individuals carry many of these resources with them both in and out of public office. Many important members of the political stratum never hold public office at all. Statist perspectives contrast individuals in and out of public office. Political leadership is closely related to official position. The administrative apparatus and legal order constrain preferences and provide means of influence. Political leaders are state actors pursuing either particular state goals or collective societal objectives and utilizing resources primarily derived from their official positions.

A third distinction between pluralist and statist approaches is that pluralist theories of leadership see public officials as relatively more constrained by societal pressures. Dahl argues that the support of the business community as well as other societal elements was a necessary condition for the urban renewal program. Lee was able to alter the societal forces he confronted by activating slack or latent resources. However, Lee is not seen as being able to change the underlying distribution of political resources. The ability of leaders to alter the preferences of citizens depends upon the extent of agreement among leaders, and this in turn depends in large part on the degree to which they are drawn from the same "social strata" (Dahl 1961: 165). Only a coherent leadership cadre can change the desires of citizens. In contrast, statist orientations see political leaders as less constrained by societal forces. They can alter preferences using the state's own resources. They may even be able to change the distribution of political resources possessed by societal groups.

In sum, the pluralist tradition in America has not simply ignored the role of political leaders. However, it has seen these leaders as being substantially constrained by societal forces, commanding resources that are derived from a wide variety of public and private sources, and functioning in a fluid, institutional environment, which has a limited impact on the power and interests of actors.

These characteristics are shared by most of the major theoretical perspectives that blossomed in the 1960s, including studies of mass behavior, political development, and bureaucratic politics, as well as pluralism. The general rejection of "the state" as a meaningful analytic concept by all of these modes of analysis was not coincidental. They were part of a larger intellectual change—the behavioral revolution. Behaviorism was a reaction against formal legalism, the approach that had dominated the discipline of political science in the United States from its inception during the last part of the nineteenth century through the 1940s. Formal legalism virtually identified political life with the state, understood as an institution that promulgated binding laws and stood in a superior hierarchical position to other parts of the polity. Formal rules were seen as independent variables. The statement of rules was "treated as tantamount to the explanation for behavior" (Eckstein 1979).

Behaviorism rejected the identity between rules and behavior. Empirical studies did not demonstrate a close relationship between formal rules and political activity. Rules did not necessarily lead to regularities; and regularities existed without rules. In a world that included polities as different as the United States, the Soviet Union, and Upper Volta, behaviorism suggested that it was impossible to understand much about actual political life simply by studying formal legal institutions (Eckstein 1979: 10–11; Almond 1973: 245–47).

As a corollary to rejecting formal legalism, behaviorist approaches focused on the society. They reversed the causal relationship that had been posited by formal legalism. Societal forces were viewed as the independent variable. Political outcomes were determined primarily by the preferences and power capabilities of societal actors. Furthermore, the introduction of statistical methods and the computer made it much more attractive to collect data on many variables from a large number of cases. Such an empirical strategy was peculiarly compatible with a pluralistic view of the political universe as heterogeneous and atomistic. (Obviously statistical methodology and theoretical perspectives are not linked in any rigid way. But computers and statistics did facilitate the acceptance of pluralist arguments by making it easier to publish and conduct research.) Hence pluralism is part of a more general intellectual orientation that has dominated American political science for the last twenty years. The new concern with the state must be seen, in the first instance, as a reaction against prevailing fashion.

Two central concerns have informed this new literature. The first involves the autonomy of the state, its ability to formulate and implement public policy. The second involves the extent of congruity between the state and its environment, a central issue for the study of political development. These issues are addressed in the next two sections of this essay.

Public policy: the state as exogenous variable

Both Nordlinger and Geertz are concerned with public policy broadly defined, that is, with authoritative actions taken by public institutions. Nordlinger investigates the relationship between state and private actors in modern industrialized democracies, arguing that if the autonomy of the state can be demonstrated in this political setting it should hold in others as well. Nordlinger notes that this is the case most likely to disprove assertions that public officials can formulate and authoritatively implement their preferences. Geertz guides his readers into a much more exotic political environment, nineteenth-century Bali, to show that symbolic activities, which have been largely ignored by Western political theory for several hundred years, can be the consummatory end of public life and the central attribute of the state.

Nordlinger's basic objective is to demonstrate that

> the preferences of the state are at least as important as those of civil society in accounting for what the democratic state does and does not do; the democratic state is not only frequently autonomous insofar as it regularly acts upon its preferences, but also markedly autonomous in doing so even when its preferences diverge from the demands of the most powerful groups in civil society.
>
> (Nordlinger 1981: 1)

The preferences of the state, which Nordlinger defines as "all those individuals who occupy offices that authorize them, and them alone, to make and apply decisions that are binding upon any and all segments of society" (Nordlinger 1981: 11), may be generated within the state itself or from the wider society. The critical point with regard to state autonomy is that these preferences not simply be designed to curry favor or avoid punishment from particular societal groups. The final measure of autonomy is the ability of state officials to translate their weighted preferences into authoritative actions.

The heart of *On the Autonomy of the Democratic State* is three chapters delineating state autonomy under different relationships between the preferences of state and societal actors. Type III state autonomy refers to situations in which there is non-divergence between the preferences of the state and the society. Nordlinger argues that even under these conditions state-oriented accounts can explain authoritative actions at least as well as society-oriented ones. The state may initiate policy and provide access for particular societal groups. The state can reinforce a weak level of convergence by manipulating information, inflating the success of ongoing programs, setting agendas, appealing to widely shared symbols, playing upon deference to official expertise, and deflecting potential opposition. In all, Nordlinger lists fifteen specific tactics that state officials can use to reinforce convergence (Nordlinger 1981: 91–98).

Type II state autonomy refers to situations in which state action changes divergent societal preference to convergent ones. The state can use four general strategies to effect such changes: altering the views of societal opponents; limiting the deployment of resources by societal opponents; gaining the support of indifferent actors; and increasing the resources of societal actors holding convergent views (Nordlinger 1981: 109–17).

Type I state autonomy refers to situations in which state actors translate their preferences into authoritative action despite divergent societal preferences. They can accomplish this by using the resources of the state to neutralize societal opponents by measures such as deploying public capital, threatening to withhold specific government programs, and masking the state's decision-making procedures. The state may even be able to act peremptorily by relying upon its inherent powers. Public officials have the authority "to take any and all actions other than those which violate the constitutional format and other legitimized procedural principles" (Nordlinger 1981: 128–39).

Nordlinger's book is at once the most and least ambitious of the studies under review. It is the most ambitious with regard to specifying the wide array of resources that public officials can use to secure their preferences and in arguing for their autonomy even in those settings where it has been most strongly denied. It is the least ambitious with regard to delineating the institutional arrangements that constrain political actors. Nordlinger's view of the political universe is not qualitatively different from earlier pluralist positions. Nordlinger does place much greater emphasis on the role of the state. This is an important departure from prevailing traditions. But like the pluralists, he sees a world of atomistic political actors, albeit one in which relatively more of the atoms are public officials. Nordlinger conceptualizes the "state as government;" the state is defined as a collection of individuals in official positions. It includes mayors as well as presidents, prefects as well as cabinet ministers. These individuals may derive their preferences from a variety of sources including other public officials, bureaucratic interests, distinctive experience and information, some conception of the public interest, and a desire for greater autonomy (Nordlinger 1981: 32–33). When more than one state unit is involved in a policy, "state preferences are based exclusively upon the weighted intrastate resources of those public officials who have an interest in the issue at hand" (Nordlinger 1981: 16). Nordlinger endorses the pluralist image of politics as a resolution of vectors (Skocpol 1982).

Nordlinger explicitly rejects state structures as an explanation for variation in the degree of state autonomy. He argues that the ability of state officials to carry out their preferences is not a function of the institutional structure within which they must function but rather of the amount of societal resistance that they encounter (Nordlinger 1981: 192–97). Nordlinger does note that it may be easier for a strong state than for a weak one to change preferences, that appeals to common values may enhance support for the state, and that the inherent power of public officials is limited by constitutional rules; but he does not give much credence to such institutional constraints. The political world is fluid; the preferences and capabilities of actors shift across issue areas and over time. *On the Autonomy of the Democratic State* is focused more on the state than even nuanced pluralist arguments; it is concerned more with state–society relations than with bureaucratic politics perspectives; but it does not differ from these orientations in its basic depiction of the atomistic character of political life.

Clifford Geertz's *Negara: The Theater State in Nineteenth Century Bali* is concerned with a political world and a conception of politics very different from Nordlinger's, and for that matter from conventional Western political thought. It is a brilliant, evocative, and poetic book, a book that at once draws the reader into a totally alien world and draws out of that world enduring insights about the nature of political life. Geertz shows that the essence of the state in nineteenth-century Bali was not allocation but ceremony.

> Court ceremonialism was the driving force of court politics; and mass ritual was not a device to shore up the state, but rather the state, even in its final gasp, was a device for the enactment of mass ritual. Power served pomp, not pomp power.
>
> (Geertz 1980: 13)

The Balinese state, the negara, was "a constellation of enshrined ideas," whose central precept was that "worldly status has a cosmic base, that hierarchy is the governing principle of the universe, and that the arrangements of human life are but approximations, more close or less, to those of the divine" (Geertz 1980: 102, 135). The main mechanism of political struggle in Bali was the court ceremony, especially cremation, designed to demonstrate the relative status of a particular noble house. These ceremonies were "not merely the drapery of political order, but its substance" (Geertz 1980: 32).

The negara was only one of several authoritative, decision-making institutions in Bali. Issues involving civil society, including public works, local security, and civil disputes, were the preserve of the village. Wet rice cultivation, or more precisely the allocation of water rights, was regulated by irrigation societies. Religious commitments were defined by the temple congregation. Membership in these three groups intersected and overlapped (Geertz 1980: 153).

The defining authoritative relationship between the negara, composed of the noble houses, and the rest of Balinese society was the obligation of individual commoners to specific lords for service in ceremonial functions and war. These commoners could be drawn from a number of different villages. They could belong to different irrigation societies and temple congregations. The overriding objective of each noble house was to control more men and resources in order to stage more elaborate ceremonies to demonstrate a higher position in the social order, which was seen as a reflection or mirror of a more encompassing hierarchical cosmos that linked man and the gods.

In the concluding chapter of *Negara*, entitled "Bali and Political Theory," Geertz muses upon the broader implications of his presentation. He argues that since the sixteenth century Western political thought has identified the state with governance or statecraft, with rule and control. However, Bali "exposes the symbolic dimensions of state power." It "restores our sense of the ordering force of display, regard, and drama" (Geertz 1980: 122). Western analysis has been utterly incapable of providing an adequate account of this force. The ceremonial functions of the state have been regarded, as in Hobbes, as a device to reinforce the power of the monarch, or in Marx or Pareto as "great frauds" designed to facilitate the extraction of resources by the elite. "Political symbology is political ideology, and political ideology is class hypocrisy" (Geertz 1980: 122). Symbolic activities have not been regarded as ends in themselves.

Geertz conceives of the state as a normative order. His observations about the central importance of symbolic activities in Bali are not merely of anti-quarian interest, and he does not mean them to be so. Even in the modern era they are a common defining characteristic of the state. In its simplest form, what is universal and distinctive to what Harry Eckstein has called the princely realm is that it symbolizes and represents in rules and laws the existence of a separate society. Rules "stand for the fact that a common, thus, moral life exists, and they celebrate the common life and make it compelling." (Eckstein 1982: 472). This symbolic function is the core activity of barely differentiated political institutions in primitive societies. While many other activities have entered the princely realm, the visible celebration of the polity's identity has not disappeared.

Symbols embodied in the state and representing basic political and ethical sentiments that permeate the polity can be seen as a fundamental institu-tional constraint that channels the behavior of individuals even to the point of endangering or sacrificing their lives. (Hobbes was too worried about desertion, at least once the existence of a moral community has been estab-lished.) Dahl's democratic creed cannot be dismissed because of disagreement over specific applications, because this creed defines a set of non-decisions that cannot be revealed by simple behavioral observation (Bachrach and Baratz 1962). David Truman's latent groups are not groups at all, but rather generally accepted societal beliefs that are enshrined in the decorative activities and specific laws of the state and that delineate the acceptable range of political behavior.

The central importance of symbols illuminated by Geertz provides greater insight into the much maligned concept of the common good or the national interest. In allocative terms, promoting the common good can be conceived of as a policy that makes some or all actors better off without making any worse off. But seeing the state as the institution where the common identity and moral beliefs of the polity are embodied in ceremony and practice goes beyond questions of resource distribution among groups or of rectification of Pareto's suboptimal conditions. Political activity focused on the state sustains the ethical and moral needs of citizens, not just their material ones. The destruction of the state by, for instance, alien conquest, is a loss for all citi-zens because it means the destruction or severe weakening of the individual's social and moral community.

Political development: the state as an intervening variable

The arguments presented by Nordlinger and Geertz do not address questions of political development: they do not explain how various forms of the state that exist in the contemporary world took their present shape. Especially for Nordlinger, the focus of concern is the causal arrow from the state to the society. In contrast, for Skowronek and the other authors discussed in this section the focus of attention is on the causal arrow from the broader environment, both international and domestic, to the nature of state institutions. The state (understood as an administrative apparatus and legal order) is treated initially as the dependent variable, although in subsequent time periods changed institutional capabilities alter the state's ability to influence economic and social behavior.

All of the authors discussed here reject functional explanations of state development. Institutional structures do not respond in any rapid and fluid way to alterations in the domestic or international environment. Change is difficult. Incongruence between the needs and expressed demands of the state and various societal groups is the norm, not the exception. Institutional change is episodic and dramatic rather than continuous and incremental. Crises are of central importance. Skowronek defines a crisis as

> a sporadic, disruptive event that suddenly challenges a state's capacity to maintain control and alters the boundaries defining the legitimate use of coercion. Crisis situations tend to become the watersheds in a state's institutional development. Actions taken to meet the challenge often lead to the establishment of new institutional forms, powers, and precedents.
>
> (Skowronek 1982: 10)

During periods of crisis politics becomes a struggle over the basic rules of the game rather than allocation within a given set of rules. However, once crises are past, institutional arrangements tend to rigidify. Institutions reproduce themselves and respond more to their own needs than to those of their domestic society or the international environment. Thus, different kinds of causal variables are appropriate for explaining the creation, as opposed to the maintenance, of state institutions.

Crisis may be generated internally or externally. Skowronek is concerned with the former case, the other authors discussed here with the latter. Internally generated crises are precipitated by dynamic changes in the society; externally generated crises by threats from the international system that lead to state efforts to increase extraction, efforts that can precipitate societal resistance. Hence, two patterns of incongruence between the state and its environment can be identified. Pattern I, public stasis and private dynamism, occurs when the exogenous sources of change are internal. Pattern II, state demands and societal resistance, occurs when the exogenous sources of change emanate from the international system.

Pattern I: Public stasis and private dynamism

The state as administrative apparatus and legal order will *not* smoothly adjust to changes in its domestic environment. Once institutions are in place they will perpetuate themselves. Power holders strive to select their own successors. Elaborate educational structures, such as France's *grands écoles*, may be created to socialize members of the higher civil service (Suleiman 1978). One of Skowronek's major points of emphasis is that, short of a total overthrow of the old regime, reforms must be carried out in the context of existing institutional structures. Some individuals occupying positions in these institutions are bound to resist change because it can undermine their budgetary support, policy scope, and personal status. The natural path for institutions is to act in the future as they have acted in the past.

Institutional statis is also encouraged by sunk costs. Once a given set of institutional structures is in place, it embodies capital stock that cannot be recovered. This stock takes primarily the form of information trust and shared expectations. Long-established institutional structures facilitate the exchange of information and tacitly coordinate behavior. There is more information, and therefore less uncertainty, about existing programs than proposed ones. If new institutions are created, these infrastructures must be re-created. Thus, even if there is widespread societal dissatisfaction with a particular set of institutions, it may be irrational to change them. The variable costs of maintaining the existing institutions may be less than the total costs of creating and maintaining new ones (Keohane 1982; Stinchcombe 1968: 120ff). Moreover, when pressures are emanating from a rapidly changing domestic environment, it may be difficult to know whether to commit substantial resources to create new institutions because it may not be possible to distinguish transitory from enduring change.

The United States offers an example of a pattern of national development in which the society has changed more dramatically than the institutional structures of the state. Skowronek suggests that there are four characteristics that can be used to describe any state:

> the concentration of authority at the national center ... , the penetration of institutional controls from the governmental center throughout the territory ... , the centralization of authority within the national government ... , the specialization of institutional tasks and roles within the government.
>
> (Skowronek 1982: 10)

The state that evolved in early nineteenth-century America rated low on all of these dimensions. Most governing tasks were carried out by state and local governments. The only national institutions of serious import were the parties and the courts. The courts became "the American surrogate for a more fully developed administrative apparatus" (Skowronek 1982: 28). The parties helped to link the national and local levels through patronage. However, these were weak foundations upon which to develop national administrative capacity: the courts and parties were centered at the local level, and their operations were fluid and malleable. Even the Civil War did not lead to any permanent increase in the institutional capability of central governmental institutions (Skowronek 1982: Ch. 2).

There are straightforward functional explanations for the creation and reinforcement of a weak and fragmented state in eighteenth- and early nineteenth-century America. The American Revolution was a reaction against British efforts to increase penetration and control of American society. The United States was not confronted with any persistent external threat. Aristocratic traditions were weak, so it was not necessary to have a strong state to facilitate socioeconomic transformation. The frontier offered a safety valve for societal pressures that might otherwise have been directed at the central government. The physical abundance of the United States made it easier to resolve conflict by increasing the size of the pie rather than by asking authoritative institutions to alter the relative distribution of the segments.

These social and economic conditions existed in symbiotic relationship with a pervasive set of values that legitimated a weak state. Louis Hartz has argued that the United States is a fragment society whose political beliefs were determined by its initial settlers. In leaving Europe, these settlers escaped not only from their contemporary conservative opponents but also from their future socialist ones (Hartz 1955). The American creed implanted "liberal, democratic, individualistic, and egalitarian values" (Huntington 1982: 2). It is not necessary to hold that this ideology was merely a handmaiden of economic interest, or conversely that beliefs were entirely independent of societal conditions. Through the middle of the nineteenth century, Lockean liberal principles were particularly well suited to the social structure and economic conditions that existed in the United States. The liberal fragment could take root and flourish precisely because it legitimated prevailing social relationships. Thus, at its premier constitutional moment, in the period of its birth, the American state was congruent with its environment. State structures were consistent with the functional needs of society, the preferences of state officials, and basic political beliefs.

However, over time the society and economy changed. Industrialization involved greater economic centralization and concentration in the United States, as in other areas of the world. Commercial networks became more complex. Conflicts between labor and management became more frequent. Externalities multiplied. Market imperfections became more common. Information was no longer readily available. The United States became a significant actor in the international economy. The fundamentally rural, agrarian society of early nineteenth-century America was supplemented by an industrialized, urban society populated by diverse ethnic groups that had unevenly assimilated the American creed. Such an environment constantly placed strains on the weak and fragmented political system.

The response to industrialization is the major concern of *Building a New American State: The Expansion of National Administrative Capacities, 1877–1920*. Skowronek examines the way in which institutional structures changed in three major issue areas: business regulation, the military, and the civil service. A functional orientation suggests a major adjustment in institutional structures to bring them into congruence with the changing society; functionalist logic would predict the creation of a strong state to meet new societal needs and demands. But this did not happen.

Skowronek refers to the period 1877–1900 as one of "state building as patchwork." New institutions simply patched up the existing polity dominated by locally oriented political parties and the courts. The Interstate Commerce Commission, the major institutional innovation in government regulation of business, was gutted by a series of Supreme Court decisions. A new civil service system was created, but it was used only to fill in the interstices around the patronage appointments from which the political parties drew much of their strength. The army was made more professional, but at the same time the national guard, the representative institution of political localism, was maintained and even strengthened.

The development of stronger national capabilities was impeded not simply by the opposition of specific groups but more fundamentally by the existing institutional structure. "Institutions and procedures once created to serve socioeconomic development now appeared as self-perpetuating perversions of that purpose" (Skowronek 1982: 40). Local interests, especially in the South, opposed a strong, professional, national army. The political parties resisted a civil service system that would deny them patronage appointments. The courts "vigorously asserted and jealously guarded the prerogatives of the judiciary in regulating economic affairs" (Skowronek 1982: 122). The outcome of the struggle between these interests of the old order and the proponents of the new, including upper middle-class professionals, regular army officers, government officials, and businessmen, was determined not just by the relative power of each faction but by the institutional structure within which the struggle took place. This was especially true for the fate of the Interstate Commerce Commission. Skowronek writes that

> the key to understanding the early regulatory effort is not to be found in the interests themselves but in the structure of the institutions they sought to influence. In an archetypical case of the pluralist paradigm, each of the interests contesting the railroad issue found representation in American national government, and each was able to make its mark on the blank slate of national regulatory policy. Yet, in this new regulatory situation, the sum of the interests could not possibly serve any of them, let alone some "public interest" standing apart from each; it only promised an incoherent, unworkable policy from which no one stood to benefit. A state that promoted pluralism promoted a formula for failure in regulation.
>
> (Skowronek 1982: 131)

Public policy cannot be viewed simply as the resolution of a set of vectors. The interests and political resources of actors are a function of existing institutions, and this may make it impossible for any given actor or coalition of actors, whether state or private, to implement their preferences.

Skowronek argues that a more powerful set of state institutions was created between 1900 and 1920. However, even after the New Deal, more recent bursts of social legislation, and two world wars, there is still no effective, consistent, and coherent control of the national administrative apparatus. The old order of localistic parties and courts was destroyed, but the "reconstituted" American state, to use Skowronek's terms, did not successfully concentrate power. "Beyond the state of courts and parties lay a hapless administrative giant, a state that could spawn bureaucratic goods and services but that defied authoritative control and direction" (Skowronek 1982: 290). In the area of national administrative capability, institutions that were created or strengthened after 1900 included the Civil Service Commission, the Bureau of the Budget, and the General Accounting Office. However, the specific positions of these agencies "within the federal establishment were all somewhat obscure," and they all functioned in environments characterized by "parallel sets of controls pitted against each other" (Skowronek 1982: 208). "In the area of the military nationalism came to mean a proliferation of semi-independent and competing power centers at the national level rather than the establishment of a national center of power" (Skowronek 1982: 247).

Thus, the institutional structures of the past placed constraints on the possibilities for the future. The preferences and capabilities of political actors cannot be treated as exogenous variables; they can only be understood within the context of a given set of institutional arrangements. Although Skowronek does not place much emphasis on enduring political beliefs, these too have played a continuing and central role in the development of the American state. Huntington has pointed to the persistent tensions between beliefs and institutional development that have erupted during periods of creedal passion (Huntington 1982). The attack on the national bureaucracy by the Reagan administration only serves to underline the enduring, deep resistance to the concentration of political power at the center. The sinister connotations of the term "military–industrial complex" as well as the failure to agree on a consistent policy toward military service are constant reminders that even in the area of national defense the United States has failed to develop a coherent and legitimate set of institutional arrangements. Judicial activism remains a powerful tradition for American courts. And lest anyone think that localism is dead, consider the following statement from the preliminary report of a commission established by the State of Alaska to study deteriorating relations with the rest of the United States:

> If Alaska wants to protect its resources, its revenues and its state prerogatives, the state government must vigorously defend [itself] against

federal encroachments. It should not be afraid of suing, of mounting a national information campaign, of building political coalitions, or taking what otherwise might seem to be drastic steps, with the exception of secession.

(*Wall Street Journal* 1983: 18 January)

In sum, Skowronek's study complements the work of other scholars, such as Huntington and Hartz, who see varying degrees of tension between state institutions and their environment as a constant theme of American political history. Skowronek's underlying causal model is one in which the outcome of institution-building during any particular period of crisis is a function of both contemporaneous environmental factors, such as industrialization, and existing institutional structures that are a product of past conditions, such as the nineteenth-century state of parties and courts. Crises reduce incongruence between state structures and the domestic environment. But during subsequent periods institutional structures reproduce themselves while society changes, leading to increased tensions which eventually precipitate another crisis.

Pattern II: State demands and societal resistance

Incongruity between the state and civil society can also arise because the state increases its demands upon the society. Such policies can lead to great social unrest, not simply because the level of extraction increases, but also because legitimacy is placed at risk by the imposition of new state practices. Political leaders do not bring such difficulties upon their heads for nothing.

Throughout the history of the Western state system the most persistent sources of pressure on the state have been external. It is the threat of invasion, or the desire to act efficaciously in the international system, that has prompted rulers to increase their level of extraction from the society. This is a major theme of a number of studies published during the last decade. In the penultimate volume of the Social Science Research Council's (SSRC) series Studies in Political Development, *The Development of National States in Western Europe*, the editor Charles Tilly argues that the need to maintain and increase military establishments was the major impetus for the growth of the state's administrative apparatus. Greater military capacity required higher levels of taxation. Higher levels of taxation required a more extensive bureaucracy. Extractive capacities initially used for military purposes could be applied in other areas as well. Taxes that began as extraordinary levies to fight specific wars often became normal and continuing sources of revenue (Tilly 1975: 42, 54, 73–74).

One of the repetitive patterns noted in *The Formation of National States in Western Europe*, the last volume of the SSRC series, is that external threats lead to crises of penetration. The articles on Germany and Russia by John R. Gillis and Walter M. Pintner, respectively, place particular emphasis on this point. Gillis argues that nineteenth-century German reforms were designed to increase the power of the state, not to create a more liberal society. The humiliation of Prussia at Jena in 1806 convinced leading members of the elite that rigid absolutism would perpetuate military inferiority. Reforms were initiated by military leaders and bureaucrats to mobilize the population in the service of the state. Citizenship was defined as a set of duties, not rights. Legislative changes and the extension of the franchise were introduced from above, not only to stave off the possibility of domestic unrest, but also to increase the state's level of extraction. Similarly, Pintner shows that the perennial Russian problem was that the needs of the state, prompted by external threats, exceeded its extractive capacity. Russian rulers strove to maintain a large army on an anemic agrarian economic base. Nineteenth-century social reforms were prompted by external failures. Defeat in the Crimean War convinced the ruling elite (composed of the tsar and a small group of high officials) that basic change was necessary. Economic reform, including the emancipation of the serfs, was initiated from above to increase the level of resources that the state could secure from its society.

Ellen Kay Trimberger's *Revolution from Above: Military Bureaucrats and Development in Japan, Turkey, Egypt, and Peru* examines four cases of major social change initiated from above by military bureaucrats. Trimberger defines a revolution as "an extralegal takeover of the central state apparatus which destroys the economic and political power of the dominant social group of the old regime" (Trimberger 1978: 2). There are two basic preconditions for revolution from above: the military and civilian administration must be bureaucratized in a Weberian sense, and they must be independent of the dominant class. Given these preconditions a revolution from above can be precipitated "only in a crisis situation—when the existing social, political, and economic order is threatened by external forces and by upheaval from below" (Trimberger 1978: 4–5). Foreign pressures lead to internal disorder which undermines the military's position. National degradation spawns nationalist ideologies that unite the military internally and provide a rationale for dramatic action. In Japan, Turkey, Peru, and Egypt the military initiated major social and economic changes after they had taken power. The purpose of these changes was to enhance the power of the state by promoting economic development. However, Trimberger is skeptical of the long-term impact of these initiatives because of the tendency of subsequent leaders to ally with the dominant economic forces and because of the constraining influence of the world economic system.

In sum, a number of studies point to external pressures as a major cause of the development of new state capacity. Such external pressures are almost certainly more compelling than internal ones. The failure to act effectively, as in Geertz's *Negara* and in eighteenth-century Poland, means the destruction of the polity. But in cases of both external and internal environmental pressures, a similar pattern emerges, characterized by rapid change during periods of crisis followed by consolidation and stasis. To borrow a metaphor from work in evolutionary biology, such a pattern can be labeled "punctuated equilibrium."

Punctuated equilibrium

All of these studies of political development point to differential rates of change in social and political structures over time. A basic analytic distinction must be made between periods of institutional creation and periods of institutional stasis. The kinds of causal factors that explain why a set of state structures is created in the first place may be quite distinct from those that explain its persistence over time. New structures originate during periods of crisis. They may be imposed through conquest or be implanted by a particular fragment of the existing social structure. But once institutions are in place they can assume a life of their own, extracting societal resources, socializing individuals, and even altering the basic nature of civil society itself. The causal dynamics associated with a crisis of the old order and the creation of a new one are different from those involved in the perpetuation of established state institutions.

Furthermore, once a critical choice has been made it cannot be taken back. There may be a wide range of possible resolutions of a particular state-building crisis. But once a path is taken it canalizes future developments. Sidney Verba has referred to this conceptualization as the branching tree model of sequential development. A critical choice forecloses other options in part because the "choice to set up a program in relation to a particular problem area may lead almost inevitably to the maintenance and even expansion of the program because of the vested interests it creates" (Verba 1971: 308). It is not possible in human affairs to start *de novo* with every change in wants, needs, and power capabilities. Past choices preclude certain strategies or make them very costly. Institutions generated by functional demands of the past can perpetuate themselves into a future whose functional imperatives are radically different.

One of the clearest examples of a branching tree argument is Lipset and Rokkan's model of the development of European party systems (Lipset and Rokkan 1968). They argue that there were three crucial historical junctures: first, the Reformation involving the struggle for control of the church; second, the democratic revolution after 1789 involving the struggle for control of the rapidly expanding educational system; and third the industrial revolution involving conflict between the urban center and agrarian periphery. At each of these critical junctures the nation-building elite that controlled the state machinery had alliance options. Once a particular alliance was chosen, however, it set the agenda for future party development. Thus, the settlement of the sixteenth-century struggle between the church and the state "gave a very different structure to the cleavages of the nineteenth" century in Protestant and Catholic Europe (Lipset and Rokkan 1968: 38).

In a particularly provocative set of analyses Charles Sabel and his collaborators have argued that the organization of industrial society has also followed a branching tree pattern. Fordism, the use of mass-production techniques involving special-purpose machines and unskilled labor to produce standardized products, was not foreordained by the nature of technology. Flexible specialization involving small firms using skilled workers and general-purpose machines to produce more specialized products was a viable alternative. However, as a result of the distribution of property rights and income in Britain and the United States, Fordism became the dominant mode of industrial production. Once this choice was made, economic and political institutions were shaped to guarantee the existence of stable mass markets. Thus, an historically contingent set of conditions in the nineteenth century set the path for the future evolution of industrial society (Sabel 1982: Chs 4 and 5; Piore and Sabel 1984; Sabel and Zeitlin 1985).

Fernand Braudel has argued that one of the critical determinants of the rise of capitalism in the West was that for a set of fortuitous reasons cities revived faster than states in the Middle Ages. Revivals, Braudel maintains, always feature two runners, the state and the city. The state usually won and the city then remained subject and under a heavy yoke. The miracle of the first great urban centuries in Europe was that the city won hands down, at least in Italy, Flanders, and Germany. Braudel goes on to suggest that the existence of free cities created a new state of mind, "broadly that of an early, still faltering, Western capitalism—a collection of rules, possibilities, calculations, the art both of getting rich and living" (Braudel 1981: 511–13). Thus, small initial differences promoted a new kind of institutional structure with profound consequences over the long term.

Moreover, choices made by leading states at a particular point in time influence not only their future range of options, but also the options of later developing states. The functions that are viewed as proper and legitimate for the state are influenced by general international norms and practices. In the modern system the institutional characteristics of states in more industrially developed areas have set an agenda for states in less developed areas. These characteristics come to be associated with the essential nature of the "modern" state and cannot be ignored even by states with very different needs. In his study of social security systems in Britain and Sweden, Hugh Heclo points out that the options pursued by the Swedes were heavily influenced by the bureaucracy's assessment of policies that had been adopted in countries with more developed industrial structures. "Because of a process of transnational learning Sweden found unemployment insurance on its national agenda at about the same time that Britain did even though Sweden's level of economic development and industrialization lagged considerably behind Britain's" (Heclo 1974: 66). Virtually every country today has, at least on paper, some kind of social security system, even though the economic resources of many Third World countries are totally incapable of actually implementing such a program. The organization of educational systems throughout the world has not only been seen as a responsibility of the state (as opposed to the church or some other private organization), but has also mimicked the characteristics of systems in the more developed countries (Meyer 1980; Meyer and Rowan 1977; Ramirez and Boli-Bennett 1982).

Even the state itself can be seen in this light. The concept of a single hierarchical ruling structure governing a defined territorial area developed out of feudal Europe. New military technologies in the late Middle Ages were characterized by economies of scale providing an incentive to form larger territorial units. The revival of trade offered economic benefits to those political actors that could assure the safe movement of goods over longer distances. States, especially nation-states, were able to secure more intense affective commitment from their inhabitants than were empires.

Over time the national state has pushed aside all other forms of political organization. After the Second World War demands for decolonization could only be met by granting formal independence, even though many of the areas that achieved this status lacked the economic, military, and bureaucratic capability to function effectively. Some intermediate form of political organization that divided functions between colonial territories and their home governments would almost certainly have been more politically and economically efficacious. But such solutions were not possible. They lacked legitimacy. They could not have commanded the support of colonial populations. The triumph of the national state in Europe became a triumph of the national state around the globe. Choices made in Europe's past dictated the possibilities for Africa's future. Once a particular path had been chosen, other paths, perhaps more functionally appropriate for contemporary problems, were foreclosed.

To borrow a term from another discipline, an imagery that expects short bursts of rapid institutional change followed by long period of stasis can be termed "punctuated equilibrium." Punctuated equilibrium refers to a set of arguments about evolution whose main proponents are Stephen Jay Gould and Niles Eldredge. Gould and Eldredge have attacked the conventional Darwinian synthesis which pictures evolutionary progress as a slow, continuous process of change in which entire species slowly adapt to environmental conditions. They have argued instead that change tends to take place rapidly in geographically isolated groups which may then displace their ancestral populations. Such displacements are rare. Generally species do not change substantially over very long periods of time. Evolutionary change, Gould and Eldredge argue, is concentrated in geographically instantaneous events (Eldredge and Gould 1972; Gould 1982; Gould and Eldredge 1977).

Gould has noted that the gradualist–punctualist debate in the largest sense

> is but one small aspect of a broader discussion about the nature of change:
> Is our world (to construct a ridiculously oversimplified dichotomy) primarily one of constant change (with structure as a mere incarnation of the moment), or is structure primary and constraining, with change as a

> "difficult" phenomenon, usually accomplished rapidly when a stable
> structure is stressed beyond its buffering capacity to resist and absorb?
>
> (Gould 1982: 383)

This description of the basic nature of the debate in evolutionary theory has
its close analog in social and political analysis. Punctuated equilibrium is an
apt description of an analytic stance that sees political institutions enduring
over long periods once they are established.

Critics of the Darwinian synthesis have also made branching tree arguments.
Once a particular evolutionary path is taken, the direction of future evolutionary developments is constrained by the available genetic pool (Gould
1982: 303). If the same set of environmental conditions exists at two different
points in time or at two geographically isolated areas of the globe, they will
not give rise to the same set of species. Speciation is a function not only of
the contemporary environment, but also of past environments, of paths that
have been followed and of paths that have not been followed. While the
long time frames and slow change of the conventional Darwinian model
offer the possibility of optimal functional adjustment (at least over the eons),
such optimality is not anticipated by alternative approaches. In a world
characterized by punctuated equilibrium there is more uncertainty and
chance. A particular structural development reflecting marginal advantages at
a particular point in time may constrain future evolutionary developments.

The metaphor of punctuated equilibrium suggests a very different world
from that of pluralism and other orientations that emerged out of the behavioral persuasion. Central to these approaches was not simply a societally
oriented focus but also reservations about institutional constraints. If institutions adjusted relatively quickly to societal changes, and if formal institutions did not explain political behavior, there was little point in making them
an object of scholarly investigation. Attention could be focused on the
motivations of individuals or groups. Even the state, which Geertz refers to
as "that master noun of modern political discourse," could be ignored
(Geertz 1980: 121). But if institutions—the administrative apparatus, legal
order, and political beliefs—are seen as basic determinants of both the
interests and the power of political actors, a different agenda is suggested for
political research. How can political institutions, including the state, be adequately described? How do institutional structures constrain the behavior of
individual actors? What factors best explain the creation of new institutions?
What resources enable institutions, especially the state, to perpetuate themselves? What is the duration of lags between different kinds of environmental
changes and changes in different kinds of institutional arrangements? When
do state institutions fail to change, even when the polity's survival is at stake?
When state institutions are suboptimal or even counter-productive for those
individuals living within a given territory, what possibilities are there for
change? The books discussed in this essay have taken important steps in
offering answers to these questions.

4 Sovereignty

An institutional perspective

Organisms are not putty before a molding environment or billiard balls before the pool cue of natural selection. Their inherited forms and behaviors constrain and push back; they cannot be quickly transformed to new optimality every time the environment alters.

(Stephen Jay Gould 1985b: 53)

Alternative perspectives

Over the last 500 years, the sovereign state has been a powerful instrument of human progress, or, at a minimum, human progress has occurred while sovereign states have been the dominant mode of political organization. The existence of an international system composed of many states facilitated economic development by preventing the consolidation of a single absolutist empire that would have stultified private initiative and by providing an environment sufficiently orderly to permit rational economic calculations (Wallerstein 1974a; North 1981; Mann 1986; Hall 1985).

This sovereign state system, however, also has some less benign consequences. Because the state system as a whole lacks a sovereign, wars are always a possibility. The severity of wars has increased over time, as measured by casualties rather than the frequency of conflict (Goldstein 1985). With the advent of nuclear weapons, major interstate conflict threatens to destroy human existence. Moreover, even very large states may not be able to cope with economic and other disturbances emanating from the international environment, and the opportunity cost of pursuing autarky is increasing, in part because technological changes in communication and transportation have reduced the transactions costs of international commercial activities (R. Cooper 1968). It is no longer obvious that the state system is the optimal way to organize political life.

The existence of a suboptimal institutional structure presents an anomaly for most of the theoretical orientations that inform social science research. These perspectives adopt a static viewpoint that is either utilitarian or functional. For both of these orientations, actors are adaptive and outcomes are optimal. History is not particularly important; institutional structures and policies will change if environmental incentives change. A social fact is explained by some other social variable that belongs to the same time period. For contemporary social science, this is a "natural" mode of explanation (Harsanyi 1960: 136).

In investigating the basic mode of political organization in the contemporary world, the national state, these conventional approaches are not likely to provide either adequate prescriptive guidance or satisfactory explanations. It will be necessary to deploy an institutionalist perspective to construct a suitable explanation for the development and persistence of the sovereign state. An institutionalist perspective regards enduring institutional structures as the building blocks of social and political life. The preferences, capabilities, and basic self-identities of individuals are conditioned by these institutional structures. Historical developments are path-dependent; once certain choices are made, they constrain future possibilities. The range of options available to policy makers at any given point in time is a function of institutional capabilities that were put in place in some earlier period, possibly in response to very different environmental pressures.

Conventional approaches

James March and Johan Olsen have argued that in one form or another, utilitarian or functional approaches dominate American social science. These orientations see political activity as an integral part of civil society. Outcomes are the result of individual choice. History is understood as functionalist in the sense that anticipated outcomes result in one single, most-efficient equilibrium. And finally, these perspectives are instrumentalist in that allocation is viewed as the major concern of political activity (March and Olsen 1984: 735). The pervasive impact of these orientations, especially utilitarian arguments, is particularly apparent in political science and economics.

In microeconomic theory, market outcomes are a product of the behavior of individual firms and consumers whose preferences and capabilities are taken as given. The realism of the assumption of egoistic individualism is not part of the inquiry of modern economics (Sen 1977: 322; Moe 1984: 741). The most pristine and imperialistic form of this argument, exemplified in the work of the Chicago School, applies microeconomic analysis to all aspects of human behavior. It assumes that preferences are universal. Gary Becker (1976: 5) argues that since

> economists generally have had little to contribute, especially in recent times, to the understanding of how preferences are formed, preferences are assumed not to change substantially over time, nor to be very different between wealthy and poor persons, or even between persons in different societies and cultures.

Customs and traditions, which might from other perspectives be thought of as determinants of values, are seen as devices for dealing with imperfect information (Stigler and Becker 1977: 82). Stigler and Becker (1977: 76) argue that the assumption of unchanging and common preferences makes it possible to avoid the intellectually flaccid position of explaining changes in behavior in terms of unexplained changes in tastes and to abstain from appealing to "whoever studies and explains tastes (psychologists? anthropologists? phrenologists? sociobiologists?)". (Stigler and Becker, of course, realize how much other social scientists cherish being identified with phrenologists.)

For the Chicago School, institutions play very little role either because they accept Coase's theorem that states that in the absence of transactions costs optimal allocation can be achieved through the market, or because they believe that in the not-so-long run, institutions, like any other outcome of behavior, must reflect the preferences and capabilities of individual actors (Moe 1987: 276–77). A shift in incentives or resources will quickly lead to a shift in behavior. In such a fluid environment, the concept of institutional structures becomes illusory and meaningless. The utilitarian perspective has also produced arguments that are more sympathetic to the importance of institutions and that potentially complement the perspective elaborated in this article. Moe (1987) has referred to this line of argument as the positive theory of political institutions. This mode of analysis treats institutional structures, which cannot be easily changed, as constraining individual actors by eliminating the viability of certain options and influencing resource availability. A stable outcome is one in which none of the individual actors have an incentive to change their behavior (Ferejohn 1987: 2). But even this more institutionally oriented utilitarian perspective must be distinguished from an institutional perspective because it takes preferences and the nature of actors as given. Institutional structures are seen as constraining actors rather than constituting them.

The utilitarian perspective, whether in its more or less institutional version, does not have much to say about failure. It cannot explain why some actors fail while others succeed, except to say that those who fail did not act to maximize their utility. Actors may not adjust to environmental opportunities or institutional constraints. Some firms go bankrupt while others thrive. Failures have to be written off as random events (Hogarth and Reder 1986: SI87, S190). Violations of basic assumptions, such as transitivity of preferences, are glossed over by arguing that, in the long run, there is learning or that, in any event, outcomes are not affected because market forces act as a corrective (Tversky and Kahneman 1986: S273).

Moreover, even those utilitarian approaches that are sympathetic to institutions regard them as being always up for grabs. Institutions are not taken for granted. Violating some established pattern of behavior is merely one cost among others. The principal agent literature is the clearest example of this perspective. Even actors in formal hierarchical relationships are presented as calculators and connivers—weasels always looking for a way to increase their utility if principles fail to monitor them effectively. Hence utilitarian theory describes a world in which actors are given and unproblematic and in which behavior is fluid and, for the Chicago School, constrained only by resource availability and relative prices.

Examples of this approach abound. In interest group pluralism, public policy is understood as a product of the pulling and hauling of particular societal groups. These groups are taken as a natural component of the political landscape. Human activity constantly produces changes in power, privilege, and welfare. Political and social structures are never permanent and never the starting point for an analysis. Institutions are at best arenas within which group activity takes place (Binder 1986: 7–10; March and Olsen 1984: 735–36).

In structural or realist theories of international politics, behavior is analyzed as a function of the distribution of power among states and the relative position of a given state. Shifts in the distribution of power will lead to changes in foreign policy and outcomes. The state, understood as a bundle of capabilities within a given territory that are deployed as if they were under the control of a unified rational actor, is taken as a given (Waltz 1979). Institutional constraints are entirely absent from this analysis. For realists, international politics is a self-help system in which individual states autonomously determine their own actions.

While utilitarian approaches, in various guises, are now the prevailing perspective in American social science, functional arguments still exert some influence, particularly in sociology and, to a lesser extent, in political science. Such theories also posit a world that is fluid and optimizing. Structures, although they may not always be readily visible, develop to fulfill different functions. Change is the result of adaptation to environmental incentives. Prevailing modes of analysis in organizational theory explain organizational structures as rational adaptations to environmental circumstances. They differ more in their descriptions of the environment than they do in their analyses of how the environment affects organizations: Weberians see rational bureaucratic modes of organization as functionally optimal in complex modern societies; Marxists argue that organizations change in response to the needs of capitalist society (DiMaggio and Powell 1983: 156). Although functional theories have been applied to social aggregates and utilitarian theory to individuals, they share a view of human behavior in which the struggle to maximize utility is pursued through adaptation of one form or another to environmental incentives.

Adherents of neoclassical economic theory, interest group pluralism, structural realism, and structural functionalism have modified their basic arguments in a variety of ways that attempt to take account of factors such as property rights, asymmetrical information, political institutions, and international regimes. But these departures do not violate the Lakatosian hard core of the actor-oriented approach. Even very sophisticated presentations take actor preferences as given, rather than as an endogenous product of an institutional structure, an assumption that makes it possible to understand actors as searching for an optimal outcome. If preferences are endogenous, this mode of analysis makes little sense. Furthermore, even arguments such as principal agent analysis in the new economic theory of the firm, or the investigation of equilibrium political institutions (Shepsle 1986), or the examination of international regimes (Keohane 1984; Krasner 1983) tend to be static in that independent and dependent variables are drawn from the same time period.

From an actor-oriented utilitarian or functional perspective, unambiguously dysfunctional behavior presents an anomaly. The most spectacular historical examples of such behavior occur when polities collapse in the face of pressure from some external force that could have been resisted given available material resources, but these resources could not be deployed because of institutional or cognitive constraints. At the end of the eighteenth century, the Polish nobility was unable to overcome a legislative system that gave every member of parliament a veto. Even in the face of extreme external threats, coherent and unified military action was impossible and the Polish state was dismembered and disappeared from the map of Europe for 120 years.

At the end of the nineteenth century, the Balinese ruling class failed to effectively unite despite pressures from the Dutch. The indigenous system collapsed when one of the major noble houses appealed to the Dutch for support in 1899, a policy which could not be reconciled with the hierarchical cosmology upon which the Balinese theater state was based (Geertz 1980: 39). The indigenous civilizations of the Western hemisphere were unable to comprehend the Spanish. They had only two classifications for human beings, the sedentary civilized and the barbarians. The Spanish were neither one of these, therefore they had to use the only other category available to them, the sacred. They thought the Spaniards were gods because they had no cognitive alternative, and Aztec civilization was destroyed (Paz 1987: 7). The nation-state system has not yet presented quite so extreme an example of dysfunctional behavior, but one is not hard to imagine, and military conflicts and state repression in the twentieth century have taken millions of individual lives even if they have not destroyed the nature of the state system itself.

An institutional perspective

This article is an effort to spell out an alternative approach to understanding how the sovereign state, and social structures more generally, might be understood, an approach that focuses on institutional change and inertia as a major explanatory variable. Institutional arguments have been given greater attention by political scientists in recent years. The basic characteristic of an institutional argument is that prior institutional choices limit available future options. There are two basic reasons why outcomes at some given point in time cannot be understood in terms of the preferences and capabilities of actors existing at that same point in time. First, capabilities and preferences, that is, the very nature of the actors, cannot be understood except as part of some larger institutional framework. Second, the possible options available at any given point in time are constrained by available institutional capabilities and these capabilities are themselves a product of choices made during some earlier period. Thus an institutional perspective requires, first, a careful delineation of the nature of particular institutional arrangements because such arrangements are both a dependent variable at time t and an independent variable at time t+1; and second, an explication of how institutional arrangements perpetuate themselves across time, even in situations where utilitarian calculations would suggest that they are dysfunctional.

An institutionalist perspective implies that it is necessary to unpack the notion of the sovereign state. What precisely does "sovereignty" mean and how has this meaning changed? More precisely, how have issues of extra-territoriality and transborder control varied across states and over time? Have state assertions to the exercise of final authority within their own territorial boundaries been challenged by external actors? What kind of transborder movements have states tried to control and how successful have they been? Once unpacked and made problematic, it is necessary to examine how the particular institutional structures of sovereignty regenerate themselves and delimit the range of available policy options and institutional changes.

While social science understands actor-oriented utilitarian and functional perspectives very well, institutional approaches are more illusive. There is variation across different social sciences with regard to the frequency with which institutionalist perspectives are invoked. They almost never appear in economics. They are also rarely invoked in political science. They are, however, much more prevalent in sociology in which the work of the founders of the discipline, especially Durkheim and Weber, rejected static utilitarian arguments, including the notion that the market could be self-regulating. Organizational sociologists have come to take for granted the notions that organizations are not fully flexible and cannot respond instantaneously to changes in environmental conditions, and that existing organizational strategies constrain the options open at any given point in time (Carroll 1984: 1272). J. Cooper and Brady (1981: 994) point out that

> institutional analysis has lagged behind behavioral analysis since the advent of the behavioral revolution in the early 1950s. Our ability to handle questions that posit individuals, whether in small numbers or large aggregates, as the units of analysis is far greater than our ability to handle questions that posit institutionalized collectivities in complex environments as the units of analysis.

There is no commonly agreed definition of what an institution structure is. Oran Young (1986: 107) states that "social institutions are recognized practices consisting of easily identifiable roles coupled with collections of rules or conventions governing relations among occupants of these roles." Sidney Verba (1971: 300) argues that institutions refer to "generally accepted regular procedures for handling a problem and to normatively sanctioned behavior patterns." Alford and Friedland (1985: 16) are more expansive, stating that the "concept of 'institution' refers to a pattern of supraorganizational relations stable enough to be described—polity, family, economy, religion, culture." Finally, Stinchcombe (1968: 107) says that an institution can be defined as "a structure in which powerful people are committed to some value or interest."

Despite their differences, these statements do suggest that there are two interrelated characteristics that are central to an institutionalist perspective: the derivative character of individuals and the persistence of something— behavioral patterns, roles, rules, organizational charts, ceremonies—over time. Sociologists have frequently argued that individuals are extremely sensitive to consensual norms. These norms are internalized through socialization. Behavior cannot be understood by examining atomized individuals. At the very least, individuals are confronted with a limited repertoire of social roles and values from which to choose. A particular role or enduring pattern of behavior can be comprehended adequately only as part of a larger social structure. Preferences are developed through involvement in political activity that is structured by institutional arrangements. Routinized procedures for hiring, promotion, and dismissal based on qualifications and performance would, for instance, be standard operating procedure for any formally established corporation in late twentieth-century America; such procedures would have been incomprehensible in medieval Europe (Katznelson 1986: 319–20; Granovetter 1985: 483; Alford and Friedland 1985: 7–8). John Meyer and his colleagues have asserted that

> a central concern of our analysis is the way in which the institutional structure of society creates and legitimates the social entities that are seen as "actors." That is, institutionalized cultural rules define the meaning and identity of the individuals and patterns of appropriate economic, political, and cultural activity. They similarly constitute the purposes and legitimacy of organizations, professions, interest groups, and states.
>
> (Meyer *et al.* 1987: 12)

Alexander Wendt (1987), applying structuration theory that more explicitly focuses on the interaction between macro and micro phenomena, maintains that behavior can be understood only in terms of the interaction between social structures that constitute individual actors and are, in turn, constituted by the actions of these actors.

Second, an institutionalist perspective implies that something persists over time and that change is not instantaneous and costless. If patterns of behavior, roles, collectivities, or formal organizations change rapidly and frequently, then there is little use in invoking an institutionalist argument. It is better under such circumstances to focus on individuals without regard to some larger context. Invoking some notion of enduring institutions can only obscure understanding in an environment where patterns of behavior and what are commonly termed institutions are rapidly changing in response to environmental pressures. While an institutionalist argument does not maintain that such rapid change never occurs, it does imply that such episodes are infrequent and are followed by long periods of either relative stasis or path-dependent change. Changes, from an institutionalist perspective, can never be easy, fluid, or continuous, and are more likely to occur at the level of the whole population of organizations, as some types are selected out, than as a result of individual adaptation (Carroll 1984; Hannan and Freeman 1977).

Dimensions of institutionalization

Institutionalization, the tendency of patterns of behavior, norms, or formal structures to persist through time, depends on two dimensions, vertical depth and horizontal linkage. Depth refers to the extent to which the institutional structure defines the individual actors. Breadth refers to the number of links that a particular activity has with other activities, to the number of changes that would have to be made if a particular form of activity were altered.

The definition of actors involves a specification of (1) endowments in the form of property rights, (2) utilities in the sense of preferences, (3) capabilities in the form of material, symbolic, and institutional resources, and (4) self-identity in that the way in which individuals identify themselves is affected or determined by their place within an institutional structure. Holding environmental pressures and horizontal links constant, the more individuals' basic self-definitions are determined by a given institutional structure, the more difficult it will be for that institution to change. Such an institution may collapse because it fails to adapt to changed environmental circumstances, but it will not be undermined by its own members.

With regard to sovereignty, the notion of citizenship is one example of institutional depth. The state bestows citizenship. The very notion of citizen in the modern world is intimately linked with the existence of sovereign states. Without such political entities, citizenship as we know it would have no meaning. The depth of citizenship, the extent to which it becomes an important part of an individual's self-definition, varies both across and within countries. Nevertheless, it is a powerful source of identity for many people, powerful enough to make many subject themselves to the dangers of violent death, Hobbes's baddest of the bad. States also constitute political communities that define what Michael Walzer (1983) has called "spheres of justice." The conception that individuals have of what is just, a basic component of any preference structure, is determined by membership in a particular political community.

Other examples of institutional structures defining the identity of individuals are even more compelling. Geertz's description of the Balinese aristocracy marching into Dutch machine guns because this was more consistent with their cosmology than capitulation to foreign rule is a powerful illustration of the ability of particular self-identities to lead individuals to accept death rather than what would be, for them, dishonor (Geertz 1980). The long list of martyrs shows that violent death is not, for some individuals, the worst possible outcome.

The concept of organizational depth reflects an epistemological stance that is skeptical of assertions of objective reality. It views reality as a social construct. This construction may arise either from the interaction of individuals who attribute meaning to certain events or from a general consensus on the meaning of events that is produced by shared paradigms or shaped by roles. In an uncertain or even unknowable external environment, meaning does not simply present itself in the form of some objective social reality. It is contingent on individual cognitions and possibly, with regard to the depth of institutionalization, on the extent to which these cognitions are determined by the immediate institutional environment within which the individual functions (Meyer *et al.* 1987: 5).

Horizontal linkage refers to the density of links between a particular activity and other activities. If a particular activity can be changed without altering anything else, then there is no linkage. If one modification requires changes in many others, then a particular activity is densely linked. Holding other things constant, the greater the number of links, the higher the level of institutionalization. For instance, the legal requirements for changing the American Constitution are much more stringent than those needed to promulgate a law: that is, many more individuals and legislative bodies must be involved to alter the Constitution. These legal demands do correspond to our commonplace understanding of what we mean by stating that a particular practice or norms is institutionalized. We mean that it is hard to change.

The breadth of institutionalization will be influenced by the way in which a particular institution fits into a broader institutional framework. In the case of sovereignty, there are two relevant sets of networks or links. First, national arrangements related to the scope and nature of authoritative control are tied to other arrangements within that same country. States may, for instance, assert control in some areas but not in others because of national legal arrangements, bureaucratic structures, or policing capabilities. The United States, for instance, has been very reluctant to move toward a system of identity cards to control illegal migration because this would conflict with liberal values that are deeply enshrined in individual beliefs and embedded in the legal system. The treatment of women's issues in Sweden and Great Britain has reflected more general attitudes toward social welfare (M. Ruggie 1984).

Second, the authority claims of a particular state are also linked to international regimes and the practices of other states. National actions that are consistent with the principles and norms of existing international regimes, and that are reinforced by the behavior and policies of other states, will be more difficult to change than assertions of sovereign authority that are antithetical to existing regimes and contradict or undermine the practices of other states. Some actions inevitably require agreement between two or more states, such as the setting of exchange rates; others are not necessarily contingent on the behavior of other actors but enforcement may be facilitated by general agreement, such as establishing the limits of the territorial sea.

In sum, institutionalization can be conceived of along two dimensions, breadth and depth. Breadth refers to the number of links an institution has, the number of other changes that would have to be made if that institution were to be changed. Depth refers to the extent to which the self-identities of individuals are determined by their participation in some larger social arrangement. This discussion is illustrated in Table 4.1.

With regard to both breadth and depth, sovereign states have become increasingly formidable institutions. They influence the self-image of those individuals within their territory through the concept of citizenship, as well as by exercising control, to one degree or another, over powerful instruments of socialization. With regard to breadth, states are the most densely linked institutions in the contemporary world. Change the nature of states and virtually everything else in human society would also have to be changed. Hence, even though environmental incentives have dramatically changed since the state system began to evolve several hundred years ago, there is little reason to believe that it will be easy to replace sovereign states with some alternative structure for organizing human political life.

Institutions that have high degrees of breadth and depth, that define the nature of actors and have many links with other institutions, are not up for grabs. They are taken for granted. Support does not have to be continually mobilized to sustain them. They are not challenged, either because actors accept them as if given by nature (they do not even conceive of alternatives), or because particular behaviors and outcomes seem so fixed that the costs of changing appear to be prohibitive (Jepperson 1987: 4–6). It is exactly this taken-for-granted quality that distinguishes institutional analysis from even those utilitarian perspectives that recognize the importance of institutions but regard that as being constantly under challenge, constantly subject to the rational maximizing calculations of their members.

Table 4.1 Dimensions of institutionalization

| | | Breadth: density of links | |
		Low	High
Depth: extent of vertical embeddedness	Low	Medieval long distance luxury trade	Urban traffic system
	High	Pennsylvania Dutch	The modern state

(In my subsequent work on sovereignty written after this essay in the 1990s it became apparent to me that the principles of sovereignty were not so taken for granted as I had imagined. Sovereignty is characterized by organized hypocrisy. Material incentives can lead political leaders to act in ways that are inconsistent with sovereignty's logics of appropriateness especially with regard to violating the rule of non-interference in the internal affairs of other states.)

An evolutionary analogy

Metaphors and analogies cannot be a substitute for analysis: that is, for specifying the relationships between clearly conceptualized variables (Snidal 1985a). But when theoretical conceptualizations are weakly developed, metaphors and analogies can clarify the underlying logic of an argument. One analogy that does help to illuminate the reasoning of an institutionalist perspective is offered by the evolutionary theories of Stephen Jay Gould and Niles Eldredge.

Gould and Eldredge have argued that evolutionary change is characterized by what they term "punctuated equilibrium." They contrast their position with the Darwinian synthesis. An evolutionary process characterized by punctuated equilibrium is one in which long periods of stasis are broken by short, in geologic time, episodes of rapid speciation. This allotropic speciation occurs in geographically isolated subpopulations usually living at the environmental margin of a particular species.

Sharp breaks occur in fossil records because one variant of a species quickly replaces its ancestor as a result of shifts in environmental conditions (Eldredge 1985: Ch. 3, 148–50; Gould 1982: 383; Gould and Eldredge 1977: 116–17).

In the Darwinian synthesis, change is slow, steady, and gradual. Darwin's commitment to gradualism reflected his social environment and his theories parallel those of Smith, Bentham, and other eighteenth- and nineteenth-century European thinkers who saw history as a pattern of moderate evolution. The Darwinian synthesis, like Adam Smith's political economy, also focused attention on the individual. The mechanism for change was mutation in particular individuals, rather than changes in whole species more or less at the same time. Adaptation would be optimal because individual variations provided a very rich repertoire of possible solutions that could be selected in response to changed environmental incentives. Alterations in the environment would ultimately produce the most functionally efficient biological stock as different responses were played out slowly over a long period of time (Gould 1982: 381; Gould and Eldredge 1977: 145; Eldredge 1985: 21–22).

Eldredge and Gould have criticized such adaptationist arguments on several grounds. The Darwinian synthesis ignores constraints imposed by previous choices. An optimally adaptive response may not be possible because the gene stock necessary for such a change is simply not present. Earlier adaptations, or even elimination of certain species, channel subsequent developments. The constraints of this channeling must be placed alongside environmental incentives to explain evolutionary change. Gould argues, for instance, that

> we should not conclude that Darwinian adaptation to local environments has unconstrained power to design theoretically optimum shapes for all situations. Natural selection, as a historical process, can only work with material available ... The resulting imperfections and odd solutions, cobbled together from parts on hand, record a process that unfolds in time from unsuited antecedents, not the work of a perfect architect creating *ab nihilo*.
>
> (Gould 1985a: 34–35)

Adaptationalist arguments also ignore the possibility that some changes are fortuitous. They may have occurred because two particular structures were genetically bound together and change in one inevitably induced change in the other. Structures originally developed for one purpose may ultimately come to serve another. One of Gould's most fascinating examples is that wings developed from protuberances, the initial purpose of which was to facilitate heat regulation for warm-blooded animals. Indeed, it is difficult to imagine, Gould argues, how wings could have developed in any other way, for they are too large to have sprung full blown as it were from the skeletal structures of terrestrial animals (Gould 1982: 383; Gould 1985b).

Gould and Eldredge developed their theory of punctuated equilibrium in response to these and other problems, as well as in reaction to the fact that the fossil record was more incomplete than the Darwinian synthesis suggested that it should be. If the Darwinian synthesis were correct and change was constant, gradual, and optimally adaptive, then it should be possible to find more or less complete fossil records. But this has not been the case. Missing links are typical rather than the exception. Such gaps in the fossil record are more easily explained by a pattern of development in which change takes place rapidly over a limited period of time and often in a limited geographic area. Evolutionary paleontologists would have to be extremely lucky to construct a complete fossil record.

Gould notes that the gradualist–punctuationalist debate in the largest sense

> is but one small aspect of a broader discussion about the nature of change: Is our world (to construct a ridiculously oversimplified dichotomy) primarily one of constant change (with structure as a mere incarnation of the moment), or is structure primary and constraining, with change as a "difficult" phenomenon, usually accomplished rapidly when a stable structure is stressed beyond its buffering capacity to resist and absorb.
>
> (Gould 1982: 383)

Punctuated equilibrium is not a perfect analogy for an institutionalist argument. There is no parallel between the concept of allotropic speciation, with its focus on alterations in geographically isolated subpopulations as the driving mechanism for change, and an institutionalist perspective. Evolutionary theory does not claim that biological structures can consciously alter their environments in ways that enhance their viability. But other aspects of Gould and Eldredge's approach are extremely germane. First, an adequate explanation must take into consideration both structures (institutions or biological stocks) and environmental incentives. Second, change is difficult; once a particular institutional structure (biological stock) is established, it tends to maintain itself—or at the very least to channel future change. Third, optimal adaptation is not always possible because the institutional stock is not available. Features selected during one point in time impose limits on future possibilities. Fourth, historical origin and present utility may require different explanations. A particular structural feature that evolved for one reason (or an institution that was established to cope with certain environmental incentives) may later be put to very different uses. "These evolutionary shifts," Gould (1983: 63) argues, "can be quirky and unpredictable as the potentials for complexity are vast." Credit cards can be used to open doors. The balancing fins of fish became the limbs for land-based vertebrates. Roman law became one of the pillars upon which notions of private property essential for capitalism were based (Anderson 1974).

Finally, punctuated equilibrium suggests that explanation rather than prediction ought to be the primary objective of science. In a world of organisms in which present behavior is constrained by structures that evolved in response to past conditions, adaptation will be imperfect and therefore unpredictable. Chance and quirkiness heavily influence the organic universe (Gould 1983: 65). This orientation does not imply that all search for regularities should be given up, that history, whether evolutionary or human, can only be a collection of individual stories. It is possible to delineate general principles and regularities that underlie a variety of unique responses. But a recognition of the importance of *fortuna* does suggest that prediction will inevitably be very difficult. Knowledge of existing institutional stock delimits a range of possible responses to environmental incentives, but does not necessarily determine any particular path. The punctuated equilibrium approach to evolutionary theory of Gould and Eldredge is a better model for social science than the logical deductive, determinative, and predictive orientation of theoretical physics to which many social scientists aspire, if only rhetorically.

Institutional persistence

Species reproduce themselves biologically; we know something about how genes work. An institutionalist perspective must delineate mechanisms that account for the perpetuation of institutions over time. Arthur Stinchcombe (1968: 102–3) describes historicist causal imagery in the following way:

Some set of causes *once* determined a social pattern (e.g., the Reformation determined Protestantism in North Europe, Catholicism in South Europe). Then ever since, what existed in one year produced the same thing the next year (e.g. each year each country has the same dominant religion it had the year before).

In such an approach, Stinchcombe goes on to argue, the problem of explanation "breaks down into two causal components. The first is the particular circumstances which caused a tradition to be started. The second is the general process by which social patterns reproduce themselves."

Arguments about how particular institutions originate are familiar enough in political science. Certainly, the most conventional are actor-oriented utilitarian or functionalist analyses. The explanation for how institutions or enduring patterns begin is no different from explanations for policy change or other, more transitory phenomena. Such explanations are not inconsistent with an institutionalist perspective. But an institutionalist perspective suggests that they must be supplemented with an examination of how preexisting structures delimit the range of possible options. An effort to explain origins would have to take account not only of environmental incentives but also of extant institutional structures—of the genetic stock, not just external conditions.

The second task of an institutionalist perspective involves explaining how institutions persist over time, even though their environments may change. If institutional arrangements change readily when environmental conditions change (or, in the language of the Chicago School, when prices change), then there is little use in invoking an institutionalist perspective; indeed, under such conditions it is not even clear that the very concept of institutions is of any use because the study of what would commonly be called institutions would be no different from the analysis of other social phenomena such as policy choices, Congressional voting, or profit maximization.

A number of mechanisms can contribute to institutional persistence and inertia. One factor is the ability of an institution to alter its environment. Statist and corporatist explanations have emphasized such possibilities. Legal rules and administrative regulations affect the barriers to entry and exit in different sectors of the economy, and, therefore, the political capabilities and external legitimacy claims of actors (Hannan and Freeman 1977: 932). Public officials actively cultivate support from private groups, and in doing so may alter not only the balance of capabilities but also conceptions of self-interest. Central decision makers can invoke symbols of national unity and thereby influence the attitudes of individual citizens toward specific policy issues. At the very least, there is likely to be a symbiosis between public and private institutions in which preferences and organizational structures are conditioned by long-standing relationships and shared political values (Katzenstein 1985; Stepan 1978; Badie and Birnbaum 1983). Hence, at least at the national level, the depth and breadth of public institutions may increase over time as a result of conscious policies to alter the distribution of power in civil society or to reinforce existing patterns of behavior.

Institutions may also increase their depth through effective recruitment of personnel. In highly professional state agencies with selective recruitment, socialization into the bureaus' ethos can be intense. The more the individuals governing an institution can socialize and select their successors, control the conditions of incumbency, and depict themselves as models for subsequent generations, the easier it is for an institution to be effectively maintained (Poggi 1978: 138; Stinchcombe 1968: 112).

An institution may persist because it can mitigate problems associated with incomplete information. Decisions in complex environments inevitably must be made without full information. Institutions can increase information and distribute it more symmetrically. Robert Keohane has argued that such activities are a central purpose of international regimes, some of which reduce the probability of cheating by establishing monitoring mechanisms and reducing suspicion. This is, as Keohane (1984) notes, a purely function-alist explanation, although one that recognizes that sunk costs can lead to a situation in which all members of an organization might prefer different arrangements but none has the incentive to initiate changes. Oliver Williamson (1975: 25) has made similar arguments with regard to the relative merits of hierarchical, as opposed to market, forms of organization. Hierarchical forms of organization, such as the firm, may be more efficient than markets when there is incomplete information because firms can more easily develop internal mechanisms that diminish or overcome the problems posed by bounded rationality.

But such functional analyses do not necessarily imply that organizational structures can be easily adapted if environmental circumstances change. Once commitments are made regarding expertise and standard operating procedures, certain kinds of information processing will be facilitated, but others kinds will be inhibited. In large organizations, many different procedures have to be coordinated. Coordination can be accomplished only if the rules are stable, but such stability may lead organizations to persist in behavior that appears to be stupid or counterproductive (Steinbrunner 1974: 78; Nelson and Winter 1982: 37). Locked-in standard operating procedures can potentially yield catastrophic outcomes if environmental conditions rapidly change (Bracken 1983).

Mark Granovetter (1985) offers a different argument about the way in which organizations contribute to resolving problems of bounded rationality. He argues that the level of shirking, cheating, and dissimulation that occurs in economic relationships (although there is no logical or empirical reason to limit his argument to such activities) is heavily influenced by the extent to which transactions are embedded in a network of personal ties. These personal relationships provide information. They also spill over into noninstrumental activities. The relationships become valued as an end in themselves and they become freighted with concerns that extend beyond short-term utility maximization. Such embedded structures tend to persist because they are functionally useful and become valued in their own right.

Internal resistance to organizational restructuring is another cause of inertia. Such restructuring is designed to benefit the whole organization over the long term. But in the short term it will disadvantage particular subunits by changing their ability to control resources and invoke legitimating norms. Disadvantaged groups are likely to resist change, and their objections will be particularly telling in environments characterized by high levels of uncertainty because the beneficial consequences of change cannot be persuasively demonstrated (Hannan and Freeman 1977: 931).

Nelson and Winter (1982: 14) make an explicit analogy between their theory of the firm and evolutionary theory. They argue that a "routine" is a regular and predictable pattern of behavior. For business firms, routines are applied to all aspects of the activity, including production and personnel policies. These routines are the equivalent of genes in evolutionary theory.

> They are a persistent feature of the organism and determine its possible behavior (though actual behavior is determined also by the environment); they are heritable in the sense that tomorrow's organisms generated from today's (for example, by building a new plant) have many of the same characteristics, and they are selectable in the sense that organisms with certain routines may do better than others, and, if so, their relative importance in the population (industry) is augmented over time.

Institutions may also persist because they follow path-dependent patterns of development. Path-dependent patterns are characterized by self-reinforcing positive feedback. Initial choices, often small and random, may determine future historical trajectories. Once a particular path is chosen, it precludes other paths, even if these alternatives might, in the long run, have proven to be more efficient or adaptive.

Alexis de Tocqueville finds America a fascinating case because the initial conditions, which he sees constraining future patterns of development, are so evident. He argues that:

> If we were able to go back to the elements of states to examine the oldest monuments of their history, I doubt not that we should discover in them the primal cause of the prejudices, the habits, the ruling passions, and, in short, all that constitutes what is called the national character. We should there find the explanation of certain customs which now seem at variance with the prevailing manners; of such laws as conflict with established principles; and of such incoherent opinions as are here and there to be met with in society, like those fragments of broken chains which we sometimes see hanging from the vaults of an old edifice, supporting nothing. This might explain the destinies of certain nations

which seem borne on by an unknown force to ends of which they themselves are ignorant.

(Tocqueville 1945: 280)

Increasing returns of various kinds lead to path-dependent patterns of development in which random initial choices preclude future options, including those that would have been more efficient over the long run. Path-dependency can arise for several reasons. There may be increasing returns to adoption: Once particular routines are adopted they may become more efficient over time. Because potentially more efficient routines were not chosen in the first place, there is no opportunity to ride them down a learning curve. The system is locked in by small initial choices (Arthur 1985: 5).

Path-dependency may also result from network externalities. The more people that choose a particular institutional structure, such as a given telephone system, the more efficient that structure becomes. Other possible routines are frozen out. Over time, the changeover gap—the amount that would have to be spent to make some alternative routines equally attractive—increases. Initially, decisions may also be locked in by economies of agglomeration. Once a choice is made, other institutions reorient themselves or new services are created. Once particular forms of economic activity, for instance, become concentrated in a Silicon Valley or Route 128, it is difficult to relocate them because of the network of financial, legal, and other services that have been created (Arthur 1984: 10; Arthur 1986: 2).

W. Brian Arthur has summarized, in Table 4.2, the differences between constant returns, diminishing returns, and increasing returns for different kinds of technological regimes. The same differences could also exist for institutional structures.

With increasing returns institutions are not necessarily efficient or flexible. Once initial choices are made, it is difficult to explore alternatives because their competitive positions are weakened by the increasing efficiency over time of the initial choice. Final outcomes are not predictable because processes are nonergodic: that is, initial small random shocks do not average out but rather establish long-term trajectories.

Finally, there are circumstances in which classes of institutions, if not particular members of that class, are very likely to persist, namely situations in which competition is limited, survival is not an issue, and the most

Table 4.2 Consequences of increasing returns

	Necessarily efficient	*Necessarily flexible*	*Predictable*	*Ergodic*
Constant returns	yes	yes	yes	yes
Diminishing returns	yes	yes	yes	yes
Increasing returns	no	no	no	no

Source: W. Brian Arthur (1984)

important element of the environment is other organizations. Under such circumstances, institutions tend toward isomorphism, not because of competition over limited material resources but because of their need to fit into a larger organizational environment. DiMaggio and Powell (1983: 150–54) point to three mechanisms for what they term "institutional isomorphic change." First, coercion arising either from political pressures from other organizations or from widely shared expectations about legitimate modes of action. Second, mimetic processes in which organizations imitate existing forms, a pattern that is likely to be particularly powerful when goals are unclear. Third, normative pressures that are often embodied in professional associations and selective mechanisms of recruitment. In the vocabulary developed earlier in this article, institutional isomorphism refers to a situation in which the density of links among organizations is high, implying that structural change will be difficult.

In sum, from a functionalist or utilitarian perspective, organizations persist so long as they contribute to the achievement of some desired goal. An institutionalist perspective need not ignore such considerations. But at a minimum an institutionalist argument must assert that institutions will not change in lock step with every change in environmental conditions, including prices. An institutionalist perspective also points to some more ambitious lines of reasoning. First, institutions may alter their own environment. States (here meaning central decision-making institutions) may, for instance, be able to alter the distribution of power among groups in civil society. Second, institutions may persist because, in a world of imperfect information, altering established routines will be costly and time-consuming and the consequences of change cannot be fully predicted. Third, certain institutional choices may determine the future trajectory of developments because of path-dependencies generated by increasing returns. Institutional structures are locked in, even though there might have been some more efficient alternative. Finally, institutional structures may persist because the material environment is permissive; horizontal links with other organizations then constrain the range of institutional possibilities.

Sovereignty

"Sovereignty" is a term that makes the eyes of most American political scientists glaze over. It has lost meaning and analytic relevance. Scholars now do talk of the state, by which they usually mean either a central administrative and legal apparatus, including especially central decision-making institutions, or a polity, the network of institutional ties, behavioral regularities, and values that knit together public and private actors who play some role in formulating the implementing authoritative decisions.

Analysts interested in comparative politics in particular have illuminated the relationship between the state apparatus and civil society and the rules that govern interactions between different components of the polity. With few exceptions, such as John Ruggie, Friedrich Kratochwil and Richard Ashley, international relations scholars have been content to take the state, here often defined as a bearer of power capabilities in the international system, as a given (J.G. Ruggie 1986; Ashley 1986; Kratochwil 1986).

The growing disjuncture, however, between the nature of sovereignty in the contemporary world and functional objectives—both security and economic—suggests that it is time to reflect on the nature of sovereignty, to make problematic for the study of international relations what has previously been taken as an analytic given. More specifically, it is necessary to examine how the authoritative claims of states (taken here to mean the central administrative and legal apparatus), and their ability to implement such claims, have changed with regard to international or transnational, as opposed to domestic, activities. Two issues are involved: First, the assertion of final authority within a given territory; second, efforts to control the transborder movements of people, goods, capital, and culture.

The assertion of final authority within a given territory is the core element in any definition of sovereignty. Strayer (1970: 58) avers that "sovereignty requires independence from any outside power and final authority over men who live within certain boundaries" (also see Finer 1974: 79; Dyson 1980: 34). The alternative to sovereignty is either a world in which there are no clear boundaries or a world in which there is no final authority within a given territory. Empires offer an example of the first form of political organization. Empires have borderlands but not boundaries and demand varying kinds of deference from groups within or even beyond these borderlands. The Roman and Chinese empires are two examples of political entities that did not recognize clear territorial boundaries (Kratochwil 1986: 33–36). Feudalism is an example of a polity in which authority varies across issue areas (the church for some questions, the nobility for others), and in which there is not necessarily a transitive ordering of authority within a given issue areas. To assert, however, that the core of sovereignty is final authority within a given territory does not exhaust the problem either behaviorally or conceptually. Behaviorally, final authority within a given territory has been challenged in one way or another throughout the history of the state system. This issue was not resolved in the late medieval struggle between secular rules and religious authorities. In the nineteenth and even the twentieth centuries, the European powers and the United States asserted extraterritorial rights in China, the Ottoman Empire, Egypt, and areas of the Persian Gulf, as well as dictating the customs policies of several Latin American states and Japan. The United States has affirmed the right to issue authoritative directives to the foreign subsidiaries of American corporations, sometimes with success, as with the freezing of Iranian assets on deposit in the overseas branches of American banks, and sometimes without success, as in the attempt to prevent the European subsidiaries of American corporations from providing material for the natural gas pipeline from the Soviet Union. A second problem with simply treating final authority within a defined territory as unproblematic is that there are territories and spheres of human activity in which only partial sovereignty—that is, control over only some issues—is claimed. The exclusive economic zone agreed to in the Law of the Sea Treaty, and accepted even by those states that have rejected the treaty itself, give littoral states economic control over an area extending out at least 200 miles but denies them the right to regulate shipping in this same area. Here is a form of territorial control that is not fully sovereign. The signatories to the Antarctic Treaty have sidestepped the issue of whether states have the right to assert sovereign claims over parts of Antarctica. The European Convention on Human Rights gives individual citizens of the European Community countries the right to appeal directly to the European Court. Conceptually, the core definition of sovereignty is not concerned with explaining the actual claims that states have made with regard to the exercise of final authority. It is one thing to say that states will deny any other entity final authority within their territory; it is another to delineate the actual scope of activities over which states have asserted authority. The public debate over abortion and welfare in the United States illustrates the depth of passion that questions related to the scope of state authority can arouse, because such issues affect not only specific instrumental outcomes but also basic conceptions about the nature of political life.

Questions related to transborder control, as opposed to purely domestic issues, have also exercised states. The claims that states have made with regard to the authoritative control of movements of people, commodities, investments, and information, ideas, or culture across their international boundaries have changed across time and over countries. In some issue areas all states have accepted the same rules; in others they have followed different norms and practices. One example of variation is the rules governing the entry and exit of people. While there is general agreement that states can regulate entry, there is no agreement on rules of exit, with some states advocating free exit and others denying that individuals are entitled to such a right. The variation can be explained by a utilitarian calculus: National laws reflect either ethnic preferences or economic interests (Weiner 1985: 443–45). Institutionalist arguments hardly seem germane for this issue. But consider a possible counterfactual. What if all states save one had opted for migration rules that provided for the free movement of individuals across borders? It would, then, be difficult for the last state to promulgate regulations that prohibit entry because the costs of enforcement could be high. On the other hand, if all states save one have adopted rules that prohibit exit, it would be less costly for the last state to enforce a rule prohibiting entry. Rules governing the exit and entry of people do involve network externalities: The utility of a particular policy does depend on the choices that have been made by other states.

More generally, if externalities are significant, and choices are irreversible, then small random events at the beginning of a process may be very important in determining the final outcome. For instance, if one or two states opt

for a certain pattern of control in a given issue-area, and there are substantial network externalities, then all other states may eventually make the
same choice, even though they would have chosen a different option had
they had the opportunity to go first. If there are path-dependent sequences,
then initial institutional choices can determine final institutional and behavioral outcomes. Choices that at first blush appear to be fully explicable in
terms of a utilitarian calculus, such as policies toward the entry and exit of
individuals, may be better understood if the impact of sequences and
externalities are investigated.

Finally, consider the dominance of the state system itself, the notion that
political life must be territorially organized with one final authority within a
given territory. Even if this vision is sometimes challenged, no alternative has
been effectively articulated and legitimated. Can the dominance of the
sovereign state in the late twentieth century be explained from a utilitarian/
functionalist perspective? I began this essay by suggesting that such an
approach posed difficulties because nuclear weapons and economic interdependence made it impossible for even the most powerful states to guarantee the lives and, possibly, the well-being of their citizens. But the triumph of
sovereignty over other possible forms of political organization in the recent
past is even more striking. Efforts to convert colonial empires into com-
monwealths have failed. The Soviet effort to base relations in Eastern
Europe on transnational functional agencies rather than state-to-state agreements has eroded over time, despite the continued material domination of
the Soviet Union. Most strikingly, decolonization has led to the creation of a
large number of states with only the most limited resources and populations.
The existence of these states can hardly be explained by their material capabilities. Their survival and being are a function of the larger institutional
framework in which they are embodied. Their most potent asset is not their
tax base, population, or army, but rather the juridical sovereignty that is
accorded by the international community: that is, by the willingness of other
states to endorse their existence and the absence of any alternative legitimate
form for organizing political life (Jackson and Rosberg 1982).

The triumph of the sovereign state cannot be understood from a utilitar-
ian/functionalist perspective. The breadth of the state in terms of its links
with other social entities, and the depth of the state reflected in the very
concept of citizenship as a basic source of individual identity, make it very
hard to dislodge. Path-dependent patterns of development have been important; once Europe was committed to a form of political organization based
on sovereign states, other possibilities were foreclosed. In earlier historical
periods, this was a result of the imposition of the state system, or derivatives
thereof, such as colonialism, through conquest. More recently, it has reflected the unwillingness to consider other forms of political organization as
fully legitimate. The problem of the West Bank, for instance, would be easier
to resolve if there were some legitimate option to either full sovereignty for
the Palestinians or continued Israeli occupation; but no such possibility is

acceptable, not simply because of the utilitarian calculus of the actors involved but also because the sovereign state is the only universally recognized way of organizing political life in the contemporary international system. It is now difficult to even conceive of alternatives. The historical legacy of the development of the state system has left a powerful institutional structure, one that will not be dislodged easily, regardless of changed circumstances in the material environment.

Part II
International politics

5 Structural causes and regime consequences
Regimes as intervening variables

Defining regimes and regime change

Regimes can be defined as sets of implicit or explicit principles, norms, rules, and decision-making procedures around which actors' expectations converge in a given area of international relations. Principles are beliefs of fact, causation, and rectitude. Norms are standards of behavior defined in terms of rights and obligations. Rules are specific prescriptions or proscriptions for action. Decision-making procedures are prevailing practices for making and implementing collective choice.

This usage is consistent with other formulations. Keohane and Nye, for instance, define regimes as "sets of governing arrangements" that include "networks of rules, norms, and procedures that regularize behavior and control its effects" (Keohane and Nye 1977: 19). Haas argues that a regime encompasses a mutually coherent set of procedures, rules, and norms (Haas 1980a: 553). Hedley Bull, using a somewhat different terminology, refers to the importance of rules and institutions in international society where rules refer to "general imperative principles which require or authorize prescribed classes of persons or groups to behave in prescribed ways" (Bull 1977: 54). Institutions for Bull help to secure adherence to rules by formulating, communicating, administering, enforcing, interpreting, legitimating, and adapting them.

Regimes must be understood as something more than temporary arrangements that change with every shift in power or interests. Keohane notes that a basic analytic distinction must be made between regimes and agreements. Agreements are ad hoc, often "one-shot," arrangements. The purpose of regimes is to facilitate agreements. Similarly, Jervis argues that the concept of regimes "implies not only norms and expectations that facilitate cooperation, but a form of cooperation that is more than the following of short-run self-interest" (Jervis 1982: 357). For instance, he contends that the restraints that have applied in Korea and other limited wars should not be considered a regime. These rules, such as "do not bomb sanctuaries," were based purely on short-term calculations of interest. As interest and power changed, behavior changed. Waltz's conception of the balance of power, in which states are driven by systemic pressures to repetitive balancing behavior, is not a regime; Kaplan's conception, in which equilibrium requires commitment to rules that constrain immediate, short-term power maximization (especially not destroying an essential actor), is a regime (Waltz 1979; Kaplan 1957: 23; Kaplan 1979: 66–69, 73).

Similarly, regime-governed behavior must not be based solely on short-term calculations of interest. Since regimes encompass principles and norms, the utility function that is being maximized must embody some sense of general obligation. One such principle, reciprocity, is emphasized in Jervis's analysis of security regimes. When states accept reciprocity they will sacrifice short-term interests with the expectation that other actors will reciprocate in the future, even if they are not under a specific obligation to do so. This formulation is similar to Fred Hirsch's brilliant discussion of friendship, in which he states:

> Friendship contains an element of direct mutual exchange and to this extent is akin to private economic good. But it is often much more than that. Over time, the friendship "transaction" can be presumed, by its permanence, to be a net benefit on both sides. At any moment of time, though, the exchange is very unlikely to be reciprocally balanced.
>
> (Hirsch 1976: 78)

It is the infusion of behavior with principles and norms that distinguishes regime-governed activity in the international system from more conventional activity, guided exclusively by narrow calculations of interest.

A fundamental distinction must be made between principles and norms on the one hand, and rules and procedures on the other. Principles and norms provide the basic defining characteristics of a regime. There may be many rules and decision-making procedures that are consistent with the same principles and norms. Changes in rules and decision-making procedures are changes within regimes, provided that principles and norms are unaltered. For instance, Benjamin Cohen points out that there has been a substantial increase in private bank financing during the 1970s. This has meant a change in the rules governing balance-of-payments adjustment, but it does not mean that there has been a fundamental change in the regime. The basic norm of the regime remains the same: access to balance-of-payments financing should be controlled, and conditioned on the behavior of borrowing countries. John Ruggie argues that in general the changes in international economic regimes that took place in the 1970s were norm-governed changes. They did not alter the basic principles and norms of the embedded liberal regime that has been in place since the 1940s.

Changes in principles and norms are changes of the regime itself. When norms and principles are abandoned, there is either a change to a new regime or a disappearance of regimes from a given issue-area. For instance, J.G. Ruggie contends that the distinction between orthodox and embedded liberalism involves differences over norms and principles. Orthodox liberalism endorses increasing the scope of the market. Embedded liberalism prescribes state action to contain domestic social and economic dislocations generated by markets. Orthodox and embedded liberalism define different regimes. The change from orthodox liberal principles and norms before World War II to embedded liberal principles and norms after World War II was, in J.G. Ruggie's terms, a "revolutionary" change (Ruggie 1982).

Fundamental political arguments are more concerned with norms and principles than with rules and procedures. Changes in the latter may be interpreted in different ways. For instance, in the area of international trade, recent revisions in the Articles of Agreement of the General Agreement on Tariffs and Trade (GATT) provide for special and differential treatment for less developed countries (LDCs). All industrialized countries have instituted generalized systems of preferences for LDCs. Such rules violate one of the basic norms of the liberal postwar order, the MFN treatment of all parties. However, the industrialized nations have treated these alterations in the rules as temporary departures necessitated by the peculiar circumstances of poorer areas. At American insistence the concept of graduation was formally introduced into the GATT Articles after the Tokyo Round. Graduation holds that as countries become more developed they will accept rules consistent with liberal principles. Hence, Northern representatives have chosen to interpret special and differential treatment of developing countries as a change within the regime.

Speakers for the Third World, on the other hand, have argued that the basic norms of the international economic order should be redistribution and equity, not nondiscrimination and efficiency. They see the changes in rules as changes of the regime because they identify these changes with basic changes in principle. There is a fundamental difference between viewing changes in rules as indications of change within the regime and viewing these changes as indications of change between regimes. The difference hinges on assessments of whether principles and norms have changed as well. Such assessments are never easy because they cannot be based on objective behavioral observations. "We know deviations from regimes," J.G. Ruggie avers, "not simply by acts that are undertaken, but by the intentionality and acceptability attributed to those acts in the context of an intersubjective framework of meaning" (Ruggie 1982: 380).

Finally, it is necessary to distinguish the weakening of a regime from changes within or between regimes. If the principles, norms, rules, and decision-making procedures of a regime become less coherent, or if actual practice is increasingly inconsistent with principles, norms, rules, and procedures, then a regime has weakened. Special and differential treatment for developing countries is an indication that the liberal regime has weakened, even if it has not been replaced by something else. The use of diplomatic cover by spies, the bugging of embassies, the assassination of diplomats by terrorists, and the failure to provide adequate local police protection are all indications that the classic regime protecting foreign envoys has weakened. However, the furtive nature of these activities indicates that basic principles and norms are not being directly challenged. In contrast, the seizure of American diplomats by groups sanctioned by the Iranian government is a basic challenge to the regime itself. Iran violated principles and norms, not just rules and procedures.

In sum, change within a regime involves alterations of rules and decision-making procedures, but not of norms or principles; change of a regime involves alteration of norms and principles; and weakening of a regime involves incoherence among the components of the regime or inconsistency between the regime and related behavior.

Do regimes matter?

It would take some courage, perhaps more courage than this editor possesses, to answer this question in the negative. This project began with a simple causal schematic. It assumed that regimes could be conceived of as intervening variables standing between basic causal variables (most prominently, power and interests) and outcomes and behavior. The first attempt to analyze regimes thus assumed the set of causal relationships shown in Figure 5.1.

Regimes do not arise of their own accord. They are not regarded as ends in themselves. Once in place they do affect related behavior and outcomes. They are not merely epiphenomenal.

The independent impact of regimes is a central analytic issue. The second causal arrow implies that regimes do matter. However, there is no general agreement on this point, and three basic orientations can be distinguished. The conventional structural views the regime concept as useless, if not misleading. Modified structural suggests that regimes may matter, but only under fairly restrictive conditions. And Grotian sees regimes as much more pervasive, as inherent attributes of any complex, persistent pattern of human behavior.

Susan Strange represents the first orientation. She has grave reservations about the value of the notion of regimes. Strange argues that the concept is pernicious because it obfuscates and obscures the interests and power relationships that are the proximate, not just the ultimate, cause of behavior in the international system. "All those international arrangements dignified by the label regime are only too easily upset when either the balance of bargaining power or the perception of national interest (or both together) change among those states who negotiate them" (Strange 1982: 487). Regimes, if they can be said to exist at all, have little or no impact. They are merely epiphenomenal. The underlying causal schematic is one that sees a direct connection between changes in basic causal factors (whether economic

Basic Causal Variables ⟶ Regimes ⟶ Related Behavior and Outcomes

Figure 5.1 Regimes as intervening variables.

or political) and changes in behavior and outcomes. Regimes are excluded completely, or their impact on outcomes and related behavior is regarded as trivial.

The second orientation to regimes, modified structural, is most clearly reflected in the essays of Keohane and Stein (Keohane 1982; Stein 1982). Both of these authors start from a conventional structural realist perspective, a world of sovereign states seeking to maximize their interest and power. Keohane posits that in the international system regimes derive from voluntary agreements among juridically equal actors. Stein states that the "conceptualization of regimes developed here is rooted in the classic characterization of international politics as relations between sovereign entities dedicated to their own self-preservation, ultimately able to depend only on themselves, and prepared to resort to force" (Stein 1982: 116).

In a world of sovereign states the basic function of regimes is to coordinate state behavior to achieve desired outcomes in particular issue-areas. Such coordination is attractive under several circumstances. Stein and Keohane posit that regimes can have an impact when Pareto-optimal outcomes could not be achieved through uncoordinated individual calculations of self-interest. Prisoner's Dilemma is the classic game-theoretic example. Stein also argues that regimes may have an autonomous effect on outcomes when purely autonomous behavior could lead to disastrous results for both parties. The game of Chicken is the game-theoretic analog.

However, regimes cannot be relevant for zero-sum situations in which states act to maximize the difference between their utilities and those of others. Jervis points to the paucity of regimes in the security area, which more closely approximates zero-sum games than do most economic issue-areas. Pure power motivations preclude regimes. Thus, the second orientation, modified structuralism, sees regimes emerging and having a significant impact, but only under restrictive conditions. It suggests that the first cut should be amended as in Figure 5.2.

For most situations there is a direct link between basic causal variables and related behavior (path a); but under circumstances that are not purely conflictual, where individual decision making leads to suboptimal outcomes, regimes may be significant (path b).

The third approach to regimes, most clearly elaborated in the essays of Raymond Hopkins and Donald Puchala, and Oran Young, reflects a fundamentally different view of international relations than the two structural

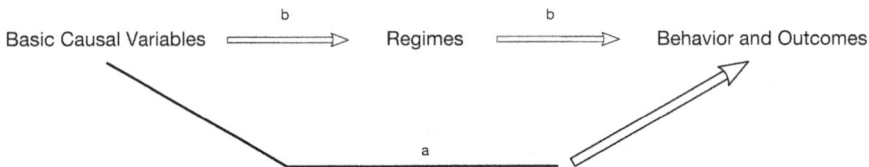

Figure 5.2 Regimes as causal variables.

arguments just described (Hopkins and Puchala 1982; Young 1982). These two essays are strongly informed by the Grotian tradition, which sees regimes as a pervasive phenomenon of all political systems. Hopkins and Puchala conclude that

> regimes exist in all areas of international relations, even those, such as major power rivalry, that are traditionally looked upon as clear-cut examples of anarchy. Statesmen nearly always perceive themselves as constrained by principles, norms, and rules that prescribe and proscribe varieties of behavior.
>
> (Hopkins and Puchala 1982: 270)

The concept of regime, they argue, moves beyond a realist perspective, which is "too limited for explaining an increasingly complex, interdependent, and dangerous world" (Hopkins and Puchala 1982: 245).

Oran Young argues that patterned behavior inevitably generates convergent expectations. This leads to conventionalized behavior in which there is some expectation of rebuke for deviating from ongoing practices. Conventionalized behavior generates recognized norms. If the observer finds a pattern of interrelated activity, and the connections in the pattern are understood, then there must be some form of norms and procedures.

While the modified structural approach does not view the perfect market as a regime, because action there is based purely upon individual calculation without regard to the behavior of others, the third orientation does regard the market as a regime. Patterns of behavior that persist over extended periods are infused with normative significance. A market cannot be sustained by calculations of self-interest alone. It must be, in J.G. Ruggie's terms, embedded in a broader social environment that nurtures and sustains the conditions necessary for its functioning. Even the balance of power, regarded by conventional structural realist analysts as a purely conflictual situation, can be treated as a regime (Bull 1977: Ch. 5). The causal schema suggested by a Grotian orientation either closely parallels the first cut shown in Figure 5.1, or can be depicted as in Figure 5.3.

Patterned behavior reflecting calculations of interest tends to lead to the creation of regimes, and regimes reinforce patterned behavior.

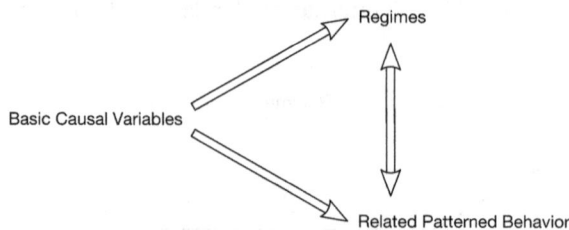

Figure 5.3 Regimes as autonomous variables.

The Grotian tradition that Hopkins and Puchala, and Young draw upon, offers a counter to structural realism of either the conventional or the modified form. It rejects the assumption that the international system is composed of sovereign states limited only by the balance of power. Rather, Hopkins and Puchala suggest that elites are the practical actors in international relations. States are rarified abstractions. Elites have transnational as well as national ties. Sovereignty is a behavioral variable, not an analytic assumption. The ability of states to control movements across their borders and to maintain dominance over all aspects of the international system is limited. Security and state survival are not the only objectives. Force does not occupy a singularly important place in international politics. Elites act within a communications net, embodying rules, norms, and principles, which transcends national boundaries.

This minimalist Grotian orientation has informed a number of theoretical postulates developed during the postwar period. Functionalism saw the possibility of eroding sovereignty through the multiplication of particularistic interests across national boundaries. Karl Deutsch's 1957 study of integration, with its emphasis on societal communication, made a distinction between security communities and anarchy (Lijphart 1974: 64–65). Some authors associated with the concept of transnationalism have posited a web of interdependence that makes any emphasis on sovereignty analytically misleading and normatively questionable. Keohane and Nye's discussion of complex interdependence rejects the assumptions of the primacy of force and issue hierarchy assumed by a realist perspective (Keohane and Nye 1977: Ch. 8). Ernst Haas points out that what he calls organic theories— eco-environmentalism, eco-reformism, and egalitarianism—deny conventional power-oriented assumptions.

Regimes are much more easily encompassed by a Grotian worldview. But the concept is not inconsistent with a realist perspective. The issue is not so much whether one accepts the possibility of principles, norms, rules, and decision-making procedures affecting outcomes and behavior, as what one's basic assumption is about the normal state of international affairs. Adherents of a Grotian perspective accept regimes as a pervasive and significant phenomenon in the international system. Adherents of a structural realist orientation see regimes as a phenomenon whose presence cannot be assumed and whose existence requires careful explanation. The two "standard cases" are fundamentally different, and it is the definition of the standard case that identifies the basic theoretical orientation. Stephen Toulmin writes that "any dynamical theory involves some explicit or implicit reference to a standard case or 'paradigm.' This paradigm specifies the manner in which, in the course of events, bodies may be expected to move." It is deviation from that movement which needs to be explained (Toulmin 1961: 56–57). From a realist perspective, regimes are phenomena that need to be explained; from a Grotian perspective, they are data to be described.

In sum, conventional structural arguments do not take regimes seriously: if basic causal variables change, regimes will also change. Regimes have no independent impact on behavior. Modified structural arguments see regimes as mattering only when independent decision making leads to undesired outcomes. Finally, Grotian perspectives accept regimes as a fundamental part of all patterned human interaction, including behavior in the international system.

Explanations for regime development

For those authors who see regimes as something more than epiphenomena, the second major issue posed by a schematic that sees regimes as intervening variables between basic causal factors and related outcomes and behavior becomes relevant. What is the relationship between basic causal factors and regimes? What are the conditions that lead to regime creation, persistence, and dissipation? Here regimes are treated as the dependent variable.

A wide variety of basic causal variables have been offered to explain the development of regimes. The most prominent are egoistic self-interest, political power, norms and principles, habit and custom, and knowledge. The last two are seen as supplementary, augmenting more basic forces related to interest, power, and values.

Egoistic self-interest

The prevailing explanation for the existence of international regimes is egoistic self-interest. By egoistic self-interest I refer to the desire to maximize one's own utility function where that function does not include the utility of another party. The egoist is concerned with the behavior of others only insofar as that behavior can affect the egoist's utility. All contractarian political theories from Hobbes to Rawls are based on egoistic self-interest. In contrast, pure power seekers are interested in maximizing the difference between their power capabilities and those of their opponent.

Keohane and especially Stein most fully adopt and elaborate an interest-oriented perspective. Stein avers that

> the same forces of autonomously calculated self-interest that lie at the root of the anarchic international system also lay the foundation for international regimes as a form of international order ... [T]here are times when rational self-interested calculation leads actors to abandon independent decision making in favor of joint decision making.
>
> (Stein 1982: 316)

Stein elaborates two circumstances under which unconstrained individual choice provides incentives for cooperation. The first occurs when such choice leads to Pareto-suboptimal outcomes: Prisoner's Dilemma and the provision of collective goods are well-known examples. Stein refers to this as the dilemma of common interests. Its resolution requires "collaboration," the active construction of a regime that directs individual decision making. Unconstrained individual decision making may also be eschewed when it would lead to mutually undesired outcomes and where the choice of one actor is contingent on the choice made by the other: the game of chicken is a prominent example. Stein refers to this as the dilemma of common aversions; it can be resolved through "coordination." Coordination need not be formalized or institutionalized. So long as everyone agrees to drive on the right side of the road, little more is needed. (Stein's concept of collaboration conforms with the definition of regimes used here. It is not so clear that coordination involves regimes. Coordination may only require the construction of rules. If these rules are not informed by any proximate principles or norms, they will not conform to the definition of regimes set forth earlier.)

Keohane utilizes insights from microeconomic theories of market failure to examine dilemmas of common interests. He is primarily concerned with the demand for regimes, the conditions under which ad hoc agreements fail to provide Pareto-optimal outcomes. He maintains that

> Regimes can make agreement easier if they provide frameworks for establishing legal liability (even if these are not perfect); improve the quantity and quality of information available to actors; or reduce other transactions costs, such as costs of organization or of making side-payments.
>
> (Keohane 1982: 338)

These benefits provided by regimes are likely to outweigh the costs of regime formation and maintenance when there is asymmetric information, moral hazard, potential dishonesty, or high issue density. In addition, the costs of forming regimes will be lower when there is a high level of formal and informal communication among states, a condition more likely to be found in open political systems operating under conditions of complex interdependence.

Political power

The second major basic causal variable used to explain regime development is political power. Two different orientations toward power can be distinguished. The first is cosmopolitan and instrumental: power is used to secure optimal outcomes for the system as a whole. In game-theoretic terms power is used to promote joint maximization. It is power in the service of the common good. The second approach is particularistic and potentially consummatory. Power is used to enhance the values of specific actors within the system.

Power in the service of the common good

The first position is represented by a long tradition in classical and neo-classical economics associated with the provision of public goods. The hidden hand was Adam Smith's most compelling construct: the good of all from the selfishness of each; there could be no more powerful defense of egoism. But Smith recognized that it was necessary for the state to provide certain collective goods. These included defense, the maintenance of order, minimum levels of welfare, public works, the protection of infant industries, and standards for commodities. Economists have pointed to the importance of the state for establishing property rights and enforcing contracts; that is, creating conditions that prevent predatory as opposed to market behavior. The state must create institutions that equate public and private rates of return (Hirschleifer 1977; Weber 1930: 336–37; North and Thomas 1973: Ch. 1). Keynesian analysis gives the state a prominent role in managing macroeconomic variables. For all of these arguments the purpose of state action is to further general societal interests.

The economist who has become most clearly associated with arguments emphasizing the instrumental role of power for cosmopolitan interests in the international system is Charles Kindleberger. In *The World in Depression* Kindleberger argues that the Depression of the 1930s could have been prevented by effective state leadership (Kindleberger 1986). An effective leader would have acted as a lender of last resort and provided a market for surplus commodities. In the interwar period the United States was able but unwilling to assume these burdens, and Great Britain was willing but unable. The result was economic chaos. Kindleberger has listed the following functions that states perform for the international trading system:

1 Protecting economic actors from force.
2 Cushioning the undesirable effects of an open system by, for instance, providing adjustment assistance for import-competing industries.
3 Establishing standards for products. In the absence of such standards inordinate energy may be wasted finding information about products.
4 Providing a national currency that can be used as an international reserve and transactions currency.
5 Constructing public works such as docks and domestic transportation systems.
6 Compensating for market imperfections by, for instance, becoming a lender of last resort when private financial institutions become so cautious that their conservatism could destroy global liquidity.

(Kindleberger 1978a)

Despite its emphasis on political action, Kindleberger's perspective is still profoundly liberal. The purpose of state intervention is to facilitate the creation and maintenance of an environment within which a market based on individual calculations of self-interest can flourish. The market, like the human body, is basically healthy, but occasionally the intervention of some external agent (the state, a doctor) may be necessary (Kindleberger 1978b). A market economy will maximize the utility of society as a whole. Political power is put at the service of the common good.

Power in the service of particular interests

A game-theoretic analogy makes it easier to distinguish between two important variants of the viewpoint of power in the service of particular interests. The first assumes that pay-offs are fixed and that an actor's choice of strategy is autonomously determined solely by these pay-offs. The second assumes that power can be used to alter pay-offs and influence actor strategy.

The first approach closely follows the analysis that applies when purely cosmopolitan objectives are at stake, except that political power is used to maximize individual, not joint, pay-offs. Under certain configurations of interest, there is an incentive to create regimes and the provision of these regimes is a function of the distribution of power. Hegemons, for instance, can play a critical role in supplying the collective goods that are needed for regimes to function effectively. Hegemons provide these goods not because they are interested in the well-being of the system as a whole, but because regimes enhance their own national values (Krasner 1976).

This emphasis on the need for asymmetric power distributions (supply-side considerations) should be contrasted with Stein's assertions concerning the efficacy of demand. The theory of hegemonic leadership suggests that under conditions of declining hegemony there will be a weakening of regimes. Without leadership, principles, norms, rules, and decision-making procedures cannot easily be upheld. No one actor will be willing to provide the collective goods needed to make the regime work smoothly and effectively. Stein's analysis, on the other hand, suggests that as hegemony declines there will be greater incentives for collaboration because collective goods are no longer being provided by the hegemon. The international system more closely resembles an oligopoly than a perfect market. Actors are aware of how their behavior affects others. When smaller states perceive that a hegemon is no longer willing to offer a free ride, they are likely to become paying customers. For Stein, interests alone can effectively sustain order. Hegemonic decline can lead to stronger regimes.

The second line of argument associated with power in the service of specific interests investigates the possibility that powerful actors may be able to alter the pay-offs that confront other actors or influence the strategies they choose. Here power becomes a much more central concept and compulsion is close at hand. Weaker actors may not be able to make autonomous choices. The values assigned to a particular cell may be changed.

Oran Young develops the notion of imposed regimes. Dominant actors may explicitly use a combination of sanctions and incentives to compel other actors to act in conformity with a particular set of principles, norms, rules, and decision-making procedures. Alternatively, dominant actors may secure de facto compliance by manipulating opportunity sets so that weaker actors are compelled to behave in a desired way.

When a hegemonic state acts to influence the strategy of other actors the regime is held hostage to the persistence of the existing distribution of power in the international system. If the hegemon's relative capabilities decline, the regime will collapse. Young argues that imposed orders are likely to disintegrate when there are major shifts in underlying power capabilities. Hopkins and Puchala suggest that regimes that are highly politicized, diffuse, and biased in their distribution of values are likely to undergo radical transformation when power distributions change. For instance, the norms of the colonial regime collapsed because the power of its supporter, the major European states, eroded. This set of arguments about regime change and hegemonic decline differs from the analysis emerging from a focus on the provision of collective goods for either cosmopolitan or particularistic reasons. Here a decline in power leads to a change in regime because the hegemon is no longer able to control the pay-off matrix or influence the strategies of the weak, not because there is no actor to provide the collective goods needed for efficient regime functioning.

Norms and principles

To this point in the discussion, norms and principles have been treated as endogenous: they are the critical defining characteristics of any given regime. However, norms and principles that influence the regime in a particular issue-area but are not directly related to that issue-area can also be regarded as explanations for the creation, persistence, and dissipation of regimes. The most famous example of such a formulation is Max Weber's *Protestant Ethic and the Spirit of Capitalism*. Weber argues that the rise of capitalism is intimately associated with the evolution of a Calvinist religious doctrine that fosters hard work while enjoining profligacy and uses worldly success as an indication of predestined fate (Laitin 1978: 368–69; Hirschman 1977). Fred Hirsch has argued that without precapitalist values such as hard work, self-sacrifice, loyalty, and honor, capitalist systems would fall apart. Such values are critical constraints on self-interested calculations that would too often lead to untrustworthy and dishonest behavior (Hirsch 1976: Ch. 11; Walzer 1980).

Financing by various pariah groups around the world offers a clear example of the way in which noneconomic norms have facilitated market activity. For instance, bills of exchange were devised by Jewish bankers during the late Middle Ages to avoid violence and extortion from the nobility: safer to carry a piece of paper than to carry specie. However, the piece of paper had to be honored by the recipient. This implied a high level of trust and such trust was enhanced by conventions: established practices were reinforced by the exclusionary nature of the group, which facilitated surveillance and the application of sanctions. The importance of conventions for the use of bills of exchange is reflected in the fact that they were frequently used in the Mediterranean basin in the sixteenth century but they were not used at the interface with the non-Mediterranean world in Syria where, according to Braudel, "two mutually suspicious worlds met face to face." Here all dealings were in barter, or gold and silver (Braudel 1975: 370; Hirschman 1977: 72; Wallerstein 1974a: 147).

John Ruggie's highly original analysis of the postwar economic regime argues that it was founded upon principles of embedded rather than orthodox liberalism. The domestic lesson of the 1930s was that societies could not tolerate the consequences of an untrammeled market. This set of diffuse values, which permeated the capitalist world, was extended from the domestic to the international sphere in the Bretton Woods agreement.

Usage and custom

The last two sets of causal variables affecting regime development are usage and custom, and knowledge. Usage and custom will be discussed in this section, knowledge in the next. Usage and custom and knowledge supplement and reinforce pressures associated with egoistic self-interest, political power, and diffuse values.

Usage refers to regular patterns of behavior based on actual practice; custom, to long-standing practice (Weber 1930). The importance of routinized behavior is particularly significant in the position taken by Hopkins and Puchala and by Young (Hopkins and Puchala 1982; Young 1982). For these authors, patterned behavior, originally generated purely by considerations of interest or power, has a strong tendency to lead to shared expectations. Patterned behavior accompanied by shared expectations is likely to become infused with normative significance: actions based purely on instrumental calculations can come to be regarded as rule-like or principled behavior. They assume legitimacy. A great deal of Western commercial law, in fact, developed out of custom and usage initially generated by self-interest. Practices that began as ad hoc private arrangements later became the basis for official commercial law (Trakman 1980; Berman and Kaufman 1978).

In Oran Young's discussion of both spontaneous and imposed regimes, habits and usage play a significant role (Young 1982). Young does not make any strong claims for the specific conditions that lead to spontaneous regimes. However, the literature to which he refers—Schelling, Lewis, and Hayek—is oriented toward a microeconomic perspective focusing on egoistic self-interest. Certain patterns of behavior are first adopted because they promote individual utility. Once established, such practices are reinforced by the growth of regimes. Most American drivers (outside New York City) would feel at least a twinge of discomfort at driving illegally through a red light at an empty intersection. Behavior that was originally only a matter of egoistic self-interest is now buttressed by widely shared norms. Similarly, Young argues that successful imposed orders are bolstered eventually by habits of obedience. A pattern of behavior initially established by economic coercion or force may come to be regarded as legitimate by those on whom it has been imposed. Usage leads to shared expectations, which become infused with principles and norms.

Knowledge

The final variable used to explain the development of regimes is knowledge. Like usage and custom, knowledge is usually treated as an intervening, not an exogenous, variable. In an earlier study Ernst Haas defined knowledge as "the sum of technical information and of theories about that information which commands sufficient consensus at a given time among interested actors to serve as a guide to public policy designed to achieve some social goal" (Haas 1980b: 367–68). Haas points to the potentialities inherent in a stance of "cognitive evolutionism," which emphasizes sensitivity to the consequences of the generation of new knowledge (Haas 1982). Knowledge creates a basis for cooperation by illuminating complex interconnections that were not previously understood. Knowledge can not only enhance the prospects for convergent state behavior, it can also transcend "prevailing lines of ideological cleavage" (Haas 1980b: 368). It can provide a common ground both for what Haas calls mechanical approaches (most conventional social science theories) and for organic approaches (egalitarianism and various environmentally oriented arguments).

For knowledge to have an independent impact in the international system, it must be widely accepted by policy makers. Stein points out that rules concerning health, such as quarantine regulations, were radically altered by new scientific knowledge such as the discovery of the microbe that causes cholera, the transmission of yellow fever by mosquitoes, and the use of preventive vaccines (Stein 1982). Prior to developments such as these, national health regulations were primarily determined by political concerns. After these discoveries, however, national behavior was determined by an international regime, or at least a set of rules, dictated by accepted scientific knowledge. Jervis argues that in the present security arena the possibilities for an arms control regime may depend on whether the Soviet Union and the United States view strategy in the same way. In particular, mutual acceptance of Mutual Assured Destruction (MAD) can provide the basis for a regime (Jervis 1982). Without consensus, knowledge can have little impact on regime development in a world of sovereign states. If only some parties hold a particular set of beliefs, their significance is completely mediated by the power of their adherents.

New knowledge can provide the basis for what Hopkins and Puchala call evolutionary change, which usually involves altering rules and procedures within the context of a given set of principles and norms. In contrast, revolutionary change, which generates new principles and norms, is associated with shifts in power. As an example of evolutionary change, Benjamin Cohen points out that the fixed exchange rate system agreed to at Bretton Woods was based upon understandings derived from the interwar experience and then-current knowledge about domestic monetary institutions and structures. States were extremely sensitive to competitive devaluation and were not confident that domestic monetary policy could provide insulation from external disturbances. It was much easier to accept a floating exchange rate regime in the 1970s because the knowledge and related institutional capacity for controlling monetary aggregates had substantially increased (Cohen 1982). In a highly complex world, where goals are often ill-defined and many links are possible, consensual knowledge can greatly facilitate agreement on the development of an international regime. Such knowledge can light a clear path in a landscape that would otherwise be murky and undifferentiated.

In sum, there are several explanations for the development of regimes. The two most prominent exogenous variables are egoistic self-interest, usually economic, and political power. In addition, diffuse values and norms such as sovereignty and private property may condition behavior within specific issue-areas. Finally, usage and custom and knowledge may contribute to the development of regimes.

Conclusion

In approaching the two basic questions that guided this exercise—the impact of regimes on related behavior and outcomes, and the relationship between basic causal variables and regimes—there are two different orientations to international relations. The Grotian perspective, which informs the essays of Hopkins and Puchala and of Young, sees regimes as a pervasive facet of social interaction. It is catholic in its description of the underlying causes of regimes. Interests, power, diffuse norms, customs, and knowledge may all play a role in regime formation. These causal factors may be manifest through the behavior of individuals, particular bureaucracies, and international organizations, as well as states (Hopkins and Puchala 1982; Young 1982).

The structural realist orientation, which infuses the other essays in this volume, is more circumspect. The exemplar or standard case for the realist perspective does not include international regimes. Regimes arise only under restrictive conditions characterized by the failure of individual decision making to secure desired outcomes. The basic causal variables that lead to the creation of regimes are power and interest. The basic actors are states.

The arguments presented by Stein, Keohane, Jervis, Ruggie, Lipson, and Cohen do press beyond conventional realist orientations (Stein 1982; Keohane 1982; Jervis 1982; J.G. Ruggie 1982; Lipson 1982; Cohen 1982). They reject a narrow structural analysis that posits a direct relationship between changes in basic causal variables and related behavior and outcomes, and denies the utility of the regime concept. For this they are taken to task in Susan Strange's critique (Strange 1982). However, the basic parametric constraints for these analyses are identical with those applied by more conventional structural arguments. The basic analytic assumptions are the same. Arguments that treat regimes as intervening variables, and regard state interests and state power as basic causal variables, fall unambiguously within the structural realist paradigm. A more serious departure from structural reasoning occurs when regimes are seen as autonomous variables independently affecting not only related behavior and outcomes, but also the basic causal variables that led to their creation in the first place.

6 State power and the structure of international trade

Introduction

In recent years, students of international relations have multinationalized, transnationalized, bureaucratized, and transgovernmentalized the state until it has virtually ceased to exist as an analytic construct. Nowhere is that trend more apparent than in the study of the politics of international economic relations. The basic conventional assumptions have been undermined by assertions that the state is trapped by a transnational society created not by sovereigns, but by nonstate actors. Interdependence is not seen as a reflection of state policies and state choices (the perspective of balance-of-power theory), but as the result of elements beyond the control of any state or a system created by states.

This perspective is at best profoundly misleading. It may explain developments within a particular international economic structure, but it cannot explain the structure itself. That structure has many institutional and behavioral manifestations. The central continuum along which it can be described is openness. International economic structures may range from complete autarky (if all states prevent movements across their borders), to complete openness (if no restrictions exist). In this paper I will present an analysis of one aspect of the international economy—the structure of international trade; that is, the degree of openness for the movement of goods as opposed to capital, labor, technology, or other factors of production.

Since the beginning of the nineteenth century, this structure has gone through several changes. These can be explained, albeit imperfectly, by a state-power theory: an approach that begins with the assumption that the structure of international trade is determined by the interests and power of states acting to maximize national goals. The first step in this argument is to relate four basic state interests—aggregate national income, social stability, political power, and economic growth—to the degree of openness for the movement of goods. The relationship between these interests and openness depends upon the potential economic power of any given state. Potential economic power is operationalized in terms of the relative size and level of economic development of the state. The second step in the argument is to relate different distributions of potential power, such as multipolar and hegemonic, to different international trading structures. The most important conclusion of this theoretical analysis is that a hegemonic distribution of potential economic power is likely to result in an open trading structure. That argument is largely, although not completely, substantiated by empirical data. For a fully adequate analysis it is necessary to amend a state-power argument to take account of the impact of past state decisions on domestic social structures as well as on international economic ones. The two major organizers of the structure of trade since the beginning of the nineteenth century, Great Britain and the United States, have both been prevented from making policy amendments in line with state interests by particular societal groups whose power had been enhanced by earlier state policies.

The causal argument: state interests, state power, and international trading structures

Neoclassical trade theory is based upon the assumption that states act to maximize their aggregate economic utility. This leads to the conclusion that maximum global welfare and Pareto optimality are achieved under free trade. While particular countries might better their situations through protectionism, economic theory has generally looked askance at such policies. In his seminal article on the optimal tariff, Harry Johnson was at pains to point out that the imposition of successive optimal tariffs could lead both trading partners to a situation in which they were worse off than under competitive conditions (Johnson 1967a: 31–61). Neoclassical theory recognizes that trade regulations can also be used to correct domestic distortions and to promote infant industries, but these are exceptions or temporary departures from policy conclusions that lead logically to the support of free trade (Hagen 1958: 496–514; Bhagwati 1969: 295–308).

State preferences

Historical experience suggests that policy makers are dense, or that the assumptions of the conventional argument are wrong. Free trade has hardly been the norm. Stupidity is not a very interesting analytic category. An alternative approach to explaining international trading structures is to assume that states seek a broad range of goals. At least four major state interests affected by the structure of international trade can be identified. They are: political power, aggregate national income, economic growth, and social stability. The way in which each of these goals is affected by the degree of openness depends upon the potential economic power of the state as defined by its relative size and level of development.

Let us begin with aggregate national income because it is most straightforward. Given the exceptions noted above, conventional neoclassical theory demonstrates that the greater the degree of openness in the international trading system, the greater the level of aggregate economic income. This conclusion applies to all states regardless of their size or relative level of development. The static economic benefits of openness are, however, generally inversely related to size. Trade gives small states relatively more welfare benefits than it gives large ones. Empirically, small states have higher ratios of trade to national product. They do not have the generous factor endowments or potential for national economies of scale that are enjoyed by larger—particularly continental—states.

The impact of openness on social stability runs in the opposite direction. Greater openness exposes the domestic economy to the exigencies of the world market. That implies a higher level of factor movements than in a closed economy, because domestic production patterns must adjust to changes in international prices. Social instability is thereby increased, since there is friction in moving factors, particularly labor, from one sector to another. The impact will be stronger in small states than in large, and in relatively less developed than in more developed ones. Large states are less involved in the international economy: a smaller percentage of their total factor endowment is affected by the international market at any given level of openness. More developed states are better able to adjust factors: skilled workers can more easily be moved from one kind of production to another than can unskilled laborers or peasants. Hence social stability is, *ceteris paribus*, inversely related to openness, but the deleterious consequences of exposure to the international trading system are mitigated by larger size and greater economic development.

The relationship between political power and the international trading structure can be analyzed in terms of the relative opportunity costs of closure for trading partners (Hirschman 1945; Tucker 1972; Waltz 1970: 205–23). The higher the relative cost of closure, the weaker the political position of the state. Hirschman has argued that this cost can be measured in terms of direct income losses and the adjustment costs of reallocating factors (Hirschman 1945: 13–34). These will be smaller for large states and for relatively more developed states. Other things being equal, utility costs will be less for large states because they generally have a smaller proportion of their economy engaged in the international economic system. Reallocation costs will be less for more advanced states because their factors are more mobile. Hence a state that is relatively large and more developed will find its political power enhanced by an open system because its opportunity costs of closure are less. The large state can use the threat to alter the system to secure economic or noneconomic objectives. Historically, there is one important exception to this generalization—the oil-exporting states. The level of reserves for some of these states, particularly Saudi Arabia, has reduced the economic opportunity costs of closure to a very low level despite their lack of development.

The relationship between international economic structure and economic growth is elusive. For small states, economic growth has generally been empirically associated with openness (Kuznets 1966: 302). Exposure to the international system makes possible a much more efficient allocation of resources. Openness also probably furthers the rate of growth of large countries with relatively advanced technologies because they do not need to protect infant industries and can take advantage of expanded world markets. In the long term, however, openness for capital and technology, as well as goods, may hamper the growth of large, developed countries by diverting resources from the domestic economy, and by providing potential competitors with the knowledge needed to develop their own industries. Only by maintaining its technological lead and continually developing new industries can even a very large state escape the undesired consequences of an entirely open economic system. For medium-size states, the relationship between international trading structure and growth is impossible to specify definitively, either theoretically or empirically. On the one hand, writers from the mercantilists through the American protectionists and the German historical school, and more recently analysts of *dependencia*, have argued that an entirely open system can undermine a state's effort to develop, and even lead to underdevelopment (Calleo and Rowland 1973: Pt II; Heckscher 1955; Coleman 1969; Frank 1969; Emmanuel 1972; Galtung 1971: 81–117). On the other hand, adherents of more conventional neoclassical positions have maintained that exposure to international competition spurs economic transformation (Haberler 1959; Diaz-Alejandro 1972: 223–55). What may be said confidently is that openness furthers the economic growth of small states and of large ones so long as they maintain their technological edge.

From state preferences to international trading structures

The next step in this argument is to relate particular distributions of potential economic power, defined by the size and level of development of individual states, to the structure of the international trading system, defined in terms of openness.

Let us consider a system composed of a large number of small, highly developed states. Such a system is likely to lead to an open international trading structure. The aggregate income and economic growth of each state are increased by an open system. The social instability produced by exposure to international competition is mitigated by the factor mobility made possible by higher levels of development. There is no loss of political power from openness because the costs of closure are symmetrical for all members of the system.

Now let us consider a system composed of a few very large but unequally developed states. Such a distribution of potential economic power is likely to lead to a closed structure. Each state could increase its income through a more open system, but the gains would be modest. Openness would create more social instability in the less developed countries. The rate of growth for more backward areas might be frustrated, while that of the more advanced ones would be enhanced. A more open structure would leave the less developed states in a politically more vulnerable position, because their greater factor rigidity would mean a higher relative cost of closure. Because of these disadvantages, large but relatively less developed states are unlikely to accept an open trading structure. More advanced states cannot, unless they are militarily much more powerful, force large backward countries to accept openness.

Finally, let us consider a hegemonic system—one in which there is a single state that is much larger and relatively more advanced than its trading partners. The costs and benefits of openness are not symmetrical for all members of the system. The hegemonic state will have a preference for an open structure. Such a structure increases its aggregate national income. It also increases its rate of growth during its ascendancy—that is, when its relative size and technological lead are increasing. Further, an open structure increases its political power, since the opportunity costs of closure are least for a large and developed state. The social instability resulting from exposure to the international system is mitigated by the hegemonic power's relatively low level of involvement in the international economy, and the mobility of its factors.

What of the other members of a hegemonic system? Small states are likely to opt for openness because the advantages in terms of aggregate income and growth are so great, and their political power is bound to be restricted regardless of what they do. The reaction of medium-size states is hard to predict; it depends at least in part on the way in which the hegemonic power utilizes its resources. The potentially dominant state has symbolic, economic, and military capabilities that can be used to entice or compel others to accept an open trading structure.

At the symbolic level, the hegemonic state stands as an example of how economic development can be achieved. Its policies may be emulated, even if they are inappropriate for other states. Where there are very dramatic asymmetries, military power can be used to coerce weaker states into an open structure. Force is not, however, a very efficient means for changing economic policies, and it is unlikely to be employed against medium-size states.

Most importantly, the hegemonic state can use its economic resources to create an open structure. In terms of positive incentives, it can offer access to its large domestic market and to its relatively cheap exports. In terms of negative ones, it can withhold foreign grants and engage in competition, potentially ruinous for the weaker state, in third-country markets. The size and economic robustness of the hegemonic state also enable it to provide the confidence necessary for a stable international monetary system, and its currency can offer the liquidity needed for an increasingly open system.

In sum, openness is most likely to occur during periods when a hegemonic state is in its ascendancy. Such a state has the interest and the resources to create a structure characterized by lower tariffs, rising trade proportions, and less regionalism. There are other distributions of potential power where openness is likely, such as a system composed of many small, highly developed states. But even here, that potential might not be realized because of the problems of creating confidence in a monetary system where adequate liquidity would have to be provided by a negotiated international reserve asset or a group of national currencies. Finally, it is unlikely that very large states, particularly at unequal levels of development, would accept open trading relations.

These arguments, and the implications of other ideal typical configurations of potential economic power for the openness of trading structures, are summarized in Table 6.1.

The structure of international trade has both behavioral and institutional attributes. The degree of openness can be described both by the *flow* of goods and by the *policies* that are followed by states with respect to trade barriers and international payments. The two are not unrelated, but they do not coincide perfectly.

In common usage, the focus of attention has been upon institutions. Openness is associated with those historical periods in which tariffs were substantially lowered: the third quarter of the nineteenth century and the period since the Second World War.

Tariffs alone, however, are not an adequate indicator of structure. They are hard to operationalize quantitatively. Tariffs do not have to be high to be effective. If cost functions are nearly identical, even low tariffs can prevent trade. Effective tariff rates may be much higher than nominal ones. Non-tariff barriers to trade, which are not easily compared across states, can substitute for duties. An undervalued exchange rate can protect domestic markets from foreign competition. Tariff levels alone cannot describe the structure of international trade (Johnson 1967b: 90–94; Belassa 1967: Ch. 3; Schmitt 1974: 200).

A second indicator, and one which is behavioral rather than institutional, is trade proportions—the ratios of trade to national income for different states. Like tariff levels, these involve describing the system in terms of an

Table 6.1 Probability of an open trading structure with different distributions of potential economic power

		Relatively equal		Very unequal
		Small	Large	
Level of development of states	Equal	Moderate–high	Low–moderate	High
	Unequal	Moderate	Low	Moderate–high

agglomeration of national tendencies. A period in which these ratios are increasing across time for most states can be described as one of increasing openness.

A third indicator is the concentration of trade within regions composed of states at different levels of development. The degree of such regional encapsulation is determined not so much by comparative advantage (because relative factor endowments would allow almost any backward area to trade with almost any developed one), but by political choices or dictates. Large states, attempting to protect themselves from the vagaries of a global system, seek to maximize their interests by creating regional blocs. Openness in the global economic system has in effect meant greater trade among the leading industrial states. Periods of closure are associated with the encapsulation of certain advanced states within regional systems shared with certain less developed areas.

A description of the international trading system involves, then, an exercise that is comparative rather than absolute. A period when tariffs are falling, trade proportions are rising, and regional trading patterns are becoming less extreme will be defined as one in which the structure is becoming more open.

Tariff levels

The period from the 1820s to 1879 was basically one of decreasing tariff levels in Europe. The trend began in Great Britain in the 1820s, with reductions of duties and other barriers to trade. In 1846 the abolition of the Corn Laws ended agricultural protectionism. France reduced duties on some intermediate goods in the 1830s, and on coal, iron, and steel in 1852. The *Zollverein* established fairly low tariffs in 1834. Belgium, Portugal, Spain, Piedmont, Norway, Switzerland, and Sweden lowered imposts in the 1850s. The golden age of free trade began in 1860, when Britain and France signed the Cobden–Chevalier Treaty, which virtually eliminated trade barriers. This was followed by a series of bilateral trade agreements between virtually all European states. It is important to note, however, that the United States took little part in the general movement toward lower trade barriers (Kindleberger 1975: 20–55; Pollard 1974: 117; Condliffe 1950: 212–23, 229–30).

The movement toward greater liberality was reversed in the late 1870s. Austria–Hungary increased duties in 1876 and 1878, and Italy also in 1878; but the main breach came in Germany in 1879. France increased tariffs modestly in 1881, sharply in 1892, and raised them still further in 1910. Other countries followed a similar pattern. Only Great Britain, Belgium, the Netherlands, and Switzerland continued to follow free-trade policies through the 1880s. Although Britain did not herself impose duties, she began establishing a system of preferential markets in her overseas empire in 1898 (Kindleberger 1951: 33; Condliffe 1950: 498; Pollard 1974: 121; Gourevitch

1973). The United States was basically protectionist throughout the nineteenth century. The high tariffs imposed during the Civil War continued with the exception of a brief period in the 1890s. There were no major duty reductions before 1914.

During the 1920s, tariff levels increased further. Western European states protected their agrarian sectors against imports from the Danube region, Australia, Canada, and the United States, where the war had stimulated increased output. Great Britain adopted some colonial preferences in 1919, imposed a small number of tariffs in 1921, and extended some wartime duties. The successor states of the Austro-Hungarian Empire imposed duties to achieve some national self-sufficiency. The British dominions and Latin America protected industries nurtured by wartime demands. In the United States the Fordney–McCumber Tariff Act of 1922 increased protectionism. The October Revolution removed Russia from the Western trading system (Kindleberger 1973: 171; Condliffe 1950: 478–81).

Dramatic closure in terms of tariff levels began with the passage of the Smoot–Hawley Tariff Act in the United States in 1930. Britain raised tariffs in 1931 and definitively abandoned free trade at the Ottawa Conference of 1932, which introduced extensive imperial preferences. Germany and Japan established trading blocs within their own spheres of influence. All other major countries followed protectionist policies (Condliffe 1950: 498; Gilpin 1971: 407; Kindleberger 1973: 132, 171).

Significant reductions in protection began after the Second World War; the United States had foreshadowed the movement toward greater liberality with the passage of the Reciprocal Trade Agreements Act in 1934. Since 1945 there have been seven rounds of multilateral tariff reductions. The first, held in 1947 at Geneva, and the Kennedy Round, held during the 1960s, have been the most significant. They have substantially reduced the level of protection (Evans 1971: 10–20).

The present situation is ambiguous. There have recently been some new trade controls. In the United States these include a voluntary import agreement for steel, the imposition of a 10 per cent import surcharge during four months of 1971, and export controls on agricultural products in 1973 and 1974. Italy imposed a deposit requirement on imports during parts of 1974 and 1975. Britain and Japan have engaged in export subsidization. Nontariff barriers have become more important. On balance, there has been movement toward greater protectionism since the end of the Kennedy Round, but it is not decisive. The outcome of the multilateral negotiations that began in 1975 remains to be seen.

In sum, after 1820 there was a general trend toward lower tariffs (with the notable exception of the United States), which culminated between 1860 and 1879; higher tariffs from 1879 through the interwar years, with dramatic increases in the 1930s; and less protectionism from 1945 through the conclusion of the Kennedy Round in 1967.

Trade proportions

With the exception of one period, ratios of trade to aggregate economic
activity followed the same general pattern as tariff levels. Trade proportions
increased from the early part of the nineteenth century to about 1880.
Between 1880 and 1900 there was a decrease, sharper if measured in current
prices than constant ones, but apparent in both statistical series for most
countries. Between 1900 and 1913—and here is the exception from the tariff
pattern—there was a marked increase in the ratio of trade to aggregate economic activity. This trend brought trade proportions to levels that have
generally not been re-attained. During the 1920s and 1930s the importance
of trade in national economic activity declined. After the Second World War
it increased. Figure 6.1 presents these findings in greater detail. There are
considerable differences in the movement of trade proportions among states.
They hold more or less constant for the United States; Japan, Denmark, and
Norway (the last not shown on the graph) are unaffected by the general
decrease in the ratio of trade to aggregate economic activity that takes place
after 1880. The pattern described in the previous paragraph does, however,

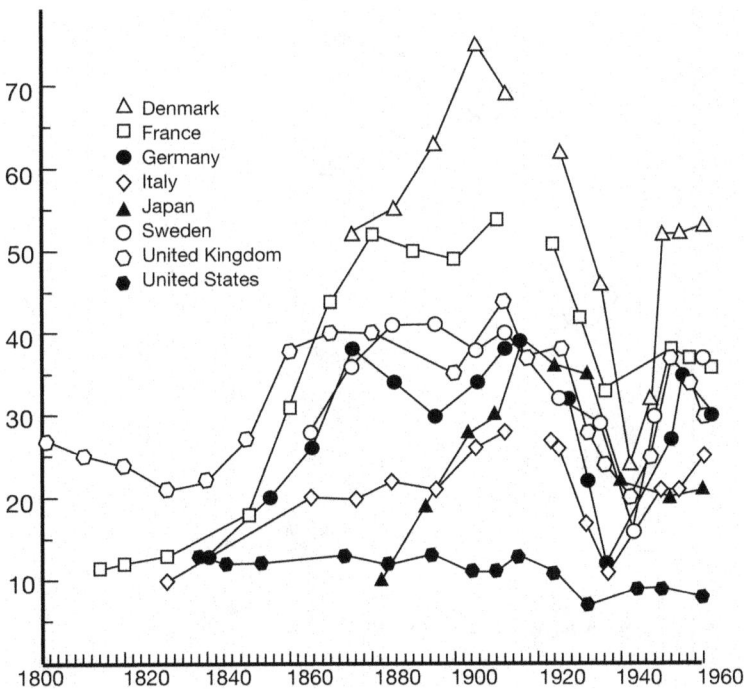

Figure 6.1 Ratio of trade to economic activity, nineteenth century to 1960, at current
prices.

Source: Kuznets 1967: Appendix 1. In all cases the mid-points of Kuznets' periods
were used.

hold for Great Britain, France, Sweden, Germany, and Italy. Figure 6.2 shows postwar developments. Because of the boom in commodity prices that occurred in the early 1950s, the ratio of trade to gross domestic product was relatively high for larger states during these years, at least in current prices. It then faltered or remained constant until about 1960. From the early 1960s through 1972, trade proportions rose for all major states except Japan. Data for 1973 and 1974 show further increases. For smaller countries the trend was more erratic, with Belgium showing a more or less steady increase, Norway vacillating between 82 and 90 per cent, and Denmark and the Netherlands showing higher figures for the late 1950s than for more recent

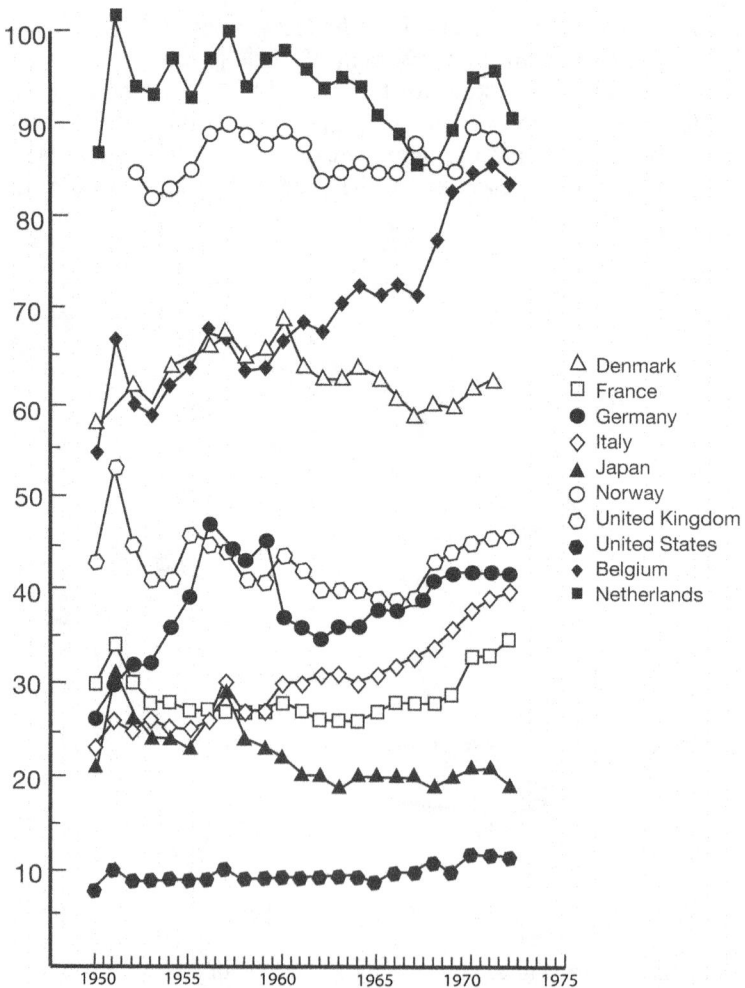

Figure 6.2 Ratio of trade to gross domestic product, 1950–1972, at current prices.
Source: United Nations Yearbook of National Account Statistics, various years.

years. There is then, in current prices, a generally upward trend in trade proportions since 1960, particularly for larger states. This movement is more pronounced if constant prices are used.

Regional trading patterns

The final indicator of the degree of openness of the global trading system is regional bloc concentration. There is a natural affinity for some states to trade with others because of geographical propinquity or comparative advantage. In general, however, a system in which there are fewer manifestations of trading within given blocs, particularly among specific groups of more and less developed states, is a more open one. Over time there have been extensive changes in trading patterns between particular areas of the world whose relative factor endowments have remained largely the same.

Richard Chadwick and Karl Deutsch have collected extensive information on international trading patterns since 1890. Their basic datum is the relative acceptance indicator (RA), which measures deviations from a null hypothesis in which trade between a pair of states, or a state and a region, is precisely what would be predicted on the basis of their total share of international trade (Savage and Deutsch 1960: 551–72; Chadwick and Deutsch 1973: 84–109). When the null hypothesis holds, the RA indicator is equal to zero. Values less than zero indicate less trade than expected, greater than zero more trade than expected. For our purposes the critical issue is whether, over time, trade tends to become more concentrated as shown by movements away from zero, or less as shown by movements toward zero.

Table 6.2 presents figures for the years 1890, 1913, 1928, 1938, and 1959 through 1968, the set collected by Chadwick and Deutsch, for the following pairs of major states and regions: Commonwealth–United Kingdom; United States–Latin America; Russia–Eastern Europe; and France–French-speaking Africa. The region's percentage of exports to the country, and the country's percentage of imports from the region, are included along with RA indicators to give some sense of the overall importance of the particular trading relationship.

There is a general pattern. In three of the four cases, the RA value closest to zero—that is the least regional encapsulation—occurred in 1890, 1913, or 1928; in the fourth case (France and French West Africa), the 1928 value was not bettered until 1964. In every case there was an increase in the RA indicator between 1928 and 1938, reflecting the breakdown of international commerce that is associated with the Depression. Surprisingly, the RA indicator was higher for each of the four pairs in 1954 than in 1938, an indication that regional patterns persisted and even became more intense in the postwar period. With the exception of the Soviet Union and Eastern Europe, there was a general trend toward decreasing RAs for the period after 1954. They still, however, show fairly high values even in the late 1960s.

Table 6.2 Regional trading patterns

	Commonwealth to United Kingdom			Latin America* to United States		
	Relative acceptance indicator	*Percentage of Commonwealth exports to United Kingdom*	*Percentage of United Kingdom imports from Commonwealth*	*Relative acceptance indicator*	*Percentage of Latin America exports to United States*	*Percentage of United States imports from Latin America*
1890	1.64	6.51	9.83	.14	9.86	2.91
1913	1.49	17.74	28.97	.45	19.47	8.05
1928	.72	17.55	26.49	1.27	30.21	17.41
1938	1.28	25.44	35.44	1.54	26.59	16.56
1954	1.60	18.54	38.47	2.04	42.76	19.07
1958	1.89	15.91	36.82	1.86	42.95	13.00
1959	1.77	15.78	36.79	1.68	42.87	11.66
1960	1.74	15.68	33.96	1.89	40.39	11.56
1961	1.66	14.27	33.15	2.03	39.78	11.82
1962	1.72	13.47	32.24	1.81	38.05	10.87
1963	1.62	13.06	31.67	1.84	37.02	11.13
1964	1.59	13.66	31.85	1.71	34.45	10.07
1965	1.47	11.53	27.42	1.43	32.66	9.01
1966	1.26	10.24	25.09	1.18	31.86	8.09
1967	1.08	9.82	22.90	1.13	31.47	7.26
1968	1.02	8.74	21.55	1.11	35.85	6.02

	Russia to Eastern Europe			France to French Africa		
	Relative acceptance indicator	*Percentage of Eastern Europe exports to Russia*	*Percentage of Russian imports from Eastern Europe*	*Relative acceptance indicator*	*Percentage of French African exports to France*	*Percentage of French imports from French Africa*
1890	.42	1.04	.58	9.57	100.0	.08
1913	.07	1.07	.79	7.24	53.59	.89
1928	.57	1.53	5.86	5.85	39.09	3.03
1938	.25	.70	3.75	7.22	44.12	5.02
1954	9.94	22.78	60.89	7.76	41.25	10.73
1958	8.85	23.13	55.01	7.77	41.13	8.14
1959	8.40	22.51	55.17	7.34	34.62	6.78
1960	8.48	22.73	56.08	6.87	35.16	7.15
1961	9.04	24.12	61.76	6.85	36.60	7.13
1962	9.01	25.55	63.00	6.60	38.76	6.34
1963	9.09	26.84	65.28	6.14	38.92	5.63
1964	9.22	26.73	64.18	5.55	36.41	5.28
1965	9.44	26.00	65.68	5.48	34.19	4.86
1966	9.90	24.24	64.77	4.90	32.64	4.69
1967	9.98	25.34	67.37	3.85	26.74	3.40
1968	11.78	33.84	67.06	7.58	46.18	2.57

Note:
* Includes Argentina, Bolivia, Brazil, Chile, Colombia, Ecuador, Mexico, Paraguay.

If we put all three indicators—tariff levels, trade proportions, and trade patterns—together, they suggest the following periodization.

Period I (1820–79): Increasing openness—tariffs are generally lowered; trade proportions increase. Data are not available for trade patterns. However, it is important to note that this is not a universal pattern. The United States is largely unaffected: its tariff levels remain high (and are in fact increased during the early 1860s) and American trade proportions remain almost constant.

Period II (1879–1900): Modest closure—tariffs are increased; trade proportions decline modestly for most states. Data are not available for trade patterns.

Period III (1900–13): Greater openness—tariff levels remain generally unchanged; trade proportions increase for all major trading states except the United States. Trading patterns become less regional in three out of the four cases for which data are available.

Period IV (1918–39): Closure—tariff levels are increased in the 1920s and again in the 1930s; trade proportions decline. Trade becomes more regionally encapsulated.

Period V (1945–c. 1970): Great openness—tariffs are lowered; trade proportions increase, particularly after 1960. Regional concentration decreases after 1960. However, these developments are limited to non-communist areas of the world.

The independent variable: describing the distribution of potential economic power among states

Analysts of international relations have an almost pro forma set of variables designed to show the distribution of potential power in the international *political* system. It includes such factors as gross national product, per capita income, geographical position, and size of armed forces. A similar set of indicators can be presented for the international *economic* system.

Statistics are available over a long time period for per capita income, aggregate size, share of world trade, and share of world investment. They demonstrate that, since the beginning of the nineteenth century, there have been two first-rank economic powers in the world economy—Britain and the United States. The United States passed Britain in aggregate size sometime in the middle of the nineteenth century, and in the 1880s became the largest producer of manufactures. America's lead was particularly marked in technologically advanced industries turning out sewing machines, harvesters, cash registers, locomotives, steam pumps, telephones, and petroleum (League of Nations 1945: 13; Wilkins 1970: 45–65). Until the First World War, however, Great Britain had a higher per capita income, a greater share of world trade, and a greater share of world investment than any other state. The peak of British ascendance occurred around 1880, when Britain's relative per capita income, share of world trade, and share of investment flows reached their highest levels. Britain's potential dominance in 1880 and 1900 was particularly striking in the international economic system, where her share of trade and foreign investment was about twice as large as that of any other state.

It was only after the First World War that the United States became relatively larger and more developed in terms of all four indicators. This potential dominance reached new and dramatic heights between 1945 and 1960. Since then, the relative position of the United States has declined, bringing it quite close to West Germany, its nearest rival, in terms of per capita income and share of world trade. The devaluations of the dollar that have taken place since 1972 are reflected in a continuation of this downward trend for income and aggregate size.

The relative potential economic power of Britain and the United States is shown in Table 6.3 and Table 6.4.

In sum, Britain was the world's most important trading state from the period after the Napoleonic Wars until 1913. Her relative position rose until about 1880 and fell thereafter. The United States became the largest and most advanced state in economic terms after the First World War, but did not equal the relative share of world trade and investment achieved by Britain in the 1880s until after the Second World War.

Testing the argument

The contention that hegemony leads to a more open trading structure is fairly well, but not perfectly, confirmed by the empirical evidence presented

Table 6.3 Indicators of British potential power (ratio of British value to next highest)

	Per capita income	Aggregate size	Share of world trade	Share of world investment*
1860	.91 (US)	.74 (US)	2.01 (Fr.)	n.a.
1880	1.30 (US)	.79 (1874–83 US)	2.22 (Fr.)	1.93 (Fr.)
1900	1.05 (1899 US)	.58 (1899 US)	2.17 (1890 Ger.)	2.08 (Fr.)
1913	.92 (US)	.43 (US)	1.20 (US)	2.18 (1914 Fr.)
1928	.66 (US)	.25 (1929 US)	.79 (US)	.64 (1921–29 US)
1937	.79 (US)	.29 (US)	.88 (US)	.18 (1930–38 US)
1950	.56 (US)	.19 (US)	.69 (US)	.13 (1951–55 US)
1960	.49 (US)	.14 (US)	.46 (1958 US)	.15 (1956–61 US)
1972	.46 (US)	.13 (US)	.47 (1973 US)	n.a.

Notes:
* Stock 1870–1913; flow 1928–1950
Years are in parentheses when different from those in first column.
Countries in parentheses are those with the largest values for the particular indicator other than Great Britain.

Table 6.4 Indicators of US potential power (ratio of US value to next highest)

	Per capita income	Aggregate size	Share of world trade	Share of world investment flows
1860	1.10 (GB)	1.41 (GB)	.36 (GB)	Net debtor
1880	.77 (GB)	1.23 (1883 GB)	.37 (GB)	Net debtor
1900	.95 (1899 GB)	1.73 (1899 GB)	.43 (1890 GB)	n.a.
1913	1.09 (GB)	2.15 (Russ.)	.83 (GB)	Net debtor
1928	1.51 (GB)	3.22 (USSR)	1.26 (GB)	1.55 (1921–29 UK)
1937	1.26 (GB)	2.67 (USSR)	1.13 (GB)	5.53 (1930–38 UK)
1950	1.78 (GB)	3.15 (USSR)	1.44 (GB)	7.42 (1951–55 UK)
1960	2.05 (GB)	2.81 (USSR)	2.15 (1958 GB)	6.60 (1956–61 UK)
1972	1.31 (Ger.)	n.a.	1.18 (1973 Ger.)	n.a.

Notes: Years are in parentheses when different from those in first column.
Countries in parentheses are those with the largest values for the particular indicator
  other than United States.

in the preceding sections. The argument explains the periods 1820 to 1879, 1880 to 1900, and 1945 to 1960. It does not fully explain those from 1900 to 1913, 1919 to 1939, or 1960 to the present.

1820–79

The period from 1820 to 1879 was one of increasing openness in the structure of international trade. It was also one of rising hegemony. Great Britain was the instigator and supporter of the new structure. She began lowering her trade barriers in the 1820s, before any other state. The signing of the Cobden–Chevalier Tariff Treaty with France in 1860 initiated a series of bilateral tariff reductions. It is, however, important to note that the United States was hardly involved in these developments, and that America's ratio of trade to aggregate economic activity did not increase during the nineteenth century.

Britain put to use her internal flexibility and external power in securing a more open structure. At the domestic level, openness was favored by the rising industrialists. The opposition of the agrarian sector was mitigated by its capacity for adjustment: the rate of capital investment and technological innovation was high enough to prevent British agricultural incomes from falling until some thirty years after the abolition of the Corn Laws. Symbolically, the Manchester School led by Cobden and Bright provided the ideological justification for free trade. Its influence was felt throughout Europe where Britain stood as an example to at least some members of the elite.

Britain used her military strength to open many backward areas: British interventions were frequent in Latin America during the nineteenth century, and formal and informal colonial expansion opened the interior of Africa. Most importantly, Britain forced India into the international economic system (Gallagher and Robinson 1953: 1–15). British military power was also a factor in concluding the Cobden–Chevalier Treaty, for Louis Napoleon was more concerned with cementing his relations with Britain than he was in the economic consequences of greater openness. Once this pact was signed, however, it became a catalyst for the many other treaties that followed (Kindleberger 1975: 41).

Britain also put economic instruments to good use in creating an open system. The abolition of the Corn Laws offered continental grain producers the incentive of continued access to the growing British market. Britain was at the heart of the nineteenth-century international monetary system which functioned exceptionally well, at least for the core of the more developed states and the areas closely associated with them. Exchange rates were stable, and countries did not have to impose trade barriers to rectify cyclical payments difficulties. Both confidence and liquidity were, to a critical degree, provided by Britain. The use of sterling balances as opposed to specie became increasingly widespread, alleviating the liquidity problems presented by the erratic production of gold and silver. Foreign private and central banks increasingly placed their cash reserves in London, and accounts were cleared through changing bank balances rather than gold flows. Great Britain's extremely sophisticated financial institutions, centered in the City of London, provided the short-term financing necessary to facilitate the international flow of goods. Her early and somewhat fortuitous adherence to the gold—as opposed to the silver or bimetallic—standard proved to be an important source of confidence as all countries adopted at least a de facto gold standard after 1870 because of the declining relative value of silver. In times of monetary emergency, the confidence placed in the pound because of the strength of the British economy allowed the Bank of England to be a lender of last resort (Triffin 1964: 2–20; Hawtrey 1947: 69–80; Yeager 1966: 251–61; Rolfe and Burtle 1973: 10–11; Condliffe 1950: 343–80).

Hence, for the first three-quarters of the nineteenth century, British policy favored an open international trading structure, and British power helped to create it. But this was not a global regime. British resources were not sufficient to entice or compel the United States (a country whose economy was larger than Britain's by 1860 and whose technology was developing very rapidly) to abandon its protectionist commercial policy. As a state-power argument suggests, openness was only established within the geographical area where the rising economic hegemony was able to exercise its influence.

1880–1900

The last two decades of the nineteenth century were a period of modest closure which corresponds to a relative decline in British per capita income, size, and share of world trade. The event that precipitated higher tariff levels was the availability of inexpensive grain from the American Midwest, made possible by the construction of continental railways. National responses

varied. Britain let her agricultural sector decline, a not unexpected development given her still dominant economic position. Denmark, a small and
relatively well-developed state, also refrained from imposing tariffs and
transformed its farming sector from agriculture to animal husbandry. Several
other small states also followed open policies. Germany, France, Russia, and
Italy imposed higher tariffs, however. Britain did not have the military or economic power to forestall these policies. Still, the institutional structure of the
international monetary system, with the City of London at its center, did not
crumble. The decline in trade proportions was modest despite higher tariffs.

1945–60

The third period that is neatly explained by the argument that hegemony
leads to an open trading structure is the decade and a half after the Second
World War, characterized by the ascendancy of the United States. During
these years the structure of the international trading system became increasingly open. Tariffs were lowered; trade proportions were restored well above
interwar levels. Asymmetrical regional trading patterns did begin to decline,
although not until the late 1950s. America's bilateral rival, the Soviet Union,
remained—as the theory would predict—encapsulated within its own regional
sphere of influence.

Unlike Britain in the nineteenth century, the United States after World
War II operated in a bipolar political structure. Free trade was preferred, but
departures such as the Common Market and Japanese import restrictions
were accepted to make sure that these areas remained within the general
American sphere of influence (Aron 1973: 191; Gilpin 1971: 409–12; Calleo
and Rowland 1973: Ch. 3). Domestically the Reciprocal Trade Agreements
Act, first passed in 1934, was extended several times after the war. Internationally the United States supported the framework for tariff reductions
provided by the General Agreement on Tariffs and Trade. American policy
makers used their economic leverage over Great Britain to force an end to
the imperial preference system (Gardner 1964: 389; Gilpin 1971: 409). The
monetary system established at Bretton Woods was basically an American
creation. In practice, liquidity was provided by the American deficit, confidence by the size of the American economy. Behind the economic veil stood
American military protection for other industrialized market economies—an
overwhelming incentive for them to accept an open system, particularly one
which was in fact relatively beneficial.

The argument about the relationship between hegemony and openness is not
as satisfactory for the years 1900 to 1913, 1919 to 1939, and 1960 to the present.

1900–13

During the years immediately preceding the First World War, the structure
of international trade became more open in terms of trade proportions and

regional patterns. Britain remained the largest international economic entity, but her relative position continued a decline that had begun two decades earlier. Still, Britain maintained her commitment to free trade and to the financial institutions of the City of London. A state-power argument would suggest some reconsideration of these policies.

Perhaps the simplest explanation for the increase in trade proportions was the burst of loans that flowed out of Europe in the years before the First World War, loans that financed the increasing sale of goods. Germany and France as well as Britain participated in this development. Despite the higher tariff levels imposed after 1879, institutional structures—particularly the monetary system—allowed these capital flows to generate increasing trade flows. Had Britain reconsidered her policies, this might not have been the case.

1919–39

The United States emerged from the First World War as the world's most powerful economic state. Whether America was large enough to have put an open system in place is a moot question. As Tables 6.3 and 6.4 indicate, America's share of world trade and investment was only 26 and 55 per cent greater than that of any other state, while comparable figures for Great Britain during the last part of the nineteenth century are 100 per cent. What is apparent, though, is that American policy makers made little effort to open the structure of international trade. The call for an open door was a shibboleth, not a policy. It was really the British who attempted to continue a hegemonic role.

In the area of trade, the US Fordney–McCumber Tariff of 1922 increased protection. That tendency was greatly reinforced by the Smoot–Hawley Tariff of 1930, which touched off a wave of protective legislation. Instead of leading the way to openness, the United States led the way to closure.

In the monetary area, the American government made little effort to alter a situation that was confused and often chaotic. During the first half of the 1920s, exchange rates fluctuated widely among major currencies as countries were forced, by the inflationary pressures of the war, to abandon the gold standard. Convertibility was restored in the mid-1920s at values incompatible with long-term equilibrium. The British pound was overvalued, and the French franc undervalued. Britain was forced off the gold standard in September 1931, accelerating a trend that had begun with Uruguay in April 1929. The United States went off gold in 1933. France's decision to end convertibility in 1936 completed the pattern. During the 1930s the monetary system collapsed (Triffin 1964: 22–28; Rolfe and Burtle 1973: 13–55; Yeager 1966: 278–317; Kindleberger 1973: 270–71).

Constructing a stable monetary order would have been no easy task in the political environment of the 1920s and 1930s. The United States made no effort. It refused to recognize a connection between war debts and reparations, although much of the postwar flow of funds took the form of American loans to Germany, German reparations payments to France and Britain, and French and British war-debt payments to the United States. The Great Depression was in no small measure touched off by the contraction of American credit in the late 1920s. In the deflationary collapse that followed, the British were too weak to act as a lender of last resort, and the Americans actually undercut efforts to reconstruct the Western economy when, before the London Monetary Conference of 1933, President Roosevelt changed the basic assumptions of the meeting by taking the United States off gold. American concern was wholly with restoring the domestic economy (Kindleberger 1973: 199–224; Yeager 1966: 314; Condliffe 1950: 499).

That is not to say that American behavior was entirely obstreperous; but cooperation was erratic and often private. The Federal Reserve Bank of New York did try, during the late 1920s, to maintain New York interest rates below those in London to protect the value of the pound (Triffin 1964: 2). Two Americans, Dawes and Young, lent their names to the renegotiations of German reparations payments, but most of the actual work was carried out by British experts (Kindleberger 1973: 296). At the official level, the first manifestation of American leadership was President Hoover's call for a moratorium on war debts and reparations in June 1931; but in 1932 the United States refused to participate in the Lausanne Conference that in effect ended reparations (Condliffe 1950: 494–97).

It was not until the mid-1930s that the United States asserted any real leadership. The Reciprocal Trade Agreements Act of 1934 led to bilateral treaties with twenty-seven countries before 1945. American concessions covered 64 per cent of dutiable items, and reduced rates by an average of 44 per cent. However, tariffs were so high to begin with that the actual impact of these agreements was limited (Evans 1971: 7). There were also some modest steps toward tariff liberalization in Britain and France. In the monetary field, the United States, Britain, and France pledged to maintain exchange-rate stability in the Tripartite Declaration of September 1936. These actions were not adequate to create an open international economic structure. American policy during the interwar period, and particularly before the mid-1930s, fails to accord with the predictions made by a state-power explanation of the behavior of a rising hegemonic power.

1960–70

The final period not adequately dealt with by a state-power explanation is the last decade or so. In recent years, the relative size and level of development of the US economy has fallen. This decline has not, however, been accompanied by a clear turn toward protectionism. The Trade Expansion Act of 1962 was extremely liberal and led to the very successful Kennedy Round of multilateral tariff cuts during the mid-1960s. The protectionist Burke–Hartke Bill did not pass. The 1974 Trade Act does include new protectionist aspects, particularly in its requirements for review of the removal of non-tariff barriers by Congress and for stiffer requirements for the imposition of countervailing duties, but it still maintains the mechanism of presidential discretion on tariff cuts that has been the keystone of postwar reductions. While the Voluntary Steel Agreement, the August 1971 economic policy, and restrictions on agricultural exports all show a tendency toward protectionism, there is as yet no evidence of a basic turn away from a commitment to openness.

In terms of behavior in the international trading system, the decade of the 1960s was clearly one of greater openness. Trade proportions increased, and traditional regional trade patterns became weaker. A state-power argument would predict a downturn or at least a faltering.

In sum, although the general pattern of the structure of international trade conforms with the predictions of a state-power argument—two periods of openness separated by one of closure—corresponding to periods of rising British and American hegemony and an interregnum, the whole pattern is out of phase. British commitment to openness continued long after Britain's position had declined. American commitment to openness did not begin until well after the United States had become the world's leading economic power and has continued during a period of relative American decline. The state-power argument needs to be amended to take these delayed reactions into account.

Amending the argument

The structure of the international trading system does not move in lockstep with changes in the distribution of potential power among states. Systems are initiated and ended, not as a state-power theory would predict, by close assessments of the interests of the state at every given moment, but by external events—usually cataclysmic ones. The closure that began in 1879 coincided with the Great Depression of the last part of the nineteenth century. The final dismantling of the nineteenth-century international economic system was not precipitated by a change in British trade or monetary policy, but by the First World War and the Depression. The potato famine of the 1840s prompted abolition of the Corn Laws; and the United States did not assume the mantle of world leadership until the world had been laid bare by six years of total war. Some catalytic external event seems necessary to move states to dramatic policy initiatives in line with state interests.

Once policies have been adopted, they are pursued until a new crisis demonstrates that they are no longer feasible. States become locked in by the impact of prior choices on their domestic political structures. The British decision to opt for openness in 1846 corresponded with state interests. It also strengthened the position of industrial and financial groups over time, because they had the opportunity to operate in an international system that furthered their objectives. That system eventually undermined the position of

British farmers, a group that would have supported protectionism if it had survived. Once entrenched, Britain's export industries, and more importantly the City of London, resisted policies of closure (Gilpin 1975: Ch. 3; Kindleberger 1973: 294). In the interwar years, the British renter class insisted on restoring the prewar parity of the pound—a decision that placed enormous deflationary pressures on the domestic economy—because they wanted to protect the value of their investments (Yeager 1966: 279).

Institutions created during periods of rising ascendancy remained in operation when they were no longer appropriate. For instance, the organization of British banking in the nineteenth century separated domestic and foreign operations. The Court of Directors of the Bank of England was dominated by international banking houses. Their decisions about British monetary policy were geared toward the international economy (Condliffe 1950). Under a different institutional arrangement more attention might have been given after 1900 to the need to revitalize the domestic economy. The British state was unable to free itself from the domestic structures that its earlier policy decisions had created, and continued to follow policies appropriate for a rising hegemony long after Britain's star had begun to fall.

Similarly, earlier policies in the United States begat social structures and institutional arrangements that trammeled state policy. After protecting import-competing industries for a century, the United States was unable in the 1920s to opt for more open policies, even though state interests would have been furthered thereby. Institutionally, decisions about tariff reductions were taken primarily in Congressional committees, giving virtually any group seeking protection easy access to the decision-making process. When there were conflicts among groups, they were resolved by raising the levels of protection for everyone. It was only after the cataclysm of the Depression that the decision-making processes for trade policy were changed. The presidency, far more insulated from the entreaties of particular societal groups than Congressional committees, was then given more power (Lowi 1972: 298–310; Schattschneider 1935). Furthermore, the American commercial banking system was unable to assume the burden of regulating the international economy during the 1920s. American institutions were geared toward the domestic economy. Only after the Second World War, and in fact not until the late 1950s, did American banks fully develop the complex institutional structures commensurate with the dollar's role in the international monetary system (Kelly 1975).

Having taken the critical decisions that created an open system after 1945, the American government is unlikely to change its policy until it confronts some external event that it cannot control, such as a worldwide deflation, drought in the great plains, or the malicious use of petrodollars. In America perhaps more than in any other country "new policies," as E.E. Schattschneider wrote in his brilliant study of the Smoot–Hawley Tariff in 1935, "create new politics" (Schattschneider 1935: 288), for in America the state is weak and the society strong (Katzenstein 1976; Huntington 1974: 16–17;

Huntington 1968: Ch. 2). State decisions taken because of state interests reinforce private societal groups that the state is unable to resist in later periods. Multinational corporations have grown and prospered since 1950. International economic policy making has passed from the Congress to the Executive. Groups favoring closure, such as organized labor, are unlikely to carry the day until some external event demonstrates that existing policies can no longer be implemented.

The structure of international trade changes in fits and starts; it does not flow smoothly with the redistribution of potential state power. Nevertheless, it is the power and the policies of states that create order where there would otherwise be chaos or at best a Lockian state of nature. The existence of various transnational, multinational, transgovernmental, and other nonstate actors that have riveted scholarly attention in recent years can only be understood within the context of a broader structure that ultimately rests upon the power and interests of states, shackled though they may be by the societal consequences of their own past decisions.

Acknowledgements

I would like to thank Robert Art, Peter Gourevitch, Samuel Huntington, Robert Keohane, Rachel McCulloch, Joseph Nye, Ronald Rogowski, and Robert W. Tucker for their comments. My greatest intellectual debt is to Robert Gilpin. Completion of this paper was made possible by support from the Washington Center of Foreign Policy Research of the Johns Hopkins School of Advanced International Studies and the Center for International Affairs at Harvard University.

7 Global communications and national power

Life on the Pareto frontier

Introduction

There is no single international regime for global communications. Radio and television broadcasting, electromagnetic spectrum allocation, telecommunications (telephone, telegraph, communications satellites, transborder data flows), and remote sensing are governed by a variety of principles, norms, rules, and decision-making procedures—or, in some cases, by no regime at all. Variation in outcomes can be explained by the interests and relative power capabilities of the actors in each case.

Global communications have been characterized not by Nash equilibria that are Pareto suboptimal but rather by disagreements over which point along the Pareto frontier should be chosen, that is, by distributional conflicts rather than by market failure. Changes in the relative power of states have led to changes in international regimes. The apparatus of economics, which has been so heavily deployed in regime analysis, has focused on information and monitoring rather than power, implying, if not explicitly arguing, that intelligence (figuring out the right institutional structure) is more important than the underlying distribution of capabilities. Regime analyses based upon market failure inevitably obscure issues of power because, given a Pareto-suboptimal situation and a concern with absolute not just relative gains, it is possible to make at least one actor better off without making others worse off—an outcome that can be resolved through cleverness rather than by resort to power, threat, and coercion.

Information flows and knowledge have been less important than relative power capabilities for international communications regimes or the lack thereof. Where there have been disagreements about basic principles and norms and where the distribution of power has been highly asymmetrical, international regimes have not developed. Stronger states have simply done what they pleased. Radio broadcasting and remote sensing offer the clearest examples.

Where there are coordination problems and the distribution of power has been more symmetrical, however, regimes have been established. The level of conflict has varied according to whether states were dealing with pure coordination problems or with coordination problems that had distributional consequences. The resolution of the former has caused little conflict because the purpose of the regime has been to avoid mutually undesirable outcomes. The allocation of the radio spectrum before the 1970s and the telecommunications regime before the 1980s offer two examples.

By contrast, in cases that have had distributional consequences, conflict has been more intense: though the states agreed on mutually undesirable outcomes, they disagreed on their preferred outcome. Controversies were triggered by changes in power, usually resulting from the development of new technologies. In recent years distributional questions have precipitated conflict over the allocation of the radio spectrum and over international telecommunications. The outcome of these disputes has been determined primarily by the relative bargaining power of the states involved. Whereas previous institutional choices had not imposed much constraint, new interests and power capabilities conferred by new technologies have led to new institutional arrangements.

This is not to say that institutional arrangements were ever irrelevant: indeed, they were necessary to resolve coordination problems and to establish stability. Without regimes all parties would have been worse off. There are, however, many points along the Pareto frontier: the nature of institutional arrangements is better explained by the distribution of national power capabilities than by efforts to solve problems of market failure.

Explaining international regimes

The consequences of different configurations of interests for the creation and maintenance of international regimes has been elaborated in a number of studies. There are four possible configurations of interests, two of which can give rise to international regimes. Regimes are irrelevant for situations characterized by either harmony or pure (zero-sum) conflict. Rather, regimes can arise under what Arthur Stein has called dilemmas of common aversions or dilemmas of common interests (Stein 1982; Snidal 1985b: 923–42).

Under zero-sum conditions there is no basis for regimes and no reason to coordinate policies, because one actor's loss is another's gain (Waltz 1979; Grieco 1988: 923–42). In a situation of harmony, too, there is no reason to create a regime, because each individual player, acting without regard for the behavior of others, maximizes both its own utility and that of the system as a whole. Purely self-regarding behavior produces both a Nash and Pareto-optimal equilibrium (Keohane 1984: 51).

By contrast, dilemmas of common aversions and dilemmas of common interests are distributions of preferences that do create incentives to establish and maintain international regimes. Both involve strategic interaction. Dilemmas of common aversions refer to situations in which actors must coordinate their policies by agreeing on some set of rules or conventions, to avoid mutually undesirable outcomes. The specific content of these rules will matter only if the actors disagree about which is the most desirable outcome. If there is no disagreement, then the outcome is a Nash equilibrium and is Pareto optimal: there is no incentive for any actor to defect and no opportunity to increase any actor's utility without damaging that of another. Cheating is therefore not a problem. There is no need to develop elaborate mechanisms for generating and monitoring information, because there is no sucker's pay-off to worry about. One set of rules is as good as any other, provided that all states agree to do the same thing. For instance, starting from a situation in which no prior investments have been made, it does not matter whether cars drive on the left or right side of the road provided that all drivers adopt the same rule. It may not matter to a couple whether they go to the mountains or the ocean for a vacation, provided that they go to the same place. Such a configuration of interests is shown in Figure 7.1.

With a minimal level of coordination (actors need only avoid switching back and forth at the same time when one starts from the right and the other from the left), all actors will end up driving on either the left or the right, or both members of a couple will go to either the mountains or the ocean. As Snidal (1985b: 931) notes:

> Sometimes coordination is presented simply as the problem of two or more actors matching policies where they are indifferent about where they match ... Here there is no disjuncture between individual and collective rationality and no problem of collective action. It requires not more than communication and common sense to achieve an outcome that is both individually and collectively optimal.

Dilemmas of common aversions, however, can involve questions of distribution in addition to those of coordination. Although actors may recognize that all would be worse off without some agreement, they may disagree about precisely what the terms of that agreement ought to be. There are many points along the Pareto frontier.

Such a distribution of interests is shown in Figure 7.2. This game is commonly referred to as the Battle of the Sexes. The story line here is as follows: Both members of a couple prefer to do something together, but they disagree on their preferred outcome, vacationing in the mountains or at the ocean.

	Mountains Left		Oceans Right	
Mountains Left	1	1	0	0
Oceans Right	0	0	1	1

Figure 7.1 Simple coordination problem

	Mountains Left	Oceans Right
Mountains Left	3 2	0 0
Oceans Right	0 0	2 3

Figure 7.2 Battle of the Sexes

With such a distribution of interests, the choice of mountains or ocean, or left or right, matters, for vacationing in the mountains gives the column player a higher pay-off than going to the ocean and vice versa. Both parties are averse to an absence of coordination in which they take different vacations, but the pay-off matrix itself provides no information about which of the two equilibrium points will be chosen. The problem is not how to get to the Pareto frontier but which point along the frontier will be chosen.

In the international relations literature that has evolved since Schelling, commitment has been the analytic device that has most commonly been used to understand which outcome will be chosen, and commitment has usually referred to cleverness (such as throwing a steering wheel out the window in a game of Chicken). Similar kinds of reasoning about commitment have been used in the recent literature on strategic trade theory. One element of this analysis is that state intervention to promote a particular industry is desirable because it demonstrates a level of national commitment that could not be provided by the action of private firms (Brander 1986: 30). The resolution of distributional conflicts could, however, be resolved through a very different route: the exercise of state power, which could be manifest in at least three ways.

1 Power may be used to determine who can play the game in the first place. In international relations less powerful actors are often never invited to the table (Snidal 1985b: 938).
2 Power may also be used to dictate rules of the game: for instance, who gets to move first. In Figure 7.2 the player who moves first can dictate the outcome, provided that the other player is convinced that the first player's strategy is irrevocable.
3 Power may be used to change the pay-off matrix or underlying power capabilities or size may determine the pay-off matrix in the first place (Conybeare 1987: 2). For instance, a more powerful row player might use tactical linkage to change, or credibly threaten to change, the pay-off matrix in Figure 7.2 to the one presented in Figure 7.3. A large importer (read the United States) might threaten to bar imports from an exporter (read Japan) if the latter failed to make basic changes in the structure of its domestic economy, such as the distribution system.

	Mountains Left	Oceans Right
Mountains Left	1 2	0 0
Oceans Right	0 0	2 3

Figure 7.3 Battle of the Sexes with tactical linkage

One of the two forms of coordination (right right) is now unambiguously superior for both players, even though both forms of coordination are Nash equilibria. The players can secure the right outcome with a minimum level of coordination, for instance by playing the game in an extended form in which either player has the option of going first. Once this outcome is reached, it is both Nash and Pareto optimal; there is no incentive for either actor to change.

In contrast to situations involving distributional choices along the Pareto frontier, such as the Battle of the Sexes pay-off structure, problems of collaboration, which are generated by dilemmas of common interests, are concerned with market failure (Stein 1982). They are characterized by Pareto-suboptimal outcomes; at least one actor can gain without compromising the utility of others. The locus classicus of this set of problems is Prisoner's Dilemma.

A great deal of the cooperation and regime literature in international relations has been devoted to analyzing how actors can escape from a situation in which there are incentives to cheat but in which mutual cooperation is better than mutual defection. Robert Axelrod and Robert O. Keohane point to Pareto suboptimality in general as the defining problem for the cooperation literature, arguing that

> what is important for our purposes is not to focus exclusively on Prisoner's Dilemma per se, but to emphasize the fundamental problem that it (along with Stag Hunt and Chicken) illustrates. In these games, myopic pursuit of self-interest can be disastrous. Yet both sides can potentially benefit from cooperation—if they can only achieve it.
>
> (Axelrod and Keohane 1985: 226–54)

The fundamental question has been: How can players move toward the Pareto optimal outcome of mutual cooperation? Charles Lipson, for instance, argues that

> because the Prisoner's Dilemma highlights both the potential gains from cooperation and the temptations that prevent it, it has been taken as an

elegant expression of the most profound political dilemmas, including that of the social contract. Indeed, Jon Elster once defined politics as "the study of ways of transcending the Prisoner's Dilemma."

(Lipson 1984: 1–23)

Several answers have emerged. Cooperation is more likely when there is iteration and no defined number of plays, and when discount rates are low and the difference between the pay-offs for cooperation and defection are modest (Oye 1985: 1–24).

Most important for the international relations research program growing out of the literature on market failure is the investigation of the way in which cooperation can be facilitated by institutions that reduce the temptation to lie, cheat, and dissimulate by increasing the symmetry and amount of information, raising the cost of illegitimate behavior, promoting convergent expectations, and fostering cross-issue-area linkages (Keohane 1984: Ch. 6.). The central normative concern of cooperation theory is to develop institutional mechanisms that inhibit cheating.

Market failure analyses, which have dominated the literature on international regimes, pay little attention to power. Once the game is defined, all actors are treated symmetrically with regard to their capabilities. Both the row and the column player have the same competence to play the game. No one is eliminated through brute force as opposed to choosing a bad strategy. In this game, clubs are never trump (Grieco 1990: 38). Everyone could be better off if only market failure problems were solved. Power—which can be understood as the ability to determine who plays the game, or to define the rules, or to change the values within the pay-off matrix—does not matter as much as information and monitoring capabilities. When analysts working within the cooperation research program have discussed the larger question of the context within which the game is specified, they have pointed to the ways in which issue linkage or limiting the number of players might facilitate cooperation rather than the distributional consequences of power.

Global communications

For international communications, however, market failure problems have been irrelevant. Monitoring and information were never a central consideration. Power, not just interest, did matter, though. And the question was not how to move to the Pareto frontier, but rather which point along the frontier would be chosen.

In the four issue-areas considered in this paper—radio and television broadcasting, remote sensing, allocation of the electromagnetic spectrum, and telecommunications (telephone and telegraph links including communications satellites)—there are no examples of harmony. And in two cases, radio broadcasting and remote sensing, there are no international regimes: there has been no agreement on principles and norms because more powerful states have been able to secure their first best outcome through unilateral action. The critical weakness of some states in these issue-areas was their inability to regulate access to their own territory because they could not effectively block all broadcasting signals or remote sensing probes.

In the other two issue-areas—allocation of the electromagnetic spectrum and telecommunications—there have been international regimes. Both initially posed pure coordination problems; actors wanted to avoid the mutually undesirable outcomes of radio interference and incompatible national communications systems. In recent years, however, distributional issues have become more consequential. Third World statesmen have worried that the entire electromagnetic spectrum would be allocated without taking account of the future needs of their countries. The regime has responded to these concerns because in this case Third World countries have power conferred by their ability to interfere with other states' broadcasts and by their membership in the International Telecommunication Union (ITU).

In the area of telecommunications, technological change has altered the capabilities of actors and increased distributional conflicts. International regimes, in turn, have changed in response to these changes in capabilities. More precisely, technological innovation gave some private actors, primarily domiciled in the United States, an incentive to press for a more competitive telecommunications regime both domestically and internationally. The direct and indirect economic bargaining power conferred by these new technologies gave the United States the leverage to secure some changes in the extant regime (which had legitimated national monopolies) either through direct pressure or by changing the international market incentives confronting other actors (Cowhey 1990: 169–99).

Modifications of the regime have been initiated by public threats of defection or unilateral action. Cooperation theory—which has focused heavily on market failures arising from dilemmas of common interests and on the need for regimes that provide information to facilitate monitoring and enforcement—is not relevant for global communications.

Radio and television broadcasting

Radio broadcasting

There is no international agreement on the fundamental issue associated with international radio broadcasting: the right to transmit signals across state boundaries without the prior consent of the target country. States have not agreed on basic principles and norms, save that of noninterference with existing transmissions. Some states, notably Western market-oriented democracies, have defended the right to the free and open dissemination of information. Others, the Soviet Union and some Third World states, urged either that prior consent be obtained before broadcasting across international boundaries or that the content of international broadcasts be controlled. Although states have episodically condemned the broadcasting of hostile propaganda, they have failed to move toward any operational defini- tion. Those few international agreements that have been endorsed are filled with the kind of confusing and contradictory language that betrays under- lying disagreements about principles and norms. For instance, Article 44 of the Atlantic City Telecommunications Convention, which was endorsed by the UN General Assembly in December 1950, condemns the jamming of radio broadcasts, but it also cautions that states should "refrain from radio broadcasts that would mean unfair attacks or slanders against other peoples anywhere" (Gross 1979: 208–9; Murty 1968: 3–4, 109–10; D. Marks 1983: 46–55; Martin 1958: 78–79).

Given these disagreements, as well as the inability of states to block access to their own territory completely, the advocates of open dissemination have prevailed. In radio broadcasting, technology provides senders with more capability than is available to their targets. One of the basic attributes of de facto sovereignty, the ability to regulate transborder flows, has been com- promised by the international transmission of hertzian waves. States with adequate resources can build globe-spanning transmitting facilities, but tar- gets cannot completely block access to their own territory. Inexpensive radio receivers, compatible with international as well as national broadcasts, are readily available. Transmitting units are much cheaper than those for televi- sion. Radio signals can travel long distances without resort to satellites or other devices that might be monitored or controlled by national authorities. Unlike telephone and transborder data flows, it is not necessary to be hooked into a national network that can be regulated by state authorities. Jamming is difficult and expensive.

On the basis of the principle that states had sovereign control over their own airspace, the initial reaction to international radio in the 1920s and 1930s was that states had the right to control hertzian waves moving through their atmosphere. At the same time, however, states asserted the right to assign any frequency, provided that it did not interfere with broadcasts ori- ginating in another state. It was this principle that prevailed. By exercising the power to send out signals, subject only to the proviso of noninterference, states tacitly rejected sovereign control over radio waves transmitted through territorial airspace. Despite a number of vaguely worded resolutions about war propaganda in both the League of Nations and the United Nations, there has been no international agreement on norms that would limit the content of international radio broadcasting (Martin 1958: 71–75, 78–81).

There is a great deal of international broadcasting. During the First World War, Germany used radio for propaganda purposes. The earliest broadcasts were in Morse code and, hence, accessible to only a very small audience. In the 1920s the Soviet Union began the systematic use of radio as a pro- paganda tool. In the following decade the use of radio for international propaganda increased dramatically: by 1939 some 25 countries had interna- tional transmissions. And all of the major combatants in the Second World

War broadcast propaganda messages. The United States, which had relied on commercial stations before the war, created the Voice of America in 1942. Another burst of activity was prompted by the beginning of the Cold War in the late 1940s. By 1983 there were at least eighty countries with international services, and the major broadcasters—the United States, the Soviet Union, China, Germany, and the United Kingdom—were sending signals in more than thirty languages. There are also large commercial stations that beam their signals to other countries, such as Radio Luxembourg, Radio Monte Carlo, and various international religious broadcasters (Bumpus and Skelt 1985: 7–11, 20–31, 31–46, Chs 7–8).

Efforts by receiving countries to block international radio transmissions have had only limited success. Jamming has been used almost since the inception of international broadcasting. Austria, Germany, and Italy jammed foreign broadcasts during and before the Second World War. The Soviet Union has jammed since the 1930s. Spain under Franco, some Middle Eastern countries, and China have also engaged in jamming (Bumpus and Skelt 1985: 100–102; Murty 1968: 56; Martin 1958: 85–86).

States have also attempted to control what their citizens can hear by limiting the capacity of radio receivers. In 1951, according to one study, only 18 per cent of radio receivers in the Soviet Union were capable of direct reception; the rest could receive only over wires. South Africa developed an ultrahigh frequency network and produced sets with only one wave band, making it impossible to receive international broadcasts. Ghana at one time sold sets capable of receiving only a few stations.

Efforts to impede the reception of radio transmissions have never been fully effective, however. Jamming requires both long- and short-range stations, and, even with extensive capital investment, it is difficult to block all signals. Western broadcasts to the Soviet Union, for instance, have operated on as many as sixty frequencies and can cozy up to Soviet stations (Eyal 1986: 2). Furthermore, efforts at state control may only increase the curiosity of potential listeners. Radio receivers are too widely available and too easily altered to permit effective state regulation.

States have even had difficulty coping with pirate stations. Northern Europe has been the most fertile ground for pirate radio stations, because government-based monopolies limit options for listeners. In Italy and France land-based pirates were so successful that the respective governments were forced to legitimate them. Spain refused to sign a European agreement that would have prohibited Spanish subjects from supplying and repairing pirate stations at sea. British regulations impeded, but did not eliminate, pirate stations in the London area (Boyd 1986: 83–94).

In sum, the technology of radio broadcasting has made state control of transborder radio transmissions extremely difficult. Hertzian waves do not recognize political boundaries. The technology of radio, unlike that of television, developed one universal standard: a receiver that worked in one country would also work in another. Radio signals could be transmitted over very long distances. Because states have disagreed about the basic principles and norms that should govern radio broadcasts and because the available technology gives senders more power than receivers, there is no international regime for radio broadcasting. Those states that favor the open dissemination of information (or propaganda, depending on one's perspective) have prevailed.

Television broadcasting

The international spillover of signals has been less problematic for television than for radio. This difference, however, is more a reflection of the relative power imparted by technology than of any agreement on principles and norms: television is less geographically promiscuous. As ground-based television broadcasts do not travel long distances, spillovers have been limited to contiguous geographic areas. Even with the larger footprint of direct broadcasting satellites, signals are still regionally contained.

Although terrestrial TV signals can travel only a few hundred miles, there have been at least 24 cases in which broadcasting affected another country. The United States licensed TV stations aiming at a primarily Canadian audience. Israel initially tried to keep out television entirely because it was regarded as lowering cultural standards, but the government ultimately capitulated because Israeli citizens were receiving broadcasts from stations in Arab countries that carried many American programs. Hungarian and Czechoslovakian televisions were converted so that they could receive broadcasts from neighboring Western countries, a more complicated procedure than altering a radio, but one that could be performed by many television technicians. Most significantly, West German television could be received in most of East Germany. It was so popular that the East German government was compelled to install cable around Dresden, the one part of the country that could not directly receive Western broadcasts—this, to attract workers to the area (Quester 1990: 30, 105, 113–14, 126–30). The development of direct-broadcasting satellites (DBS) posed more substantial challenges to national control. Initially, DBS, like radio, appeared to be a technology that could circumvent state control, because any individual with a television receiver could access transmissions from other countries. This fear has proven to be unfounded, though; interstate agreements have effectively regulated most satellite television broadcasts.

International agreements have endorsed the principle that television signals should be limited as much as possible to national markets. The 1971 World Administrative Radio Conference (WARC) on space telecommunications concluded in part that DBS spillover should be minimized unless there was an explicit agreement among countries. WARC delegates have agreed to utilize different channels, different orbital positions, and different polarizations for their transmissions from direct-broadcasting satellites. If these provisions were breached there would be interference with the broadcasts. Implied by the WARC agreements, therefore, was the de facto acceptance of the principle of no broadcasting without prior consent (Gorove 1985: 8, 58; Blatherwick 1987: 42, 47).

Agreement, however, has been limited to areas where states have shared interests and relatively equal power. Europe offers the prime example. European states have authorized the expansion of direct-broadcasting satellites as one manifestation of a more integrated Europe; they have also, however, imposed restrictions on advertising and content and encouraged the development of more European programming. Commenting on American objections to a Community directive that at least 50 per cent of programming— excluding sports, game shows, and advertisements—be produced in Europe, Jacques Delors, the president of the European Commission, stated: "I say to the United States, 'Have we the right to exist, to perpetuate our traditions?'" (*Europe* 1989, April: 29; *Financial Times* 1989, 15 June; *New York Times* 1989, 4 October: C17).

In contrast, there has been no agreement on broadcasting between Cuba and the United States. The United States has beamed television signals at Cuba, and the Cuban government has jammed them. Likewise, West Germany consciously acted to penetrate East Germany. When East Germany adopted a color TV system that was incompatible with West German broadcasts (the black and white systems had been the same), the West Germans began broadcasting on both their own and the East German standard (Quester 1990: 126).

In sum, land-based television broadcasting has presented less of a problem than radio because the available technology has limited reception; nevertheless, politically controversial spillovers did occur in the Middle East and Europe. When direct-broadcasting satellites increased the footprint of signals, states with the same preferences and the mutual ability to interfere with each other's broadcasts, such as the members of the European Community (EC), could coordinate, but those with disagreements, such as Cuba and the United States, could not. Where disagreements on the principle of prior consent existed, the pay-off matrix was Deadlock. There was no agreement because for both parties the first best choice was unilateral uncoordinated action. Those states favoring open access prevailed because the distribution of power, derived from the available technology, made it easier to transmit successfully than to block radio and television transmissions. The issue was where states would end up on the Pareto frontier, not how to get there. Assuming no agreement on principles, the future of state control will depend on power derived from technological choices. It would, for instance, be easier to regulate transmissions sent through fiber-optic cables than those sent via satellites (Quester 1990: 138–39).

Remote sensing

Remote sensing is another issue-area in which there is no agreement on basic principles and therefore no foundation for an international regime. Remote sensing involves electronic information-gathering from satellites. States have disagreed about basic principles and norms—the right to sense versus the need to secure prior consent from the target state. Power is asymmetrically distributed: target states have not been able to block sensing probes. The behavior of those more powerful states that are able to engage in remote sensing has been constrained only by the need to secure territorial access to make use (usually commercial) of some of the data secured from satellite probes.

The first American remote sensing satellite was launched in 1972. A number of countries, including India, China, France, and Japan, have their own programs. These satellites can gather important strategic and commercial data from anywhere. It is very difficult, and in many cases impossible, for sensed states to disrupt this process (as distinct, say, from the possibilities in systems with gateways such as oceanic cables that are easily accessible to state authorities). While some commercial applications of data gathered by remote sensing, such as the exploitation of minerals, do ultimately require territorial access, other kinds of information, such as the deployment of military forces or the prospects for crop yields, do not.

The international rules that have evolved in the area of remote sensing are not constraining (Soroos 1986: 340). The UN General Assembly has endorsed the following principles: remote sensing is not to be carried out in a way that would be detrimental to the sensed state; sensed states are to be allowed to participate in programs and are to be given access to processes as well as raw data; sensing states are to notify the UN of their programs. The United States, the Soviet Union, and Japan, however, have stated that they do not regard these rules as legally binding (Blatherwick 1987: 72–76).

A number of possible regimes were rejected. Developing countries had initially endorsed the view that there should be no remote sensing without the prior approval of the sensed state (Blatherwick 1987: 62–64). But without the ability to block satellite probes, states could not enforce such a rule or compel others to accept it. Sweden had advocated the creation of an international regime similar to that for satellite communications, in which control over the gathering and dissemination of remote sensing data would be subject to a formal international agreement. This too failed (Blatherwick 1987: 74–77). Unlike telecommunications, where the technology would be useless or its benefits severely curtailed without state-authorized territorial access, remote sensing allowed actors in one state to secure useful information about conditions in another without formal approval.

Nonetheless, remote sensing has not entirely evaded the control of sensed states. From the outset, the United States accepted the fact that the commercial benefits of its remote sensing program would be limited unless it engaged the support of other countries. It backed the development of local receiving stations and made the raw data secured from its LANDSAT available to all comers at affordable prices, an approach that coincided with the traditional American commitment to the free flow of information. Not surprisingly, this openness was not extended to the security arena; satellite photographs with very fine resolution remain highly classified (Blatherwick 1987: 57, 77).

Hence in the area of remote sensing, as with radio and television broadcasting, there is no agreement with regard to the basic principle of prior consent, that is, the right of a national state to control access to its own territory. Remote sensing is an area in which more powerful states have not confronted problems of coordination or distribution. Consequently, their first best solution was to act unilaterally; they have provided target states with some information because the latter had the power to control the territorial access necessary to realize some of the commercial benefits of remote sensing.

The electromagnetic spectrum

In the last two issue-areas related to international communication considered in this paper—allocation of the electromagnetic spectrum and telecommunications—no state could achieve its objectives through purely unilateral action. The allocation of the electromagnetic spectrum involves a classic coordination problem. If there is no general agreement on frequency allocation, then broadcasts can interfere with each other. This can happen even if states agree on the principle of the open dissemination of information without prior consent. Distributional issues, which are also a factor, include determining which groups of broadcasters should have standing, allocating geosynchronous orbit slots for broadcast satellites, and, most important, defining the principle that should be used for partitioning the electromagnetic spectrum. Since the spectrum is a limited resource, who gets how much and why?

The International Telecommunication Union (ITU)—an intergovernmental organization and the various World Administrative Radio Conferences (WARCS) that it sponsors—has been the venue within which these issues have been resolved. States have played the decisive role because they are the only actors capable of enforcing agreements, that is, of controlling broadcasts emanating from within their own territory.

The major question associated with the electromagnetic spectrum has been the determination of principles and rules upon which allocation should be based. Occasionally this matter has been resolved on technical grounds; for instance, the spark wireless sets used on ships at the beginning of the twentieth century were inexpensive but very wasteful of the radio spectrum. They were eventually phased out.

Most competing claims have not been so easily settled, however: for instance, the allocation of geosynchronous orbits, which are the most efficient locations for broadcasting satellites. The claims of some equatorial states to sovereign control of slots above their own territory have simply been ignored by more powerful states. The allocation of these slots has been made at World Administrative Radio Conferences dealing with space orbits. These deliberations have given INTELSAT, an international consortium that controls most communications satellites, priority rights over national and binational satellite systems. INTELSAT had the support of Third World and other countries (Kavanaugh 1986: 93–106). The regime clearly mattered here because the venue for making this decision, the ITU, which sponsors WARCS, is a universal international organization based on the principle of sovereign equality: one nation, one vote. The issue here is not whether the Pareto-optimal frontier would be reached but which point along the frontier would be chosen.

In dividing up the spectrum there have been two rival positions. The first, which dominated allocation until very recently, has been that frequencies should be designated on a first-come-first-served basis, provided claimants could make effective use of the resource. The second, championed by less developed countries, has been that at least some portion of the spectrum should be allocated on the basis of sovereign equality. The concern of the developing countries is that by the time their needs increase, already developed countries will have claimed virtually all usable frequencies.

The principle of basing allocation on usage was agreed to very early. The 1906 convention on radiotelegraphy specified that certain radio bands be used for certain types of services. Radio frequencies were registered on a first-come-first-served basis. Countries notified the Bureau of the International Telegraph Union (the predecessor of the International Telecommunications Union) in Berne that they had established a communications channel. Other countries, in turn, were prohibited from interfering with stations that were on the Berne list (Codding and Rutkowski 1982: 13, 25–26). By 1980 this first-come-first-served set of rules had resulted in a situation in which the Soviet Union and the United States claimed half of the available frequencies and 90 per cent of the spectrum was allocated to provide benefits for 10 per cent of the world's population. (Krasner 1985: 229).

Developing countries have challenged the rules of the game based solely on present need, arguing that some part of the spectrum should be reserved for future demand. Delegates to recent WARCS have accepted this principle. Developing countries derived leverage from the fact that, as states, they had a presumptive right to participate in ITU conferences, which afforded them access to the relevant decision-making forums and facilitated coordination of their strategies. Unlike many other areas, in which least-developed countries (LDCs) have little or no directly relevant power capabilities (they cannot, with two or three exceptions, for instance, launch satellites, nor can they shoot them down), developing states can interfere with the signals of neighboring countries.

The political issues involving the international regime for allocating the radio spectrum were not generated by market failures leading to Pareto-suboptimal outcomes. Rather, they grew out of matters involving coordination with distributional consequences. Unilateral action would leave all actors worse off, but any form of coordination would privilege some over others. This is a classic Battle of the Sexes pay-off matrix. The point along the Pareto frontier that has been chosen—one at which most frequencies are still allocated on a first-come-first-served basis that benefits industrialized countries—reflects the existing distribution of power capabilities as manifested by the present demand for communications channels. Nevertheless, the preferences of developing countries have not been completely ignored; unlike the cases of radio broadcasting and remote sensing, where targets had little power, in the case of the electromagnetic spectrum Third World states could exercise some leverage through their votes in the ITU and their ability to interfere with broadcasts from other states.

Telecommunications

International telecommunications—telegraph, telephone, and transborder data flows—pose a fundamental coordination problem: assuring the economic and technical compatibility of international links. Choices also have distributional consequences. In recent years the most controversial aspect of these choices has concerned which actors could participate in global telecommunications and whether prices should be set by market competition or administrative fiat. The major impetus for change came from technological innovations that altered the interests, and ultimately the power, of the various public and private players. These technological changes led some actors, especially in the United States, to press for a more market-oriented regime, as opposed to one that legitimated national monopolies.

Despite astonishing technological changes beginning with the invention of the telegraph in 1836 and continuing through the initial deployment of high-quality fiber-optic cables and satellites in the 1960s, the international regime for telecommunications remained fundamentally stable. It was a regime based on national monopolies, usually public post and telephone and telegraph agencies (PTTS) but occasionally privately owned firms, as with American Telephone and Telegraph (ATT) in the United States. Prices were set through administrative fiat both nationally and internationally. The sending country could charge whatever it wanted for a call and paid a fixed fee to the receiving country. Senders were prohibited from routing calls along cheaper paths or from selling blocks of calls, which together essentially precluded price competition. Within countries, at least in the case of many industrialized countries, suppliers of telecommunications equipment were usually limited to national entities such as Western Electric, the equipment-manufacturing subsidiary of ATT before the latter was broken up (Cowhey 1990: 177–80; Drake 1989: 3–4, 11–15).

The history of international organizations dealing with telecommunications began with the International Telegraph Union, which was created after a meeting called by Napoleon III in 1865. (The name was changed to the International Telecommunications Union in 1932, when radio transmission was formally added to its portfolio.) The inaugural session dealt with such coordination problems as designating hours for sending and receiving, agreeing on a common code (the international Morse code), and setting technical standards. International cable links (the first telegraph cable was laid under the English Channel in 1851) were jointly owned by the operating entities at the termini of the cables. Like cables, international wireless communication, which was first developed at the end of the nineteenth century, had to be tied into national communications networks at a limited number of gateways, to provide telegraph or telephone service. States jealously guarded their right to regulate wireless communication, even between ships. National regulations frustrated an effort by the Marconi company, the original developer of such equipment, to set its own international rules (Codding and Rutkowski 1982: 19; Feldman 1975: 23–29, 48; Luther 1988: 19).

The International Telecommunication Union (ITU) and INTELSAT, the consortium created to launch and operate communications satellites, were designed to reinforce this system. INTELSAT was a common carrier for common carriers, not a rival for established national monopolies. Peter Cowhey has argued that the "regime was in fact a political invention so successful that it eventually disappeared from sight" (Cowhey 1990: 169). The old regime legitimated a system of national monopolies and administered prices so successfully that the ITU and its committees came to be viewed as little more than agencies for dealing with questions of technical compatibility.

In recent years the fundamental principles and rules of the old regime—national monopolies and administered prices—have been challenged by new actors with new power capabilities, the result of technological change. Telecommunications is eroding the distinction between voice and data forms of transmission. The microchip revolution created potent new equipment manufacturers. Communications systems have been linked with computers. Fax machines have obscured the difference between conventional mail and telecommunications.

New technologies gave large users and new equipment producers an incentive to change the extant system of national monopolies. Large users could reduce their communications costs by developing alternatives to those services offered by national PTTS. The producers of new equipment could realize greater economies of scale by accessing foreign as well as domestic markets (Cowhey 1990: 188; Drake 1989: 40–42, 46–48). More efficient telecommunications services could enhance the competitiveness of particular companies or even national economies. Unlike even the dramatic technological changes of the 1830s through the 1950s, the more recent developments have made it possible for individual companies to achieve greater efficiencies by developing their own telecommunications systems rather than relying entirely on national monopolies. For instance, beginning in the 1960s IBM developed its own communications system based on satellites and lines leased from PTTS. This system now extends to 145 countries (*Business Week*, special issue no. 3033–44, January–March 1988, p. 141).

It is not surprising that changing incentives have changed national policies. The United States has been at the forefront of the demands for a more competitive international system, one that would be based more on market competition than on public or private monopolies imposing state-authorized tariffs. Many of the large users and manufacturers that would benefit from a more competitive environment are domiciled in the United States. Moreover, the United States had already deregulated its domestic regime for telephone communications. Once the United States opened its own market to foreign manufacturers of equipment, it had an incentive to pry open the markets of its competitors as well (Aronson and Cowhey 1988: 218–23).

The United States has not been alone in pushing for a more competitive international environment. The United Kingdom and Japan have also supported change. Like the United States, these two countries are hubs of global communications and the home countries for major international financial and manufacturing companies that can derive large savings by introducing new communications facilities and services. The United States, the United Kingdom, and, to a lesser extent, Japan have supported what Cowhey has called the big bang—a major move away from national monopolies (Cowhey 1990: 191–95).

There was initially little support for the Anglo-American position. The European PTTS were not anxious to open their national markets to competition. But some of the large European companies supported change, if only because they feared that national restrictions would give an advantage to their American competitors, who worked in a more market-oriented system. The European Community eventually supported American initiatives to place services, including telecommunications, in the GATT negotiations, where the prevailing principles and norms were market-oriented, rather than solely within the purview of the ITU, which had historically legitimated national monopolies. Even within the ITU there has been some change. A 1989 agreement recognized the right of new entities, such as IBM, to operate under the same rules as established private phone companies (Cowhey 1990: 196; Drake 1989: 49, 66).

In response, the PTTS and their national governments have not simply acceded to demands for a purely market-oriented regime. They have used regulations and standards to maintain their national control, for example, prohibiting the connection of private lines to publicly switched networks, banning independent transmission facilities, and requiring PTT equipment for initial connections. Because of anxiety about budget deficits, pressure from manufacturers of new equipment, and perhaps the insistence of the United States, the Japanese government has privatized Nippon Telephone and Telegraph (NTT) and permitted some competition for international services, but it has not yet endorsed a free and open market. The EC is committed to introducing a free market for terminals, private branch exchanges (PBXS), and value-added services as part of the 1992 program. PTT monopolies may be limited to such basic services as telephones (H. Bauer 1990: 33–35).

Although the Canadian system is more open than those in Europe, it has more restrictions than that of the United States (Aronson and Cowhey 1988: 162, 178–80).

Changing national policies in the area of telecommunications reflect the way in which technological innovation can alter national power and policies. Once domestic deregulation had eliminated ATT's long-distance monopoly, the company's interest in preserving monopolies in other countries disappeared. Indeed, many American producers and users would be better off under a more competitive international system, but the United States could not impose a competitive system on other countries. It could, however, pressure other actors, most obviously by threatening to block access to the very large American market for equipment but also by adopting national regulations that would leave more restricted foreign telecommunications users at a competitive disadvantage. In sum, the international regime has changed. Although national monopolies still control basic domestic services in most countries, a wider range of telecommunications facilities has been introduced. There has been movement toward a more market-oriented international regime. A few large countries, especially the United States, have changed the incentives offered to other actors in the international system. Whatever the final outcome of the movement toward a more market-oriented system, the issues involved have not been ones of market failure. Nor is this a situation of harmony in which unilateral choices maximize both individual and collective interest. The tough bilateral and international negotiations over the rules governing the provision of telecommunications equipment and services suggest that while states need to coordinate their behavior, they also differ in their views about which is the most desirable point on the Pareto frontier.

Satellite communications

The case of the development and deployment of communications satellites raised issues of coordination yet again. On the one hand, the absence of coordination would have left all actors worse off; on the other hand, the choice of which form of coordination to adopt would inevitably have distributional consequences.

The initial international regime for communications satellites departed from existing practices in significant ways. International cables, the first means of transmitting messages across open waters, were usually jointly owned by various national operating entities. For satellites, INTELSAT, a new entity organized as a consortium of member states, was created. Instead of placing communications satellites under the purview of the ITU, where one-nation-one-vote practices would have given Third World and Eastern bloc countries some leverage, the new consortium distributed votes according to usage. This gave the heaviest users the largest number of votes. INTELSAT itself, rather than national operating entities, owned satellites, a departure from the practice governing international cables. Nevertheless, INTELSAT reinforced rather than challenged the prevailing system of national monopolies. Satellites that had at least the potential for point-to-point communication were not initially allowed to disturb the prevailing regime of national monopolies (Cowhey 1990: 181).

The United States, the prime mover in the creation of INTELSAT, had originally hoped to handle satellite communications through a series of bilateral agreements that would have maximized the bargaining power of the United States, with its substantial technological lead in the early 1960s. The Europeans countered with a proposal to create a new international organization that would constrain American influence. The idea of a consortium, the institutional arrangement that was ultimately accepted, was also proposed by the Europeans.

Given a new set of problems in which the power resources of the actors were different from those affecting radio and cable communications, the US and the major Western European states acted on their own to create a new organization rather than rely on an existing entity, such as the ITU or the United Nations Committee on the Peaceful Uses of Outer Space. The consortium reflected a distribution of power in which the United States controlled vital technology but other states still regulated access to their national systems. The Soviet Union and LDCs were excluded from the opening negotiations, although the United States did conduct bilateral talks with the Soviet Union. Japan, Australia, and Canada played peripheral roles.

In June 1964 the participants concluded an interim five-year agreement. Ownership and voting power would be based on usage, which gave the United States 61 per cent and Western Europe 30.5 per cent of the votes. Australia, Canada, and Japan received 8.5 per cent. Quotas could be adjusted to give developing countries up to 17 per cent, but no more. These arrangements allowed the United States to maintain a secure controlling interest—but with limitations. If there was disagreement on important issues, voting rules mandated that passage required 12.5 per cent of votes over and above the votes of the member with the largest number of votes. Hence, the United States could not act alone (Pelton 1974: 54–59).

Nineteen official actors (eighteen countries and the Vatican) signed the final agreement in July 1964. Membership in INTELSAT grew to more than a hundred countries. Voting power continued to be based on usage until INTELSAT was privatized in 2001.

The national power capabilities provided by technological and financial resources initially gave the United States the dominant role in INTELSAT, even if American policy makers failed to secure their first best institutional preference of bilateral arrangements. Not only did the United States have more voting power, but its designated operating entity, COMSAT (the Communications Satellite Corporation established as a joint venture for American participation in communications satellites), was recognized in the 1964 Interim Agreement as the operational manager for INTELSAT. Daily operations were entirely in COMSAT's hands. No INTELSAT secretariat or international civil service was specified by the Interim Agreement (Pelton 1974: 82). Over time, the influence of the United States eroded, as the underlying power capabilities of other states increased with the diffusion of technology. Negotiations for a permanent agreement to supplant the 1964 Interim Agreement took place between 1969 and 1973. These discussions resulted in a decrease in American control including a reduction in the role of COMSAT (Pelton 1974: 123; Kavanaugh 1986: 97).

By the 1980s INTELSAT actually hindered American efforts to create a more competitive market-oriented regime. The director general of INTELSAT argued in a 1986 article that

> one other conclusion which may be reached is that foreign policies and relations should not be the product of a "Johnny-one-note" economic philosophy. US estrangement from INTELSAT is not a desirable or viable alternative for world peace and understanding. And, while the currently popular economic trilogy—deregulation, pro-competition, and private sector predominance—may have its value and applicability, it is simply insufficient to serve as a complete litmus test for enlightened and effective foreign relations.
>
> (Colino 1986: 208)

The United States itself approved some new satellite operations in the 1980s, but with substantial restrictions that recognized the central role of INTEL-SAT. The FCC ruled that new operations could not connect with public switching networks, because they would have directly competed with INTELSAT's services. New systems could be established only with the permission of a foreign government and if they went through an INTELSAT review of coordination (Aronson and Cowhey 1988: 121–32).

By the 1990s, however, competition among satellite providers was growing. New companies complained about the privileged position of INTELSAT because of its intergovernmental status. Within INTELSAT there was concern that the cumbersome nature of decision making would damage INTELSAT's position in an increasingly competitive market. In 2000, the Congress passed the Open-market Reorganization for the Betterment of International Telecommunications Act (ORBIT Act), which required the privatization of INTELSAT. The importance of the American market and voting power within the organization gave the United States significant leverage. INTELSAT became a private company in 2001 (United States, Government Accountability Office 2004: 5–8).

The issue in the case of communications satellites was not market failure or monitoring adherence to agreements. Rather, it concerned the distribution of rewards. There are many points along the Pareto frontier. Those that have been chosen have reflected the relative bargaining power of states.

Conclusions

The literature on international regimes has focused on market failures. It has emphasized the possibility of mutual gains. When the logic of individual utility maximization leads to Pareto-suboptimal outcomes, appropriate institutional constructs can enhance well-being. Power, the conventional focus of the literature on international relations, is not necessarily inconsistent with this perspective. Robert Keohane has argued that what he calls the contractual approach is not a substitute for a power-oriented or interdependence position, but is rather a supplement to these "traditional modes of political analysis" (Keohane 1990: 746; Keohane 1984: 21).

Research programs, however, have both a denotation and a connotation. While the denotation, or explicit logic, of a research program based on the investigation of market failure is not inconsistent with a power-oriented analysis, the connotation of this research program is that power can be ignored. The connotation of a research program suggests which questions are most important, what kind of evidence should be gathered, and, often tacitly, which issues should be ignored. In a penetrating analysis of the positive theory of institutions, Terry Moe argues that

> over the last decade, as the positive theory of political institutions has developed as an intellectual enterprise ... [t]he theme that gets driven home again and again is that political institutions help mitigate collective action problems—and that this is why they exist and take the forms they do. While the positive theorists are well aware that politics is a game of winners and losers and that institutions are crucial means by which winners win and losers lose, this is not an equally important theme. All too often, it is not discussed at all.
>
> (Moe 1990: 1–2)

The research program that emerges from an emphasis on market failure, one specific manifestation of the problem of social choice, suggests that the most important issue is how to reach the Pareto frontier. Prisoner's Dilemma is the exemplary pay-off matrix, but other situations such as Stag Hunt or Chicken, all of which can result in Pareto-suboptimal outcomes, are also examined. Deadlock, the one other game that has been mentioned with any frequency in the cooperation under anarchy literature, is not extensively discussed because it is not analytically interesting. Battle of the Sexes is hardly noted at all as a possible pay-off matrix (Oye 1985: 12–18). Analysis involves investigating the kinds of institutional arrangements that can overcome the problem presented by a pay-off structure in which the Pareto-optimal outcome is not a Nash equilibrium. For example, although Keohane explicitly argues in *After Hegemony* that both power and exchange determine outcome, the most heuristically compelling section of the book, Chapter 6, examines the ways in which institutions can overcome problems of market failure by, for instance, increasing the symmetry and amount of information, making it easier to establish reputation across several issue-areas, and promoting convergent expectations. It is this chapter that has influenced the research program on cooperation, not Keohane's recognition of the fact that institutions are created within a power-driven context.

Power is ignored because the research program based on the analysis of market failure does not provide either heuristic insights or analytic techniques for investigating relative capabilities. Power recedes into the background not only because scholars have studied absolute rather than relative gains, but also because it is not evident how power is relevant for solving problems of market failure. If the purpose of international regimes is to enhance both the amount and the symmetry of information so that states can be more confident that they can prevent cheating, then the cognitive ability to construct efficacious institutional arrangements is more important than national power capabilities. Cleverness can make everyone better off.

Conversely, a power-oriented research program is not logically inconsistent with the analysis of market failure. But again, the connotation of such a research program pushes issues of Pareto suboptimality, cheating, and monitoring into the background. The most important issue for a power-oriented analysis is the distribution of capabilities and benefits. Charles Perrow, for instance, argues that there is always a struggle within an institution because control of the institution can bring with it a variety of rewards including security, power, and survival. Perrow criticizes economic analyses, such as the principal-agent literature, for ignoring the distribution of power (Perrow 1986: 132, 230, 257–58). For a power-oriented research program, power is exercised not to facilitate cooperation but to secure a more favorable distribution of benefits. And analysis seeks to explain outcomes in terms of interests and relative capabilities rather than in terms of institutions designed to promote Pareto optimality.

The primary motivation for establishing international regimes for international telecommunications has been to solve coordination problems that have distributional consequences—not to address problems of market failure. States wanted some set of rules for the allocation of the electromagnetic spectrum and international telecommunications including satellites, because the failure to coordinate policies on noninterference and on the compatibility of national networks would have left everyone worse off. But because the decisions would be consequential for the distribution of rewards, conflict arose over how such coordination problems should be resolved, that is, where along the Pareto frontier they would end up. While all actors were better off with some form of coordination rather than none, the form of coordination adopted would affect them differently.

The regimes that have been established for the allocation of the radio spectrum and international telecommunications have reflected the relative power of states and have changed as the distribution of power has changed. Regimes were not irrelevant; without at least some shared rules all actors would have been worse off. Power has been determined by three considerations: technology and market size, which have influenced the relative opportunity costs of change and therefore the ability to make credible threats; membership in universal international organizations, which has given states the presumptive right to influence policies that are affected by one-nation-one-vote decision-making procedures; and control over territorial access provided by juridical sovereignty.

For instance, INTELSAT became much less of an American preserve as the technological capabilities of other states improved. Third World states were able to secure some changes in the first-come-first-served principle of allocating the electromagnetic spectrum because they had a presumptive right to membership in the ITU and because, once they had their own broadcasting facilities, they could interfere with the radio signals of others. The United States was able to secure movement toward a more market-oriented regime for global telecommunications because some actors in other states feared that they would be put at a competitive disadvantage by unilateral American action, but US leverage was limited by the fact that state authorities controlled access to their own national networks.

In two cases—radio broadcasting and remote sensing—there has been no agreement with regard to the basic issue of whether sending states have to secure the prior consent of targets. States opposed to prior consent could secure a better distribution of rewards through unilateral action, that is, by broadcasting or sensing without the prior consent of target countries rather than by attempting to coordinate with those opposed to the free dissemination of information. Third World states secured some data from remote sensing because their approval for territorial access was needed to realize the commercial benefits of some information.

There has been no systematic classification of international regimes with regard to whether market failure, coordination, or distributional questions have been central. Are interactions among states best characterized by Prisoner's Dilemma, Stag Hunt, Deadlock, the Battle of the Sexes, or some other pay-off matrix? The literature on cooperation has focused on pay-off matrices in which cheating is a central problem because the Pareto-optimal outcome is not a Nash equilibrium. One of the attractions of Prisoner's Dilemma is that it lends itself to interesting manipulations (Jervis 1988: 317–49). The cooperation research program is academically attractive because it allows political scientists to deploy a heuristically powerful array of analytic tools developed by economists, not to speak of the appeal of identifying with a discipline higher on the social science pecking order and better able to present itself as a true science, Nobel prize and all.

How important is market failure for the study of international relations? It is illusory to suppose that this issue will be resolved on the basis of empirical studies. The literature now contains enough examples to suggest that both market failure and power-oriented research programs can present plausible analyses, often about the same issue.

There are, however, three aspects of the international system that suggest that a power-oriented approach is, in many cases, more appropriate than analyses based on market failure. First, there are some issues in international politics, especially but not exclusively related to security, that are zero sum. What is at stake is the power, that is, the relative capacity, of actors. Power-oriented concerns may be directed either toward altering the behavior of others or toward preserving one's own autonomy. Market failure is never at issue here; one actor's gain is another's loss (Jervis 1988: 33; Grieco 1990).

Second, in international relations it is possible to eliminate some players through the use of force or to compel an actor to accept an outcome that it would never agree to voluntarily. This is an option that is not analytically tractable for a market failure research program, which assumes that actors are in a position to make voluntary choices. The Austro-Hungarian Empire did not chose to dismantle itself after the First World War. Munich compelled Czechoslovakia to accept an outcome that left it absolutely worse off.

Third, even if states are interested in absolute rather than relative gains, the initial allocation of property rights will have distributional consequences, even if any particular specification of such rights can lead to a Pareto-optimal outcome (Coase 1960: 1–44; Conybeare 1980: 307–34). Different choices will differentially privilege different actors. For instance, Joseph Grieco's study of the nontariff barrier codes negotiated during the Tokyo Round suggests that conventional concerns about relative power are a more persuasive explanation of outcomes than neoliberal considerations involving cheating and information. Grieco argues that both absolute and relative gains must be included in the utility function of states (Grieco 1990: 40–49). Changing the rules for using the radio spectrum, or setting tariffs for INTELSAT, or lending IMF resources, or assigning landing rights for international airlines, or limiting whale catches would benefit some actors at the expense of others. The issue here is movement along the Pareto frontier, not how to reach the frontier. Power and interests, not monitoring capacity, determine outcomes. These three characteristics—concern with relative power, the ability to eliminate actors, and the assignment of property rights—are the core of much of the literature on international relations.

This is not to say that institutions or market failure problems are irrelevant. First, as John Ruggie, in particular, has elegantly argued, the existence of the basic actors in the contemporary international system—national states—must be understood in a larger, historically grounded institutional context. The issue here, however, is not the temptation to cheat and the ability to monitor but rather an understanding of how the players in the game came to exist in the first place (J.G. Ruggie 1983: 261–85). Second, the free-rider problem that emerges when there is a very asymmetrical distribution of power will lead to the Pareto-suboptimal provision of collective goods. In these circumstances, however, the problem is not cheating and monitoring but rather the fact that the more powerful state (or small group of states) prefers to provide the collective good regardless of what the smaller states do, and the smaller states prefer to defect regardless of what the larger state does. A situation of Prisoner's Dilemma arises only if there are a larger number of smaller states, no one of which is willing to provide collective goods unilaterally. Third, past institutional choices do influence the contemporary interests and power of actors exactly because such choices privilege some players at the expense of others.

Nevertheless, for a very large class of global issues, indeed the classic agenda of the study of international politics—security, autonomy, and the distribution of valued resources—power needs to be given pride of place. These issues are not characterized by the fact that Pareto-optimal outcomes are not Nash equilibria. Neoliberal speculations about the positive consequences of greater information are fascinating (even if empirical demonstrations of such benefits are scarce). But they obscure considerations of relative power capabilities, which draw attention to how the pay-off matrix was structured in the first place, how the available options are constrained, who can play the game, and, ultimately, who wins and who loses.

Acknowledgments

I would like to thank Peter Cowhey, John Ferejohn, Robert Jervis, Robert Keohane, Terry Moe, and especially William Drake, who is also especially absolved of any responsibility for the conclusions of this paper.

Part III
Sovereignty

8   Sovereignty and its discontents

Some analysts have argued that sovereignty is being eroded by one aspect of the contemporary international system, globalization, and others that it is being sustained, even in states whose governments have only the most limited resources, by another aspect of the system, the mutual recognition and shared expectations generated by international society. Some have pointed out that the scope of state authority has increased over time, and others that the ability of the state to exercise effective control is eroding. Some have suggested that new norms, such as universal human rights, represent a fundamental break with the past, while others see these values as merely a manifestation of the preferences of the powerful. Some students of international politics take sovereignty as an analytic assumption, others as a description of the practice of actors, and still others as a generative grammar (Cerny 1990: 13).

This muddle in part reflects the fact that the term "sovereignty" has been used in different ways, and in part it reveals the failure to recognize that the norms and rules of any international institutional system, including the sovereign state system, will have limited influence and always be subject to challenge because of logical contradictions (nonintervention versus promoting democracy, for instance), the absence of any institutional arrangement for authoritatively resolving conflicts (the definition of an international system), power asymmetries among principal actors, notably states, and the differing incentives confronting individual rulers. In the international environment actions will not tightly conform with any given set of norms regardless of which set is chosen. The justification for challenging specific norms may change over time but the challenge will be persistent.

The term "sovereignty" has been used in four different ways—international legal sovereignty, Westphalian sovereignty, domestic sovereignty, and interdependence sovereignty. International legal sovereignty refers to the practices associated with mutual recognition, usually between territorial entities that have formal juridical independence. Westphalian sovereignty refers to the exclusion of external actors from authority structures within a given territory. Domestic sovereignty refers to the formal organization of political authority within the state and the ability of public authorities to exercise effective control within the borders of their own polity. Finally, inter-dependence sovereignty refers to the ability of public authorities to regulate the flow of information, ideas, goods, people, pollutants, or capital across the borders of their state.

International legal sovereignty and Westphalian sovereignty involve issues of authority and legitimacy, but not control. They both have distinct rules or logics of appropriateness. The rule for international legal sovereignty is that recognition is extended to territorial entities that have formal juridical independence. The rule for Westphalian sovereignty is the exclusion of external authority from the territory of a state. Domestic sovereignty involves both authority and control, both the specification of legitimate authority within a polity and the extent to which that authority can be effectively exercised. Interdependence sovereignty is exclusively concerned with control and not authority, with the capacity of a state to regulate movements across its borders.

The various kinds of sovereignty do not necessarily covary. A state can have one but not the other. The exercise of one kind of sovereignty—for instance, international legal sovereignty—can undermine another kind of sovereignty, such as Westphalian sovereignty, if the rulers of a state enter into an agreement that recognizes external authority structures, as has been the case for the members of the European Union. A state such as Taiwan can have Westphalian sovereignty, but not international legal sovereignty. A state can have international legal sovereignty, be recognized by other states, but have only the most limited domestic sovereignty either in the sense of an established structure of authority or the ability of its rulers to exercise control over what is going on within their own territory. In the 1990s some failed states in Africa, such as Somalia, served as unfortunate examples. A state can have international legal, Westphalian, and established domestic author-ity structures and still have very limited ability to regulate cross-border flows and their consequent domestic impacts, a situation that many contemporary observers conceive of as a result of globalization.

This study focuses primarily on Westphalian sovereignty and, to a lesser extent, on international legal sovereignty. Domestic authority and control and the regulation of transborder movements are examined only insofar as they impinge on questions associated with recognition and the exclusion of external actors from domestic authority structures.

All political and social environments are characterized by two logics of actions, what James March and Johan Olsen have called logics of expected consequences and logics of appropriateness. Logics of consequences see political action and outcomes, including institutions, as the product of rational calculating behavior designed to maximize a given set of unex-plained preferences. Classical game theory and neoclassical economics are well-known examples. Logics of appropriateness understand political action as a product of rules, roles, and identities that stipulate appropriate behavior in given situations. The question is not how can I maximize my self-interest but rather, given who or what I am, how should I act in this particular circumstance (March and Olsen 1989: 24–26; March 1994: 57–58; March and Olsen 1998).

These two logics are not mutually incompatible but their importance varies across environments. If a logic of appropriateness is unambiguous and the consequences of alternative courses of action unclear, the behavior of actors (primarily rulers for this study) is likely to be determined by their roles. If actors find themselves in a situation in which they have multiple and contradictory roles and rules, or no rules at all, but the results of different courses of action are obvious, a logic of consequences will prevail (March and Olsen 1998). In a well-established domestic polity a logic of appropriateness will weigh heavily, although within the confines imposed by specific roles (president, general, senator, voter) actors will also calculate the course of action that will maximize their interests. Even in very well-settled situations, such as Swedish local governments, which Nils Brunsson uses to motivate his study of what he has ingeniously termed the organization of hypocrisy, actors never fully conform with the logic of appropriateness associated with their specific roles; they also engage in purely instrumental behavior generated by a logic of expected consequences (Brunsson 1989).

The basic contention of this study is that the international system is an environment in which the logics of consequences dominate the logics of appropriateness. Actors embody multiple roles, such as head of state, diplomatic representative, government leader, party organizer, ethnic representative, revolutionary avatar, or religious prophet, that imply conflicting rules for action. International rules can be contradictory—nonintervention as opposed to the protection of human rights, for example—and there is no authority structure to adjudicate such controversies. In most cases domestic roles will be more compelling than international ones, because domestic rather than international logics of appropriateness are most likely to dominate the self-conceptualization of any political leader. Moreover, the international system is characterized by power asymmetries. Stronger actors can, in some cases, conquer weaker ones, eliminating the existence of a particular state, although not necessarily challenging the general principles associated with Westphalian or international legal sovereignty. Conquest simply changes borders. But rulers might also choose to reconfigure domestic authority structures in other states, accepting their juridical independence but compromising their de facto autonomy, a policy that does violate Westphalian sovereignty. Stronger states can pick and choose among different rules selecting the one that best suits their instrumental objectives, as the European powers did during the era of colonialism when they "resuscitated pre-Westphalian forms of divided sovereignty" such as protectorates and subordinate states (Strang 1996: 24). In the international environment roles and rules are not irrelevant. Rulers do have to give reasons for their actions, but their audiences are usually domestic. Norms in the international system will be less constraining than would be the case in other political settings because of conflicting logics of appropriateness, the absence of mechanisms for deciding among competing rules, and power asymmetries among states.

The prevailing approaches to international politics in the United States, neorealism and neoliberalism, properly deploy a logic of consequences, although their ontology, states conceived of as unified rational autonomous actors, is not suitable for understanding some elements of sovereignty, especially the extent to which the domestic autonomy of states has been compromised. Various efforts to employ a logic of appropriateness, reflected most prominently in the English school and more recent constructivist treatments, understate the importance of power and interest and overemphasize the impact of international, as opposed to domestic, roles and rules.

Both international legal sovereignty and Westphalian sovereignty can be defined by clear rules or logics of appropriateness, recognize juridically independent territorial entities, and exclude external authority structures from the territory of the state. Yet both of these logics have been violated, more frequently for Westphalian sovereignty than international legal sovereignty, because logics of consequences can be so compelling in the international environment. Rulers have found that it is in their interest to break the rules. Violations of international legal sovereignty have taken place through mutual agreement, since recognition depends on the voluntary acceptance of other states. Violations of Westphalian sovereignty have occurred through both voluntary agreements, and coercion and imposition.

The starting point for this study, the ontological givens, are rulers, specific policy makers, usually but not always the executive head of state. Rulers, not states—and not the international system—make choices about policies, rules, and institutions. Whether international legal sovereignty and Westphalian sovereignty are honored depends on the decisions of rulers. There is no hierarchical structure to prevent rulers from violating the logics of appropriateness associated with mutual recognition or the exclusion of external authority. Rulers can recognize another state or not; they can recognize entities that lack juridical independence or territory. They can intervene in the internal affairs of other states or voluntarily compromise the autonomy of their own polity.

Any actor-oriented approach must start with simple assumptions about the underlying preferences of actors. These preferences must be applicable to all actors across space and time. If the preferences, the underlying interests of actors, are problematic, then the preferences become something to be explained rather than something that can do the explaining. The assumption of this study is that rulers want to stay in power and, being in power, they want to promote the security, prosperity, and values of their constituents. The ways in which they accomplish these objectives will vary from one state to another. Some rulers need to cultivate their military; others seek a majority of votes. Some will enhance their position by embracing universal human rights; others succeed by endorsing exclusionary nationalism. Some are highly dependent on external actors for their financial support; others rely almost exclusively on domestic sources.

International legal sovereignty has been almost universally desired by rulers, including rulers who have lacked juridical independence. Recognition provides benefits and does not impose costs. Recognition facilitates treaty making, establishes diplomatic immunity, and offers a shield against legal actions taken in other states. International legal sovereignty can indicate to domestic actors that a particular ruler is more likely to remain in power, if only because that ruler can more easily secure external resources.

The basic rule of international legal sovereignty, that mutual recognition be extended among formally independent territorial entities, has never been universally honored. The fact that rulers want recognition does not mean that they will always get it. Nonrecognition has been used as an instrument of policy. Rulers with territory and juridical and de facto autonomy, such as the Chinese communist regime from 1949 to the 1970s, have not been recognized. At the same time rulers have recognized entities lacking in formal juridical autonomy—Byelorussia and the Ukraine were members of the United Nations. Even entities without territory have been recognized. The Iranian mullahs had a better chance of staying in power in 1979 by violating diplomatic immunity (a long-standing rule associated with international legal sovereignty) than by honoring it. These departures from the standard norm have not, however, generated alternative logics of appropriateness.

While almost all states in the international system have enjoyed international recognition (even if other kinds of entities are sometimes recognized as well), many fewer states have enjoyed Westphalian sovereignty. Rulers have frequently departed from the principle that external actors should be excluded from authority structures within the territory of their own or other states. Westphalian sovereignty can be violated through both intervention and invitation. More powerful states have engaged in intervention, coercing public authorities in weaker states to accept externally dictated authority structures. Rulers have also issued invitations, voluntary policies that compromise the autonomy of their own polity, such as signing human rights accords that establish supranational judicial structures, or entering into international loan agreements that give the lender the right not just to be paid back but also to influence domestic policies and institutions. The norm of autonomy, the core of Westphalian sovereignty, has been challenged by alternatives including human rights, minority rights, fiscal responsibility, and the maintenance of international stability. Moreover, in the international system principled claims have sometimes merely been a rationalization for exploiting the opportunities presented by power asymmetries.

The multiple pressures on rulers have led to a decoupling between the norm of autonomy and actual practice. Talk and action do not coincide. Rulers might consistently pledge their commitment to nonintervention but at the same time attempt to alter the domestic institutional structures of other states, and justify this practice by alternative norms such as human rights or opposition to capitalism. Rulers must speak to and secure the support of different constituencies making inconsistent demands (Brunsson 1989: 27–31). Nationalist groups agitate for an end to external influence; the International Monetary Fund (IMF) insists on a legitimated role in domestic policy formation. Rulers might talk nonintervention to the former, while accepting the conditionality terms of the latter. For rulers making choices in an anarchic environment in which there are many demands, multiple norms, power asymmetries, and no authoritative decision-making structures, adhering to Westphalian sovereignty might, or might not, maximize their utility.

Outcomes in the international system are determined by rulers whose violation of, or adherence to, international principles or rules is based on calculations of material and ideational interests, not taken-for-granted practices derived from some overarching institutional structures or deeply embedded generative grammars. Organized hypocrisy is the normal state of affairs.

Violations of the basic rule of Westphalian sovereignty have occurred more frequently than violations of the basic rule of international legal sovereignty and have been more explicitly justified by alternative principles. Departures from the logic of appropriateness associated with international legal sovereignty have often been unproblematic because they involve agreements among rulers that are mutually beneficial; everyone is better off and no one needs to be convinced. In contrast, coercive violations of the logic of appropriateness associated with Westphalian sovereignty can leave some actors worse off; justifications in the form of alternative principles or rules have been offered, sometimes to convince targets and sometimes to ensure support from domestic constituents in those states engaged in coercion.

Four meanings of sovereignty

The term "sovereignty" has been commonly used in at least four different ways: domestic sovereignty, referring to the organization of public authority within a state and to the level of effective control exercised by those holding authority; interdependence sovereignty, referring to the ability of public authorities to control transborder movements; international legal sovereignty, referring to the mutual recognition of states or other entities; and Westphalian sovereignty, referring to the exclusion of external actors from domestic authority configurations. These four meanings of sovereignty are not logically coupled, nor have they covaried in practice.

Embedded in these four usages of the term is a fundamental distinction between authority and control. Authority involves a mutually recognized right for an actor to engage in specific kinds of activities. If authority is effective, force or compulsion would never have to be exercised. Authority would be coterminous with control. But control can be achieved simply through the use of brute force with no mutual recognition of authority at all. In practice, the boundary between control and authority can by hazy. A loss of control over a period of time could lead to a loss of authority. The effective exercise of control, or the acceptance of a rule for purely instrumental reasons, could generate new systems of authority. If a practice works, individuals might come to regard it as normatively binding, not just instrumentally efficacious; conversely, if a mutually accepted rule fails to control behavior, its authority might be rejected over time (Sugden 1989). In many social and political situations a logic of consequences, in which control is the key issue, and a logic of appropriateness, associated with authority, can both affect the behavior of actors (Wendt and Friedheim 1996: 246, 251; Onuf 1991: 430; Wendt 1992: 412–13; Shue, 1997: 348).

Westphalian sovereignty and international legal sovereignty exclusively refer to issues of authority: does the state have the right to exclude external actors, and is a state recognized as having the authority to engage in international agreements? Interdependence sovereignty exclusively refers to control: can a state control movements across its own borders? Domestic sovereignty is used in ways that refer to both authority and control: what authority structures are recognized within a state, and how effective is their level of control? A loss of interdependence sovereignty (control over transborder flows) would almost certainly imply a loss of domestic sovereignty in the sense of domestic control but would not necessarily imply that the state had lost domestic authority.

Domestic sovereignty

The intellectual history of the term "sovereignty" is most closely associated with domestic sovereignty. How is public authority organized within the state? How effectively is it exercised? Bodin and Hobbes, the two most important early theorists of sovereignty, were both driven by a desire to provide an intellectual rationale for the legitimacy of some one final source of authority within the state. Both were anxious to weaken support for the religious wars that tore France and Britain apart by demonstrating that revolt against the sovereign could never be legitimate (Skinner 1978: 287). Strayer, in his study of the early state, suggests that

> For those who were skeptical about the divine right of monarchs there was the theory that the state was absolutely necessary for human welfare, and that the concentration of power which we call sovereignty was essential for the existence of the state.
>
> (Strayer 1970: 108)

F.H. Hinsley writes,

> at the beginning, at any rate, the idea of sovereignty was the idea that there is a final and absolute political authority in the political community; and everything that needs to be added to complete the definition is added if this statement is continued in the following words: "and no final and absolute authority exists elsewhere."
>
> (Hinsley 1986: 25–26)

Later theorists from Locke, to Mill, to Marx, to Dahl have challenged the notion that there has to be some one final source of authority, but the work of all of these writers is concerned primarily with the organization of authority within the state.

Polities can be organized in many different ways without raising any issues for either international legal or Westphalian sovereignty. Authority may be concentrated in the hands of one individual, as Bodin and Hobbes advocated, or divided among different institutions, as is the case in the United States. There can be federal or unitary structures. The one point at which the organization of domestic authority could affect international legal sovereignty occurs in the case of confederations in which the individual units of the state have some ability to conduct external relations. This was the case, for instance, for Bavaria, which retained the right to independent foreign representation, although largely for honorary purposes, after German unification in 1870 (Oppenheim 1992, 247; Brierly 1963: 127–28).

The effectiveness of political authorities within their own borders may also vary without empirically or logically influencing international legal or Westphalian sovereignty. Whether operating in a parliamentary or presidential, monarchical or republican, or authoritarian or democratic polity, political leaders might, or might not, be able to control developments within their own territory. They might, or might not, be able to maintain order, collect taxes, regulate pornography, repress drug use, prevent abortion, minimize corruption, or control crime. A state with very limited effective domestic control could still have complete international legal sovereignty. It could still be recognized as a juridical equal by other states, and its representatives could still exercise their full voting rights in international organizations. The Westphalian sovereignty of an ineffective state would not necessarily be compromised. Domestic leaders might continue to exclude external actors, especially if these actors were not much interested in local developments. Domestic sovereignty, the organization and effectiveness of political authority, is the single most important question for political analysis, but the organization of authority within a state and the level of control enjoyed by the state are not necessarily related to international legal or Westphalian sovereignty.

Interdependence sovereignty

In contemporary discourse it has become commonplace for observers to note that state sovereignty is being eroded by globalization. Such analysts are concerned fundamentally with questions of control, not authority (Thomson 1995: 216). The inability to regulate the flow of goods, persons, pollutants, diseases, and ideas across territorial boundaries has been described as a loss of sovereignty (Mathews 1997; Wriston 1997). In his classic study, *The Economics of Interdependence,* Richard Cooper argued that in a world of large open capital markets smaller states would not be able to control their own monetary policy because they could not control the transborder movements of capital. James Rosenau suggests in *Turbulence in World Politics* that the basic nature of the international system is changing. The scope of activities over which states can effectively exercise control is declining. New issues have emerged such as "atmospheric pollution, terrorism, the drug trade, currency crises, and AIDs," which are a product of interdependence or new technologies and which are transnational rather than national. States cannot provide solutions to these and other issues (Rosenau 1990: 13).

While a loss of interdependence sovereignty does not necessarily imply anything about domestic sovereignty understood as the organization of authoritative decision making, it does undermine domestic sovereignty comprehended simply as control. If a state cannot regulate what passes across its borders, it will not be able to control what happens within them.

It is nowhere near as self-evident as many observers have suggested that the international environment at the end of the twentieth century has reached unprecedented levels of openness that are placing new and unique strains on states. By some measures international capital markets were more open before the First World War than they are now (Obstfeld and Taylor 1997). The importance of international trade has followed a similar trajectory, growing during the last half of the nineteenth century, then falling from the first to the fifth decades of the twentieth century, then growing after 1950 to unprecedented levels for most but not all states (Thomson and Krasner 1989). International labor movements were more open in the nineteenth century than they are now (Williamson 1996: 16, 18). Some areas have become more deeply enmeshed in the international environment, especially East Asia; others, notably most of Africa, remain much more isolated. Regardless of the conclusions that are reached about changes in international flows, there have still been considerable variations in national political responses. Increases in transnational flows have not made states impotent with regard to pursuing national policy agendas; increasing transnational flows have not necessarily undermined state control. Indeed, the level of government spending for developed countries has increased along with various measures of globalization since 1950 (Garrett 1998).

Interdependence sovereignty, or the lack thereof, is not practically or logically related to international legal or Westphalian sovereignty. A state can be recognized as a juridical equal by other states and still be unable to control movements across its own borders. Unregulated transborder movements do not imply that a state is subject to external structures of authority, which would be a violation of Westphalian sovereignty. Rulers can lose control of transborder flows and still be recognized and be able to exclude the authority of external actors.

In practice, however, a loss of interdependence sovereignty might lead rulers to compromise their Westphalian sovereignty. Indeed, neoliberal institutionalism suggests that technological changes, which have reduced the costs of transportation and communication, have led to a loss of interdependence sovereignty, which, in turn, has prompted states to enter into agreements (an exercise of international legal sovereignty) to create international institutions, some of which have compromised their Westphalian sovereignty by establishing external authority structures (Keohane 1984: 1995).

Thus the first two meanings of sovereignty, interdependence sovereignty and domestic sovereignty, are logically distinct from the basic concerns of this study—international legal sovereignty and Westphalian sovereignty. The structure of domestic political authority and the extent of control over activities within and across territorial boundaries are not necessarily related to international recognition or the exclusion of external actors, although behaviorally the erosion of domestic or interdependence sovereignty can lead rulers to compromise their Westphalian sovereignty.

International legal sovereignty

The third meaning of sovereignty, international legal sovereignty, has been concerned with establishing the status of a political entity in the international system. Is a state recognized by other states? Is it accepted as a juridical equal? Are its representatives entitled to diplomatic immunity? Can it be a member of international organizations? Can its representatives enter into agreements with other entities? This is the concept used most frequently in international legal scholarship, but it has been employed by scholars and practitioners of international relations more generally.

The classic model of international law is a replication of the liberal theory of the state. The state is treated at the international level as analogous to the individual at the national level. Sovereignty, independence, and consent are comparable with the position that the individual has in the liberal theory of the state (Weiler 1991: 2479–80). States are equal in the same way that individuals are equal. The concept of the equality of states was introduced into international law by Vattel in *Le Droit de gens,* first published 1758. Vattel reasoned from the logic of the state of nature. If men were equal in the state of nature, then states were also free and equal and living in a state of nature. For Vattel a small republic was no less a sovereign state than was a powerful kingdom (Brierly 1963: 37–40).

The basic rule for international legal sovereignty is that recognition is extended to entities, states, with territory and formal juridical autonomy. This has been the common, although as we shall see, not exclusive, practice. There have also been additional criteria applied to the recognition of specific governments rather than states: the communist government in China, for instance, as opposed to the state of China. These additional rules, which have varied over time, have included the ability to defend and protect a defined territory, the existence of an established government, and the presence of a population (Fowler and Bunck 1995: Ch. 2; Thomson 1995: 228; Oppenheim 1992: 186–90; Crawford 1996: 500).

The supplementary rules for recognizing specific governments, as opposed to states, have never been consistently applied. The decision to recognize or withhold recognition can be a political act that can support or weaken a target government. Weaker states have sometimes argued that the recognition of governments should be automatic, but stronger states, who might choose to use recognition as a political instrument, have rejected this principle. States have recognized other governments even when they did not have effective control over their claimed territory, such as the German and Italian recognition of the Franco regime in 1936, and the American recognition of the Lon Nol government in Cambodia in 1970. States have continued to recognize governments that have lost power, including Mexican recognition of the Spanish republican regime until 1977, and recognition of the Chinese Nationalist regime by all of the major Western powers until the 1970s. States have refused to recognize new governments even when they have established effective control, such as the British refusal in the nineteenth century to recognize the newly independent Latin American states until a decade after they had established effective control, the Russian refusal to recognize the July monarchy in France until 1832, and the US refusal to recognize the Soviet regime until 1934. The frequency and effectiveness of the use of recognition or nonrecognition as a political instrument have depended both upon the distribution of power (conflicting policies by major powers reduce the impact of recognition policies) and the degree of ideological conflict (Peterson 1982: 328–36; Peterson 1997: 32, 90–91, 187; Strang 1996: 24).

More interesting from the perspective of this study is not the fact that specific governments have been denied or given recognition, but rather that even entities, as opposed to specific governments, that do not conform with the basic norm of appropriateness associated with international legal sovereignty have been recognized. Entities that lack either formal juridical autonomy or territory have also been recognized. India was a member of the League of Nations and a signatory of the Versailles settlements even though it was a colony of Britain. The British Dominions were signatories at Versailles and members of the League even though their juridical independence from Britain was unclear. India and the Philippines were founding members of the United Nations even though they did not become formally independent until 1946 and 1947 respectively. The Palestinian Liberation Organization (PLO) was given observer status in the United Nations in 1974 and this status was changed to that of a mission in 1988 coincident with the declaration of Palestinian independence even though the PLO did not have any independent control over territory. Byelorussia and the Ukraine were members of the United Nations even though they were part of the Soviet Union (Oppenheim 1992: 145–46). Andorra became a member of the United Nations in 1993 even though France and Spain have control over its security affairs and retain the right to appoint two of the four members of its Constitutional Tribunal (Andorra 1993: Article 66). Hong Kong, a British colony and then part of China, became a founding member of the World

Trade Organization even though China was not. The Order of Malta is recognized as a sovereign person by more than sixty states even though it lost control of Malta in 1798 and holds no territory other than some buildings in Rome (Bradford 1972: 63–67, 117–23, 220, 226).

The uncertainty surrounding the recognition of specific governments, and even the violations of the principle that recognition should be limited to territorial entities that are juridically independent, has not reduced the attractiveness of international legal sovereignty for rulers or created an environment in which basic institutional arrangements have been challenged.

Almost all rulers have sought international legal sovereignty, the recognition of other states, because it provides them with both material and normative resources. Sovereignty can be conceived of as "a ticket of general admission to the international arena" (Fowler and Bunck 1995: 12). All recognized states have juridical equality. International law is based on the consent of states. Recognized states can enter into treaties with each other, and these treaties will generally be operative even if the government changes. Dependent or subordinate territories do not generally have the right to conclude international agreements (although, as with everything else in the international system, there are exceptions), giving the central or recognized authority a monopoly over formal arrangements with other states (Oppenheim 1992: 158, 245, 339–40; Thomson 1995: 219).

Even though the differences in treatment can be blurred, it is better to be recognized than not. Nonrecognition is not a bar to the conduct of commercial and even diplomatic discourse, but it can introduce an element of uncertainty into the calculations of actors. Ex ante they may not be able to predict how particular governments or national court systems will respond to an unrecognized government. Multinational firms might be more reluctant to invest.

By facilitating accords, international legal sovereignty offers the possibility for rulers to secure external resources that can enhance their ability to stay in power and to promote the security, economic, and ideational interests of their constituents. The rulers of internationally recognized states can sit at the table. Entering into certain kinds of contracts, such as alliances, can enhance security by reducing uncertainty about the commitment of other actors (Fowler and Bunck 1995: 142). Membership in international financial institutions opens the possibility, although not the assurance, of securing foreign capital. Even if rulers have entered into accords that have far-reaching effects on their domestic autonomy, such as the European Union, they have nothing to lose by retaining their international legal sovereignty, including their formal right to withdraw from any international agreements.

Recognition also provides a state, and by implication its rulers, with a more secure status in the courts of other states. The act of state doctrine holds, in the words of one US Supreme Court decision, *Underhill* vs *Hernandez*, that "Every sovereign State is bound to respect the independence of every other sovereign State, and the courts of one country will not sit in judgment

on the acts of the government of another done within its own territory"
(quoted in Oppenheim 1992: 365–67). In British and American courts,
recognition is consequential because the sovereign or public acts of a recognized state, as opposed to its private or commercial acts, cannot be challenged, and the property of a recognized state is immune from seizure.
Traditionally only the citizens of recognized states have been able to appear
as parties to litigation in the United States. If a government or state is not
recognized either de jure or de facto, then American and British courts need
not consider its legislation valid—for instance, in deciding whether a piece of
property has been legally transferred (Brierly 1963: 149–50).

Recognition also provides immunity for diplomatic representatives from
both civil and criminal actions. Representatives are not subject to any form
of arrest or detention, although the host country can refuse to receive, or
can expel, specific individuals. Diplomatic premises cannot be entered by
representatives of the host country. Diplomatic bags cannot be opened
(Oppenheim 1992: 1072–97).

The attractiveness of international legal sovereignty can also be understood from a more sociological or cognitive perspective. Recognition as a
state is a widely, almost universally understood construct in the contemporary world. A ruler attempting to strengthen his own position by
creating or reinforcing a particular national identity is more likely to be
successful if his state or his government enjoys international recognition.
Recognition gives the ruler the opportunity to play on the international
stage; even if it is only a bit part, parading at the United Nations or shaking
hands with the president of the United States or the chancellor of Germany
can enhance the standing of a ruler among his or her own followers. In an
uncertain domestic political situation (a situation in which domestic sovereignty is problematic), international recognition can reinforce the position of
rulers by signaling to constituents that a ruler may have access to international resources, including alliances and sovereign lending. Hence, international legal sovereignty can promote the interests of rulers by making it
easier for them to generate domestic political support not just because
they are in a better position to promote the interests of their constituents but
also because recognition is a signal about the viability of a political regime
and its leaders.

Like other institutional arrangements in the international environment,
however, international recognition is not a constitutive act in the sense that
the absence of recognition precludes the kinds of activities that recognition
itself facilitates. Governments have maintained administrative contacts and
signed agreements with governments they have not recognized; they have
exchanged trade missions, registered trademarks, accepted consular missions,
and concluded arrangements for the exchange of prisoners of war. Representatives of one state have had contacts with representatives of other states
that they have not recognized; for instance, the United States sent a personal
representative to the Holy See when the Vatican was not recognized by the

United States; US and mainland Chinese officials met in Geneva in 1954; the Vietnam peace negotiations in Paris from 1970 to 1973 took place when the United States did not recognize the North Vietnamese government; President Nixon went on an official visit to China in 1971 when the two countries did not recognize each other. National court systems have increasingly been given discretion by their own governments to decide whether the actions of nonrecognized governments will be given special legal standing. The US Protection of Diplomats Act of 1971 provides for the protection of diplomats even if their governments have not been recognized by the United States. When the United States recognized the People's Republic of China as the legitimate government of China in 1979 and withdrew recognition from the Republic of China (ROC), it established a special status for Taiwan. The Taiwan Relations Act stipulated that the legal standing of the ROC in American courts would not be affected, that Taiwan would continue to be a member of international financial institutions, and that the American Institute in Taiwan, a nongovernmental agency, would be created, in effect, to conduct the functions of an embassy (Oppenheim 1992: 158–73; Peterson 1997: 107–108, 140, 148–52, 197; United States, Congress 1979).

Whatever international recognition has meant, it has not led rulers to eschew efforts to alter the domestic authority structures, policies, or even personnel of other states, or to enter into contractual relationships that compromise the autonomy of their own state. International legal sovereignty does not mean Westphalian sovereignty. Moreover, it does not guarantee that legitimate domestic authorities will be able to monitor and regulate developments within the territory of their state or flows across their borders; that is, it does not guarantee either domestic sovereignty or interdependence sovereignty.

For instance, with American troops about to leave Italy in the summer of 1947 following the ratification of the Italian Peace Treaty, George Marshall, the American secretary of state, indicated to the US embassy in Rome that it must be stressed to General Lee (commander of allied forces) that "Govt Allied mil in Italy must respect scrupulously restoration Ital sovereignty upon coming into force treaty" (United States, FRUS: 1947, vol. 3 1972: 931). This message was sent at a time when the United States was intervening in Italian domestic politics by supporting the Christian Democrats, trying to restructure the Socialist Party, and attempting to weaken the position of the Communist Party. Marshall wanted to recognize Italy's international legal sovereignty, but he was completely unconcerned with Italy's Westphalian sovereignty, with the exclusion of American influence from Italy's domestic authority formations (Miller 1986: 243–63).

Indeed, international legal sovereignty is the necessary condition for rulers to compromise voluntarily aspects of their Westphalian sovereignty. Nowhere is this more apparent than in the European Union. In an interview shortly before the opening of the April 1996 European Union conference on governance in Turin, Jacques Chirac, the president of France, stated that:

"*Um sich erweitern zu können, muss sich Europa zunächst vertiefen, wobei es die Souveränität seiner Staaten respektieren muss*" ("In order for Europe to be widened it must in the first instance be deepened, but the sovereignty of each state must be respected") (*Frankfurter Allgemeine Zeitung*, 26 March 1996: 1). Chirac was arguing that the member states of the European Union must retain their international legal sovereignty, even while they were entering into agreements that compromised their Westphalian interdependence and domestic sovereignty, since the European Union can regulate transborder movements, the European Court exercises transnational authority, and some European Union decisions can be taken by a majority vote of the member states.

Finally, it should be obvious that international legal sovereignty does not guarantee the territorial integrity of any state or even the existence of a state. Recognized states have been dismembered and even absorbed, although this happened much more frequently before 1945 than since (Fazal 2007). The conquest of any particular state extinguishes the sovereignty of that state (domestic, Westphalian, interdependence, and usually international legal), but conquest is not a challenge to Westphalian and international legal sovereignty as institutional forms. It reconfigures borders but does not create new principles and norms.

Westphalian sovereignty

Finally, sovereignty has been understood as the Westphalian model, an institutional arrangement for organizing political life that is based on two principles: territoriality and the exclusion of external actors from domestic authority structures. Rulers may be constrained, sometimes severely, by the external environment, but they are still free to choose the institutions and policies they regard as optimal. Westphalian sovereignty is violated when external actors influence or determine domestic authority structures.

Domestic authority structures can be infiltrated through both coercive and voluntary actions, through intervention and invitation. Foreign actors, usually the rulers of other states, can use their material capabilities to dictate or coerce changes in the authority structures of a target; they can violate the rule of nonintervention in the internal affairs of other states. Rulers may also themselves establish supranational or extranational authority structures that constrain their own domestic autonomy; they can extend invitations, sometimes inadvertent, that result in compromises of their own Westphalian sovereignty. While coercion, intervention, is inconsistent with international legal as well as Westphalian sovereignty, voluntary actions by rulers, invitations, do not violate international legal sovereignty although they do transgress Westphalian sovereignty.

The norm of nonintervention in internal affairs had virtually nothing to do with the Peace of Westphalia, which was signed in 1648. It was not clearly articulated until the end of the eighteenth century by Emmerich de Vattel and might more accurately be referred to as Vattelian or even Westphalian/ Vattelian sovereignty. Nevertheless, the common terminology is used here because the Westphalian model has so much entered into common usage, even if it is historically inaccurate.

The fundamental norm of Westphalian sovereignty is that states exist in specific territories, within which domestic political authorities are the sole arbiters of legitimate behavior. While autonomy can be compromised as a result of both intervention and invitation, the former has gotten much more attention. For many observers, the rule of nonintervention—which is always violated through coercion or imposition, as opposed to voluntary invitation—is the key element of sovereign statehood. Robert Jackson writes that:

> The *grundnorm* of such a political arrangement (sovereign statehood) is the basic prohibition against foreign intervention which simultaneously imposes a duty of forbearance and confers a right of independence on all statesmen. Since states are profoundly unequal in power the rule is obviously far more constraining for powerful states and far more liberating for weak states.
>
> (Jackson 1990: 6)

The principle of nonintervention was first explicitly articulated by Wolff and Vattel during the last half of the eighteenth century. Wolff wrote in the 1760s that "To interfere in the government of another, in whatever way indeed that may be done is opposed to the natural liberty of nations, by virtue of which one is altogether independent of the will of other nations in its action" (quoted in A. Thomas and Thomas 1956: 5). Vattel argued that no state had the right to intervene in the internal affairs of other states. He applied this argument to non-European as well as European states, claiming that

> The Spaniards violated all rules when they set themselves up as judges of the Inca Athualpa. If that prince had violated the law of nations with respect to them, they would have had a right to punish him. But they accused him of having put some of his subjects to death, of having had several wives, &c—things, for which he was not at all accountable to them; and, to fill up the measure of their extravagant injustice, they condemned him by the laws of Spain.
>
> (Vattel 1852: 155)

Weaker states have always been the strongest supporters of the rule of nonintervention. During the nineteenth century the Latin American states endorsed this rule at international meetings in 1826 and 1848. In 1868 the Argentine jurist Carlos Calvo published a treatise in which he condemned intervention by foreign powers to enforce contractual obligations of private parties. The foreign minister of Argentina, Luis Drago, argued in a note to the American government in 1902 that intervention to enforce the collection of public debts was illegitimate. The Calvo and Drago doctrines became recognized claims in international law. At the sixth International Conference of American States held in Havana in 1928, the Commission of Jurists recommended adoption of the principle that "No state has a right to interfere in the internal affairs of another." This proposal, however, was rejected, in large part because of the opposition of the United States. The United States had engaged in several interventions in Central America and the Caribbean. The American secretary of state, Charles Evans Hughes, argued that the United States had a right to intervene to protect the lives of its nationals should order break down in another country. At the seventh International Conference of American States held in 1933, the United States finally accepted the principle of nonintervention. The wording that "no state has the right to intervene in the internal or external affairs of another" was included in the Convention on Rights and Duties of States and accepted by the United States (A. Thomas and Thomas 1956: 56–62). The Charter of the Organization of American States (OAS) stipulates that

> No State or group of States has the right to intervene, directly or indirectly, for any reason whatever, in the internal or external affairs of any other State. The foregoing principle prohibits not only armed force but also any other form of interference or attempted threat against the personality of the State or against its political, economic, and cultural elements.

In the latter part of the twentieth century nonintervention has been routinely endorsed in major international agreements such as the United Nations Charter and the 1975 Helsinki agreement, albeit often along with other principles such as human rights that are in tension with nonintervention.

While Westphalian sovereignty can be compromised through invitation as well as intervention, invitation has received less notice in the literature because observers have confounded international legal and Westphalian sovereignty. Intervention violates both. Invitation violates only Westphalian sovereignty. Invitation occurs when a ruler voluntarily compromises the domestic autonomy of his or her own polity. Free choices are never inconsistent with international legal sovereignty (Oppenheim 1992: 431).

Invitations can, however, infringe domestic autonomy. Rulers may issue invitations for a variety of reasons, including tying the hands of their successors, securing external financial resources, and strengthening domestic support for values that they themselves embrace. The rulings of the European Court of Justice, for instance, have legitimacy in the judicial systems of the member states of the European Union. IMF conditionality agreements, which may include stipulations requiring changes in domestic structures, carry weight because they are attached to the provision of funding.

Violations of Westphalian sovereignty can arise in a sovereign state system because the absence of a formal hierarchical system of authority, the defining characteristic of any international system, does not mean that the authority structures in any given political entity will be free of external influence. Wendt and Friedheim have defined informal empires as "trans-juridically sovereign states" (Wendt and Friedheim 1996). Formal constitutional independence does not guarantee de facto autonomy. A recognized international legal sovereignty will not necessarily be a Westphalian sovereignty.

In recent years a number of analysts have used the Westphalian model as a benchmark to assert that the character of the international system is changing in some fundamental ways. Writing of the pre-1950s world, James Rosenau contends that

> In that system, legitimate authority was concentrated in the policy-making institutions of states, which interacted with each other on the basis of equality and accepted principles of diplomacy and international law. Their embassies remained inviolable and so did their domestic affairs. Intrusion into such matters were met with protests of violated sovereignty and, not infrequently, with preparations for war. For all practical purposes, the line between domestic and foreign affairs was preserved and clearly understood by all. The norms of the Western state system lodged control over external ties in the state and these were rarely defied and even more rarely revised.
>
> (Rosenau 1990: 109)

Philip Windsor states that

> It is fashionable, at present, to suggest that the old Westphalian system of a world of non-interventionist states is on the decline, and that the dangers of growing intervention by different powers in the affairs of other states have been on the increase. The Westphalian system represented some remarkable achievements: the absolute sovereignty of a state rested on a dual basis whereby internal authority was matched by freedom from external interference; and in this way the principle of *cuius regio, eius religio*, codified in the Religious Peace of Augsburg, laid the foundation of the modern states system.
>
> (Windsor 1984: 45)

The way in which some analysts have understood sovereignty in terms of the Westphalian model is brought out clearly by authors who have studied minority or human rights, because claims about such rights are seen as a contradiction of sovereignty. In one of the most important studies of minority rights in the interwar period C.A. Macartney writes, "The doctrine of state sovereignty does not admit that the domestic policy of any state—the policy which it follows towards its own citizens—can be any concern of any other state" (Macartney 1934: 296). In a more recent study of human rights Forsythe suggests that

> The most fundamental point about human rights law is that it establishes a set of rules for all states and all people. It thus seeks to increase world unity and to counteract national separateness (but not necessarily national distinctions). In this sense, the international law of human rights is revolutionary because it contradicts the notion of national sovereignty— that is, that a state can do as it pleases in its own jurisdiction.
>
> (Forsythe 1983: 4)

Writing in the 1990s about the status of minority groups Kay Hailbronner claims that "Modern public international law seems to have broken through the armour of sovereignty" (Hailbronner 1992: 117). Similarly Brian Hehir has asserted that "In the Westphalian order both state sovereignty and the rule of nonintervention are treated as absolute norms." He then goes on to suggest that this Westphalian system is under an unprecedented level of assault (Hehir 1995: 6).

Despite these claims about unparalleled change, the most important empirical conclusion of the present study is that the principles associated with both Westphalian and international legal sovereignty have always been violated. Neither Westphalian nor international legal sovereignty has ever been a stable equilibrium from which rulers had no incentives to deviate. Rather, Westphalian and international legal sovereignty are best understood as examples of organized hypocrisy. At times rulers adhere to conventional norms or rules because it provides them with resources and support (both material and ideational). At other times, rulers have violated the norms, and for the same reasons. If rulers want to stay in power and to promote the security, material, and ideational interests of their constituents, following the conventional practices of Westphalian and international legal sovereignty might or might not be an optimal policy.

In sum, analysts and practitioners have used the term "sovereignty" in four different and distinct ways. The absence or loss of one kind of sovereignty does not logically imply an erosion of others, even though they may be empirically associated with each other. A state can be recognized, but its authority structures can be de facto subject to external authority or control. It can lose control of transborder movements but still be autonomous. Rulers have recognized entities that lack formal juridical autonomy or even territory, and they have denied recognition to governments that have exercised effective control over the territory of a recognized state.

The international system is complex. Information is imperfect. There are no universal structures that can authoritatively resolve conflicts. Principles and rules can be logically contradictory. Power asymmetries can be high. Widely recognized and endorsed principles will not always promote the interests of rulers. Logics of consequences can trump logics of appropriateness.

Modalities of compromise

Deviations from institutional norms and rules, whether of international legal or Westphalian sovereignty (or any other institutional arrangement for that matter) can occur in four ways: conventions, contracts, coercion, and imposition. These four modalities are distinguished along two underlying dimensions. First, does the behavior or policy of one ruler depend on that of another: is it contingent? Second, is at least one of the parties better off and none worse off: is the transgression Pareto-improving?

Rulers can join international *conventions* in which they agree to abide by certain standards regardless of what others do. Rulers can enter into *contracts* in which they agree to specific policies in return for explicit benefits. Rulers can be subject to *coercion,* which leaves them worse off, although they do have some bargaining leverage. Finally, rulers or would-be rulers can suffer *imposition*, a situation that occurs when the target ruler cannot effectively resist.

The Westphalian model has been violated through all four of these modalities: rulers have issued invitations that compromise their autonomy by joining conventions or signing contracts, and they have intervened in the internal affairs of other states through coercion and imposition. Departures from international legal sovereignty, especially with regard to recognizing entities that lack juridical independence or autonomy, have occurred less frequently and have depended primarily on contracts, Pareto-improving mutual agreements.

A convention makes rulers better off—otherwise they would not have accepted it—even if not all parties honor its terms. Contracts make at least one ruler better off and none worse off, but only if the participants honor their commitments. If one party reneges, so will the other. For rulers contemplating entering into conventions and contracts, the status quo remains available. Rulers are no worse off if they do not participate. Conventions and contracts are voluntary accords.

Coercion and imposition leave one of the parties worse off. In situations of coercion one ruler threatens to impose sanctions on another if the target ruler does not alter his or her policies. The target can reject these demands, in which case it suffers sanctions, or accept them. In either case the target is worse off. The status quo ante is no longer an option.

Imposition involves a situation in which the target has no choice. New authority structures may be imposed on the target state. Rulers may be forcibly removed.

Invitations, which compromise autonomy through conventions and contracts, violate Westphalian sovereignty but not international legal sovereignty; in fact, all contracts and conventions are facilitated by and are a confirmation of international legal sovereignty. What is critical for international legal sovereignty is that the contract or convention is voluntary.

Coercion and imposition involving issues of autonomy are violations of both international legal sovereignty and Westphalian sovereignty. Both coercion and imposition leave one of the parties worse off. The weaker actor would not have accepted an outcome inferior to the status quo ante if it were not faced with the threat of sanctions, possibly including the use of force. In the most extreme case, the target could be eliminated. Coercion and imposition violate a basic norm of international legal sovereignty, which is that states have the right to act voluntarily. Rulers would never voluntarily accept an arrangement that leaves them worse off.

The modality through which norms might be violated depends on configurations of power and interest. Imposition can only occur when interests are different and power asymmetries high. The initiator must have overwhelming power, the ability to determine the life or death, figuratively and sometimes literally, of rulers in the target entity (state or would-be state). Often this power takes the form of military resources, but in some cases it has involved the initial recognition not just of a particular government but of the state itself. Already established and powerful states have engaged in imposition by conditioning recognition on the target's acceptance of conditions related to domestic political structures. Rejection would mean that the target never becomes an actor. The status quo is an option, but the status quo, an absence of international recognition, would leave the ruler without a state to rule.

Coercion also can take place if the preferences of rulers are different and if there are asymmetries of power. For coercion, however, the asymmetries are less than is the case for imposition. The initiator cannot annihilate the target. The target ruler is worse off if he or she resists and suffers the imposition of sanctions, but the ruler does not cease to exist. The target is faced not with the alternatives of capitulation or nonexistence but with a choice between suffering the costs of sanctions or the costs of acceding to the initiator's demands. In situations of coercion the status quo ante is no longer an option.

For contracting to occur, there must be opportunities for cooperation; actors must have complementary interests, but power can also matter. All rulers are better off as a result of a contract, although some may be better off than others. Acceptance is always voluntary. The status quo ante remains an option; the ruler is no worse off if the contract is rejected. The terms of a specific contract may depend on the bargaining power of rulers, their ability to threaten credibly to stay with the status quo rather than conclude an agreement. In contracting, however, one ruler is never worse off.

Conventions only involve interests, usually ideational rather than material. Power is irrelevant. Rulers are not forced to join conventions; they can remain with the status quo and be no worse off. The behavior of one ruler, the extent to which he (or she) implements a convention, is not contingent on the behavior of others. Conventions are not likely to involve security or economic interests where contingent behavior matters; if one actor reneges, so will others. Rulers may, however, find that their ideational interests can be furthered, regardless of whether other signatories to a convention honor their commitments. Conventions can only occur if rulers have complementary or identical interests.

Violations of Westphalian sovereignty have been almost routine in international politics even though observers have been blinded to their frequency by the assumption that the Westphalian model has been operative. Violations of international legal sovereignty have been less common and have almost always been the result of voluntary decisions, contracting or conventions; rulers have mutually agreed to departures from the norm that international recognition should be accorded to juridically autonomous territorial entities.

Conventions

The conventions examined in this book relate to Westphalian sovereignty. These conventions are voluntary agreements in which rulers make commitments to follow certain kinds of practices involving relations between rulers and ruled within their own borders: commitments that are not contingent on the extent to which other signatories honor the same accord. These agreements can expose domestic practices to external scrutiny. To one degree or another a convention can violate Westphalian principles by undermining the autonomy of the state; conventions invite, although do not inevitably result in, external actors having some influence on domestic authority structures. In the most compelling example of a convention that violates Westphalian sovereignty, the European Human Rights regime, individuals within signatory states can bring cases against their own government in the European Court of Human Rights and the decisions of the court are binding on national judiciaries. In the weakest cases, signing a convention might have no effect on the de facto autonomy of a signatory state whose rulers might simply ignore its provisions.

Conventions are primarily a development of the twentieth century. The only example of a convention in the nineteenth century that I have discovered involves the rights of Polish nationals after the Napoleonic Wars. As part of the Vienna settlement, the rulers of the major powers committed themselves to preserving the national institutions of the Poles, even though Poland itself had been partitioned among Russia, Prussia, and Austria.

Many conventions have been signed in the twentieth century. In 1926 the League of Nations adopted a convention outlawing slavery. The International Labor Organization, which was created after the First World War, endorsed a number of agreements regarding the treatment and conditions of workers, all of which were conventions. For instance, the fact that one state violated the terms of the 1930 Convention Regarding Forced and Compulsory Labor, which stipulated that forced labor was to be paid at prevailing wages and would never be used in mines, did not mean that others would do so as well (Convention on Forced and Compulsory Labor, reprinted in Brownlie 1992: 246–56).

After the Second World War, the number of conventions increased dramatically. About fifty agreements involving relations between rulers and ruled have been ratified. Most have been adopted within the United Nations system, including broad statements of general principle such as the commitment to human rights in the Preamble to the Charter of the United Nations, and the United Nations conventions dealing with political rights and with social and economic rights, as well as accords on more specific issues such as slavery, women, children, refugees, stateless persons, genocide, and torture. There have been a number of regional conventions as well, the most consequential of which have been adopted in the Western hemisphere and Europe.

The enforcement and monitoring mechanisms for these conventions vary enormously. Some, such as the Universal Declaration of Human Rights, do not have the status of a formal treaty and are devoid of monitoring provisions. Others—for example, the conventions on slavery, the status of refugees, and political rights of women—provide that disputes can be referred to the International Court of Justice. No human rights cases have, however, been referred to the court. Others, such as the conventions on racial discrimination, apartheid, and the rights of the child, provide for the creation of committees that receive information and can, with the approval of the concerned states, investigate alleged violations.

The European Convention on Human Rights, which entered into force in 1953, and subsequent protocols have by far the most wide-ranging enforcement provisions and most elaborated organizational structure. The European Commission on Human Rights can hear complaints from individuals, non-governmental organizations (NGOs), and states; it receives about four thousand communications a year. The European Court of Human Rights can make decisions that are binding on national jurisdictions. The jurisdiction of the commission (composed of independent experts) and the court has been recognized by more than twenty signatories to the convention. Decisions of the commission and the court have led to legal changes in Belgium, Switzerland, Germany, and Sweden (Donnelly 1992: 82–83; Forsythe 1989: 19).

None of these conventions violates international legal sovereignty. The extent to which they have violated Westphalian sovereignty is an empirical question that can only be answered by examining behavior, not simply by looking at the terms of the agreement. Andrew Moravcsik has pointed out that the formal provisions of the Inter American human rights regime are as, or more, organizationally elaborated than the European regime, but have been less consequential because there has been less domestic political support (Moravcsik 1994: 54–55). In general, there has been no relationship between signing human rights agreements and respect for human rights.

There is no single explanation for why countries sign conventions. Rulers could sign because they expect that this would strengthen values and practices that they are committed to by tying the hands of their successors or making particular principles and norms more attractive to other rulers.

In the case of the European regime, the rulers of Western Europe, especially in those countries where democracy was fragile, wanted to reinforce democratic values. The existence of the regime made it more likely that citizens would have a clearer view of what constituted illegitimate state acts (Moravcsik 1998).

Where enforcement and monitoring provisions have been weak, as has generally been the case for human rights regimes, rulers might sign because, even though they are indifferent or antipathetic to human rights within their own state, they might believe that signing would make their regime appear more palatable to external and internal actors. Stalin's willingness to sign on to some human rights conventions could be viewed as a cynical act designed to make the Soviet Union more attractive to communist sympathizers in other countries. The Helsinki accords, which included human rights provisions, altered the behavior of groups in civil society in Eastern Europe, much to the dismay and surprise of their communist overlords, who had signed because they believed that the provisions of the accord dealing with borders and economic exchange would strengthen their position (D.C. Thomas 2001).

Rulers might also sign a convention because it is part of the script of modernity; it is something that a modern state does. When cognitive models provide the motivation for signing a convention, participation might, or might not, actually have an impact on domestic authority structures. In many cases, talk and action have been completely decoupled.

Contracts

A contract is an agreement between two or more rulers, or a ruler and another international actor, such as an international financial institution, that is mutually acceptable, Pareto-improving, and contingent. Contracts are always consistent with international legal sovereignty. Indeed, the ability to enter into agreements is one of the advantages of international legal sovereignty.

Contracts might, or might not, be consistent with Westphalian sovereignty. A contract can violate the Westphalian model if it alters domestic conceptions of legitimate behavior, subjects domestic institutions and personnel to external influence, or creates transnational authority structures. Obviously, many contracts between states do not transgress the Westphalian model. A military alliance, for instance, might commit one state to come to the aid of another, a trade agreement to end export subsidies, a financial accord to specify capital requirements for banks, an environmental treaty to limit fishing in international waters. Such arrangements do not alter domestic authority structures.

Rulers must regard a contract as Pareto-improving; otherwise they would not enter into it, since the status quo remains available. In contrast with conventions, however, the behavior of actors is mutually contingent. In contractual arrangements affecting Westphalian sovereignty rulers would not compromise the autonomy or territorial authority of their state unless the behavior of others also changed. If one actor abrogates the contract, others would do so as well. For both contracts and conventions rulers compromise Westphalian sovereignty through invitation; they are not the targets of intervention but rather voluntarily choose to insinuate external factors into their domestic structures of authority.

For more than three hundred years there have been contracts, often major international treaties, that have compromised Westphalian principles. It should hardly be surprising that under some circumstances rulers would find that their prospects for retaining office, or promoting the material, security, and ideational interests of their constituents, would be enhanced by entering into contractual arrangements that conceded domestic autonomy. The Peace of Westphalia contained extensive provisions for religious toleration between Catholics and Protestants in Germany. Germany had been devastated by the Thirty Years War, whose intensity was exacerbated by religious conflict. While Ferdinand III, the Habsburg ruler and Holy Roman emperor, would have preferred to repress the Lutherans and Calvinists, he lacked the resources to do so and, instead, accepted institutional changes in the empire that specified a consociational decision-making structure for religious questions (Lehmbruch 1997). In the Peace of Utrecht of 1713, the rulers of Europe agreed that France and Spain would never be unified under a single king, a decision that reflected a desire to enhance security by maintaining a system that could sustain a balance of power. The Treaty of Utrecht of 1731, in which France ceded Arcadia and the Hudson Bay to Britain, provided for the protection of the rights of Catholics living in these areas, a constraint on British autonomy that was accepted as part of the more general settlement from which Britain benefited. The Peace of Vienna protected the rights of Catholics living in the Netherlands; clauses stipulating religious toleration were included in the basic law of the Netherlands and could not, according to the treaty, be unilaterally changed by the Dutch themselves, because the major powers wanted to limit the possibilities of religious strife in the Low Countries.

Sovereign lending to weaker states in the nineteenth century, as well as the twentieth, frequently was conducted through contracts that violated Westphalian principles. When Greece was recognized as an independent state in 1832, it accepted a 60,000-franc loan, but the terms involved a commitment of specific revenues as well as the presence of foreign officials approved by the major powers of Europe. In 1881 the Ottoman Empire established the Council of the Public Debt controlled by foreign bondholders, which collected revenues and even engaged in development projects. By 1910 it had more employees than the Ministry of Finance. Again, the Ottoman rulers would have preferred to control their own finances, but it was better to have the foreign loan with the Debt Council than not to have the loan without it. In 1895 Serbia accepted a six-member Monopolies Commission, two of whose members were appointed by France and Germany, which controlled revenues from the tobacco, salt, and petroleum monopolies, revenue that went directly to foreign bondholders and not into the treasury of Serbia.

In the twentieth century sovereign lending routinely involved violations of Westphalian autonomy. International financial institutions, such as the World Bank and the International Monetary Fund, have institutionalized and rou- tinized practices that are inconsistent with Westphalian autonomy. These institutions do not simply offer funds on the condition that they be repaid; they extend resources only if borrowers are willing to accept changes in their domestic policies and often institutional structures as well. The European Bank for Reconstruction and Development, created after the collapse of the Soviet bloc, explicitly requires that member states have democratic regimes. Conditionality attached to loans from international financial institutions was initially supported by the United States but resisted at Bretton Woods by the representatives of European and Latin American states, who correctly assumed that they would be the targets of policies that were heavily influenced by American decision makers. Ultimately, the Americans succeeded in having conditionality written into the Articles of Agreement of the fund because the United States was the only source of significant capital in the 1950s.

Minority and human rights have also been promoted through contracts that violate Westphalian autonomy. Extensive minority rights agreements were concluded with all of the new states that were created at the end of the First World War. Most were the result of intervention through coercion or imposition. The leaders of most of the newly created states felt that they had no alternative but to accept the demands of the major powers. They did not want to guarantee minority rights but they were desperate for recognition. In a few cases, however, notably Czechoslovakia, Hungary, and the Baltic states, rulers offered invitations, voluntarily accepted protection for mino- rities, as part of a more general settlement that included their recognition as international legal sovereigns. After the Second World War Austria and Italy concluded treaties, contracts, covering the rights of the German-speaking minority in the South Tyrol. Germany and Denmark have made joint declarations about the status of minority speakers in the border areas of the two states.

Contracts have also been concluded that affected basic constitutional structures, not just specific institutions or policies. American practices in Italy and Germany after the Second World War involved contracts with national leaders that were designed to promote democratic regimes, or at least to exclude or repress communist influence; national leaders invited the influence of their American counterparts. In Italy, the Christian Democrats were happy to enter into these arrangements, which enhanced their own ability to stay in power. American rulers also assiduously cultivated non- communist leaders in Germany. They supported the Christian Democrats and other non-communist parties. Even in Germany, which was formally occupied until 1955, American rulers could not simply dictate outcomes. They had to contract with local leaders.

The European Union, which raises issues about the principles of both territoriality and autonomy, has been created through contracts entered into by the rulers of the European states. In the Treaty of Rome, the Single European Act, Maastricht, and other agreements, rulers have promoted their interests by establishing new institutional arrangements, some of which transcend territorial boundaries and compromise their domestic autonomy.

The regime for the law of the seas was developed in the 1980s and 1990s through a series of tacit and explicit contracts—that is, coordinated national policies and international agreements. One element of this regime is the exclusive economic zone (EEZ), which generally extends from 12 to 200 nautical miles from the shore. Within the EEZ littoral states have authority over mineral and fishing resources, but they do not have control over shipping. The EEZ does not violate autonomy; there is no exercise of external authority, but it does violate territoriality by creating an area within which states have authority over some issues but not others.

Hence, rulers have frequently concluded contracts that violate the principle of autonomy, and in some cases territoriality as well. They are better off with these agreements than without them, otherwise they would have stayed with the status quo. Better to have financial resources at lower interest rates and conditionality than to pay much higher rates or have no access to international capital markets at all. Better to have the European Court and mutual recognition (both of which violate autonomy) than not. Better for the rulers of Czechoslovakia to have an international regime for minority protection in 1919 than to leave the large German minority in the Sudetenland without any international guarantees, although in 1938 this did Czechoslovakia no good. Better for Italian Christian Democrats to accept aid and guidance from the Americans than to confront Italy's large Communist Party without external support.

Coercion and imposition

Coercion and imposition, both examples of intervention, exist along a continuum determined by the costs of refusal for the target state. With regard to Westphalian principles, coercion occurs when rulers in one state threaten to impose sanctions unless their counterparts in another compromise their domestic autonomy. The target can acquiesce or resist, but is always worse off than in the status quo ante. Imposition occurs when the rulers or would-be rulers of a target state have no choice; they are so weak that they must accept domestic structures, policies, or personnel preferred by more powerful actors, or else be eliminated, or, if they are polities that have not been recognized, remain in oblivion. The higher the cost of refusal for the target, the more a particular situation moves toward the pole of imposition. When applied against already established states, coercion and imposition are violations of the international legal, as well as Westphalian, sovereignty. When applied against the would-be rulers of not yet created states, coercion and imposition are violations of Westphalian sovereignty because the autonomy of any state that does emerge has been constrained by external actors, but not of international law concepts of sovereignty, which only apply once a state has secured international recognition.

Coercion and imposition, unlike conventions and contracts, must involve power asymmetry. Imposition entails forcing the target to do something that it would not otherwise do. There is no bargaining. Effective coercion can only occur if the initiator can make credible threats. The initiator has the ability, the power, to remove the status quo from the set of available options.

Coercion is not a common occurrence in the international system; the initiator must be able to make a credible threat. The clearest cases of coercion with respect to the Westphalian model have involved the use or threat of economic sanctions. In the twentieth century, sanctions were applied more than twenty times in attempts to improve human rights or alter the domestic regime of the target either by removing the ruler or changing institutional structures. Collective sanctions against South Africa with the aim of ending apartheid were authorized by the United Nations from 1962 until 1994. The United Kingdom enacted sanctions against Uganda from 1972 to 1979 to force out Idi Amin. The European Community used economic pressure against Turkey in 1981–82 to encourage the restoration of democracy. Between 1970 and 1990 the United States imposed sanctions against more than a dozen countries for human rights violations (Hufbauer *et al.* 1990). In all of these cases the target, even if it did not comply with the sanctions, was worse off than it had been because it could not both avoid sanctions and maintain its ex ante policies. Either it suffered sanctions, at least for some period of time, or it had to change its policies.

Imposition occurs when the target is so weak that it has no choice but to accept the demands of the more powerful. Force is the most obvious instrument of imposition. Imposition has been possible when there has been either a condominium among the major powers or the acceptance of spheres of influence. Great powers have been cautious about attempting to impose violations of the Westphalian model when such policies have been opposed by their major rivals, because mutual antagonism among the strong gives potential targets opportunities to maneuver.

Imposition has been employed in cases associated with minority rights, sovereign lending, and the basic constitutional structures of weaker states. In the nineteenth century the British not only signed agreements, contracts, with major European powers to end the slave trade; they also used military force. In 1839 Britain unilaterally authorized its ships to board suspected slavers flying the Portuguese flag, arguing that Portugal had failed to honor its treaty commitments to end the slave trade. In 1850 British warships entered Brazilian ports and burned ships that were thought to be involved in slaving.

The United States has used military force against a number of Caribbean and Central American states. The US sent marines into the Dominican

Republic in 1911, and in 1916 forced out the president, declared martial law, and appointed US officials as ministers of war and the interior. Similar pressure was applied against Nicaragua at the same time, with American officials selecting the Nicaraguan president in 1916. American rulers made acceptance of the 1901 Platt amendment, which included provisions limiting Cuban debt, authorizing American intervention if Cuban independence was threatened, and establishing an American naval base at Guantanamo, a condition for the withdrawal of US troops. American decision makers have sent troops into Haiti almost a dozen times, wrote the Haitian constitution in 1915, and appointed the president. In 1994 American military action restored a Haitian president who had been overthrown by the military. Panama became an independent state in 1903 with the support of American leaders who wanted to build a canal across the isthmus. In 1989 American troops invaded Panama, arrested its president, Manuel Noriega, and brought him back to Florida, where he was tried and convicted of criminal drug charges.

The smaller states of Central and Eastern Europe, like their Caribbean and Central American counterparts, have also been subject to impositions that violate Westphalian sovereignty. These states all emerged from the Habsburg and Ottoman empires. The initial existence of some of these states depended on recognition by the major powers. For rulers with limited material strength, international legal sovereignty, recognition, was valued because it could provide external resources and enhance internal legitimacy. Unlike Lenin and Mao, the would-be rulers of Serbia, Greece, and Montenegro could not secure effective territorial control and authority on their own. The major powers were not willing to recognize these states unless their would-be rulers accepted externally dictated conditions regarding domestic political structures, policies, or personnel. The alternative to acceptance was nonexistence.

When Greece was created in 1832 the form of government, a monarchy, the monarch (Otho, second son of the king of Bavaria), ministers, army officers, and financial policies were all dictated by the major European states whose military intervention gave Greece life in the first place. When Otho was overthrown in 1863, the major powers appointed his successor.

The Treaty of Berlin of 1878 recognized Serbia, Montenegro, and Romania as independent states, and Bulgaria as a tributary state of the Ottoman Empire, but only after the would-be rulers of these new states had been compelled to accept limitations on their authority regarding commercial arrangements and minorities. Moreover, the lower Danube, which flowed through Romania, was to be controlled by an independent European commission. The first Albanian constitution was drafted not by Albanians, but by representatives of the major European powers in 1914.

During the Cold War the Soviet Union dictated the domestic institutional structure and the policies of its East European satellites. Poland, Hungary, Romania, Czechoslovakia, and Bulgaria were not Westphalian sovereigns. Their militaries could not operate independently. In some cases their internal security forces reported directly to Moscow (Rice 1984: Ch. 1). Although their rulers did have some autonomy they could not stray too far from the Kremlin's preferences, and abandoning communist regimes was out of the question until the late 1980s.

One of the more enduring examples of imposition under great-power condominium has involved efforts to secure minority rights in Eastern and Central Europe during the nineteenth and twentieth centuries. All of the states that emerged from the Ottoman and Habsburg empires were compelled to accept provisions for minority protection as a condition of international recognition. This was true for Greece in 1832, and for Serbia, Montenegro, Romania, and Bulgaria at Berlin in 1878. The would-be rulers of the target states did not want to grant minority rights, but they acquiesced to the demands of the rulers of the major European powers because international recognition with minority rights provisions, which might be evaded, was better than no recognition at all.

The would-be leaders of all of the states that were created after the First World War (or were successors to the defeated empires) had to accept extensive provisions for the protection of minorities. As in Greece in 1832, these would-be rulers had limited bargaining leverage. Austria, Hungary, Bulgaria, and Turkey were defeated states, and minority protections were written into their peace treaties. Poland, Czechoslovakia, Yugoslavia, Romania, and Greece were new or enlarged states. They signed minority rights treaties with the Allied and Associated Powers. Albania, Lithuania, Latvia, Estonia, and Iraq made declarations as a result of pressure that was brought upon them when they applied to join the League of Nations. With only a few exceptions, notably Czechoslovakia, Hungary, and the Baltic states, the would-be rulers of these new states were not sympathetic to minority rights (Claude 1955: 16; D. Jones 1991: 45; Bartsch 1995: 81–85).

The United States and especially the major powers of Western Europe attempted to secure minority rights in the states that emerged out of Yugoslavia after 1991. Recognition of Slovenia and Croatia by the European Community in December of 1991 was conditioned on protection for minorities, including a guaranteed number of seats in the Croatian Parliament. The 1995 Dayton accords provided for the establishment of a commission for minorities, a majority of whose members were foreign, as well as an ombudsman who was initially to be appointed by the major European states. These were highly coercive if not imposed arrangements that would have been rejected by the states that emerged from the former Yugoslavia had they not been subject to external pressure.

Conclusions

The term "sovereignty" has been used in four different ways: domestic sovereignty, interdependence sovereignty, international legal sovereignty, and Westphalian sovereignty. Both international legal and Westphalian sovereignty are best conceptualized as examples of organized hypocrisy.

Both have clear logics of appropriateness, but these logics are sometimes inconsistent with a logic of consequences. Given the absence of authoritative institutions and power asymmetries, rulers can follow a logic of consequences and reject a logic of appropriateness. Principles have been enduring but violated.

For Westphalian sovereignty the violations have taken place through conventions, contracting, coercion, and imposition. Conventions and contracting are voluntary; rulers have invited violations of the de facto autonomy of their own polities because it leaves them better off than in the status quo ante. Coercion leaves one of the parties worse off; the target must alter its domestic policies or institutions or accept the costs of sanctions. Imposition occurs when the target is so weak that it has no choice but to comply either because the ruler or would-be ruler is faced with military force or because the failure to secure international legal sovereignty, recognition, would threaten the very existence of the state. Coercion and imposition are examples of violations of Westphalian sovereignty through intervention rather than invitation.

For international legal sovereignty violations have primarily been the result of contracting and conventions. Rulers have recognized entities that lacked formal juridical autonomy or, in the case of the Knights of Malta, even territory. Rulers have also refused to recognize governments that have demonstrated domestic sovereignty, and extended recognition to governments that have not exercised effective control over their own territory. These have often been unilateral actions that have not been contingent on the policies of other states.

The logic of appropriateness that is associated with the Westphalian norm of autonomy has mattered in the calculations of rulers, but so have alternatives such as human rights, minority rights, international stability, and fiscal responsibility. Rulers have different constituencies. They respond primarily to domestic supporters who hold different values in different states. The material interests of states often clash. Power is asymmetrical. There is no hierarchical authority. Logics of consequences have trumped Westphalian logics of appropriateness.

The basic rule of international legal sovereignty has been more robust and more widely adhered to. Once rulers have recognition, they hardly ever want to give it up. International legal sovereignty provides an array of benefits, including reducing the transaction costs of entering into agreements with other entities, facilitating participation in international organizations, extending diplomatic immunity, and establishing special legal protections. Because international legal sovereignty is a widely accepted and recognized script, it makes it easier to organize support from internal as well as external sources. Especially in polities with weak domestic sovereignty, international legal sovereignty, international recognition, can provide a signal to constituents that a regime and its rulers are more likely to survive and thereby make it more likely that these constituents would support the regime.

Nevertheless, international legal sovereignty like Westphalian sovereignty is not a Nash equilibrium, nor is it taken for granted. Rulers have had reasons to deviate from the rule and have invented other institutional forms when it has suited their purpose. The British Commonwealth, with its high commissioners rather than ambassadors, was an alternative to international legal sovereignty. Meetings of the major industrialized states include not only the representatives of international legal sovereigns—the presidents, premiers, and prime ministers of this and that country—but also the commissioner of the European Union. The consequences for Taiwan of losing its international legal sovereignty in the 1970s have been mitigated by the fact that some countries, notably the United States, have invented alternative arrangements that provide the functional equivalent of recognition.

Of all the social environments within which human beings operate, the international system is one of the most complex and weakly institutionalized. It lacks authoritative hierarchies. Rulers are likely to be more responsive to domestic material and ideational incentives than international ones. Norms are sometimes mutually inconsistent. Power is asymmetrical. No rule or set of rules can cover all circumstances. Logics of consequences can be compelling. Logics of consequences and appropriateness can be decoupled.

9 Organized hypocrisy in nineteenth-century East Asia

Introduction

Every international system or society has a set of rules or norms that define actors and appropriate behaviors. These norms are, however, never obeyed in an automatic or rote fashion. Perhaps more than any other setting, the international environment is characterized by organized hypocrisy (Brunsson 1989). Actors violate rules in practice without at the same time challenging their legitimacy. Organized hypocrisy is characteristic of international environments because: (1) actors, whether they be states, city states, empires, trading leagues, or tributary states have different levels of power; (2) rulers in different political entities will be responsive to different domestic norms which may, or may not, be fully compatible with international norms; (3) situations arise in which it is unclear what rule should apply and, there is, in an international system, no authority structure that can resolve these differences (Krasner 1999: Ch. 1).

What happens when a logic of consequences designed to maximize material interests conflicts with a logic of appropriateness based on conforming with norms, rules and roles? How consequential are norms as opposed to material considerations?

East Asian international relations in the nineteenth century provide an example of a situation in which the tension between norms and material concerns was particularly acute. Two international normative constructs clashed—the European sovereign state system of formal equality and autonomy, and the Sinocentric Confucian system of hierarchy and dependency. The material interests of the protagonists were incompatible: China and Korea wanted to preserve their autonomy; the Western states wanted economic access; Japan pursued autonomy and then expansion. For none of the major players were their own logics of appropriateness fully compatible with maximizing their material interests. In nineteenth-century Asia, as in many other situations, decision makers resorted to organized hypocrisy.

Norms were never taken for granted, either by Asian rulers or by Western interlopers. Logics of consequences dictated behavior while logics of appropriateness were rhetorically embraced; organized hypocrisy was rife.

European and Asian decision makers were more than clever enough to invent alternative institutional arrangements or to provide rationales for behaviors and policies that were manifestly inconsistent with the core norms they professed to believe in. Their behavior was decoupled from their normative commitments (Scott 1995; Meyer *et al.* 1997 on decoupling). For China, as for the Western powers, when the logic of consequences clashed with logics of appropriateness, the former usually prevailed, and not just in the nineteenth century. The Western powers established a set of institutional arrangements in China through what came to be termed "the unequal treaties." These were inconsistent not just with international legal sovereignty, which holds that agreements should be voluntary, but also with the domestic autonomy of China, with its Westphalian/Vattelian sovereignty. China also abandoned, compromised or distorted traditional Confucian practices to accommodate the power of the West, not a new development since China had always episodically confronted external powers—the Mongol cavalry from the Asian steppes, the Muslim empire of Tamerlane and his successors, later tsarist Russia—which did not share China's Confucian beliefs and which were powerful enough to threaten the Middle Kingdom. Japan, the Asian state that pursued an optimal strategy with regard to the dangers of Western encroachment, chose whatever institutional forms would maximize Japanese interests, ideational as well as material.

There were, however, two ways in which logics of appropriateness constrained Asian states from pursuing what might otherwise have been their optimal strategies for obstructing the incursions of the West. First, Asian states had less information about the West than the West had about Asia. Sovereignty practices, especially the permanent stationing of official representatives, ambassadors or consuls, facilitated the transmission of information among participants in the Western state system. In contrast, Confucian norms could not readily accommodate ongoing relations between equals. There were no ambassadors, only often infrequent tributary missions. With better information, China and Korea might have been able to pursue policies that would have increased the likelihood that they could have maintained more autonomy. Second, the domestic ideational and institutional incentives facing some Asian rulers, especially those in Korea, led them to pursue policies that were suboptimal with regard to preserving the independence of the polities they governed. Given its weakness and vulnerability, the optimal policy for Korea at the end of the nineteenth century would have been to engage a number of Western powers to counterbalance the threat posed by Japan, but Korea's rulers could not do this without losing the support of the Korean literati whose beliefs and societal position depended upon upholding Confucian principles. China was also constrained by domestic values which exacerbated the impact of external defeat on internal legitimacy. During the first part of the nineteenth century the Qing committed too many resources to holding Chinese possessions in Central Asia, which could not be defended against growing Russian power, because China's rulers feared that a loss of even these distant territories would encourage domestic challengers. Norms, then, did matter, not because they were taken for granted in ways that prevented rulers from exploring foreign policies options that would have enhanced their material interests, but because cultural values influenced the behavior of domestic constituents whose support rulers needed to stay in power.

Organized hypocrisy

All political and social environments are characterized by two logics of action, which James March and Johan Olsen have called logics of expected consequences and logics of appropriateness. Logics of consequences see political action and outcomes, including institutions, as the product of rational calculating behavior designed to maximize a given set of unexplained preferences. Logics of appropriateness understand political action as a product of rules, roles and identities. Identities specify appropriate behavior in given situations. The question is not: "How can I maximize my self interest?" but rather, given my role: "How should I act in this particular circumstance?" (March and Olsen 1989: pp. 24–26; March 1994: pp. 57–58; March and Olsen 1998).

In a well-established domestic polity, logics of appropriateness prevail and will usually, but not always, be consistent with logics of consequences. Doing the right thing will usually be consistent with an actor's self-interest. Disagreements about contested rules can be resolved by institutions, such as the courts or legislatures, which all actors regard as authoritative. Coercion is illegitimate for private actors.

In any international system, logics of appropriateness and logics of consequences will more often be incompatible than is the case in a well-established domestic polity. Organized hypocrisy, saying one thing but doing another, endorsing a logic of appropriateness while acting in ways consistent with a logic of consequences, will be a more frequent phenomenon. Because socialization is less complete in international environments and there are no authority structures to resolve conflicts among competing norms, rules may be mutually inconsistent, such as the admonition against intervening in the internal affairs of other states, one of the central precepts of a sovereignty-based international system, and the promotion of human rights, a principle endorsed in many international conventions. In the traditional Sinocentric world the emperor was viewed as standing above all other rulers, but China had to accommodate other practices because it episodically had to confront more powerful external actors with different logics of appropriateness, as happened between China and the Islamic empires of Central Asia in the fourteenth and fifteenth centuries, and between the East Asian and Western worlds in the eighteenth and nineteenth centuries. Under such circumstances organized hypocrisy is inevitable unless one of the parties abandons, or is forced to give up, its normative architecture, as China did at the beginning of the twentieth century. Organized hypocrisy is also characteristic of international affairs because domestic norms are likely to trump international ones if the two are in conflict; political leaders are more concerned about what their domestic supporters believe than about international principles per se.

Power asymmetries in the international environment and the absence of any legitimate authority that could constrain coercion means that stronger states can pick and choose from among those norms that best suit their material interests, or ignore norms altogether, because they can impose their choice on weaker actors. In an international system characterized by sovereignty norms, for instance, reconfiguring the domestic political structures of other states is illegitimate, but it is an option that the rulers of powerful states have often availed themselves of because it may be the most efficient way to promote their material objectives (Owen 2002). In the Confucian world order the rulers were, for instance, supposed to lead by example rather than to engage in threats and punishments (Confucius 1997: Book II), but, of course, Chinese emperors did use force to impose their will on weaker polities.

In the international environment, roles and rules are not irrelevant. Rulers do have to give reasons for their actions, but their audiences are usually domestic. Norms in the international system will be less constraining, organized hypocrisy more prevalent, than is the case in many domestic political settings.

Sovereign equality versus Confucian hierarchy

The core norms of the European system were international legal sovereignty and Westphalian/Vattelian sovereignty. The basic rule of international legal sovereignty is that recognition and formal legal equality should be granted to juridically independent territorial entities, sovereign states. Each state has the right to enter freely into voluntary contractual arrangements. The basic rule of Westphalian/Vattelian sovereignty is that each sovereign state is autonomous; each has the right to determine its own domestic authority structures independent from external interference. Although this norm is associated with the Peace of Westphalia, it was actually not explicitly articulated until the last part of the eighteenth century by Emmerich de Vattel (1852: 155) in his *The Law of Nations*. The Peace of Westphalia itself was inconsistent with what has come to be termed "Westphalian sovereignty." While paying lip service to the principle that the prince could set the religion of his territory, *cuius regio eius religio*, the treaties of Osnabrück and Münster (which comprised the Peace of Westphalia) included extensive provisions for religious toleration within the Holy Roman Empire that were designed to dampen the religious antagonisms that had made the Thirty Years War such a bloody and destructive conflict (Krasner 1995/96).

The core norms of the Sinocentric system were entirely different from those of the West. The Confucian system was based on hierarchy rather than equality. The principles of foreign policy were the same ones that informed domestic politics and even familial relations. Within the family the father held the superior position. In the political order the emperor stood at the pinnacle of at least the earthly hierarchy. China was the center of the civilized universe. China was not one state among many, it was the apex of civilization. The emperor was a sacred figure, the mediator between heaven and earth, as well as a temporal ruler. Confucian norms also placed great emphasis on appropriate rites and ceremonies, such as the kowtow to the emperor which embodied this hierarchical order (Hsu 1968: 3–4; Mancall 1968: 63–65; Kim 1980: 2).

Lesser political entities were tributary states offering symbolic obeisance and material tribute to the emperor. Relations among political entities within the Sinocentric world were governed by customs, rules and rituals, not by treaties. Tributary states had to adopt the Chinese calendar and to send tribute missions to China at regular intervals. In 1818, for instance, the tributary list included Korea, which sent tribute four times a year, Laos once in ten years, and Siam once in three years (Fairbank 1968: 11). The distinction between tribute and trade was opaque since commercial activities were associated with the tribute missions. Tributary missions brought tribute to the emperor and received gifts from him. Licensed trade took place in the Peking Tributary Hall for a limited number of traders who accompanied the tribute mission (Hamashita 1997: 124; Onuma 2000: 12–14).

Aside from tributary payments and associated commercial transactions, the tributary system also involved the investiture of the tributary state ruler by representatives of the emperor. In Japan this happened only during some limited periods such as the Ashikaga shogunate, but in other polities, including Korea and Vietnam, investiture missions from Beijing were more standard. Such ceremonies legitimated the local ruler. In Korea in 1875, for instance, the queen sought the investiture of her infant son as the future king, even though her husband was only in his twenties, because she feared that her father-in-law would challenge her son's right of succession (Kim 1980: 249). During the Qing dynasty, Tibet had a tributary relationship with China (at least from the Chinese perspective) and Beijing played some role in the selection of Dalai Lama in the eighteenth and early nineteenth centuries (Oksenberg 2001: 94–98). Investiture missions were sent from Beijing to the Ryukyus (the Liu-Ch'iu islands) from the fourteenth to the nineteenth centuries. During the elaborate ceremony, the Ryukyu ruler, who was only given the title of king after the investiture, kowtowed to the symbols of the emperor that were brought by the Chinese delegation (Chen 1968: 135–64; Kim 1980: 24–25).

The tributary state system did not necessarily involve any significant level of control by China. Even in Korea, the closest tributary state to Beijing not only geographically but also culturally and institutionally, there was no permanent representative during the Qing period and no significant intervention in Korean external or internal affairs until international pressures increased during the last part of the nineteenth century. Nor were there permanent officials in Vietnam or the Ryukyus, although China episodically stationed troops in Tibet. The tributary states generally had de facto autonomy over their external as well as their internal affairs. They were not protectorates in the Western sense. From the Han to the Qing dynasties, for 1,500 years, China encouraged the tributary relationship even though it often imposed financial burdens on the imperial treasury. External relations legitimated the internal position of the emperor (Suzuki 1968: 184; Wang 1968: 60; Liu 1980: viii).

In sum, the sovereign state system that originated in Europe and the East Asian Confucian system had different norms and rules for governing external relations: formal equality for the West, hierarchy for the East; independent states for the West, tributary states and an imperial center for the East. Although there had been ongoing contact between East Asia and Europe from the sixteenth century, these two cultures only began to clash in a sustained way during the nineteenth century when the West had accumulated enough military and economic power to challenge China. The European powers and the United States were never, however, strong enough simply to overrun and occupy China, and they knew it. The situation in Asia cannot be compared with the European conquest of the Americas where different cultural practices played only a limited role because the West obliterated its indigenous opponents. In Asia there was an extended period during which European and Confucian norms and institutional structures coexisted. Although the sovereign state system ultimately triumphed, nineteenth-century East Asia provides an unusual laboratory for examining the extent to which cultural values constrained the options that were available to different actors.

The West

In China the Western powers (Britain, France, Germany, Russia and the United States) confronted a problem for which the conventional rules of sovereignty—mutual recognition, equality, non-intervention—provided no solution. The major Western powers wanted commercial access to China, and in the case of Russia limited territorial acquisition, but they did not have the capability to govern China. They wanted to change Chinese domestic policies but they did not want to incur the governance costs of direct rule (Lake 1999: Ch. 3). Neither direct colonization, which is consistent with sovereignty norms, nor honoring China's autonomy, would have maximized the material interests of the West. Logics of appropriateness were inconsistent with logics of consequences. The latter prevailed.

The Western powers used military coercion to compel China to change some domestic policies, assumed control of some public functions, notably the customs service and associated activities which accounted for a quarter of the revenue for China's central government, and developed a new institutional form, the treaty ports. All of these policies violated China's Westphalian/ Vattelian sovereignty, its domestic autonomy. The West did not challenge China's right to be recognized as an independent state, but did violate China's international legal sovereignty (a concept totally alien to China) by coercing China to sign some international agreements.

During the nineteenth century China lost a series of military confrontations. When China tried to impede the flow of opium, by far the most lucrative Western export during the first part of the nineteenth century, the Western powers, especially Britain, used military force to open Chinese markets. Britain annexed Hong Kong after the first Opium War and took Kowloon after the second. After Beijing was sacked, the Chinese felt that they had to sign the Treaty of Tientsin in 1860 which gave Britain the right to have a permanent representative in Beijing, a practice completely antithetical to the Sinocentric system. The Portuguese, who had occupied Macao since 1557, rejected Chinese sovereignty in 1849. By treaty in 1858 Russia secured the northern bank of the Amur river, and in 1860 additional land between the Ussuri and the sea. Japan sent a small force to annex the Ryukyus, which it had indirectly controlled for two centuries, and China renounced its right to tribute. In 1866 and 1871 respectively, the French and Americans sent military forces into Korea, then a tributary state of China. After the Sino-French War, the French annexed Vietnam, also a tributary state of China in 1885, and took Laos in 1893. Germany used the murder of two missionaries as a pretext to threaten China, and secured through treaty the entrance and two islands in the Bay of Jiaozhou. The Germans wanted to establish a naval base for their Asian fleet there, and the right to militarily occupy an area within a radius of 50 km of the leased territory where China could not act without German approval. Shortly thereafter Russia obtained a 25-year lease on Port Arthur. During the Sino-Japanese war of 1894–95, Japanese troops from Korea crossed the Yalu and threatened Beijing. In the Treaty of Shimonoseki, essentially dictated by Japan, China renounced its suzerainty over Korea, and ceded Taiwan, the Pescadores and the Liaodong peninsula (later returned because of threats from Russia) to Japan (Hsu 1968: 68–71; Chesneaux and Bastid 1977: 53–56, 247–49, 285, 299; Fairbank 1978: 249–50, 256–59; Kim 1980: Ch. 2; Onuma 2000: 30–32).

Thus the Western powers, and by the end of the nineteenth century Japan, could militarily defeat China but they did not have the resources to govern directly. Tributary entities could be colonized—Vietnam, Korea, the Ryukyus—but not China itself. For the British in particular, the 1857 Indian Mutiny had demonstrated the high governance costs of occupying heavily populated, relatively well-developed states. To secure their material objectives, the West (and Japan) needed some institutional form that would give them control but without the costs of direct occupation.

The treaty ports, an institutional form inconsistent with sovereignty principles, were the solution they fixed upon. The system was initiated after the first Opium War with the Treaty of Nanking in 1842, concluded between

China and Britain, which established five treaty ports. France and the United States signed agreements with China shortly thereafter. In the ports foreigners enjoyed extraterritoriality; they were under the jurisdiction of their own consuls and tried under the laws of their own countries, not China. They could freely engage in commercial activity and own land, governed again by the laws of their own country. Shanghai became the center of foreign activity. In 1854 the British, Americans and French established an autonomous political body in Shanghai, the municipal council, which was elected by landholders and had a budget, police force and militia, all outside of any formal authorization from China. The Taiping rebellion led to a large influx of Chinese. In 1885 there were more than 125,000 Chinese in the international concession and about 3,600 foreigners. The Chinese, however, had no rights within the concession and were treated as foreigners and subject to high taxation. In 1858, the British and the French essentially took over Canton after the local Chinese governor had closed the port. The Europeans had a force of more than 5,000 men, enough to defeat the local Chinese militia. By the end of the century there were 85 treaty ports (Chesneaux and Bastid 1977: 61–68, 250–51; Fairbank 1978: 240–49).

The treaty port system was rationalized by making a distinction between civilized and uncivilized nations. This was completely at odds with sovereignty principles because the agreements were coerced and China's authority was compromised within its own territory. However, the ports could actually be accommodated within traditional Chinese practices. From the Chinese point of view the development of the treaty port system was a way of co-opting foreigners and limiting their penetration in China. The establishment of special residence areas had been introduced by the Chinese for Arab merchants who settled in Canton during the Tang dynasty. The consuls were completely consistent with the traditional Chinese practice of having a representative responsible for the members of a foreign community. In fact very similar practices had existed in late medieval Europe, where trading houses established in major European cities by foreign entities were expected to police their own members (Greif 1994). Overseas Chinese communities were organized in the same way. For the Chinese, the treaty ports were merely a gloss, a variant, of the traditional tribute system which allowed some commercial activity to take place far from the imperial center where the norms of ritual obeisance would have been more difficult to avoid. While foreigners took the treaties as an indication of their privileges, the Chinese viewed them as limiting what the foreigners could do (Fairbank 1968: 257–61; Chesneaux and Bastid 1977: 251; Duus 1989: xviii; Onuma 2000: 32).

While the treaty port system could be accommodated within existing Chinese practices, the assumption by the Western powers of some of China's official state functions, especially the customs service, was inconsistent with both sovereignty and Confucian norms. The Treaty of Nanking had forced China to reduce its tariff, which had been 60–70 per cent, to 5 per cent. Foreign control of customs began as a temporary measure during a period of unrest in Shanghai during the early 1850s and then became institutionalized for all of China. An Englishman became the chief of Chinese customs in 1861. By 1885 the customs service, now located in Beijing, employed 500 Westerners and 2,000 Chinese, and accounted for a quarter of the state's revenues which were collected more efficiently and honestly than had been the case under Chinese administration. The service also enforced quarantine regulations, maintained ports, paid China's foreign debt, managed the postal service, supervised emigration and conducted coastal geographic surveys. After the Sino-Japanese war, Britain attempted to extend its indirect control of the customs service by insisting that loans to China were to be repaid with revenues dedicated from the customs service, whose administration was not to be changed for the life of the loan, scheduled to last until 1943. This was a kind of nineteenth-century East Asian example of contemporary conditionality agreements negotiated by international financial institutions (Chesneaux and Bastid 1977: 175–76, 252–53, 295, 299–300).

In sum, it is hard to find any way in which sovereignty norms constrained the behavior of the West in East Asia during the nineteenth century. Treaties were coerced. Extraterritoriality was established in the treaty ports. State functions were appropriated. What limited direct colonization or further Western incursions into China's internal affairs were the governance costs that would have been incurred had the West pursued an even more aggressive policy.

China and organized hypocrisy

China, which was usually the most powerful polity in the eastern part of the Eurasian land mass, existed in a less complicated neighborhood than the states of Europe. Rather than the European world of many competing political entities, which threatened each other's security and sometimes very existence, China's external enemies came from only one direction, the Asian steppes, and then only episodically, before the nineteenth century. Hideyoshi's somewhat megalomaniacal ambitions aside, until the twentieth century Japan could not think of conquering China. Korea was always too weak. India was remote and the Himalayas were high. The polities that occupied the Malayan and Vietnamese peninsulas to the southwest were small. The islands of the Pacific posed no threat. Hierarchical Confucian principles, the tributary state system and the unique position of the Chinese emperor were often consistent with material circumstances.

Nevertheless, China sometimes confronted situations in which powerful challengers refused to honor Confucian rules. Here Chinese officials were as adept as their Western counterparts, perhaps more adept, in the exercise of organized hypocrisy. When logics of appropriateness dictated one kind of behavior and logics of consequences another, China was often able to follow the latter while rationalizing behavior in terms of the former. Confucian norms were widely recognized but Chinese policy could often as easily, perhaps more easily, be explained by power (Inoguchi n.d.)

The Chinese theory of government was in tension with the fact that the peoples of Central Asia did not share Chinese culture. During the Han dynasty in the centuries before AD 1000 relationships between the Chinese and neighboring states, especially the states to the west and north with whom China had severe conflicts, were not always hierarchical. Treaties were signed which implied equality. The Central Asian Muslim states never regarded the Chinese emperor as a superior. They regarded the Chinese as heathens who would one day be converted. They respected Chinese culture but viewed the Chinese as ignorant of the world. The emperor was seen as a great ruler but not superior to others such as the potentates of India, Russia and the Ottoman Empire. The Chinese did not, because they could not, always demand that the Central Asian monarchs regard the emperor as their suzerain. The imperial court frequently treated these countries as if they were equals, while at the same time trying to describe these relations to the Chinese as one of suzerainty. For instance, in 1394 a Chinese document relates that Tamerlane submitted to the Ming emperor and accepted him as the King of Heaven. Given that Tamerlane was a Muslim, it is highly unlikely that he would have acknowledged any such status to a pagan. But the submission, perhaps a forged document or a wrongly translated one, was accepted at court. In a letter to the Timurid ruler in 1418, the Ming emperor abandoned any formal pretense of superiority and referred to goods from the Timurid as gifts and not tribute, but at the same time the letter extended the emperor's name further into the margin, implying, at least for Chinese readers, superiority. This symbolic device allowed the Ming to claim that they were following Chinese rules of hierarchy, while in effect recognizing Timurid equality. The letter was not included in the Ming annals (Fairbank 1968: 5; Fletcher 1968: 210–24; Suzuki 1968: 185–86; Onuma 2000: 17).

Commercial relations were conducted without the Central Asians recognizing the suzerainty of China. Tribute in Chinese could mean any gift that was given to the emperor. Such gifts could come from rulers who completely accepted China's hierarchical vision of the world, but gifts could also come from rulers who did not. It was not in China's interest to make fine distinctions but rather to call everything tribute. In the early period of the Ming dynasty, goods from Central Asia were defined as tribute. For the Central Asians they were understood as trade. In many cases, missions from Central Asia bearing "tribute" were in fact nothing more than trading missions with fake papers. For the members of the Chinese court it was preferable to have trade take place in Beijing, where they could get a piece of the action, than at some distant frontier. These fake missions were an open secret (Fletcher 1968: 208–9).

The use of forged documents in Chinese relations with the Mongols, in seventeenth-century Japanese relations with the Koreans, and in late eighteenth-century relations between Britain and China (where the British translators essentially forged translations of the Chinese emperor's letter to the British envoy, which they believed would be unacceptable to the British) are all perfect examples of organized hypocrisy. The forgeries, even forgeries that were known to be forgeries, allowed the Chinese, the Japanese, the Koreans and the British to conduct trade and to claim that they were operating according to their own respective normative prescriptions (Elisonas 1991: 297–99; Onuma 2000: n. 37).

Organized hypocrisy was also evident in the empire's dealings with Russia. The 1727 Treaty of Kiakhta with Russia can be viewed as one between equals because the treaty provided for an exchange of official letters and included a clause that implied equality between the signatories. The treaty also opened trade along the border. It is not, however, clear that the Chinese regarded the treaty in this way. The border trade was described as being within the tributary system since it had been officially permitted by the emperor, even though tribute had not been sent and the Russians had not kowtowed. The border was far away and the actual nature of transactions could be obfuscated in Beijing (Fairbank 1968: 13–14; Hamashita 1997: 131–32).

Likewise, relations with Japan did not fit the Confucian model. Japan shared much of China's culture, but China was not militarily strong enough to compel Japan to acknowledge the symbolic superiority of their emperor in any consistent way. Because the two countries were sufficiently distant, this anomaly was usually easily accommodated (Suzuki 1968: 190). When there was a direct conflict between Japanese and Chinese policies before the latter part of the nineteenth century, both countries found ways of glossing over their differences. The Ryukyu islands offer one example. From the sixteenth to the nineteenth centuries these islands were both a fief of Satsuma, which was primarily interested in commercial advantage and prestige, and a tributary state of China, which continued to oversee certain ceremonial functions such as the investiture of new kings. The Ryukyu king paid tribute to Satsuma and participated in ceremonial functions in Edo as a feudatory of Satsuma. At the same time traditional relations with China were maintained. The Japanese kept out of sight during official Chinese visits to invest the king. It was not in the interests of the Chinese to investigate too closely. The Ryukyus operated with a set of institutional arrangements that defied any transitive hierarchical structure for almost 300 years (Sakai 1968).

The Chinese were, then, hardly inexperienced in dealing with powerful external actors that did not share Confucian values. What was new about the challenge of the West in the nineteenth century was not the difference in values but the difference in power. China faced a conjunction of internal and external crises in the nineteenth century. The regime confronted a number of traditional internal opponents such as the White Lotus Society, which was committed to the restoration of the Ming dynasty and organized a major revolt at the beginning of the nineteenth century. By the middle of the century there were a number of popular rebellions, including the Taiping and the Nian, fueled by discontent generated by corruption, currency debasement and economic dislocation resulting from the introduction of new crops such as corn. Christian theology, with its essentially egalitarian message which was antithetical to Confucian beliefs, was also appropriated by some rebel movements. There was a Muslim rebellion in Yunnan from 1856 to 1873. There were sporadic periods of unrest in major cities. The problems for Beijing around 1860 were first and foremost the Taiping Rebellion, which threatened to destroy Qing rule, second the territorial expansion of the Russians, and only third the British demands for trade (Chesneaux and Bastid 1977: 38–49, Ch. 4; Fairbank 1978: 253).

Despite all of this these internal disorders, and the two Opium Wars with the West, the dynasty survived and even reasserted itself after 1870. Western influence at the core of the empire remained contained even towards the end of the nineteenth century. In 1874, for instance, foreign representatives were admitted into the presence of the emperor, but they had to wait seventeen years for another audience. The ceremony where they presented their credentials lasted about ten minutes. It was held in a hall outside the palace enclosure, leading the French and Russians not to attend. Only after the Sino-Japanese war was the diplomatic corps invited to the inner palace and given the right to enter through the central gate which had been reserved for the emperor (Chesneaux and Bastid 1977: 275).

On the whole, then, the Chinese were adept at the exercise of organized hypocrisy. Behaviors inconsistent with Confucian norms were ignored or reinterpreted for domestic audiences. Yasuaki Onuma accurately captures the basic problem that China confronted throughout its long history: Sinocentric norms could not always govern relations between China and other political entities which possessed enough power to resist or threaten the imperial center and which did not share China's norms:

> Even if China was a superpower for much of human history, it was impossible for China to impose its will on all the peoples in the world with its limited military and economic powers, and cultural influence … the tribute system inherently comprised an estrangement from reality, and could function only when the parties in the system acquiesced in this estrangement.
>
> (Onuma 2000: 17)

There were, however, at least two ways in which normative structures constrained Chinese policies. First, Chinese decision-makers knew much less about the West than the West knew about China, because the Sinocentric world did not have an institutional structure that provided for regular diplomatic intercourse. There were no ambassadors, only episodic tribute missions to Beijing and investiture missions to tributary states. China sent its first foreign mission to the West, which was led by the British inspector-general for customs Robert Hart and charged with fact gathering, only in 1866. Only in the 1870s did China begin to establish permanent missions abroad (Hsu 1980: 72). Better information might have provided the Chinese leaders with more options, but it is difficult to imagine that it would have saved the empire any more than closer proximity with the West saved the Ottoman Empire.

Second, at the beginning of the nineteenth century the Qing committed too many resources to holding their possessions in Central Asia because they feared that external losses would be taken as signs of weakness that could enhance the strength of internal enemies. If the mandate of heaven was lost externally, it would also be lost internally. The regime felt compelled to hold all of its possessions, even though its material capabilities had decreased. The emperor's claim to be master of the world trapped him into defending areas that he could no longer hold in the face of local resistance and Russian expansion. Nevertheless, the Qings still had some authority and control in Central Asia in the 1860s. Finally, they incorporated eastern Turkestan into China itself as the province of Sinkiang. Western Turkestan was abandoned to the control of Russia (Fletcher 1968: 221–24; Hsu 1968: 117).

In sum, China confronted a series of internal and external challenges during the nineteenth century to which the empire and its Confucian norms ultimately succumbed. But in their confrontations with the Europeans, Chinese leaders, as in previous centuries, even millennia, were adept at the exercise of organized hypocrisy. When material circumstances demanded it they were able to adopt completely instrumental practices, such as accepting forged papers, signing treaties and engaging in trade far from Beijing, while at the same time endorsing Sinocentric values with which these practices were inconsistent. Power asymmetries, not normative constraints, led to the collapse of the East Asian international order.

Japan

If China was constrained by Confucian principles in only limited ways, Japan, after the Meiji restoration, was hardly constrained at all. Confronted with a loss of national autonomy and possibly foreign occupation, Japan's leaders initiated a set of domestic institutional reforms designed to turn Japan into a modern industrialized state, embraced Western concepts of international law, sent missions to Europe and the United States to gather information, and welcomed foreign experts. A country that had essentially abandoned the opportunity to produce modern firearms during the Togukawa period was able within four decades after the Meiji restoration to defeat Russia, a major Western power.

In international affairs Japan jettisoned Confucian practices, or, perhaps more aptly, picked and chose those institutional forms that would maximize its economic and security interests. By 1870 the new Japanese government had accepted the Western model of international relations. Japanese leaders argued that all states, at least all civilized states, were equal. Their domestic and foreign policy goal was to make it clear to the West that Japan would have to be categorized as a civilized nation entitled to treat other Asian countries as uncivilized, just as the West was doing.

The Sino-Japanese treaty of 1871 tacitly recognized the two countries as equals. The treaty provided for, for instance, mutual consular jurisdiction over nationals in the trading ports of the other country. It was the first modern international treaty signed in Asia. The Chinese justified abandoning hierarchical norms on the grounds that Japan had never been a tributary of China, although in fact Japan had episodically in the past acknowledged China's superior position (Wang 1958). The treaty was a great success for Japan, which wanted mutual acknowledgment of equal status. It was more problematic for Chinese leaders, who decided that at least tacit acceptance of Japanese equality was worth the price of discouraging alliances between Japan and the Western powers. In 1872 the Japanese representative in Beijing was given an audience with the Chinese emperor. He gave three bows, the practice for Western representatives, but did not kowtow (Kim 1980: 149–52, 156–58, 175).

In 1872 Japan declared that the Ryukyus, which had been a tributary of China but had long been subject to effective control by Satsuma, would henceforth be a tributary of Japan. This move was taken unilaterally without discussion with either the Ryukyuan king or the Chinese. The Japanese insisted that the Ryukyuan king be invested by the Japanese emperor, the role that had been played for hundreds of years by the Chinese emperor. In 1879, however, prompted in part by anxiety that Britain might attempt to take over the Ryukyus, the Japanese sent a force of 400 soldiers and 250 policemen, seized the capital, abolished the island kingdom, and established the new Japanese prefecture of Okinawa in its stead (Kim 1980: 171–72, 280–83).

Japan's adroitness at pursuing its material self-interests, and its ability to appeal to whatever principles or rules might be useful, were nowhere more in evidence than with regard to Korea. During the 1860s Japan became increasingly aware of China's weakness and Russia's expansion. Japanese authorities considered increasing their influence in Korea in order to, among other things, forestall Russian advances that could threaten Japanese security. In the late 1860s, but before Meiji, the Japanese proposed sending a mission to Korea that would mediate Korean disputes with Western powers. In 1869 several high Japanese officials suggested that Korea should be persuaded to accept Japanese control of its foreign policy, and that arrangements should be established that were a mixture of Western practices and Asian suzerainty (Kim 1980: 117–35, Ch. 3).

As a result of pressure and military threats, Korea concluded a treaty with Japan in February 1876. Some of the specific discussions were still informed by Sinocentric norms. The term "emperor of Japan" was not used because the Koreans insisted that only the ruler of China be referred to in this way. Instead, the treaty alluded to the government of Japan and the government of Korea. The treaty acknowledged that Korea was an independent state, although the Korean negotiators, who were still alienated from and antipathetic to Western norms, did not have a cognitive framework within which to situate the notion of state equality. Symmetry between Korea and Japan was entirely consistent with the Confucian norms held by Korea's governing class, and for Korea the treaty was a way to reinstitute traditional practices that had allowed trading to take place in Pusan under the Tsushima Han. Japan secured additional trading rights and extraterritorial privileges that were analogous to the rights that the Western powers had in China. Japan used Western concepts to establish its superior position rather than Sinocentric notions which would have involved a tributary relationship between Japan and Korea. The treaty "drove a major institutional wedge into the surviving traditional world order in East Asia and challenged, if it did not openly reject, China's suzerainty over the peninsula kingdom" (Kim 1980: 253).

China had supported, or at least had not objected to, the treaty because Chinese officials realized that they did not have the strength to protect Korea should Japan decide to attack. China was preoccupied with internal rebellion in the northwest. China also feared that Russia might intervene. The Treaty of Kanghwa was an example of realpolitik, at least for Japan (Kim 1980: 255). Japan's ambition to control Korea was fully realized two decades later as a result of the Sino-Japanese war.

In sum, during the last part of the nineteenth century Japanese policy was totally unconstrained by Sinocentric principles or institutions. The Japanese applied both Western and Confucian norms depending on which would better promote Japanese security and economic interests. Japan rapidly adopted Western practices and was able not only to prevent violations of its Westphalian/Vattelian sovereignty but also to turn itself into a major power, equal or superior to some of its Western challengers.

Korea

The impact of norms was minimal for the West and for Japan, and limited even for China itself, but very significant for Korea. Korea was the most isolated polity in East Asia. The Koreans still lived in what one analyst has termed a "Confucian dream world" (Kim 1980: 331). They viewed the weakness of China vis-à-vis the West as a manifestation of the corruption of the Manchus. They found the Japanese claim of superiority over Korea insulting, as they had in the sixteenth and seventeenth centuries (Elisonas 1991). They saw Christianity as an alien faith which challenged the neo-Confucian views of the Korean elite. Korea was the last polity to open to the outside. Its first treaty with a Western power, the United States, was concluded in 1882.

Isolation was not an optimal policy for Korea and it cost the country, which became a Japanese colony in 1910, dear. Korea was in a precarious position by the 1870s. It was a weak polity in an environment where power configurations were changing rapidly. Korea's best chance of maintaining its independence would have been to engage the interest of a number of foreign states. Had the Koreans been able to open their country in a way that would have given the United States, Britain, Germany, France and Russia, as well as Japan, an economic interest, this might have prevented any single state from taking over the peninsula. But such a policy would have required the employment of Western rather than Sinocentric institutional forms, a world of equal sovereign states, not a world of hierarchy in which Korea's basic identity was as a tributary of China. This the Korean elite refused to do. Korea, or more accurately the Korean ruling elite, was trapped by Sinocentric norms.

Korea resisted Western pressure in the 1860s and 1870s, leaving China, its suzerain, in a difficult position. The Chinese realized that they could not defend Korea, but they also did not want Korea to renounce its tributary status. Korea was symbolically important for the Manchus and critical for China's military security. Any foreign power occupying the peninsula could threaten the heart of the empire. Chinese decision makers knew that Korea was threatened by Japan and by the Western powers. They began to involve themselves in Korean affairs to an unprecedented extent, and encouraged Korea's leaders to open their country to the West. In 1882 Korea signed a treaty with the United States which was quickly followed by agreements with Britain and Germany (Kim 1980: 69; Liu 1980: xvi–xviii).

Both China and Korea wanted a statement in the 1882 treaties with the Western powers that would have recognized Korea as a tributary state of China, but the United States and the European states objected. Since the Europeans had themselves designated Bulgaria as a tributary state of the Ottoman Empire in the Berlin agreement of 1878, the stance of the West cannot be attributed simply to an automatic rejection of institutional forms that were inconsistent with sovereignty principles. However, at the suggestion of the Chinese, who by this time had clearly mastered some European diplomatic practices, the Koreans provided a separate note to the American president and later to European heads of state which read, in the case of America:

> Cho-sen [Korea] has been a state tributary to China from ancient times. Yet hitherto full sovereignty has been exercised by the king of Cho-sen in all matters of internal administration and foreign relations. Cho-sen and the United States, in establishing now by mutual consent a treaty, are dealing with each other upon a basis of equality ... As regards the various duties which devolve upon Cho-sen as a tributary state to China, with these the United States has no concern whatever.
>
> (Kim 1980: 315)

China's leadership wanted to employ both Confucian and Western practices, a strategy that failed not because it was inherently inconsistent (Korea could have paid tribute to China and signed trade agreements with the West) but because Japan had the military resources to make Korea a colony.

Shortly after signing treaties with the United States, Britain and Germany, rioting broke out among Korean soldiers in Seoul over the allocation of rice. The rioters blamed the influence of Queen Min and her relatives and appealed to the Taewon'gun, the father of the king, who was out of power but the leader of the conservative faction. The Taewon'gun was able to seize control of the state apparatus following further unrest that included attacks on Japanese officials. The Japanese legation in Seoul was forced to flee the country. For the Japanese these developments were an ideal pretext for military action. To pre-empt this possibility China intervened by sending 2,000 troops, arresting the Taewon'gun and sending him to China. The Chinese feared that unrest in Korea would lead to foreign control. Confronted with a clear imperative, the Chinese abandoned their traditional practices, which had left Korea more or less on its own with regard to both internal and external policies so long as it honored its tributary obligations, and acted decisively to forestall a security threat to China itself (Kim 1980: 318–27).

In the end China's policies failed. Threatened with insurrection, the king of Korea appealed to China for aid. Claiming rights under its 1885 treaty with Korea, Japan intervened. The Japanese troops drove the Chinese forces that had been sent to Korea back into China itself, crossed the Yalu, and threatened Beijing. In the Treaty of Shimonoseki, essentially dictated by Japan, China renounced its suzerainty over Korea, and ceded Taiwan, the Pescadores and the Liaodong peninsula (later returned because of pressure from Russia) to Japan. The treaty marked the end of the Confucian order. China was forced to accept Korea, which had been its most durable tributary, as an autonomous state. Defeat by Japan, an Asian country that the Chinese had always considered inferior, undermined the position of the regime more than earlier military losses to the Western powers (Chesneaux and Bastid 1977: 285; Onuma 2000: 52–53).

In Korea, then, as opposed to the Western states, Japan and China itself, logics of appropriateness prevailed over logics of consequences even in circumstances where the very existence of the polity was threatened. The most compelling explanation for this behavior is the domestic political situation in Korea. Korea during the Yi dynasty was ruled by its aristocracy, the *yangban*, a civil and military class organized according to Confucian principles. The *yangban* had embraced the Chinese tributary system at the beginning of the fifteenth century and used it to legitimate their overthrow of the previous regime. The opening of Korea to the outside world was strongly resisted by the literati. They had objected to the treaty with Japan and they were adamant in their opposition to the agreement signed with the United States in 1882. They saw Christianity, with its egalitarian precepts, as evil (Kim 1980: 5–6, 29–30, 309).

Given the internal divisions in Korea, the literati could not maintain their position if they abandoned Confucian principles. Within the domestic sphere there was no conflict for the *yangban* between logics of appropriateness and logics of consequences. For foreign policy, however, Confucian principles were incompatible with Korean independence. If the leading members of the *yangban* class had known with confidence that their policies would contribute to Korea's colonization by Japan, they might have pursued a different strategy, but the intentions of foreign actors could only be guessed at while the ambitions of their domestic enemies were more obvious.

Organized hypocrisy and contemporary East Asia

The issues that confronted East Asia in the nineteenth century, the tension between logics of consequences and logics of appropriateness, have not disappeared even though there is now only one dominant set of rules and principles, those associated with the sovereign state system. The issues confronting Japan, such as the dispute with Russia over the Kuriles, are quite conventional: who has sovereignty over a particular piece of territory? China, however, has confronted two issues—Hong Kong and Taiwan—where the imaginative exercise of organized hypocrisy appears to provide the most satisfactory outcomes. In Hong Kong solutions have been found. In Taiwan they have not.

China wanted formal control over Hong Kong. At the same time, it did not want to undermine Hong Kong's economic dynamism. These objectives could not be achieved by applying the conventional rules associated with Westphalian/Vattelian and international legal sovereignty. Simply incorporating Hong Kong as a province of China would have weakened the confidence of both local and foreign economic interests. China could have established Hong Kong as a distinct part of China governed by different rules but without any special international or transnational ties. Such an arrangement would have been perfectly consistent with international legal and Westphalian/Vattelian sovereignty, but might not have assuaged the anxiety of commercial interests. China could have accepted the continuation of British administration, but this would have been inconsistent with China's nationalist aspirations and the desire of its leaders to expunge the legacy of colonialism (Smith 2001).

Instead, China opted for an arrangement that gave Hong Kong a distinct domestic position and, with the agreement of other states, a distinct international status as well. China's commitments to Hong Kong, including continuation of a legal system based on English common law, were enumerated in the Joint Declaration concluded with Britain and in the Basic Law promulgated for Hong Kong. Hong Kong was given the right to participate in international organizations. Hong Kong is a full member of eight organizations, including the World Trade Organization, the Asian Development Bank and the World Health Organization, an associate member of six more, and a participant in nineteen as part of the Chinese delegation. In addition, Beijing gave Hong Kong the right to issue passports, to enforce its own customs procedures, to conclude visa agreements with other states and to establish foreign economic missions. All of these activities required the explicit agreement of other states. Passports are worthless unless they are recognized. An entity cannot join international organizations unless its other members agree. Hong Kong is not juridically independent but it has been given international legal sovereignty.

In addition, the judicial arrangements for Hong Kong legitimate foreign sources of authority. The Hong Kong Court of Final Appeal is authorized to call on foreign judges from common law countries to sit with the Court and can refer to precedents from common law countries in reaching decisions. In the first two years of the Court's existence the fifth position on the bench was always occupied by a Commonwealth judge. In agreeing to the use of the common law and to foreign judges, China compromised its own Westphalian/ Vattelian sovereignty. Organized hypocrisy prevailed. Because the logic of appropriateness associated with sovereignty was inconsistent with behavior that would flow from a logic of consequences designed to maximize economic growth, China created, with the compliance of other states, a unique set of institutional arrangements. China extolled sovereignty and at the same time compromised it.

Taiwan has proven to be a much more difficult situation, one in which the major parties have not been able to find a mutually satisfactory institutional arrangement. It is only a little stretch to understand Hong Kong as a modern-day tributary state left to pursue its own domestic and external policies so long as tribute, in this case in the form of trade and investment, is paid and Beijing's interests are not threatened. It is not hard to imagine a similar arrangement for Taiwan, but no such option is being actively pursued. Another alternative would be for Taiwan to be recognized as an independent and separate state. This would be perfectly consistent with conventional sovereignty norms. Some important domestic groups on Taiwan support this option. The government in Beijing is adamantly opposed. Another possibility, also consistent with conventional norms, would be for China to absorb Taiwan. Again, this would leave an entity, a marginally larger China, completely consistent with the principles of sovereignty. The political leadership in Taiwan has rejected this option, at least so long as the domestic political structure on the mainland remains unchanged.

The motivation for Taiwan's leaders and their constituents to resist a takeover by an authoritarian, more impoverished China are obvious. But why would Beijing be so adamantly committed to a conventional sovereignty solution, absorption, for Taiwan when it was so imaginative with regard to Hong Kong? Would not an agreement that symbolically accepted the unity of China while leaving Taiwan in a position of de facto independence be more consistent with a logic of consequences for Beijing? Such an arrangement would reduce the chance of a violent conflict, facilitate economic exchange and perhaps even make it more likely that Taiwan would eventually be fully rejoined with China. Obviously, the present leadership of the People's Republic has rejected this option.

The most compelling explanation here, as in the case of nineteenth-century China and especially Korea, is to be found in the domestic political sphere. Ideologically, the Chinese Communist Party is bankrupt. To legitimate its rule it has increasingly drawn on nationalist sentiments. Bringing Taiwan back into the fold would be the final step in rectifying the humiliation which the West, including Japan, imposed on China during the nineteenth and first part of the twentieth centuries. Recognizing Taiwan as an independent entity or working out some arrangement in which Taiwan would symbolically pay obeisance to Beijing but maintain effective control over its domestic and foreign affairs would deprive the Communist Party of this nationalist card.

International norms have constrained the options that have been pursued by the leadership of the People's Republic, at least with regard to Taiwan, but as in the nineteenth century only because these norms have been salient for domestic politics. Just as the Qing committed too many resources to trying to hold Central Asia because they feared that external losses would be regarded as a sign of weakness that could exacerbate domestic challenges, and as Korea's *yangban* class continued to embrace Confucian policies that legitimated their internal position, the leadership of the People's Republic have pursued policies with regard to Taiwan that may enhance their domestic position but are not optimal for China's economic development and military security.

Conclusions

Nineteenth-century Asia experienced a clash between logics of appropriateness for organizing the international system—between the Confucian world of hierarchy and deference, and the Western world of sovereignty and equality. Had either European or Asian powers honored the norms which they professed, history would have unfolded in a very different way. Either leaving China and other states to formulate their own policies, or colonizing them, would have been consistent with sovereignty principles. But the West did neither. The governance costs of taking over China were prohibitive. Recognizing China's Westphalian/Vattelian sovereignty, its right to autonomously formulate its own domestic policies, would have deprived the European powers, the United States and later Japan of the economic penetration they desired. In Asia itself, Japan, recognizing the threat from the West, radically restructured its own domestic polity and freely deployed the new principles of the sovereign state system. China also, by and large, found ways of engaging in organized hypocrisy that promoted its material objectives while at the same time not explicitly renouncing Confucian norms. Only in Korea, where abandoning Confucian practices externally could have undermined the regime internally, did Asian principles clearly constrain political leaders from pursuing policies that might have preserved Korea's independence. In nineteenth-century East Asia, as in international environments more generally, the logic of consequences usually trumps the logic of appropriateness. The most dramatic exceptions have occurred when jettisoning logics of appropriateness could lead to internal revolt even while adhering to them endangers international security.

Acknowledgement

I would like to thank Onuma Yasuaki for his helpful comments on an earlier draft of this paper.

10 Sharing sovereignty
New institutions for collapsed and failing states

Conventional sovereignty assumes a world of autonomous, internationally recognized, and well-governed states. Although frequently violated in practice, the fundamental rules of conventional sovereignty—recognition of juridically independent territorial entities and nonintervention in the internal affairs of other states—have rarely been challenged in principle. But these rules no longer work, and their inadequacies have had deleterious consequences for the strong as well as the weak. The policy tools that powerful and well-governed states have available to "fix" badly governed or collapsed states—principally governance assistance and transitional administration (whether formally authorized by the United Nations or engaged in by a coalition of the willing led by the United States)—are inadequate. In the future, better domestic governance in badly governed, failed, and occupied polities will require the transcendence of accepted rules, including the creation of shared sovereignty in specific areas. In some cases, decent governance may require some new form of trusteeship, almost certainly de facto rather than de jure (Fearon and Laitin 2004: 5–43).

Many countries suffer under failed, weak, incompetent, or abusive national authority structures. The best that people living in such countries can hope for is marginal improvement in their material well-being; limited access to social services, including health care and education; and a moderate degree of individual physical security. At worst they will confront endemic violence, exploitative political leaders, falling life expectancy, declining per capita income, and even state-sponsored genocide. In the Democratic Republic of Congo, for example, civil wars that have persisted for more than two decades have resulted in millions of deaths. In Zimbabwe the policies of President Robert Mugabe, who was determined to stay in office regardless of the consequences for his country's citizens, led to an economic debacle that began in 2000 with falling per capita income, inflation above 500 per cent, and the threat of mass starvation. In Colombia much of the territory is controlled by the Revolutionary Armed Forces of Colombia (FARC), a Marxist rebel group that derives most of its income from drug trafficking. In Rwanda more than 700,000 people were slaughtered in a matter of weeks in 1994 as a result of a government-organized genocide.

The consequences of failed and inadequate governance have not been limited to the societies directly affected. Poorly governed societies can generate conflicts that spill across international borders. Transnational criminal and terrorist networks can operate in territories not controlled by the internationally recognized government. Humanitarian disasters not only prick the conscience of political leaders in advanced democratic societies but also leave them with no policy options that are appealing to voters.

Challenges related to creating better governance also arise where national authority structures have collapsed because of external invasion and occupation rather than internal conflict. The availability of weapons of mass destruction and the presence of transnational terrorism have created a historically unprecedented situation in which polities with very limited material capability can threaten the security of much more powerful states. These polities can be conquered and occupied with relative ease, leaving the occupying power with the more challenging task of establishing an acceptable domestic governing structure. Contemporary Afghanistan and Iraq are the obvious cases in point.

Left to their own devices, collapsed and badly governed states will not fix themselves because they have limited administrative capacity, not least with regard to maintaining internal security (Fearon and Laitin 2004: 36–37). Occupying powers cannot escape choices about what new governance structures will be created and sustained. To reduce international threats and improve the prospects for individuals in such polities, alternative institutional arrangements supported by external actors, such as de facto trusteeships and shared sovereignty, should be added to the list of policy options.

The current menu of policy instruments for dealing with collapsed and failing states is paltry, consisting primarily of transitional administration and foreign assistance to improve governance, both of which assume that in more or less short order, targeted states can function effectively on their own. Nation-building or state-building efforts are almost always described in terms of empowering local authorities to assume the responsibilities of conventional sovereignty. The role of external actors is understood to be limited with regard to time, if not scope, in the case of transitional administration exercising full executive authority. Even as the rules of conventional sovereignty are de facto violated if not de jure challenged, and it is evident that in many cases effective autonomous national government is far in the future, the language of diplomacy, the media, and the street portrays nothing other than a world of fully sovereign states.

The next section of this article describes the basic elements that constitute the conventional understanding of sovereignty and provides a taxonomy of alternative institutional forms. It is followed by a discussion of the ways in which conventional sovereignty has failed in some states, threatening the well-being of their own citizens and others. The inadequacy of the current repertoire of policy options for dealing with collapsed, occupied, and badly governed states—governance assistance and transitional administration—is then assessed. The possibilities for new institutional forms—notably shared sovereignty and some de facto form of trusteeship—are examined. Included is a discussion of why such arrangements might be accepted by political leaders in target as well as intervening states.

Conventional sovereignty and some alternatives

Conventional sovereignty has three elements: international legal sovereignty, Westphalian/Vattelian sovereignty, and domestic sovereignty. The basic rule of international legal sovereignty is to recognize juridically independent territorial entities. These entities then have the right to freely decide which agreements or treaties they will enter into. In practice, this rule has been widely but not universally honored. Some entities that are not juridically independent have been recognized (e.g. Byelorussia and the Ukraine during the Cold War), and some entities that are juridically independent have not been recognized (e.g. the People's Republic of China from 1949 to the 1970s).

The fundamental rule of Westphalian/Vattelian sovereignty is to refrain from intervening in the internal affairs of other states. Each state has the right to determine its own domestic authority structures. Although the principle of nonintervention is traditionally associated with the Peace of Westphalia of 1648, the doctrine was not explicitly articulated until a century later by the Swiss jurist Emmerich de Vattel in his *The Law of Nations or Principles of the Law of Nature Applied to the Conduct and Affairs of Nations and Sovereigns*, originally published in French in 1758. In practice, Westphalian/Vattelian sovereignty has frequently been violated.

Domestic sovereignty does not involve a norm or a rule, but is rather a description of the nature of domestic authority structures and the extent to which they are able to control activities within a state's boundaries. Ideally, authority structures would ensure a society that is peaceful, protects human rights, has a consultative mechanism, and honors a rule of law based on a shared understanding of justice.

In the ideal sovereign state system, international legal sovereignty, Westphalian/Vattelian sovereignty, and domestic sovereignty are mutually supportive. Recognized authorities within territorial entities regulate behavior, enjoy independence from outside interference, and enter into mutually beneficial contractual relations (treaties) with other recognized entities. This is the conventional world of international politics in which state-to-state relations are what count. One of the most striking aspects of the contemporary world is the extent to which domestic sovereignty has faltered so badly in states that still enjoy international legal, and sometimes even Westphalian/Vattelian, sovereignty. Somalia, for instance, is still an internationally recognized entity, even though it has barely any national institutions; and external actors have not, in recent years, tried to do much about Somalia's domestic sovereignty, or the lack thereof.

Conventional sovereignty was not always the hegemonic structure for ordering political life. Obviously, the basic rules of medieval Europe or the pre-nineteenth-century Sinocentric world were very different. But even in the nineteenth century, by which time conventional sovereignty had become a well-recognized structure, there were also legitimated and accepted alternatives. Protectorates were one alternative to conventional sovereignty; the rulers of a protectorate relinquished control over foreign policy to a more powerful state but retained authority over domestic affairs. For instance, in 1899 the ruler of Kuwait signed an agreement that gave Britain control of most elements of his country's foreign policy because he needed external support against threats from both Iraq and members of his own family (Tetreault 1991: 565–91). In nineteenth-century China the major powers established treaty ports where British, French, German, and Japanese authorities regulated commerce and exercised extraterritorial authority over their own citizens and sometimes Chinese as well. In Shanghai, for instance, the British established a municipal council that regulated the activities of Chinese living within Shanghai as well as non-Chinese (Chesneaux and Bastid 1977: 61–68). Within the British Empire, Australia, Canada, and South Africa became dominions that enjoyed almost complete control over their domestic affairs, recognized the British ruler as the head of state, but to some extent deferred to Britain in matters of foreign policy. Finally, colonization was a legitimated practice in the nineteenth century that allowed powerful states to assume international legal sovereignty and regulate the domestic authority structures of far-flung territories.

Conventional sovereignty is currently the only fully legitimated institutional form, but unfortunately it does not always work. Honoring Westphalian/Vattelian sovereignty (and sometimes international legal sovereignty as well) makes it impossible to secure decent and effective domestic sovereignty, because the autochthonous political incentives facing political leaders in many failed, failing, or occupied states are perverse. These leaders are better able to enhance their own power and wealth by making exclusionist ethnic appeals or undermining even the limited legal routinized administrative capacity that might otherwise be available.

To secure decent domestic governance in failed, failing, and occupied states, new institutional forms are needed that compromise Westphalian/Vattelian sovereignty for an indefinite period. Shared sovereignty, arrangements under which individuals chosen by international organizations, powerful states, or ad hoc entities would share authority with nationals over some aspects of domestic sovereignty, would be a useful addition to the policy repertoire. Ideally, shared sovereignty would be legitimated by a contract between national authorities and an external agent. In other cases, external interveners may conclude that the most attractive option would be the establishment of a de facto trusteeship or protectorate. Under such an arrangement, the Westphalian/Vattelian sovereignty of the target polity would be violated, executive authority would be vested primarily with external actors, and international legal sovereignty would be suspended. Other analysts have made similar suggestions. Keohane has argued that there should be gradations of sovereignty. Helman and Ratner suggest that there are three forms of what they call "guardianship": governance assistance, the delegation of government authority, and trusteeship. They also suggest the term "conservatorship" as an alternative to trusteeship (Keohane 2003: 276–77; Helman and Ratner 1993: 3–21). There will not, however, be any effort to formalize through an international convention or treaty a general set of principles for such an option.

Failures of conventional sovereignty

Failed, inadequate, incompetent, or abusive national authority structures have sabotaged the economic well-being, violated the basic human rights, and undermined the physical security of their countries' populations. In some cases, state authority has collapsed altogether for an extended period, although such instances are rare. Afghanistan in the early 1990s before the Taliban consolidated power, Liberia for much of the 1990s, and the Democratic Republic of Congo and Sierra Leone in the late 1990s are just a few of the examples. Governance challenges have also arisen in Afghanistan and Iraq, where authority structures collapsed as a result of external invasion rather than internal conflict. The occupying powers, most obviously the United States, were then confronted with the challenge of fashioning decent governance structures in both countries. In some parts of the world, disorder (including civil war) has become endemic. For the period 1955 to 1998, the State Failure Task Force identified 136 occurrences of state failure in countries with populations larger than 500,000. The task force operationalized state failure as one of four kinds of internal political crisis: revolutionary war, ethnic war, "adverse regime change," or genocide (Goldstone *et al.* 2000: iv, v, 3–5). In 1955 fewer than 6 per cent of the countries were in failure. In the early 1990s the figure had risen to almost 30 per cent, falling to about 20 per cent in 1998. Adverse regime change was the most common form of state failure, followed by ethnic war, revolutionary war, and genocide. The task force identified partial democracy, trade closure, and low levels of economic well-being as indicated by high infant mortality rates as the primary causes of state failure (King and Zeng 2001: 623–28). James Fearon and David Laitin show that internal strife is more likely in countries suffering from poverty, recent decolonization, high population, and mountainous terrain. These conditions allow even relatively small guerrilla bands to operate successfully because recognized governments do not have the administrative competence to engage in effective rural policing and counterinsurgency operations (Fearon and Laitin 2004: 36–37).

States that experience failure or poor governance more generally are beset by many problems. In such states, infrastructure deteriorates; corruption is widespread; borders are unregulated; gross domestic product is declining or stagnant; crime is rampant; and the national currency is not widely accepted. Armed groups operate within the state's boundaries but outside the control of the government. The writ of the central government, the entity that exercises the prerogatives of international legal sovereignty (e.g. signing treaties and sending delegates to international meetings), may not extend to the whole country; in some cases, it may not extend beyond the capital. Authority may be exercised by local entities in other parts of the country, or by no one at all.

Political leaders operating in an environment in which material and institutional resources are limited have often chosen policies that make a bad situation even worse. For some leaders, disorder and uncertainty are more attractive than order and stability because they are better able to extract resources from a disorderly society. Decisions affecting the distribution of wealth are based on personal connections rather than bureaucratic regulations or the rule of law. Leaders create multiple armed units that they can play off against each other. They find it more advantageous to take a bigger piece of a shrinking pie than a smaller piece of a growing pie.

The largest number of poorly governed states is found on the continent of Africa. Since the mid-1950s about a third of African states have been in failure (Goldstone *et al.* 2000: 21). In constant 1995 US dollars, gross domestic product per capita for all of sub-Saharan Africa fell from $660 in 1980 to $587 in 1990 to $563 in 2000. Out of the sub-Saharan states for which data are available from the World Bank, eighteen had increases in their per capita gross domestic product from 1990 to 2000, seven had decreases of less than 5 per cent, and seventeen experienced decreases of more than 5 per cent. With the exception of the former Soviet Union, no other area of the world fared so badly with regard to economic performance (World Bank, World Development Indicators).

Sierra Leone offers one example of state collapse during the 1990s. Government revenue declined from $250 million in the mid-1970s to $10 million in 1999. Most television service ended in 1987 when the minister of education sold the country's broadcasting tower. During the 1990s, civil strife resulted in at least 50,000 deaths and many more injuries and maimings. There was a military coup in 1992, an election in 1996, and another coup in 1997. A Nigerian-led West African peacekeeping force intervened in 1998 and restored the elected president to power, but it was unable to control rebel violence. A 1999 peace agreement brought Sankoh Foday, leader of the Revolutionary United Front (RUF), into the government as vice president and minister of mines. The RUF was infamous for cutting off the limbs of its victims. This agreement collapsed after 500 UN peacekeepers were kidnapped when they entered Sierra Leone's diamond area. Charles Taylor, then president of Liberia and currently under indictment for crimes against humanity by the Special Court for Sierra Leone, supported rebel groups in Sierra Leone in 2000 and 2001 because he wanted access to the country's diamond mines. Order was finally restored in 2002 after the United Nations authorized a force that grew to 17,000 men. British units made a substantial contribution to finally defeating and disarming the rebel forces (Reno 2003: 72–73, 88; Sengupta 2003). Describing Sierra Leone in the 1990s, William Reno writes,

> The country's rulers intentionally made life for their subjects less secure and more materially poor. They became personally wealthy as a consequence of this disorder, and then sold chances to profit from disorder to those who could pay for them by providing services—as experts in violence, for example—and to those local and expatriate businessmen who traded their access to commercial networks.
> (Reno 2003: 75; see also Rotberg 2003: 14; Ignatieff 2003: 301–3)

Thus, for many countries domestic sovereignty is not working, and the situation is not improving in any substantive way. Although the number and percentage of countries suffering from civil war declined during the 1990s, the per capita gross national income in current US dollars of the least developed countries continued to drop, falling by 9 per cent from 1990 to 2000, a period of robust growth for the world as a whole (World Bank, World Development Indicators).

Why sovereignty failures matter

In the contemporary world, powerful states have not been able to ignore governance failures. Polities where domestic authority has collapsed or been inadequate have threatened the economic and security interests of these states. Humanitarian crises have engaged electorates in advanced democracies and created no-win situations for political leaders who are damned if they intervene and damned if they do not. And, most obviously, when a state has been invaded, the occupiers have been confronted with the problem of establishing effective domestic sovereignty.

The availability of weapons of mass destruction, the ease of movement across borders, and the emergence of terrorist networks have attenuated the relationship between the underlying capabilities of actors and the ability to kill large numbers of people. In the past, state and nonstate actors with limited resources could not threaten the security of states with substantial resources. The killing power of a nation's military depended on the underlying wealth of the country. Nonstate actors such as anarchist groups in the nineteenth century could throw bombs that might kill fifty or even several hundred people, but not more. This is no longer true. States with limited means can procure chemical and biological weapons. Nuclear weapons demand more resources, but they are not out of reach of even a dismally poor country such as North Korea. Weapons of mass destruction can be delivered in myriad ways, not only by missiles but also by commercial ships, trucks, planes, and even envelopes. Failed or weak states may provide terrorists with territory in which they can operate freely.

Moreover, political leaders who have effective control within their borders but limited resources to defend or deter an invasion present a tempting target if they adopt policies that threaten the core security interests of powerful states. For instance, throughout his rule Saddam Hussein sought and sometimes used weapons of mass destruction, and even when faced with invasion, failed to fully cooperate with UN inspectors. In Afghanistan the Taliban supported al-Qaeda, which had already demonstrated that it could strike core targets in the United States. Neither Iraq nor Afghanistan could defend itself against, or deter, a US attack. When the threat is high and invasion is easy, powerful states are likely to use military force to bring down a menacing regime. When, however, the old regime has collapsed, the occupiers confront the challenge of creating effective and decent domestic sovereignty.

Sovereignty failures may also present problems in the area of transnational criminality. Drug trafficking is difficult to control under any circumstances, but such activities are more likely to flourish where domestic sovereignty is inadequate. About 95 per cent of illicit drug production takes place in areas of civil strife. Colombia, where the FARC has controlled a large part of the territory, has been one of the major sources of such drugs for the United States. In the late 1990s Afghanistan cultivated 75 per cent of the world's opium poppies, and despite a ban by the Taliban at the end of its rule, production revived after the regime was overthrown because the new government in Kabul had only limited control over much of the country (United Nations, Office on Drugs and Crime 2001; Rhode 2004; Collier and Hoeffler 2004: 8–9). Transnational trafficking in persons is more likely, although not limited to, countries where domestic authority and control are weak or ineffective. A 2004 State Department report lists ten countries—Bangladesh, Burma, Cuba, Ecuador, Equatorial Guinea, Guyana, North Korea, Sierra Leone, Sudan, and Venezuela—that have not met minimum efforts to control trafficking in persons. Most of the ten are failed or badly governed states (United States, Department of State 2004). In addition, it is more difficult to trace and punish the perpetrators of transnational financial fraud in countries where the police and judiciary do not function well.

Finally, gross violations of human rights present unpleasant political choices for democratic leaders in powerful states. There have been a number of humanitarian catastrophes in recent years, with the killings in Rwanda in the mid-1990s being one of the most appalling and most widely reported. Millions of people have died in other countries as well at the hands of their own government or rival political groups. These and other humanitarian disasters have engaged attentive elites. The Canadian ministry of foreign affairs, for instance, organized the International Commission on Intervention and State Sovereignty in 2000 in response to UN Secretary-General Kofi Annan's appeal for a new consensus on the right of humanitarian intervention. The commission, composed of twelve eminent persons, produced a widely circulated report entitled *The Responsibility to Protect*. The report defends the principle of humanitarian intervention when governments abuse or fail to protect their own citizens. The outcome document adopted by the high-level plenary meeting of the General Assembly in 2005 endorsed the responsibility to protect. Samantha Power's book, *A Problem from Hell: America and the Age of Genocide*, which describes the failure of the United States to act either to prevent or to mitigate a number of genocides throughout the twentieth century, won a Pulitzer Prize in 2003 (International Commission on Intervention and State Sovereignty 2001; G. Evans and Sahnoun 2002: 99–110).

From an electoral perspective, American leaders cannot simply ignore humanitarian crises. Sowmya Anand and Jon Krosnick have shown that the US electorate is made up of a number of distinct issue publics. Individuals in each of these publics are knowledgeable about their specific issue, including where presidential aspirants stand. Anand and Krosnick asked a random sample of the electorate questions about US foreign policy before the 2000 elections such as: should the United States be "Helping poor countries provide food, clothing, and housing for their people? Helping resolve disputes between two other countries? Preventing governments of other countries from hurting [their] own citizens? Preventing people in other countries from killing each other?" On these four questions, between 7.3 per cent and 9.6 per cent of the electorate indicated that these issues were extremely important to them. These percentages are low compared with percentages on some other issues (e.g. 33.5 per cent indicated that defending the United States against missile attack was very important), but the responses do indicate that there is a significant part of the US electorate concerned with humanitarian issues in poorer countries (Anand and Krosnick 2003: Tables 2 and 3).

Humanitarian crises, then, present decision makers in democratic countries with a no-win situation. If they fail to intervene and a humanitarian disaster occurs, they may lose the votes of citizens who are attentive to and care about the fate of particular countries, regions, ethnic groups, or principled issues in general. On the other hand, if a political leader does intervene, the costs in terms of soldiers killed will be readily apparent, but the number of lives saved can never be demonstrated with certainty.

The existing institutional repertoire: governance assistance and transitional administration

Political leaders in powerful and weak states have been reluctant to challenge the conventional norms of sovereignty. The policy options currently available to repair occupied or badly governed states—governance assistance and transitional administration—are consistent with these norms. They have made some limited contribution to improving governance in badly run and collapsed states, but policy makers would be better served if they had a wider repertoire of policy choices.

Governance assistance

For the last decade international organizations, the United States, and other donor countries have devoted substantial resources to promoting better governance. US foreign aid has been given to train judges, rewrite criminal codes, increase fiscal transparency, professionalize the police, encourage an open media, strengthen political parties, and monitor elections. Since the 1950s, international financial institutions have been involved in questions of policy and sometimes institutional reform in borrowing countries. The conditions attached to lending by the World Bank and the International Monetary Fund (IMF) have covered a wide range of issues such as aggregate credit expansion, subsidies, number of government employees, indexation of salaries, tariffs, tax rates, and institution-building. International financial institutions have placed their own personnel in key bureaus (International Monetary Fund, Fiscal Affairs Department 1986: 40; Broad 1988: 51–53, Table 12). In the mid-1990s the managing director of the IMF and the president of the World Bank committed themselves to a more aggressive attack on corruption in developing states (P. Lewis 1997: 4; McKinley 1998: 4). In 1997 the World Bank subtitled its world development report *The State in a Changing World*. The report declares that the "clamor for greater government effectiveness has reached crisis proportions in many developing countries where the state has failed to deliver even such fundamental public goods as property rights, roads, and basic health and education" (World Bank 1997: 2). Further, it lists basic tasks for the state, including establishing a foundation of law, protecting the environment, and shielding the vulnerable; chastises governments for spending too much on rich and middle-class students in universities while neglecting primary education; and urges these governments to manage ethnic and social differences (World Bank 1997: 4). Finally, and most ambitiously, the 1991 Agreement Establishing the European Bank for Reconstruction and Development explicitly includes a commitment to democracy as a condition of membership. The first paragraph of the Agreement Establishing the European Bank for Reconstruction and Development, signed in Paris on 29 May 1990, states that contracting parties should be "committed to the fundamental principles of multiparty democracy, the rule of law, respect for human rights and market economics."

Foreign assistance to improve governance in weak states does not usually contradict the rules of conventional sovereignty. Governments contract with external agencies to provide training in various areas. Such contracting is a manifestation of international legal sovereignty and is consistent with Westphalian/Vattelian sovereignty, so long as the influence of external actors on domestic authority structures is limited to specific policies or improvements in the capabilities of government employees. When bargaining power is highly asymmetric, as may be the case in some conditionality agreements between international financial institutions and borrowing countries,

Westphalian/Vattelian sovereignty can be compromised. External actors can influence not just policies but also institutional arrangements in target states. The borrowing country is better off with the agreement, conditions or no, than it would have been without it; otherwise it would not have signed. Nevertheless, political leaders may accept undesired and intrusive engagement from external actors because the alternative is loss of access to international capital markets.

The effectiveness of governance assistance will always be limited. Some leaders will find the exploitation of their own populations more advantageous than the introduction of reforms. The leverage of external actors will usually be constrained. International financial institutions are in the business of lending money; they cannot put too stringent restrictions on their loans lest their customers disappear. Many IMF agreements are renegotiated, sometimes several times. Small social democratic countries in Europe have been committed, because of the views of their electorates, to assisting the poor; they will be loath to allow their funding levels to drop below the generally recognized target of 0.7 per cent of national income. The wealthier countries also routinely provide humanitarian assistance, regardless of the quality of governance in a particular country.

Moreover, those providing governance assistance are likely to adopt formulas that reflect their own domestic experience and that may be ill suited to the environments of particular target countries. The United States, for instance, has emphasized elections and independent legislatures. Interest groups have been regarded as independent of the state, whereas in European social democratic countries, they are legitimated by and sometimes created by the state (Carothers 1999).

Transitional administration

Transitional administration is the one recognized alternative to conventional sovereignty that exists in the present international environment, but it is explicitly not meant as a challenge to the basic norms of sovereignty. The scope of transitional administration or peacekeeping and peacebuilding operations has ranged from the full assertion of executive authority by the UN for some period of time, East Timor being an example, to more modest efforts involving monitoring the implementation of peace agreements, as was the case in Guatemala in the 1990s. Transitional administration, usually authorized by the UN Security Council, has always been seen as a temporary, transitional measure designed to create the conditions under which conventional sovereignty can be restored. The US occupation of Iraq has followed the same script, albeit without any UN endorsement of the occupation itself, although the Security Council did validate the restoration of international legal sovereignty in June 2004. Westphalian/Vattelian sovereignty and sometimes international legal sovereignty are violated in the short term so that they can be restored in the longer term; at least, that is the standard explanation.

The record of peacebuilding efforts since World War II has been mixed. One recent study identified 124 cases of peacebuilding by the international community. Of these, 43 per cent were judged to be successful based on the absence of hostilities. If progress toward democracy is added as a measure of success, only 35 per cent were successful (Doyle and Sambanis 2000: 779–802; Downs and Stedman 2002: 50–52).

More extensive peacekeeping operations, those that might accurately be called "transitional administration" because they involve the assertion of wide-ranging or full executive authority by the UN (or the United States), are difficult: the demands are high; advance planning, which must prejudge outcomes, is complicated, especially for the UN; and resources—economic, institutional, and military—are often limited. UN missions have run monetary systems, enforced laws, appointed officials, created central banks, decided property claims, regulated businesses, and operated public utilities. The resources to undertake these tasks have rarely been adequate. Each operation has been ad hoc; no cadres of bureaucrats, police, soldiers, or judges permanently committed to transitional administration exist; and there is a tension between devolving authority to local actors and having international actors assume responsibility for all governmental functions because, at least at the outset, this latter course is seen as being more efficient (Caplan 2002: 8–9, 50–51; United Nations 2000: 7, 14; Schrader 2003: A1).

Transitional administration is particularly problematic in situations where local actors disagree about basic objectives among themselves and with external actors. Under these circumstances, as opposed to situations in which local actors agree on goals but need external monitoring to provide reassurances about the behavior of their compatriots, the inherently temporary character of transitional administration increases the difficulty of creating stable institutions. If indigenous groups disagree about the distribution of power and the constitutional structure of the new state, then the optimal strategy for their political leaders is to strengthen their own position in anticipation of the departure of external actors. They do so by maximizing support among their followers rather than backing effective national institutions. Alternatively, local leaders who become dependent on external actors during a transitional administration, but who lack support within their own country, do not have an incentive to invest in the development of new institutional arrangements that would allow their external benefactors to leave at an earlier date (Fearon and Laitin 2004: 37; Edelstein 2004: 49–81).

Multiple external actors with varying interests and little reason to coordinate their activities have exacerbated the problems associated with transitional administration. The bureaucratic and financial interests of international organizations are not necessarily complementary. NGOs need to raise money and make a mark. The command structures for security and civilian activities have been separated. The permanent members of the Security Council, to whom UN peacekeeping authorities are ultimately responsible, have not always had the same interests (Ignatieff 2003: 27).

Bosnia, one of the most well-known peacekeeping endeavors, illustrated many of these problems. The 1995 Dayton agreement created a complicated and possibly unworkable political structure. Because of antagonisms among the groups in Bosnia, the UN high representative, who has always been a West European, has made many decisions, large and small. For instance, in 1998 the high representative, Carlos Westendorp, mandated a license plate design that did not indicate where the driver was from. Had he not done this, many Bosnians would have been reluctant to leave their local districts (Cousens 2002: 532; International Crisis Group 2002: 25, 33; Chesterman 2001: 1; Caplan 2002: 19, 39). In 2004 Paddy Ashdown, who had become the high representative two years earlier, dismissed 60 Bosnian Serb political leaders (including the interior minister and the speaker of the parliament) for failing to arrest Radovan Karadžić, twice indicted by the Hague war crimes tribunal (Wood 2004: 6).

External actors failed to establish a coherent administrative structure. The Security Council appoints the high representative for Bosnia and Herzegovina on the basis of a recommendation from the 55-member Peace Implementation Council. The high representative, however, had no authority over SFOR, the Stabilization Force. The commander of SFOR reported to NATO's commander in Europe, an American (see www.nato.int/sfor/index.htm and linked pages). Nor was there fully effective coordination among the many non-military organizations operating in Bosnia and Herzegovina. The Organization for Security and Economic Cooperation in Europe (OSCE) dealt with such issues as human rights, rule of law, security cooperation, and education reform. The European Union (EU) provided, among other things, a special police organization whose members worked side by side with local officials. The UN High Commissioner for Refugees (UNHCR) was the lead agent for refugees and internally displaced persons. The UN Development Program administered more than $100 million in reconstruction funds. The World Bank took the lead in economic reconstruction. The International Committee of the Red Cross dealt with missing persons. The policies of these different agencies were sometimes at loggerheads. For instance, EU efforts to condition aid to Mostar, the largest city in Herzegovina, on cooperation between Croats and Serbs were frustrated by the issuance of a World Bank loan for the reconstruction of a hydroelectric plant that was granted without concern for political factors (www.oscebih.org/mission/mandate.asp; UN Development Program, "UNDP BiH—It's Not Just What We Do, but Also How We Do It!" www.undp.ba/osc.asp?idItem=2; UN High Commissioner for Refugees, "History," www.unhcr.ba/history/index.htm; and Office of the High Representative, www.ohr.int/; Cousens 2002: 540; O'Neill 2002: 37–40; International Crisis Group 2002: ii; Caplan 2002: 24)

Transitional administration has been most effective when the level of violence in a country has been low, where there has been involvement by major powers, and where the contending parties within the country have reached a mutually acceptable agreement. The key role for the transitional administration is then to monitor the implementation of the agreement. For instance, in Namibia the contact group, comprising Canada, France, Germany, Great Britain, and the United States, was involved in UN discussions about the constitutional structure for an independent Namibia beginning in 1978. All of the major contending parties consented to the UN Transition Assistance Group (UNTAG) that was sent in 1989, allowing the lightly armed mission to play a neutral role between South Africa and Namibia. The strength of the major potential spoilers, hard-line whites, was undermined by the collapse of apartheid in South Africa. The major responsibility of UNTAG was to supervise the elections for the government that assumed power when Namibia secured international legal sovereignty (Downs and Stedman 2002: 59–61; Paris 2004: Ch. 8).

There were also successful missions in Central America in the 1990s. In both Guatemala and Nicaragua, government and rebel groups had reached a mutually acceptable settlement. Peacekeeping missions contributed to stability by supervising elections, helping to demobilize combatants, and training police (Downs and Stedman 2002: 62–63; Paris 2004: Ch. 7).

In sum, transitional administration has worked best for the easiest cases, those where the key actors have already reached a mutually acceptable agreement. In these situations, the transitional administration plays a monitoring role. It can be truly neutral among the contending parties. The mission does not have to be heavily armed. Transitional administration, however, is much more difficult in cases such as Bosnia, Kosovo, Afghanistan, and Iraq—that is, where local leaders have not reached agreement on what the ultimate outcome for their polity should be and where they must think about positioning themselves to win support from parochial constituencies when transitional administration, along with its large foreign military force, comes to an end.

New institutional options: de facto trusteeships and shared sovereignty

Given the limitations of governance assistance and transitional administration, other options for dealing with countries where international legal sovereignty and Westphalian/Vattelian sovereignty are inconsistent with effective and responsible domestic sovereignty need to be explored. At least two such arrangements would add to the available tool kit of policy options. The first would be to revive the idea of trusteeship or protectorate, probably de facto rather than de jure. The second would be to explore possibilities for shared sovereignty in which national rulers would use their international legal sovereignty to legitimate institutions within their states in which authority was shared between internal and external actors.

De facto trusteeships

In a prescient article published in 1993, Gerald Helman and Steven Ratner argued that in extreme cases of state failure, the establishment of trusteeships under the auspices of the UN Security Council would be necessary. By the end of the 1990s, such suggestions had become more common. Analysts have noted that de facto trusteeships have become a fact of international life. In a monograph published in 2002, Richard Caplan argues, "An idea that once enjoyed limited academic currency at best—international trusteeship for failed states and contested territories—has become a reality in all but name." Martin Indyk, an assistant secretary of state during President Bill Clinton's administration, has argued that the most attractive path to permanent peace in the Middle East would be to establish a protectorate in Palestine, legitimated by the United Nations and with the United States playing a key role in security and other areas. Even if final status talks were completed, the trusteeship would remain in place until a responsible Palestinian government was established (Helman and Ratner 1993: 3–21; Caplan 2002: 7; Ignatieff 2003: 308; Indyk 2003: 51–66).

Despite these recent observations, developing an alternative to conventional sovereignty, one that explicitly recognizes that international legal sovereignty will be withdrawn and that external actors will control many aspects of domestic sovereignty for an indefinite period of time, will not be easy. To date there has been no effort, for instance, to produce a treaty or convention that would define and embody in international law a new form of trusteeship. Just the opposite. The rhetorical commitment of all significant actors, including the United States, has been to restore authority to local actors at the soonest possible moment, a stance exemplified by the decision to give what US officials insisted was full sovereignty to Iraq in June 2004.

Codifying a general set of principles and rules for some new kind of trusteeship or protectorate would involve deciding who would appoint the authority and oversee its activities: the UN Security Council? A regional organization such as the European Union? A coalition of the willing? A single state? A treaty or convention would have to define the possible scope of authority of the governing entity: all activities of the state including security and international affairs? Only matters related to the provision of public goods such as roads, but not those related to the private sphere such as marriage? Given that there would be no fixed date for ending a trusteeship or protectorate, how would the appropriate moment for transferring authority to local actors be determined? What intermediate steps would be taken? Could a trusteeship, some aspects of domestic governance remain under the control of the trustee or conservator (Caplan 2002: 9)?

The most substantial barrier to a general international treaty codifying a new form of trusteeship or protectorate is that it will not receive support from either the powerful, who would have to implement it, or the weak, who might be subject to it. There is widespread sentiment for the proposition that Westphalian/Vattelian sovereignty is not absolute and can be breached in cases of massive human rights violations. UN Secretary-General Annan expressed this view in 1999 to widespread international acclaim (Annan 1999). The UN General Assembly endorsed the concept of the responsibility to protect in 2005. But arguing that Westphalian/Vattelian sovereignty is not absolute is quite different from codifying an explicit alternative that would deprive states of their international legal sovereignty as well as control over their domestic affairs.

An explicit and legitimated alternative to sovereignty would require, at minimum, agreement among the major powers. An arrangement supported by leading states that are not members of the OECD such as Brazil, China, India, Indonesia, Nigeria, and South Africa would be even better. Best of all would be an agreement endorsed by the Security Council and the General Assembly. There is no indication, however, that such widespread support would be given. None of the actors has a clear interest in doing so. The major powers, those with the capacity to create a trusteeship, want to be able to pick and choose not only where they intervene but also the policies they would follow. The endorsement of a new institutional arrangement would provide a new choice on the menu, but this option might make it difficult to engage in ad hoc arrangements better suited to specific circumstances. For states in the Third World, any successor to the mandate system of the League of Nations, or the trusteeship system of the UN, would smell, if not look, too much like colonialism.

Shared sovereignty

Shared sovereignty would involve the engagement of external actors in some of the domestic authority structures of the target state for an indefinite period of time (Keohane 2003: 276–77). Such arrangements would be legitimated by agreements signed by recognized national authorities. National actors would use their international legal sovereignty to enter into agreements that would compromise their Westphalian/Vattelian sovereignty with the goal of improving domestic sovereignty. One core element of sovereignty—voluntary agreements—would be preserved, while another core element—the principle of autonomy—would be violated.

National leaders could establish shared sovereignty through either treaties or unilateral commitments. To be effective, such arrangements would have to create self-enforcing equilibria involving either domestic players alone or some combination of domestic and international actors. Political elites in the target state would have to believe that they would be worse off if the shared sovereignty arrangement were violated.

For policy purposes, it would be best to refer to shared sovereignty as "partnerships." This would more easily let policy makers engage in organized hypocrisy, that is, saying one thing and doing another. Shared sovereignty or partnerships would allow political leaders to embrace sovereignty, because these arrangements would be legitimated by the target state's international legal sovereignty, even though they violate the core principle of Westphalian/Vattelian sovereignty: autonomy. Organized hypocrisy is not surprising in an environment such as the international system where there are competing norms (e.g. human rights vs Westphalian/Vattelian sovereignty), power differentials that allow strong actors to pursue policies that are inconsistent with recognized rules, and exceptional complexity that makes it impossible to write any set of rules that could provide optimal outcomes under all conditions. Shared sovereignty or partnerships would make no claim to being an explicit alternative to conventional sovereignty. It would allow actors to obfuscate the fact that their behavior would be inconsistent with their principles.

Historical examples of shared sovereignty

Shared sovereignty agreements have been used in the past. There are several late nineteenth-century shared sovereignty arrangements in which external actors assumed control over part of the revenue-generating stream of a state that had defaulted on its debt. The state wanted renewed access to international capital markets. The lenders wanted assurance that they would be repaid. Direct control over the collection of specific taxes provided greater confidence than other available measures.

For example, a shared sovereignty arrangement between external lenders and the Porte (the government of the Ottoman Empire) was constructed for some parts of the revenue system of the empire during the latter part of the nineteenth century. The empire entered international capital markets in the 1850s to fund military expenditures associated with the Crimean War. By 1875, after receiving more than a dozen new loans, the empire was unable to service its foreign debt. To again secure access to international capital markets, the Ottomans agreed in 1881 to create, through government decree, the Council of the Public Debt. The members of the council—two from France; one each from Austria, Germany, Italy, and the Ottoman Empire itself; and one from Britain and the Netherlands together—were selected by foreign creditors. Until the debt was liquidated, the Porte gave control of several major sources of revenue to the council and authorized it to take initiatives that would increase economic activity. The council promoted, for instance, the export of salt (the tax on which it controlled) to India and introduced new technologies for the silk and wine industries. It increased the confidence of foreign investors in the empire's railways by collecting revenues that the government had promised to foreign companies. In the decade before World War I, the council controlled about one-quarter of the empire's revenue. It was disbanded after the war (Blaisdell 1929: 90–120, 124–30; Feis 1965: 332–41; B. Lewis 1995: 298–99; Owen 1981: 101). International legal sovereignty was honored; Westphalian/Vattelian sovereignty was ignored. This arrangement was durable because if the empire had revoked its decree, it would have lost access to international capital markets.

The relationship of the Soviet Union to the satellite states of Eastern Europe during the Cold War is another example of shared sovereignty. For more than forty years, Soviet penetration of domestic regimes, close oversight of officials, and policy direction from Moscow kept communist regimes in power. During the 1950s the Polish secret police, for instance, reported directly to Moscow. The militaries of the satellites were integrated into the Soviet command structure and unable to operate independently. The communist regimes that Moscow had put in place and sustained by violating Westphalian/Vattelian sovereignty dutifully signed off on the security arrangements that their overlord preferred. Except in a few instances, such as the invasion of Czechoslovakia in 1968, Soviet behavior was consistent with international legal sovereignty. The implicit and sometimes explicit use of force, however, was necessary to support these regimes because many of the citizens of the satellite states were alienated from their rulers.

The shared sovereignty arrangements established by the United States after World War II were more successful. Germany is the prime example. The Western allies wanted to internationally legitimate the Federal Republic of Germany (FRG or West Germany) but at the same time constrain its freedom of action. The Bonn agreements, signed in 1952 by the FRG, France, the United Kingdom, and the United States and revised in Paris in 1954, gave West Germany full authority over its internal and external affairs but with key exceptions in the security area. Not only did the FRG renounce its right to produce chemical, biological, and nuclear weapons; it also signed a status of forces agreement that gave the allies expansive powers. These included exclusive jurisdiction over the members of their armed forces and the right to patrol public areas including roads, railways, and restaurants. Allied forces could take any measures necessary to ensure order and discipline (Germany 1959: Articles 19, 22, 28). West Germany's military was fully integrated into NATO. Article 5(2) of the Convention on Relations gave the Western powers the right to declare a state of emergency until FRG officials obtained adequate powers enabling them to take effective action to protect the security of the foreign forces ("Convention on Relations between the Three Powers and the Federal Republic of Germany" 1955: 57–69; Bishop 1955: 125–47; Katzenstein 1987). Without a clear definition of these adequate powers, the Western allies formally retained the right to resume their occupation of the Federal Republic until 1990, when the 1990 Treaty on the Final Settlement with Respect to Germany terminated the Bonn agreements.

The United States succeeded in the West German case because most Germans supported democracy, a market economy, and constraints on the FRG's security policies. Obviously the strength of this support reflected many factors, including the long-term economic success of the West relative to the Soviet bloc. Shared sovereignty arrangements for security in the FRG contributed to effective domestic governance by taking a potentially explosive issue off the table both within and, more important, without West Germany. Security dilemmas that might have strengthened undemocratic forces in the FRG never occurred because the Bonn government did not have exclusive control of the country's defense.

One recent arrangement that has included elements of shared sovereignty, albeit in watered-down form, is the program associated with the development of oil resources in Chad and the pipeline that carries this oil through Cameroon to the Atlantic. Both Chad and Cameroon have been badly governed. In the 1990s an oil company consortium led by Exxon wanted to develop Chad's oil, but it feared not only that the Chad and Cameroon governments might void any contract but also that it would be subject to public criticism and court action by human rights and environmental groups. Because of these fears, the oil companies insisted on the involvement of the World Bank as a minority partner, an involvement that they hoped would lessen any chances of unilateral contract revisions and provide cover for, perhaps even improve, human rights and environmental performance. Royal Dutch Shell withdrew from the project in the mid-1990s because it feared being targeted for human rights violations, an accusation that had already been levied against the company because of its operations in Nigeria (Silverstein 2003: 1). The World Bank in turn insisted on a modest (in the end quite modest) degree of shared sovereignty.

Under pressure from World Bank officials, Chad enacted the Revenue Management Law in 1998. The law divided oil revenues into two categories: direct (dividends and royalties) and indirect (taxes, charges, and customs duties). Direct revenues were placed in a foreign escrow account, 10 per cent of which is committed to future generations. Of the remaining 90 per cent, 80 per cent was to be used for social services (including health care and education), 15 per cent for current government expenses, and 5 per cent for the oil-exporting region. The law provided for the creation of the Oil Revenues Control and Monitoring Board or Collège, which was responsible for authorizing and monitoring disbursements from the escrow account. The board included members from Chad's judiciary, civil society, and trade unions (Uriz 2001: 223; World Bank n.d.).

In addition, in February 2001 the World Bank created an independent body known as the International Advisory Group, whose members it would appoint in consultation with national authorities. The group had access to relevant information and officials, and advised the governments of Chad and Cameroon and the World Bank about the misallocation or misuse of public funds, involvement of civil society, institution building, and governance more generally. The chair of the five-member group (which included a former deputy minister in the Canadian government, a Dutch agricultural specialist, an American anthropologist, and an African NGO leader) was Mamadou Lamine Loum, a former Senegalese prime minister (World Bank 2007).

The potential leverage of international actors before the project was put in place was significant. The project would provided Chad with a 50 per cent increase in revenue. Chad and Cameroon could not have completed the project without the oil companies, and the companies would not have invested without the involvement of the World Bank. The bank, unlike the companies, had legitimacy, which allowed it to negotiate conditions related to Chad's domestic institutional structures (Uriz 2001: 198; Raeburn 2000: 60).

Nevertheless, despite the leverage enjoyed by the World Bank and the oil companies, the extent to which external actors have intruded on Chad's domestic governance has been modest. The International Advisory Group is just advisory. Most of the members of the Chadian oversight committee have been closely associated with the government. The allocation of funds to social services was not specified with regard to areas. In January 2006 the Bank suspended the program and froze its loans to Chad, after Chad passed a new law which violated the original agreement with the Bank. The Bank's actions also resulted in the suspension of some payments to the government of Chad from the oil escrow account managed by Citibank. In June of 2006 the Bank concluded a new agreement with Chad providing for a somewhat revised allocation of funds (World Bank, Chad Cameroon Pipeline Project 2007). While the Bank's leverage remained substantial, the willingness of Chinese companies to invest in Chad strengthened the government's position.

In sum, like virtually every other institutional arrangement that can be imagined, shared sovereignty has been tried before: specific configurations of power and interest led stronger actors to introduce shared sovereignty arrangements, and weaker ones to accept them. In the late nineteenth century, lenders wanted assurance from defaulting states that if they provided new capital they would be repaid. After World War II, both the United States and the Soviet Union used shared sovereignty to undergird their preferred domestic regimes in Western and Eastern Europe. Chad accepted some constraints on its use of oil revenues because complete rejection of the World Bank's recommendations might have entirely scuttled the pipeline project.

Conclusion

During the twentieth century, the norms of international legal sovereignty and Westphalian/Vattelian sovereignty became universally accepted. It has often been tacitly assumed that these norms would be accompanied by effective domestic sovereignty, that is, by governance structures that exercised competent and ideally constructive control over their countries' populations and territory. This assumption has proven false. Poor, even malevolent, governance is a widespread problem. Badly governed states have become a threat to the interests of much more powerful actors: weapons of mass destruction have broken the connection between resources and the ability to do grievous harm; genocides leave political leaders in democratic polities with uncomfortable choices; and transnational disease and crime are persistent challenges.

The policy tools available to external actors—governance assistance and transitional administration—are inadequate, even when foreign powers have militarily occupied a country. Governance assistance can have positive results in occupied or badly governed states, but the available evidence suggests that the impact is weak. Transitional administration, which aims to restore conventional sovereignty in a relatively short time frame, can be effective only if indigenous political leaders believe that they will be better off allying with external actors, not only while these actors are present but also after they leave.

The menu of options to deal with failing and collapsed states could be expanded in at least two ways. First, major states or regional or international organizations could assume some form of de facto trusteeship or protectorate responsibility for specific countries, even if there is no general international convention defining such arrangements. In a trusteeship, international actors would assume control over local functions for an indefinite period of time. They might also eliminate the international legal sovereignty of the entity or control treaty-making powers in whole or in part (e.g. in specific areas such as security or trade). There would be no assumption of a withdrawal in the short or medium term.

Second, domestic sovereignty in collapsed or poorly governed states could be improved through shared sovereignty contracts. These contracts would create joint authority structures in specific areas. They would not involve a direct assault on sovereignty norms because they would be formally consistent with international legal sovereignty, even though they would violate Westphalian/Vattelian sovereignty.

Political leaders in target states might accept such arrangements to secure external resources, either payments for raw materials' exploitation or foreign assistance, to encourage the departure of occupying forces, or to attract voters. To be durable, shared sovereignty institutions either would require external enforcement or would have to create adequate domestic support, which would depend on the results delivered.

De facto trusteeships or protectorates and shared sovereignty hardly exhaust the possibilities for improving domestic sovereignty in poorly governed states. Leaders in some polities have already used private firms to carry out some activities that have traditionally been in the hands of state officials. Indonesia, for instance, used a Swiss firm to collect its customs for more than eleven years. Mozambique contracted with Crown Agents to operate its customs agency and train indigenous personnel in the late 1997 (James 2002; Crown Agents n.d.). A number of other countries have also contracted out their customs services. Beginning in 1998 Cambodia contracted out some of its health care services to NGOs (Bhushan *et al.* 2002). Other governments have hired private military companies (PMCs). Perhaps with stronger accountability mechanisms enforced by advanced industrial states, such as the ability to prosecute PMCs and their employees for abuses, the results might be more consistently salutary (Singer 2003).

There is no panacea for domestic sovereignty failures. Even with the best of intentions and substantial resources, external actors cannot quickly eliminate the causes of these failures: poverty, weak indigenous institutions, insecurity, and the raw materials curse. But the instruments currently available to policy makers to deal with places such as Congo, Liberia, and Iraq are woefully inadequate. De facto trusteeships, and especially shared sovereignty, would offer political leaders a better chance of bringing peace and prosperity to the populations of badly governed states and reduce the threat that such polities present to the wider international community.

Conclusion

Garbage cans and policy streams: how academic research might affect foreign policy

Introduction

In 2001 and 2002 and then again from February 2005 until April of 2007, I worked in Washington at the State Department and at the National Security Council in the White House. I joined the Policy Planning Staff at the State Department a couple of weeks before 9/11 and watched incredulously with the other members of the office the attacks on the World Trade Center and the Pentagon. In April of 2002 I moved to the National Security Council, where I became the director for governance and development (one of the nice things about the NSC is that you have some leeway in making up your title) and worked primarily for Gary Edson, the deputy national security advisor who was the principal architect of the Millennium Challenge Account. I returned to Stanford at the end of 2002. In the fall of 2004 I wrote a letter about the challenge of failed states and democratization to my old colleague and friend, Condoleezza Rice, who had been designated as the next secretary of state, and she asked me to come back to Washington as director of the Policy Planning staff, a position whose occupants have included not only the renowned George Kennan, the first director, but Paul Nitze, Walt Rostow, Paul Wolfowitz, Anthony Lake, Richard Solomon, Dennis Ross, James Steinberg, and Morton Halperin.

While many of the directors of the Policy Planning Office at the State Department, the foreign affairs office where the fit between academia and policy appears to be most natural, have had ties with the university world, I have been among the few senior international relations scholars to hold the office. Kennan was a foreign service officer and then occupied a chair of history at the Princeton Institute for Advanced Studies; Walt Rostow, an economist, was one of the leading scholars of economic growth; Richard Solomon taught at Michigan as a China expert; Morton Halperin and Paul Wolfowitz both left very promising academic careers after a few years. Of the 23 scholars identified as having the most impact over the last 25 years in a recent survey of more than 1,000 international relations scholars, only four had served in policy-making position, two at the United Nations, John Ruggie and Michael Doyle, and two in the United States government,

Joseph Nye and me (Peterson *et al.* 2005: 62). While I might like to attribute my selection to my scholarly accomplishments, the necessary if not sufficient reason for my appointment was my long friendship with the new secretary of state, a friendship that had been characterized more by long conversations about the logical coherence and heuristic power of various institutional theories, and some spirited baseline exchanges on the tennis court, than by discussions of policy issues.

No academic coming to Washington can escape reflecting on the relationship between academia and policy making. The subject has generated a small body of literature over the last decade or two, the general thrust of which is to bemoan the growing gap, which some refer to as a chasm, between Washington and universities. Most of the scholars who have looked at this issue attribute the disconnect to developments in political science such as the absence of rewards for policy-related work, too much focus on general theoretical conceptualizations, and the validation of large studies with statistically significant but small r^2s.

My own assessment is different. The disconnect between academic political science and policy making is related in part to the complexity of the problems confronting policy makers but even more to the complexity of the policy-making process. The garbage can model proposed by Cohen, March, and Olsen, and John Kingdon's notion of policy streams, provide a better framework for understanding how policy is actually made (Cohen *et al.* 1972; Kingdon 1995). Academics are a part of the stream that generates policy alternatives but given the nature of the policy-making process itself, policy alternatives never by themselves determine policy. The best policy alternative, assuming for a moment that it is even possible to determine what that alternative is, will not necessarily be chosen. There is, inescapably, a haphazard and random character to the process. The right people have to be in place at the right time. A policy window has to open for a policy alternative to be attached to a problem. The rational decision-making model, which lurks behind many of the critiques of the gap between academia and policy, assumes that if academics provided better policy inputs then policy would be better; this is not necessarily the case. The closing-the-gap model not only does not allow for chance, it also fails to recognize that outcomes reflect political bargaining and compromise and that some alternatives will never be considered because they fail to conform with the predispositions, biases, or existing commitments of key decision makers.

The gap

Almost all of the recent writings on the relationship between academia and policy making, or the lack thereof, point to a gap. Alexander George's 1993 book was famously titled *Bridging the Gap: Theory and Practice in Foreign Policy* (George 1993). Although some individuals with academic backgrounds have served as principals at the State Department and the NSC, including Condoleezza Rice, George Shultz, Brent Scowcroft, Tony Lake, Madeline Albright, and Henry Kissinger, the relationship between university international relations scholars and public officials is attenuated. There is no direct pipeline from scholarly findings to policy. For foreign affairs, there is no entity like the Council of Economic Advisors, which institutionalizes the presence of economists in government. Although a few policy makers do regularly read academic journals, and I have met some of them, the number is small. While some prominent approaches and findings in international relations are shared with the policy world, such as the democratic peace and realism, others are almost never directly alluded to, such as liberal institutionalism. Self-enforcing equilibria is a term that trips lightly off the tongues of professors; I never heard it used in policy discussions. And I can attest that in Washington addressing someone as doctor, as in Dr Rice, is an honorific; addressing that individual as professor is a put-down. The situation is different in other countries where in my experience academic standing did elicit some degree of deference even in countries that were not particularly sympathetic to the Bush administration's policies.

Most of the academics who have sought to explain the gap and suggest ways in which it might be narrowed have pointed to failings in the academic world. Alexander George and others have highlighted elements of academic work in international relations that limits its utility for policy makers. Many academic approaches search for structural factors over which policy makers have no control. Structural realism emphasizes the distribution of power among states, something that cannot be changed in the short or medium term. At best, policy makers may be able to reallocate resources between civilian and military purposes. Fearon and Laitin have identified mountainous terrains as one of the factors associated with civil wars; not something policy makers can do much about (Fearon and Laitin 2004).

Scholars will report small but significant correlation coefficients if equations are appropriately specified. Such relationships, however, George and others have noted, have limited utility for policy makers dealing with specific cases. Political leaders who lose wars usually lose office, but Saddam stayed in power after the Gulf War. A statistically significant general finding, may often be of little help for a policy maker dealing with a specific problem (Stein 2000: 60).

George believed that rich theories with many causal variables were more likely to be useful for policy makers than elegant theories with few. Academia political science, however, places more emphasis on identifying critical factors which can explain a significant amount of the variance in an outcome rather than a laundry list, which might explain a bit more (George 1997).

Other observers of the policy theory divide have pointed not so much to the nature of research but to the incentive structure in the discipline of political science. Political science places little value on policy-oriented work. An article in a refereed journal counts for a lot; an article in *Foreign Affairs* counts for a little. New PhDs are hired entirely on the basis of their scholarly work; policy-related writings or service in government counts for nothing (Jentleson 2002). The standard advice for any younger scholar interested in government service is: get tenure first.

Finally, a number of writers have noted that foreign policy is really difficult. Many different factors can impact on an outcome. Stephen Walt has written that

> States' actions, and the effects of those actions, are the product of many different factors (relative power, domestic politics, norms and beliefs, individual psychology, etc.), and scholars have therefore produced a host of different theories employing many variables. Unfortunately, we do not have a clear method for combining these partial theories or deciding when to emphasize one over another.
>
> (Walt 2005: 35)

Outcomes may be the result of complex feedback and interaction loops. Unintended consequences are to be expected (Jervis 1997: Ch. 2). It may not be clear how to classify a problem. With which class of events should the apparent lack of central state control over Pakistan's Federally Administered Tribal Area be associated: weak governance, strategic calculations about the balance of power in the region, internal dissension among domestic actors, or something else?

For most observers, then, the gap is a product of the nature of academia. Even the most convincing empirical findings may be of no practical use because they do not include factors that policy makers can manipulate. And, the theories are not that good anyway because the analysis of foreign policy and international politics is particularly challenging given the number of relevant variables and the complexity of the environment. The implication of the closing-the-gap school is that even if we cannot expect major analytic breakthroughs that would provide unassailable answers to key problems, the academy would be able to contribute more to policy if academic research were more focused on the needs of policy makers; research would be more focused on the needs of policy makers if the reward structure within the academy were changed.

An alternative view

The rational actor model, tacitly assumed by the closing-the-gap school, has, of course, been widely criticized. The conditions for fully rational decision making almost never hold. Time is short. Attention is limited. Problems cannot be clearly defined. Human beings are subject to persistent cognitive failings such as fearing losses more than they value gains or anchoring actions around some arbitrary starting point. Different agencies within a government may have their own provincial interests.

Many different alternatives to the rational decision-making model have been offered. One that particularly resonates with my own experience is John Kingdon's argument that policy is the result of the convergence, often haphazard, of three independent streams – problems, policy alternatives, and politics (Kingdon 1995). Kingdon's work draws on Cohen, March and Olsen's memorably named garbage can model (Cohen *et al.* 1972).

Cohen, March and Olsen applied their model to what they called "organized anarchies," organizations with shifting actors, problematic preferences, and trial and error decision making (Cohen *et al.* 1972: 1). In organized anarchies outcomes are the result of the convergence of problems, solutions, people, and choice opportunities. Individual actors attach solutions to problems. These actors do not necessarily have consistent preference orderings. Relevant actors change over time and across issue areas. Problems may have access to many possible solutions or to few. Higher-level decision makers have access to more solutions, but less time. Lower-level policy makers, charged with dealing with a specific problem, have more time but fewer solutions available to them. Solutions that are attached to one problem at a particular point in time may be attached to another problem at some later point.

March, Cohen, and Olsen summarize their position in the following way:

> From this point of view, an organization is a collection of choices looking for problems, issues and feelings looking for decision situations in which they might be aired, solutions looking for issues to which they might be the answer, and decision makers looking for work …
>
> To understand processes within organizations, one can view a choice opportunity as a garbage can into which various kinds of problems and solutions are dumped by participants as they are generated. The mix of garbage in a single can depends on the mix of cans available, on the labels attached to the alternative cans, on what garbage is currently being produced, and on the speed with which garbage is collected and removed from the scene.
>
> (Cohen *et al.* 1972: 2)

John Kingdon in his *Agendas, Alternatives, and Public Policies* (Kingdon 1995) reframes the garbage can model. Although Kingdon focuses on agenda setting, his framework can be applied to the entire policy process (Zahariadis 2007). Empirically, Kingdon's study, the first edition of which was published in 1984, was based largely on data collected in the 1970s and focused on two issues, health care and transportation. Kingdon's framework treats the US national government as an organized anarchy. Preferences may be opaque or contradictory. Actors move in and out of the policy process. There are disagreements among various agencies and bureaus. Jurisdictional boundaries are not clear. The administrator of USAID, for instance, formally reports to the secretary of state. At the same time the administrator and the secretary are both members of the board of directors of the Millennium Challenge Corporation, an independent government corporation. Technologies are uncertain; it is not clear how inputs into a process are turned into outputs. A particular military strategy might or might not be successfully implemented, and even if it is implemented successfully might or might not accomplish its stated objective. The National Endowment for Democracy or USAID contractors might or might not carry out programs to assist civil society organizations in ways expected by policy makers, but even if faithfully carried out such programs might or might not contribute to the development of effective democracy. Under these circumstances past experiences often guide action, and trial and error is inevitable (Zahariadis 2007: 66–67). Rational decision-making is impossible.

There are five components to Kingdon's framework: three streams and two elements that can bring the streams together. The three streams—policy recognition, policy alternatives, and politics—flow more or less independently. Each has its own dynamic. Policy windows, where the three streams can be joined to create new initiatives, can be opened by policy entrepreneurs or politicians, or forced open by problems such as 9/11 or Katrina, that must be addressed. Policy agendas and outcomes are not the result of a rationale assessment of all possible policy options. Policy windows remain open only for a limited period of time and policies must conform with the interests of key decision makers in the political stream. When a policy window does open change can be dramatic, not just incremental.

Problem recognition transforms an issue from a condition to a problem. A condition is something that cannot or need not be changed. A problem is something that policy makers must address. If health care is regarded as a right, Kingdon observes, it is a problem that needs to be dealt with. If health care is not regarded as a right, then it is a condition which policy makers can neglect (Kingdon 1995: 109–13). If the absence of democracy in the Middle East is irrelevant for American economic and security interests, then it is a condition that can be ignored; if the absence of democracy in the Middle East generates transnational terrorism which threatens the national security of the United States it is a problem that must be confronted.

Problem recognition may occur for a variety of reasons. There may be crises, dramatic and unforeseen events that demand a response: 9/11 is an obvious case in point. Alternatively, indicators, especially quantitative indicators and other kinds of feedback, may reveal that a policy is not accomplishing its intended objectives. Bureaucrats trying to expand their turf may also attempt to have an issue recognized as a problem. Politicians may try to make their mark by identifying an issue as a problem. Lobbying groups striving to further their interests may also raise the saliency of an issue (Kingdon 1995: Ch. 5).

The second stream, policy alternatives, is moved by very different currents. Policy alternatives are cooked up by policy communities in what Kingdon

refers to as the "policy primeval soup" (Kingdon 1995: Ch. 6). Policy communities exist inside and outside of government. They are composed of
experts including academics, think-tank professionals, Congressional staff
members, and bureaucrats. The communities associated with specific issues
may be coherent and easily identified, or fragmented and diffuse.

Policy alternatives are more likely to survive, Kingdon asserts, if they are
well cooked. A new proposal is more likely to be the result of recombining
well-understood existing ideas than a completely new approach that no one
had considered seriously. Policy proposals have to be technically feasible, not
only a good idea that could work, but a good idea that can be effectively
implemented and administered. To have any chance of success, they also
have to conform with the overall ideologies of policy makers. Persuasion,
Kingdon argues, is the coin of the realm in the policy alternatives stream.
Over time a consensus may develop if the proponents of a particular
approach are persuasive enough.

Consistent with the garbage can model, however, the way in which policies
are attached to problems is not systematic. Organizations can attend to
many issues in parallel. Because of time and cognitive capacity, however,
policy makers, those in the political stream, can only pay attention to a more
limited number of issues (Zahariadis 2007: 68). Individuals in the policy
community may have knowledge about many different policy alternatives,
but only a few of these can ever be presented to policy makers.

In an interesting amendment to Kingdon's original position, Robert
Durant and Paul Diehl suggest that the cooking may be less thorough in the
foreign policy arena. In foreign policy the president, the key political actor in
the United States, operates with fewer constraints and in a more hierarchical
way than is the case for domestic policy making. As commander-in-chief
the president has constitutional prerogatives with regard to national security
that have no domestic equivalent. The president can establish counter-
bureaucracies in the White House that can circumvent established agencies.
In the policy stream, officials in the White House or specifically designated bureaucracies may generate alternatives that have not been well
cooked within some larger policy community. The president may have privileged information in the foreign policy arena that is available only to a limited
number of players in both the policy alternatives and the political streams.
Foreign policy crises may demand action even if there is no well-cooked
policy alternative available (Durant and Diehl 1989).

Academics can be significant players in the policy alternative stream.
Academics can influence the public agenda, provide policy options, and
directly introduce their ideas if they are working in government. However,
there is not necessarily an embrace of academics. "In some Washington
quarters," Kingdon observes, "there is a distrust of, and even a disdain for,
academic work" (Kingdon 1995: 57). My own experience in Washington did
not suggest that academics came with any particular authority. For better or
worse, probably for better, Americans may respect academics in general, and

defer to their judgment if they have technical knowledge, but they do not regard them as deserving any particular deference. I certainly got more recognition for my academic work when I was traveling as a government official in Latin America, Europe, and Asia than I ever did in the United States. My counterparts in foreign ministries in other parts of the world would refer to my academic writing, an experience I had only once in Washington, albeit from a quite highly placed individual.

Politics is the third stream that enters into the policy process. The political stream, like the problem recognition and policy alternative streams, moves according to its own logic. The main elements affecting the flow of the political stream are: the national mood, interest group campaigns, and administrative or legislative turnover. Politicians are interested in staying in office. They are attentive to the national mood, to sentiments that they might attach to particular policy initiatives. They may be moved by interest group pressure or by communications from constituents. Attentiveness to particular problems can shift depending on which individuals hold positions of power. Such changes obviously take place when a new administration begins and hundreds, even thousands, of offices change hands. They may also take place when committee chairs change or when new appointees assume important positions in the bureaucracy (Zahariadis 2007: 73–74; Kingdon 1995: Ch. 7).

In the political stream, consensus is built primarily through bargaining rather than persuasion. Different politicians will be interested in different issues. They may be able to link issues in ways that push their own agenda items. If a particular initiative catches on, there may be a bandwagon onto which many politicians will try to jump.

The problem recognition, policy alternatives, and political streams flow along independent of each other. There may be a great policy alternative but no politician that is interested in the associated problem. There may be a serious problem but no available feasible policy alternatives that might be attached to it. There may be a politician interested in a particular problem but no feasible policy alternative that is consistent with that politician's ideological orientation (Kingdon 1995: Ch. 7).

The streams come together when a policy window opens. (The mixed metaphor here is Kingdon's, not mine.) Sometimes policy windows open for predictable reasons: for instance, a piece of legislation must be renewed, or a new administration takes office. Sometimes policy windows are opened by policy entrepreneurs, individuals that are well connected and knowledgeable. Policy entrepreneurs are familiar with what is going on in all three streams, with what kind of garbage is in the available garbage cans at any particular moment. They are most likely to be effective when they have direct access to politicians in the political stream. Policy windows cannot be opened by those exclusively involved with the generation of policy alternatives, including academics. These individuals may be constantly stirring the policy soup, but they cannot turn a policy alternative into an actual policy unless a policy window opens.

Policy windows might not stay open for very long. The public mood might shift leading politicians to lose interest. Those holding key political positions might change. A policy entrepreneur capable of linking policy alternatives with problems might lose favor.

The closing-the-gap literature assumes that if academics could generate better policy alternatives, or provide better ways of framing problems, then we would have better policy. The perspective offered by Kingdon, and by Cohen, March, and Olsen, is not inconsistent with this assertion. Better policy alternatives could, but will not necessarily, result in better policy. The solutions and the problems would have to be in the same garbage can and an appropriate policy entrepreneur would have to be able to bring them together.

In sum, the multiple streams framework provides a way of thinking about how academia can impact on policy which is very different from the closing-the-gap approach. The quality of scholarship is only one input into the policy alternatives stream. How solutions in the policy alternatives stream effect policy also depends on how problems are generated and the political calculations that key decision makers must make. The policy alternatives available to these decision makers when a policy window opens might or might not be the policy that might emerge from a rational actor model in which actors were not constrained by cognitive limitations or time.

The intellectual challenge of foreign policy research

Foreign policy is in many ways more challenging than many other kinds of issues. Kingdon interviewed people about transportation and health. These are very hard problems, and the United States has hardly even now, 30 years after Kingdon's initial research, found solutions that are satisfactory. The base of systematic knowledge, however, for the specific problems associated with transportation, health, and many other issues is more robust than is the case for most major foreign policy questions.

Systematic knowledge comes from the development of logically sound theories and empirical evidence. Such theories, and especially convincing evidence, are easier to come by when there is a large body of relevant data, when it is evident to what general class a specific case belongs. Sometimes data alone can be compelling even without an underlying causal theory: for instance, initial findings about the relationship between smoking and lung cancer. This finding did not mean that North Carolina senators would support measures to discourage smoking. They did suggest, however, that there would be major public health benefits if people did stop smoking.

Compelling systematic knowledge about foreign policy issues is harder to come by. The study of international relations has been approached in a number of different ways, few of which have provided compelling findings that would, if nothing else, at least demand the attention of policy makers. One organizing structure has been to look at competing general theories such as realism, liberalism, and constructivism. These general theories provide guidance about what factors are relevant for understanding a problem – the international distribution of power, interests, ideas, and values – but they are not blueprints. In the contemporary world, the rise of China is an obvious issue for the United States. Realism suggests an inevitable clash (Mearsheimer 2005). Liberalism suggests opportunities for cooperation generated by shared economic interests. Constructivism suggests examining the norms and values guiding China's foreign policy and providing legitimacy for the regime: nationalism could make China's leaders more risk-acceptant; concerns about weakening economic growth could make them more risk-averse. Experts working in the policy alternatives streams will almost certainly have one or more of these ideas in mind. Politicians in the political stream will, with varying degrees of explicit recognition, be guided by general theoretical orientations. These meta-theories help to frame discussions but they will not provide dispositive arguments and evidence that policy makers could ignore only at their peril.

Moreover, many of the factors that these meta-theories emphasize cannot be manipulated by policy makers. Realism is particularly hobbled in this regard. Decision makers cannot change the distribution of power although they can reallocate available resources from domestic to international purposes. Liberal institutionalism ought to be more useful since it may suggest what kinds of institutions might be created to overcome market failure problems. The creation of these institutions, however, will always pose political challenges. Different institutions may have different distributional consequences even if all actors can be made absolutely better off (Chapter 7; Gruber 2000). Different players with different utilities may condition their cooperation in one area with concessions in another. Constructivism is useful if norms and values can be manipulated, but not if they are taken for granted and impossible to change in the short and medium term.

More specific problem-oriented work in international politics, especially work using large data sets, has produced lots of statistically significant findings, but the amount of variation explained is often limited. Fearon and Laitin's work, for instance, has shown that there is no statistically significant relationship between ethnic or religious fractionalization and civil war, while there are statistically significant relationships for poverty, population size, mountainous terrain, prior war, and oil exports (Fearon and Laitin 2004). But the total amount of variance explained even by this very statistically sophisticated and empirically well-specified research project is limited. In any given situation political leaders might mobilize their followers around ethnic divisions; guerrilla groups might learn to fight in flat urban areas; regimes might be able to control opponents contemplating a grab for resource wealth. An American decision maker, in the political stream, has to make decisions about policy for a specific civil war.

Moreover, every decision maker recognizes, sometimes only implicitly, that path-dependent processes can matter. Had al-Qaeda in Iraq not succeeded in blowing up the Golden Mosque in Samarra, civil strife might have been much lower. Had Hitler been assassinated in July 1944, the course of the Second World War and its aftermath might have been very different. Had the British destroyed Washington's army in Brooklyn in 1776, the prospects for American independence would have been much reduced. Social science, including the study of international relations, which focuses on structural conditions and their consequences cannot make predictions about path-dependent processes even though it may be able to explain them in retrospect.

Decision makers must take account of the political consequences of any decision. External intervention might stop a genocide but undermine the domestic political position of a president if casualties are high. Social science findings might suggest that a particular policy is likely to fail. Nevertheless, a political leader might conclude that the expected utility of change, taking account of the consequences of appearing to be uncertain or indecisive, would be lower than the expected utility of persisting.

Policy makers in the political stream must also find framing conceptualiza-tions, which may be inconsistent with social science findings, that can steer bureaucracies and generate political support. Several studies have shown, for instance, that the success rate for democracy promotion through the use of force is low (Pickering and Peceny 2006; Pei *et al.* 2006; Brownlee 2007). There have been some successes, including Panama and Grenada and not just the much more developed and thoroughly defeated Germany and Japan, but many more failures. The United States, however, more than any other country, has made the spread of democracy an explicit part of its foreign policy (Kagan 2006). American national identity is defined by a set of beliefs associated with Lockean individualism, democracy, and a market economy (Hartz 1955). The propagation or preservation of democracy has been an explicit objective of every major war that the United States has fought. If the United States does engage in a military action that leads to occupation, even if that action is motivated by security rather than ideational con-cerns, any American leader would find it difficult, even impossible, not to make democratization a core objective regardless of what social science might suggest.

Paul Nitze wrote in 1954 when he was director of Policy Planning that:

> To deal with such problems as present themselves to S/P [the State Department designation for the policy planning office] in the full rich-ness of their reality would require methods analogous to the simulta-neous solution of an almost infinite series of equations in the higher calculus. Many of the problems are without clear precedent; they cannot be resolved solely on the basis of tradition or of historical experience. The question is not whether to use the tools of political theory and political philosophy. The question is rather what tools are applicable to what situations and to what end.

> (Nitze 1954: 1)

Three stories

The multiple streams framework has helped me to make sense of many of the projects that I was involved in while I worked in Washington. Three in particular stand out: first, the creation of the Millennium Challenge Account; second, the idea of challenging China to be a "responsible stakeholder" in the international system; and third, the creation of a new initiative, the Partnership for Democratic Governance, to help countries provide better services to their populations by contracting out some activities. I have not selected these three because they were associated with the most salient challenges facing the Bush administration, but rather because I was intimately involved in all of them and had the opportunity to see the policymaking process at close hand. All three illustrate the haphazard, the garbage can, nature of the foreign policy-making process.

The Millennium Challenge Account: social science findings and foreign assistance

In 2004 the Congress appropriated funds for a new foreign assistance program, the Millennium Challenge Account (MCA), which had first been proposed by President George W. Bush at the Inter-American Development Bank in Washington and then at the UN Financing for Development Conference held in Monterrey Mexico in March of 2002. The administration advocated, and Congress accepted, the creation of a new government corporation, the Millennium Challenge Corporation (MCC), to administer the MCA. The president had initially proposed a $5 billion budget for the MCA by fiscal year 2006. Funding, however, stayed around $2 billion, about 10 per cent of total US assistance, during the Bush years.

The MCA broke with conventional approaches to aid by basing the distribution of its funds on ex post conditionality with respect to governance. Traditional foreign assistance conditionality had always been ex ante: that is, countries promised to implement reforms in exchange for additional aid funding. The MCA, in contrast, only provided funding after countries had actually demonstrated that they had achieved good or at least better governance. The MCC measured good governance by sixteen quantified indicators, six related to governing justly, four to investing in people, and six to promoting economic freedom. To be most seriously considered for funding, countries had to score above the mean for half of the indicators in each of the three categories. All of these indicators were publicly available and came from third parties such as the World Bank, the IMF, Freedom House, and the Heritage Foundation. The US government had no control over the scores.

The basic concept for the MCA reflected the best social science thinking available about the effectiveness of foreign assistance. By the time the Bush administration came to office, skepticism about conventional foreign assistance was becoming increasingly pronounced. William Easterly's devastating critique of development aid, *The Elusive Quest for Growth*, was published in 2001. The hundreds of billions of dollars that had been given in foreign aid over several decades appeared to have done no good at all, possibly even harm. A number of World Bank studies, however, suggested that external funds could make a positive contribution if the recipient countries enjoyed good governance. If not, the money would simply be wasted through poorly conceived projects, misallocation, and corruption. The MCA took this insight about the relationship between aid, growth, and governance and operationalized it through the creation of a new assistance program. Perhaps viewed from the outside nothing could appear to be more rational.

The story from the inside, however, was not so straightforward. I got to see some although not all of it first hand. The basic concept for the MCA was developed not in a routine inter-agency process but rather by a small group of individuals at the White House in the first months of 2002. I was at that time serving as a member of the Policy Planning Staff at the State Department. Although the secretary of state Colin Powell and a few others might have known about the MCA, my colleagues and I were shocked, flabbergasted, when the president announced at a speech at the Inter-American Development Bank on 14 March 2002 that the United States would increase its core foreign assistance programs by 50 per cent or $5 billion. In his speech the president called for "a new compact for global development, defined by new accountability for both rich and poor nations alike. Greater contributions from developed nations must be linked," he argued, "to greater responsibility from developing nations." Bush underlined the relationship between good governance and growth arguing that "when nations refuse to enact sound policies, progress against poverty is nearly impossible. In these situations, more aid money can actually be counterproductive, because it subsidizes bad policies, delays reform, and crowds out private investment" (Bush, G.W. 2002).

The MCA was one aspect of the administration's effort to frame a new grand strategy for the United States in the aftermath of the terrorist attack of 9/11. Domestic political and economic conditions in the developing world were now regarded as a core concern of American national security. Transnational terrorism was understood at least in part as a reaction to repressive regimes that were not governing justly or investing in their own people. The first two sentences of President Bush's opening statement for the 2002 *National Security Strategy of the United States*, which is best remembered for its discussion of preemption, have nothing to do with military action and everything to do with domestic authority structures in other countries. Bush began:

> The great struggles of the twentieth century between liberty and totalitarianism ended with a decisive victory for the forces of freedom—and a single sustainable model for national success: freedom, democracy, and

free enterprise. In the twenty-first century, only nations that share a commitment to protecting basic human rights and guaranteeing political and economic freedom will be able to unleash the potential of their people and assure their future prosperity.

(United States, Office of the President 2002)

The 2002 report included a lengthy discussion of the MCA. In its eight years in office the Bush administration nearly tripled American foreign assistance.

The conceptualization of the MCA was led by Gary Edson, who was the deputy assistant to the president for international economic affairs and deputy national security advisor. Edson was a lawyer by training, not a development economist, although he did have an MBA from Chicago. As the sherpa for the G-8 meetings, however, Edson was familiar with the arguments about governance and growth. In the run up to the G-8 meeting in Kananaskis, Canada, in 2002, he had had discussions with his counterparts about aid selectivity. Given differences among member countries, it was clear to him that an aid program based on governance criteria would not fly as a G-8 initiative. He was, however, intrigued about the possibilities for the United States.

Edson was one of the most adept policy entrepreneurs that I encountered during my time in government. When he returned to Washington he had discussions with key figures in OMB, notably Robin Cleveland, about how a new assistance program might be budgeted, especially the question of whether appropriated funds could be isolated from the earmarking and constraints that afflict the aid budgets of State and USAID. He had off-the-record informal discussions with a small number of officials about the possibility of linking aid to performance, including Al Larson, who was then the undersecretary of state for economic affairs, Steven Radelet, a development economist who was then a deputy assistant secretary at the Treasury and later became a senior fellow at the Center for Global Development, and Clay Lowery, who was at the NSC.

The action-forcing event, in multiple streams terminology the event that turns a condition into a problem, was not only the administration's understanding of the relationship between American national security, terrorism, and repressive regimes, but also the commitment that Bush had made to attend the Financing for Development Conference which was held in Monterrey Mexico from 18 to 22 March 2002. The commitment was firm because of Bush's close relationship with President Vincente Fox of Mexico. No American president attends such a major international meeting without a deliverable. The MCA was a more dramatic deliverable than anyone outside of a narrow circle of individuals around the White House had anticipated.

Once the basic conceptualization for the MCA had been presented, a substantial increase in foreign assistance to be provided to countries that had demonstrated good governance, the NSC led an inter-agency process to determine the indicators that would be used to identify countries that might be chosen for funding, income cutoffs for possible recipients, and how the MCA would be administered. I moved from the State Department Policy Planning Staff to the National Security Council shortly after the MCA was announced and served as director of governance and development at the NSC from April through November 2002, working primarily on the MCA.

Once the MCA had entered the inter-agency process the obvious danger was that the administration's decision to constrain its own freedom of action would be undermined by bureaucracies seeking greater discretion to pursue their own particular projects. Throughout this process, Edson was very attentive to preserving the basic vision of the project. The administration proposed that the MCA would be run by a new government corporation, the Millennium Challenge Corporation, because of anxiety that if it were placed in an existing agency, USAID or State, it would succumb to business as usual. The indicators for country selection were chosen because they had wide country coverage, correlated (with the exception of the democracy indicators) with economic growth, and came from respected third-party sources. It was also decided that only lower-middle-income and lower-income countries as defined by the World Bank could receive MCA funding.

While the choice of indicators and income cutoffs was consistent with the expectations of the closing-the-gap model that policy relevant research could have an impact on actual policy, the development of the MCA can hardly be understood from a conventional rational actor model. The action-forcing event, the problem, in Kingdon's terms was the president's commitment to attend the Monterrey Conference. This opened a policy window. The policy alternatives stream was small, closed, and hierarchical flowing from the White House. The basic concept was not well cooked although it did conform with the best available social science knowledge, and this made it easier to get support from parts of the development community, Congress, and the press (Hook 2008: 158–59). The politics involved the administration's ability to take advantage after 9/11 of a national mood in which freedom, growth, and democracy around the world were central concerns. From the outside the MCA might look like an example of how the gap had been closed; from the inside its conceptualization and success depended critically on the president's predispositions and the intelligence and drive of a policy entrepreneur, Gary Edson, who was not trained as an economist and who had initially learned about the relevance of governance for aid effectiveness primarily from his counterparts in the G-8 process.

China as a responsible stakeholder: conceptual framings and foreign policy

In a speech to the National Committee on US–China Relations in September 2005 Robert Zoellick, the deputy secretary of state, urged China to be a "responsible stakeholder" in the international system. Zoellick went on to say that: "From China's perspective, it would seem that its national interest would be much better served by working with us to shape the future international system." Zoellick noted the many major international issues including transnational terrorism, disease, the proliferation of weapons of mass destruction, and poverty could be more effectively addressed if China and the United States were cooperating with each other. He was at pains to contrast differences between the American relationship with contemporary China and the Soviet Union during the Cold War, noting that China was not committed to overturning the existing international system, or to an implacable ideological struggle with the United States, or to capitalism. He stated that nineteenth-century balance of power concepts were outmoded in the contemporary globalized world. He argued that China, to address successfully its domestic problems notably rural poverty, needed a benign international environment. He then proceeded to point out a number of Chinese policies that were problematic, including insufficient transparency in its military budget, theft of intellectual property, growing mercantilism, efforts to "lock up" oil supplies through reliance on equity investments instead of the market, and contrasted them with policies of engagement such as the Six-Party Talks and foreign assistance pledges for Afghanistan and Iraq. He urged China to do more to resolve the crisis in Sudan, to work cooperatively for security in Asia, and to correct its own historical blind spots. He argued that greater democratization would be necessary for China's own growth and stability. Zoellick concluded by stating that:

> Tonight I have suggested that the US response should be to help foster constructive action by transforming our thirty-year policy of integration: We now need to encourage China to become a responsible stakeholder in the international system. As a responsible stakeholder, China would be more than just a member – it would work with us to sustain the international system that has enabled its success.
>
> (Zoellick 2005)

Although I never heard the term "neo-liberal institutionalism" uttered within the confines of the State Department, Zoellick's speech was completely consistent with the idea that international institutions were necessary for global stability and that such institutions could not survive if major players behaved as free riders. The conceptualization of China as a responsible stakeholder went beyond the notion of engagement that had been used by six previous administrations and which focused in large part on internal change in China. Zoellick argued that China was failing to act on its own self-interest as the Chinese regime itself had defined it because China's "peaceful rise" would be impossible without a stable international system, and a stable international system would be more difficult to sustain if China were not playing by—and then working to support, sustain, and adapt—the rules. Although Zoellick did not use the term "free rider," which for diplomatic discourse might have been either too wonky or too provocative, the danger for China of China's free riding was exactly what the speech was about.

Indeed, Zoellick noted that the American administration would not be able to continue to run interference in Congress for China without a change in China's behavior. Like the Millennium Challenge Account, the idea of responsible stakeholder was entirely consistent with major social science approaches to the international system. And from the outside there would be no reason to think that the idea of challenging China to be a responsible stakeholder in the international system had not emerged from a fully rational decision-making process.

The internal reality, however, is much more clearly illuminated by the multiple streams framework. In this case Evan Feigenbaum, who was then responsible for Asia on the Policy Planning staff, played a key role. Feigenbaum had written a memo for Colin Powell in 2002 about China in which he used the phrase "constructive stakeholder," followed by a transition memo for Secretary Rice in which the words "responsible" and "stakeholder" were prominent although they were not placed right next to each other, arguing that China should be challenged to "assume the responsibilities of a stakeholder" in the international system. These memos, like others from Policy Planning, had been sent to principals and others on the seventh floor, the floor where the offices of the secretary, deputy secretary, under-secretaries for management and political affairs, several assistant secretaries, and the policy planning staff are located. They had very little impact on policy.

When Zoellick arrived at the State Department in February of 2005, he made it clear that China was one of the areas that he would focus on. He expressed an interest in meeting with the Policy Planning staff and after several tries an opening was found on his schedule. Spending 45 minutes without trying to reach agreement on a specific policy question is a significant opportunity cost for the deputy secretary of state, so it came as no surprise that scheduling the meeting took some time. Feigenbaum, along with other members of the Policy Planning staff, was great at his job. He had an exceptional command of the facts and he could conceptualize problems in ways that were useful to policy makers. I am sure that the contribution that Feigenbaum could make to China policy was immediately apparent to Zoellick as the members of the staff went around the room describing their responsibilities.

Zoellick enlisted Feigenbaum to work with him on China policy. One of the first things that Feigenbaum did was, at Zoellick's request, to pull his old memo out of the drawer, tidy it up a bit so that Zoellick could use it with the secretary and others, and put on a new date. Zoellick and his principal speechwriter then put the words "responsible" and "stakeholder" right next to each other in a draft of the speech. Before the speech was made Zoellick engaged in extensive private discussions with some of his Chinese counterparts as well as with China experts in the United States. He then deployed the phrase no fewer than five times in the text.

The Chinese took the challenge of being a responsible stakeholder seriously. They were initially at pains to understand what the term meant, and the Chinese ambassador invited Feigenbaum and me to lunch and spent some time querying us about the differences between stakeholder, partner, and shareholder. They wanted to understand how Zoellick's speech related to other approaches to China such as hedging and balancing. I have been told the Chinese called others around Washington and that it took some time for the Chinese government to identify the appropriate characters for translating the term "responsible stakeholder." At one point, Feigenbaum prepared, and Zoellick cleared, a formal note walking the Chinese through different manifestations of the concept, which was then shared with the Chinese Embassy. At the next high-level meeting between Zoellick and his Chinese counterpart, Vice Foreign Minister Dai Bingguo, the Chinese went to some lengths to point out how they had acted as a responsible stakeholder, noting policies like their support for UN peacekeeping missions. On the American side, Zoellick explicated to Dai and others the implications of the phrase. The conceptualization of China as a responsible stakeholder could be used to challenge China to weigh policy tradeoffs it had hitherto avoided, for instance supporting the World Bank as a 4 per cent voting stakeholder, on the one hand, while undercutting its loan policies through no-strings bilateral soft loans, on the other. The concept could be used to persuade China to see its interests in a different light with regard to Sudan or the Extractive Industries Transparency Initiative.

As in the case of the MCC, challenging China to be a responsible stakeholder might be taken as a product of a fully rational decision-making process informed, at least to some extent, by academic work. Reality conformed much more to the garbage can model. The confluence of a problem, a solution and a person was necessary for the US to adopt this new orientation. The notion of China as a responsible stakeholder had been sitting around in the policy soup, or at least in Evan Feigenbaum's desk drawer, for several years. The conceptualization became a policy because the deputy secretary of state opened a policy window. Had the deputy's interests or orientation been different, "responsible stakeholder" would never have entered the lexicon of American foreign policy.

The Partnership for Democratic Governance: from academic idea to policy initiative

On 1 October 2007 at an event on the margins of the UN General Assembly meeting, the secretary general of the OECD, Angel Gurria, the administrator of the UNDP, Kemal Dervis, The US secretary of state, Condoleezza Rice, the foreign minister of Chile, Alejandro Foxley, and the deputy foreign minister of Poland, Andrzej Sardos, announced the creation of the Partnership for Democratic Governance. The members of the Partnership were the OECD, UNDP, Australia, Brazil, Canada, Chile, Denmark, Japan, Korea, Mexico, New Zealand, Poland, Turkey, the United States, the Organization of American States, and the Inter-American Development Bank. A publication issued by the OECD a few months later stated that the "Partnership for Democratic Governance aims to support developing countries ... in building their governance capacity and improving service delivery to their citizens." The publication indicated that the:

> PDG Advisory Unit is the operational arm of the Partnership. It collects and shares information on best practices related to contracting out. It carries our country assessments and determines whether, given the country's circumstances, direct provisions of external expertise could deliver results and help build capacity.
> (OECD, Partnership for Democratic Governance, Advisory Unit n.d.)

The PDG did not have resources to directly fund projects; the Advisory Unit was supported by modest contributions from a number of the founding members.

The first glimmer of an idea for the PDG occurred on 18 January 2006 in a van parked outside a building at Georgetown University where Secretary Rice had given a speech on transformational diplomacy. I was sitting in the van next to Sean McCormack, the assistant secretary of state for public affairs. Sean suggested that it might be worthwhile for Policy Planning to explore some possibilities for legacy initiatives for the secretary. The Policy Planning staff developed a number of possibilities in a variety of areas including energy and the treatment of orphans. The idea for the PDG came from "Sharing Sovereignty," the paper that I had published in *International Security* in 2004. The basic argument of the paper was that many of the countries around the world vested with international legal sovereignty and even Westphalian/Vattelian sovereignty lacked effective domestic sovereignty. In some cases they did not have the capacity to provide services to their own population. In other cases distrust within the polity was so high that it was impossible for political leaders to make credible commitments. The most obvious assistance tools, including governance assistance and short-term UN transitional authorities, might not be adequate. The article concluded that shared sovereignty arrangements in which countries contracted out key activities might be appropriate in some cases.

Was contracting out government service the best idea for supporting better governance in states with weak domestic sovereignty? Not necessarily. Was there some rational decision-making process that could have surveyed all of the possibilities for new US multilateral initiatives and provided the secretary of state with the best possible option? I do not think so. In an environment, however, where democracy and governance were central issues for the administration, it was an idea that had at least some initial traction.

Turning an idea into reality required, in this case, support or at least not outright hostility from a number of people at the State Department and USAID, support from the secretary of state, and ultimately approval at a principals meeting in September of 2006. More importantly, it required buy in from at least some other countries and an international home since no one wanted the PDG to be a free-standing entity. In the summer and fall of 2006 I traveled to Europe, South America, Asia, and Australia to try to sell the idea. Ultimately the PDG did get support from a number of countries. For me, the most striking was Australia, which was already engaged in an ambitious regional contracting-out project, the Regional Assistance Mission for the Solomon Islands (RAMSI). RAMSI was directly involved in running the police, judicial, and financial affairs of the Solomon Islands.

As important as individual country support was getting the backing of the OECD, which ultimately housed the PDG advisory group, and the UNDP. At the OECD, Angel Gurria, the secretary general, was critical. Gurria was attentive to new opportunities for the OECD. Moreover, when he had been finance minister in Mexico he had considered contracting out the collection of Mexican customs, something that a number of other countries around the world had done. While he did not succeed he was very familiar with the rationale for bringing in external service providers, in the case of customs because of the problem of corruption. Kemal Dervis, the administrator of the UNDP, a former finance minister in Turkey and World Bank official, and someone I had met when he was working in Washington before taking up his UN position, was also supportive.

Thus, the Partnership for Democratic Governance was one of those relatively rare instances in which an academic idea became a policy reality. Consistent with the closing-the-gap perspective this process only occurred because an academic—me—had a government position. But the idea itself was hardly enough. Problem recognition and politics were critical. Governance failures in weak states was seen as a problem by American officials. At the international level politics also mattered. Some countries, such as Australia, were very familiar with the concept. Others were happy to align themselves with an American initiative, especially one that was not particularly costly. Some countries that declined to join the PDG were skeptical of the idea, but others wanted to distance themselves from the Bush administration. Bargaining as well as persuasion, perhaps bargaining much more than persuasion, is what mattered on the political side.

Conclusion: living with the gap

Even if by some magic the style of work and career choices that have been rewarded in academic political science were changed to encourage more policy-oriented work, the impact on policy would be far from certain. Academic work is only one ingredient in the policy soup, especially in the United States with its think tanks, extensive Congressional staffs, and experienced bureaucrats. Those in the political stream, policy makers, confront multiple challenges. Some are the inevitable result of time pressure and multiple agendas. Others are the result of political calculations which no one in the political stream can avoid. In choosing a policy any president must consider its domestic political impact and be attentive to the domestic political constraints of leaders in other countries. Brilliant policy alternatives, even brilliant policy alternatives generated by academics, might be missed or might not be feasible given the political constraints under which any president must operate.

Given the rich array of institutions in the United States, both inside and outside the government, that are concerned with international affairs and foreign policy, it is not evident that much would be gained by trying to focus academic political science more on the policy world. Even within the academy, schools of public policy and policy research institutes are becoming more prominent, an inevitable trend given the need for universities to translate what they are doing into language that can be understood by their government and private supporters. More than in any other country the thousands of officials that are appointed by any president can bring a variety of perspectives into official circles. Think tanks generate their own ideas but they also translate ideas from academia into forms that might prove useful to policy makers.

Over time and in comparison with other major powers, the United States has had an exceptionally successful foreign policy. In large part this success has been a product of the country's geographic isolation, achieved size, and rich resource base. But the openness of the American policy process, even in the area of foreign policy, should not be gainsaid. In an environment as complex and challenging as the international system, having a variety of ideas swirling around in the policy soup, ideas that come from a wide variety of sources including academia, is a much better guarantee against catastrophic failures than a more closed or hierarchical system.

Acknowledgements:

Thanks to Lynn Eden, Bruce Jentleson, Robert Keohane, and Amy Zegart, as well as a number of present and former government officials, for their comments on earlier drafts of this article.

Bibliography

Abu-Lughod, J. (1989) *Before European Hegemony*, New York: Oxford University Press.

Acheson, D. (1969) *Present at the Creation: My Years in the State Department*, New York: W.W. Norton.

Alford, R.A. and Friedland, R. (1985) *Powers of Theory: Capitalism, the State, and Democracy*, Cambridge: Cambridge University Press.

Allison, G. (1971) *Essence of Decision: Explaining the Cuban Missile Crisis*, Boston: Little, Brown.

Almond, G. (1973) "Approaches to Developmental Causation," in G. Almond, S. Flannagan, and R.J. Mundt (eds) *Crisis, Choice, and Change: Historical Studies of Political Development*, Boston: Little, Brown.

Anand, S. and Krosnick, J.A. (2003) "The Impact of Attitudes toward Foreign Policy Goals on Public Preferences among Presidential Candidates: A Study of Issue Publics and the Attentive Public in the 2000 US Presidential Election," *Presidential Studies Quarterly*, 33: 31–72.

Anderson, P. (1974) *Lineages of the Absolutist State*, London: Verso.

Andorra (1993) Constitution of Andorra. Available at: www.andora.ad/consell/constituk.htm.

Annan, K. (1999) "The Legitimacy to Intervene: International Action to Uphold Human Rights Requires a New Understanding of State and Individual Sovereignty," *Financial Times*, 31 December.

Aron, R. (1973) *The Imperial Republic*, Englewood Cliffs, NJ: Prentice-Hall.

Aronson, J.D. and Cowhey, P.F. (1988) *When Countries Talk: International Trade in Telecommunications Services*, Cambridge, MA: Ballinger.

Art, R.J. (1973) "Bureaucratic Politics and American Foreign Policy: A Critique," *Policy Sciences*, 4: 467–90.

Arthur, W.B. (1984) "Competing Technologies and Economic Prediction," *Options*, 2: 10–13.

—— (1985) "Competing Technologies and Lock-in by Historical Small Events: The Dynamics of Allocation Under Increasing Returns," CEPR Publication No. 43, Stanford, CA: Stanford University, Center for Economic Policy Research.

—— (1986) "Industry Location Patterns and the Importance of History," mimeo, Stanford, CA: Stanford University, Food Research Institute.

Ashley, R. (1986) "The Poverty of Neo-realism," in R.O. Keohane (ed.) *Neorealism and Its Critics*, New York: Columbia University Press.

Axelrod, R. and Keohane, R.O. (1985) "Achieving Cooperation under Anarchy: Strategies and Institutions," *World Politics*, 38: 226–54.

Bachrach, P. and Baratz, M. (1962) "The Two Faces of Power," *American Political Science Review*, 56: 947–52.

Badie, B. and Birnbaum, P. (1983) *The Sociology of the State*, Chicago: University of Chicago Press.

Bank for International Settlements (various years) *Annual Report*, Basle.

Bartsch, S. (1995) *Minderheitenschutz in der internationalen Politik: Völkerbund und KSZE/OSZE in neuer Perspektive*, Oplanden: Westdeutscher Verlag.

Bauer, H. (1990) "Telecommunications and the United European Market," *Telecommunications*, 25: 33–35.

Bauer, R.A., Sola Pool, I. de and Dexter, L.A. (1967) *American Business and Public Policy: The Politics of Foreign Trade*, New York: Atherton.

Becker, G.S. (1976) *The Economic Approach to Human Behavior*, Chicago: University of Chicago Press.

Belassa, B. (1967) *Trade Liberalization among Industrial Countries*, New York: McGraw-Hill.

Benjamin, R. and Duvall, R. (1985) "The Capitalist State in Context," in R. Benjamin and S. Elkin (eds) *The Democratic State*, Lawrence: Kansas State University Press.

Berman, H. and Kaufman, C. (1978) "The Law of International Commercial Transactions (Lex Mercatoria)," *Harvard International Law Journal*, 19: 221–77.

Bhagwati, J. (1969) *Trade, Tariffs, and Growth*, Cambridge, MA: MIT Press.

Bhushan, I, Keller, S. and Schwartz, B.. (2002) *Achieving the Twin Objectives of Efficiency and Equity: Contracting Health Services in Cambodia*, ERD Policy Brief Series No. 6, Manila: Asian Development Bank,

Binder, L. (1986) "The Natural History of Development Theory," *Comparative Studies in Society and History*, 28: 3–33.

Bishop, Jr, J.W. (1955) "The 'Contractual Agreements' with the Federal Republic of Germany," *American Journal of International Law*, 49: 125–47.

Blair, J.M. (1976) *Control of Oil*, New York: Pantheon.

Blaisdell, D.C. (1929) *European Financial Control in the Ottoman Empire: A Study of the Establishment, Activities, and Significance of the Administration of the Ottoman Public Debt*, New York: Columbia University Press.

Blatherwick, D.E.S. (1987) *The International Politics of Telecommunications*, Research Series, Berkeley: Institute for International Studies.

Boyd, D. (1986) "Pirate Radio in Britain: A Programming Alternative," *Journal of Communication*, 36: 83–94.

Bracken, P. (1983) *The Command and Control of Nuclear Weapons*, New Haven: Yale University Press.

Bradford, E. (1972) *The Shield and the Sword: The Knights of St. John*, London: Hodder and Stoughton.

Brander, J.A. (1986) "Rationales for Strategic Trade and Industrial Policy," in P.R. Krugman (ed.) *Strategic Trade Policy and the New International Economic*, Cambridge, MA: MIT Press.

Braudel, F. (1975) *The Mediterranean and the Mediterranean World in the Age of Philip II*, New York: Harper and Row.

—— (1981) *Civilization and Capitalism, 15th–18th Century, Volume I, The Structures of Everyday Life: The Limits of the Possible*, New York: Harper and Row.

Brierly, J.L. (1963) *The Law of Nations: An Introduction to the International Law of Peace*, ed. H. Waldock, 6th edn, New York: Oxford University Press.

Brimmer, A.F. and Dahl, F.R. (1975) "Growth of American International Banking: Implications for Public Policy," *Journal of Finance*, 30: 341–63.

Broad, R. (1988) *Unequal Alliance: The World Bank, the International Monetary Fund, and the Philippines*, Berkeley: University of California Press.

Brownlee, J. (2007) "Can America Nation-Build?" *World Politics* 59: 314–40.

Brownlie, I. (ed.) (1992) *Basic Documents on Human Rights*, 3rd edn, Oxford: Clarendon Press.

Brunsson, N. (1989) *The Organization of Hypocrisy: Talk, Decisions and Actions in Organizations*, Chichester: John Wiley and Sons.

Buhl, D. (1990) "Window to the West: How Television from the Federal Republic Influenced Events in East Germany," discussion paper D-5, Cambridge, MA: Joan Shorenstein Barone Center, Kennedy School, Harvard University.

Bull, H. (1977) *The Anarchical Society: A Study of Order in World Politics*, New York: Columbia University Press.

Bull, H. and Watson, I. (1984) *The Expansion of International Society*, New York: Oxford University Press.

Bumpus, B. and Skelt, B. (1985) *Seventy Years of International Broadcasting, Communication and Society*, Paris: UNESCO.

Burnham, W.D. (1970) *Critical Elections and the Mainsprings of American Politics*, New York: W.W. Norton.

Bush, G.W. (2002) "Remarks by the President on Global Development, Inter-American Development Bank," Washington, DC; available at: www.whitehouse.gov/news/releases/2002/03/20020314–17.html.

Calleo, D.P. and Rowland, B. (1973) *America and the World Political Economy, Part II*, Bloomington: Indiana University.

Caplan, R. (2002) *A New Trusteeship? The International Administration of War-torn Territories*, London: International Institute for Strategic Studies.

Carothers, T. (1999) *Aiding Democracy Abroad: The Learning Curve*, Washington, DC: Carnegie Endowment for International Peace.

Carroll, G.R. (1984) "Organizational Ecology," *Annual Review of Sociology*, 10: 71–93.

Cerny, P.G. (1990) *The Changing Architecture of Politics: Structure, Agency, and the Future of the State*, London: Sage.

Chadwick, R. and Deutsch, K.W. (1973) "International Trade and Economic Integration: Further Developments in Trade Matrix Analysis," *Comparative Political Studies*, 6: 84–109.

Chen, T. (1968) "Investiture of Liu-Ch'iu Kings in the Qing Period," in J.K. Fairbank (ed.) *The Chinese World Order: Traditional China's Foreign Relations*, Cambridge, MA: Harvard University Press.

Chesneaux, J.M., and Bastid, M.B. (1977) *China from the Opium Wars to the 1911 Revolution*, Hassocks, Sussex, UK: Harvester.

Chesterman, S. (2001) "Kosovo in Limbo: State-Building and 'Substantial Autonomy'," New York: International Peace Academy.

Claude, Jr, I.L. (1955) *National Minorities: An International Problem*, Cambridge, MA: Harvard University Press.

Coase, R. (1960) "The Problem of Social Cost," *Journal of Law and Economics*, 3: 1–44.

Codding, Jr, G.A. and Rutkowski, A.M. (1982) *The International Telecommunication Union in a Changing World*, Dedham, MA: Artech House.

Cohen, B.J. (1973) *The Question of Imperialism: The Political Economy of Dominance and Dependence*, New York: Basic Books.

—— (1982) "Balance of Payments Financing: Evolution of a Regime," *International Organization*, 36: 457–78. Reprinted in S. D. Krasner (ed.) *International Regimes* (1983), Ithaca, NY: Cornell University Press.

Cohen, M.D., March, J.G. and Olsen, J.P. (1972) "A Garbage Can Model of Organizational Choice," *Administrative Science Quarterly*, 17: 1–25.

Coleman, D.C. (ed.) (1969) *Revisions in Mercantilism*, London: Methuen.

Colino, R.R. (1986) "Global Politics and INTELSAT: The Conduct of Foreign Relations in an Electronically Wired World," *Telecommunications Policy*, 10: 199.

Collier, P. and Hoeffler, A. (2004) *The Challenge of Reducing the Global Incidence of Civil War*, Oxford: Centre for the Study of African Economies, Department of Economics, Oxford University.

Condliffe, J.B. (1950) *The Commerce of Nations*, New York: Norton.

Confucius (1997) *The Analects of Confucius*, trans. C. Leys, New York: Norton.

"Convention on Forced and Compulsory Labor" (1992) reprinted in I. Brownlie (ed.) *Basic Documents on Human Rights*, 3rd edn, Oxford: Clarendon Press.

"Convention on Relations between the Three Powers and the Federal Republic of Germany" (1955) *American Journal of International Law*, 49, supplement: 57–69.

Conybeare, J.A.C. (1976) "United States Foreign Economic Policy and the International Capital Markets: The Case of Capital Export Controls, 1963–74," PhD dissertation, Harvard University.

—— (1980) "International Organization and the Theory of Property Rights," *International Organization*, 34: 307–34.

—— (1987) *Trade Wars: The Theory and Practice of International Commercial Rivalry*, New York: Columbia University Press.

Cooper, J. and Brady, D.W. (1981) "Institutional Context and Leadership Style: The House from Cannon to Rayburn," *American Political Science Review*, 75: 411–25.

Cooper, R. (1968) *The Economics of Interdependence*, New York: McGraw-Hill.

Cousens, E.M. (2002) "From Missed Opportunities to Overcompensation: Implementing the Dayton Agreement on Bosnia," in S.J. Stedman, D. Rothchild, and E.M. Cousens (eds) *Ending Civil Wars: The Implementation of Peace Agreements*, Boulder, CO: Lynne Rienner.

Cowhey, P. (1990) "The International Telecommunications Regime: The Political Roots of International Regimes for High Technology," *International Organization*, 44: 169–99.

Crawford, B. (1996) "Explaining Defection from International Cooperation: Germany's Unilateral Recognition of Croatia," *World Politics*, 48: 482–521.

Crown Agents (n.d.) *Customs Reform Programme: The Modernisation of Alfandegas de Mocambique*, Sutton, UK: Crown Agents.

Dahl, R. (1961) *Who Governs: Democracy and Power in an American City*, New Haven: Yale University Press.

—— (1967) *Pluralist Democracy in the United States*, Chicago: Rand McNally.

—— (1972) *Polyarchy: Participation and Opposition*, New Haven: Yale University Press.

Damrosch, L. (1993) "Changing Conceptions of Intervention in International Law," in L.W. Reed and C. Kaysen (eds) *Emerging Norms of Justified Intervention: A Collection of Essays from a Project of the American Academy of Arts and Sciences*, Cambridge, MA: American Academy of Arts and Sciences.

Dessler, D. (1989) "What's at Stake in the Agent Structure Debate," *International Organization*, 43: 441–73.

Diaz-Alejandro, C.F. (1972) "Latin America: Toward 2000 A.D.," in J. Bhagwati (ed.) *Economics and World Order from the IGYOs to the IGGOs*, New York: Macmillan.

DiMaggio, P.J. and Powell, W.W. (1983) "The Iron Cage Revisited: Institutional Isomorphism and Collective Rationality in Organizational Fields," *American Sociology Review*, 48: 147–60.

Donnelly, J. (1992) *International Human Rights*, Boulder, CO: Westview.

Downs, G. and Stedman, S.J. (2002) "Evaluating Issues in Peace Implementation," in S.J. Stedman, D. Rothchild, and E.M. Cousens (eds) *Ending Civil Wars: The Implementation of Peace Agreements*, Boulder, CO: Lynne Rienner.

Doyle, M. (1983) "Kant, Liberal Legacies, and Foreign Affairs," *Philosophy and Public Affairs*, 12: 204–35.

Doyle, M.W. and Sambanis, N. (2000) "International Peacebuilding: A Theoretical and Quantitative Analysis," *American Political Science Review*, 94: 779–802.

Drake, W.J. (1989) "Asymmetric Reregulation and the Transformation of the International Telecommunications Regime," unpublished paper, Department of Communications, University of California, San Diego.

Drezner, D. (2007) *All Politics is Global: Explaining International Regulatory Regimes*, Princeton: Princeton University Press.

Durant, R.F. and Diehl, P.F. (1989) "Agendas, Alternatives, and Public Policy: Lessons from the U.S. Foreign Policy Arena," *Public Policy*, 9: 179–205.

Duus, P. (1989) "Introduction: Japan's Informal Empire in China, 1895–1937: An Overview," in P. Duus, R.H. Myers, and M.R. Peattie (eds) *The Japanese Informal Empire in China, 1895–1937*, Princeton, NJ: Princeton University Press.

Dyson, K.H.F. (1980) *The State Tradition in Western Europe: A Study of an Idea and Institution*, New York: Oxford University Press.

Easterly, W. (2001) *The Elusive Quest for Growth: Economists' Misadventures in the Tropics*, Cambridge: MIT Press.

Eckes, Jr, A.E. (1975) *A Search for Solvency: Bretton Woods and the International Monetary System, 1941–1971*, Austin: University of Texas Press.

Eckstein, H. (1979) "On the 'Science' of the State," *Daedalus*, 108: 4.

—— (1982) "The Idea of Political Development: From Dignity to Efficiency," *World Politics*, 34: 451–86.

Edelstein, D.M. (2004) "Occupational Hazards: Why Military Occupations Succeed or Fail," *International Security*, 29: 49–81.

Eldredge, N. (1985) *Time Frames: The Rethinking of Darwinian Evolution and the Theory of Punctuated Equilibria*, New York: Simon and Schuster.

Eldredge, N. and Gould, S.J. (1972) "Punctuated Equilibria: An Alternative to Phyletic Gradualism," in T.J.M. Schopf (ed.) *Models in Paleobiology*, San Francisco: Freeman, Cooper.

Elisonas, J. (1991) "The Inseparable Trinity: Japan's Relations with China and Korea," in J.W. Hall (ed.) *The Cambridge History of Japan*, Vol. 4: *Early Modern Japan*, Cambridge: Cambridge University Press.

Emmanuel, A. (1972) *Unequal Exchange: A Study of the Imperialism of Trade*, New York: Monthly Review.

Engler, R. (1977) *The Brotherhood of Oil: Energy Policy and the Public Interest*, Chicago: University of Chicago Press.

European Bank for Reconstruction and Development (1991) *Agreement Establishing the European Bank for Reconstruction and Development*, Available at: www.ebrd.com/pubs/insti/basics.pdf.

Evans, G. and Sahnoun, M. (2002) "The Responsibility to Protect," *Foreign Affairs*, 81: 99–110.

Evans, J.W. (1971) *The Kennedy Round in American Trade Policy: The Twilight of the GATT?*, Cambridge, MA: Harvard University Press.

Evans, P., Rueschmeyer, D. and Skocpol, T. (1985) *Bringing the State Back In*, New York: Cambridge University Press.

Eyal, J. (1986) "Recent Developments in the Jamming of Western Radio Stations Broadcasting to the USSR and Eastern Europe," *Radio Liberty Research*, RL 419/86, Radio Free Europe, Radio Liberty.

Fairbank, J.K. (1968) "A Preliminary Framework," in J.K. Fairbank (ed.) *The Chinese World Order: Traditional China's Foreign Relations*, Cambridge, MA: Harvard University Press.

—— (1978) "The Creation of the Treaty System," in J.K. Fairbank (ed.) *The Cambridge History of Modern China*, Vol. 10: *Late Ch'ing, 1800–1911*, Part I, Cambridge: Cambridge University Press.

Fazal, T.M. (2007) *State Death: The Politics and Geography of Conquest, Occupation, and Annexation*, Princeton: Princeton University Press

Fearon, J.D. (1994) "Domestic Political Audiences and the Escalation of International Disputes," *American Political Science Review*, 88, 3: 577–92.

—— (2003) "Ethnicity, Insurgency, and Civil War," *American Political Science Review*, 97: 1–17.

Fearon, J.D. and Laitin, D.D. (2004) "Neotrusteeship and the Problem of Weak States," *International Security*, 28: 5–43.

Feis, H. (1965) *Europe, the World's Banker, 1870–1914: An Account of European Foreign Investment and the Connection of World Finance with Diplomacy before World War I*, New York: W.W. Norton.

Feldman, M. (1975) *The Role of the United States in the International Telecommunication Union and Pre-ITU Conferences*, Baton Rouge, LA: Mildred L. Bos Feldman.

Fenno, Jr, R.F. (1973) "The Internal Distribution of Influence: The House," in D.B. Truman (ed.) *The Congress and America's Future*, 2nd edn, Englewood Cliffs, NJ: Prentice-Hall.

Ferejohn, J. (1987) "The New Institutionalism," paper presented at the American Political Science Association Annual Meeting, Chicago, IL, September.

Financial Times, various issues.

Finer, S. (1974) "State-Building, State Boundaries and Border Control: An Essay on Certain Aspects of the First Phase of State-Building in Western Europe Considered in the Light of the Rokkan–Hirschman Model," *Social Science Information*, XIII: 79–126.

Fletcher, J.F. (1968) "China and Central Asia, 1368–1884," in J.K. Fairbank (ed.) *The Chinese World Order: Traditional China's Foreign Relations*, Cambridge, MA: Harvard University Press.

Foreign Policy (2007) *Failed States Index*, Washington, DC: Foreign Policy.

Forsythe, D.P. (1983) *Human Rights and World Politics*, Lincoln: University of Nebraska Press.

—— (1989) *Human Rights and World Politics*, 2nd edn, Lincoln: University of Nebraska Press.

Fowler, M.R. and Bunck, J.M. (1995) *Law, Power, and the Sovereign State: The Evolution and Application of the Concept of Sovereignty,* University Park: Pennsylvania State University Press.

Frank, A.G. (1969) *Latin America: Underdevelopment or Revolution,* New York: Monthly Review.

Gallagher, J. and Robinson, R. (1953) "The Imperialism of Free Trade," *Economic History Review,* 6: 1–15.

Galtung, J. (1971) "A Structural Theory of Imperialism," *Journal of Peace Research,* 8: 81–117.

Gardner, L. (1964) *Economic Aspects of New Deal Diplomacy,* Madison: University of Wisconsin Press.

Gardner, R.N. (1969) *Sterling–Dollar Diplomacy,* New York: McGraw-Hill.

Garrett, G. (1998) "Global Markets and National Politics: Collision Course or Virtuous Cycle," *International Organization,* 52: 787–824.

Geertz, C. (1964) "Ideology as a Cultural System," available at www.gongfa.com/geertz1.htm.

—— (1980) *Negara: The Theatre State in Nineteenth Century Bali,* Princeton: Princeton University Press.

George, A. (1993) *Bridging the Gap: Theory and Practice in Foreign Policy,* Washington, DC: USIP Press.

—— (1997) "Knowledge for Statecraft: The Challenge for Political Science and History," *International Security,* 22: 44–51.

Germany (Federal Republic) (1959) *Agreement to Supplement the Agreement between the Parties to the North Atlantic Treaty regarding the Status of their Forces with respect to Foreign Forces stationed in the Federal Republic of Germany,* Federal Law Gazette 1961 II: 1218.

Gerschenkron, A. (1962) *Economic Backwardness in Historical Perspective,* Cambridge, MA: Harvard University Press.

Gilpin, R. (1971) "The Politics of Transnational Economic Relations," *International Organization,* 25: 398–419.

—— (1975) *US Power and the Multinational Corporation: The Political Economy of Foreign Direct Investment,* New York: Basic Books.

Goldsmith, A.A. (2000) "Foreign Aid and Statehood in Africa," *International Organization,* 55: 135–36.

Goldstein, J.S. (1985) "Kondratieff Waves as War Cycles," *International Studies Quarterly,* 29: 411–44.

Goldstone, J.A., Gurr, T.R., Harff, B., Levy, M.A., Marshall, M.G., Bates, R.H., Epstein, D.L., Kahl, C.H., Surko, P.T., Ulfelder, Jr, J.C., and Unger, A.N. (2000) *State Failure Task Force Report: Phase III Findings,* McLean, VA: Science Applications International Corporation.

Gorove, S. (1985) "International Direct Television Broadcasting by Satellite: 'Prior Consent' Revisited," *Columbia Journal of Transnational Law,* 24: 8–58.

Gottlieb, G. (1993) *Nation against State: A New Approach to Ethnic Conflicts and the Decline of Sovereignty,* New York: Council on Foreign Relations Press.

Gould, S.J. (1982) "Darwinism and the Expansion of Evolutionary Theory," *Science,* 216: 380–87.

—— (1983) *Hen's Teeth and Horse's Toes,* New York: W.W. Norton.

—— (1985a) "Not Necessarily a Wing," *Natural History,* 94: 12–25.

—— (1985b) *The Flamingo's Smile,* New York: Norton.

282 *Bibliography*

Gould, S.J. and Eldredge, N. (1977) "Punctuated Equilibria: The Tempo and Mode of Evolution Reconsidered," *Paleobiology*, 3: 115–51.

Gourevitch, P.A. (1973) "International Trade, Domestic Coalitions, and Liberty: Comparative Responses to the Great Depression of 1873–96," paper delivered to the International Studies Association Convention, Washington. Published in (1977) *Journal of Interdisciplinary History*, 8: 281–313.

—— (1978) "The Second Image Reversed: the International Sources of Domestic Politics," *International Organization*, 32: 881–912.

Graebner, L.S. (1975) "The New Economic Policy, 1971," in US Commission on the Organization of the Government for the Conduct of Foreign Policy (ed.), *Appendices*, Vol. 3, Washington, DC: Government Printing Office.

Granovetter, M. (1985) "Economic Action and Social Structure: The Problem of Embeddedness," *American Journal of Sociology*, 91: 481–510.

Greif, A. (1994) "Cultural Beliefs and the Organization of Society: A Historical and Theoretical Reflection on Collectivist and Individualist Societies," *Journal of Political Economy*, 102: 912–41.

Grew, R. (ed.) (1978) *Crises of Political Development in Europe and the United States*, Princeton: Princeton University Press.

Grieco, J.M. (1988) "Anarchy and the Limits of Cooperation: A Realist Critique of the Newest Liberal Institutionalism," *International Organization*, 42: 485–507.

—— (1990) *Cooperation among Nations: Europe, America, and Non-Tariff Barriers to Trade*, Ithaca, NY: Cornell University Press.

Gross, L. (1948) "The Peace of Westphalia, 1648–1948," *American Journal of International Law*, 42: 21–41.

—— (1979) "Some International Law Aspects of the Freedom of Information and the Right to Communicate," in K. Nordenstreng and H.I. Schiller (eds) *National Sovereignty and International Communication*, Norwood, NJ: Ablex.

Group of Lisbon (1995) *Limits to Competition*, Cambridge, MA: MIT Press.

Gruber, L. (2000) *Ruling the World*, Princeton: Princeton University Press.

Haas, E. (1980a) "Technological Self-Reliance for Latin America: the OAS Contribution," *International Organization*, 34: 541–70.

—— (1980b) "Why Collaborate? Issue-Linkage and International Regimes," *World Politics*, 32: 357–405.

—— (1982) "Words Can Hurt You; Or, Who Said What to Whom about Regimes," *International Organization*, 36: 207–43. Reprinted in S.D. Krasner (ed.) *International Regimes* (1983), Ithaca, NY: Cornell University Press.

Haberler, G. (1959) *International Trade and Economic Development*, Cairo: National Bank of Egypt.

Hagen, E. (1958) "An Economic Justification of Protectionism," *Quarterly Journal of Economics*, 72: 496–514.

Hailbronner, K. (1992) "The Legal Status of Population Groups in a Multinational State under Public International Law," in Y. Dinstein and M. Tabory (eds) *The Protection of Minorities and Human Rights,* Dordrecht: Martinus Nijhoff.

Hall, J.A. (1985) *Powers and Liberties*, Oxford: Blackwell.

Halperin, M. (1974) *Bureaucratic Politics and Foreign Policy*, Washington: Brookings Institution.

Hamashita, T. (1997) "The Intra-regional System in East Asia in Modern Times," in P.J. Katzenstein and T. Shiraishi (eds) *Network Power: Japan and Asia*, Ithaca, NY: Cornell University Press.

Hannan, M.T. and Freeman, J. (1977) "The Population Ecology of Organizations," *American Journal of Sociology*, 82: 929–64.

Harsanyi, J.C. (1960) "Explanation and Comparative Dynamics in Social Science," *Behavioral Science*, 5: 36–45.

Hartz, L. (1955) *The Liberal Tradition in America*, New York: Harcourt, Brace.

Hawtrey, R.G. (1947) *The Gold Standard in Theory and Practice*, London: Longmans, Green.

Heckscher, E.F. (1935) *Mercantilism*, Vol. I, London: George Allen and Unwin

—— (1955) *Mercantilism*, New York: Macmillan.

Heclo, H. (1974) *Modern Social Politics in Britain and Sweden*, New Haven: Yale University Press.

Hehir, J.B. (1995) "Intervention: From Theories to Cases," *Ethics and International Affairs*, 9: 1–14.

Helman, G.B. and Ratner, S.R. (1993) "Saving Failed States," *Foreign Policy*, 89: 3–21.

Hinsley, F.H. (1986) *Sovereignty*, Cambridge: Cambridge University Press.

Hirsch, F. (1976) *The Social Limits to Growth*, Cambridge, MA: Harvard University Press.

Hirschleifer, J. (1977) "Economics from a Biological Viewpoint," *Journal of Law and Economics*, 20: 1–52.

Hirschman, A.O. (1945 and 1980) *National Power and the Structure of Foreign Trade*, Berkeley: University of California Press.

—— (1977) *The Passions and the Interests: Political Arguments for Capitalism before its Triumph*, Princeton, NJ: Princeton University Press.

Hogarth, R.M. and Reder, M.W. (1986) "Editors' Comments: Perspectives from Economics and Psychology," *Journal of Business*, 59: S185–S207.

Hook, S.W. (2008) "Ideas and Change in US Foreign Aid: Inventing the Millennium Challenge Corporation," *Foreign Policy Analysis*, 4: 147–67.

Hopkins, R. and Puchala, D. (1982) "International Regimes: Lessons from Inductive Analysis," *International Organization*, 36: 245–75. Reprinted in S.D. Krasner (ed.) *International Regimes* (1983), Ithaca, NY: Cornell University Press.

Hsu, I.C.Y. (1968) *China's Entrance into the Family of Nations: The Diplomatic Phase, 1858–1880*, Cambridge, MA: Harvard University Press.

—— (1980) "Late Ch'ing Foreign Relations, 1866–1905," in J.K. Fairbank and K. Liu (eds) *The Cambridge History of China*, Vol. 11: *Late Ch'ing 1800–1911*, Part 2, Cambridge: Cambridge University Press.

Hufbauer, G.C., Schott, J.J. and Elliot, K.A. (1990) *Economic Sanctions Reconsidered: History and Current Policy*, 2nd edn, Washington, DC: Institute for International Economics.

Huitt, R.K. (1973) "The Internal Distribution of Power: The Senate," in D.B. Truman (ed.) *The Congress and America's Future*, 2nd edn, Englewood Cliffs, NJ: Prentice-Hall.

Huntington, S.P. (1968) *Political Order in Changing Societies*, New Haven, NJ: Yale University Press.

—— (1974) "Paradigms of American Politics: Beyond the One, the Two, and the Many," *Political Science Quarterly*, 89: 16–17.

—— (1982) "American Ideals versus American Institutions," *Political Science Quarterly*, 97: 1–37.

Ignatieff, M. (2003) "State Failure and Nation-Building," in J.L. Holzgrefe and R.O. Keohane (eds) *Humanitarian Intervention: Ethical, Legal, and Political Dilemmas*, Cambridge: Cambridge University Press.

Indyk, M. (2003) "A Trusteeship for Palestine?" *Foreign Affairs*, 82: 51–66.

Inoguchi, T. (n.d.) "China's Intervention in Vietnam and its Aftermath, 1786–1802: A Re-examination of the Historical East Asian World Order," Institute of Oriental Studies, University of Tokyo.

International Commission on Intervention and State Sovereignty (2001) *The Responsibility to Protect*, Ottawa: International Development Research Centre; available at: www.dfait-maeci.gc.ca/iciss-ciise/pdf/Commission-Report.pdf.

International Crisis Group (2002) *Courting Disaster: The Misrule of Law in Bosnia and Herzegovina*, Balkans Report No. 127, Sarajevo/Brussels: International Crisis Group; available at: www.crisisweb.org//library/documents/report_archive/A400592_25032002.pdf.

International Monetary Fund *Annual Report on Exchange Restrictions*, various issues.

—— *Direction of Trade*, various issues.

—— *Survey*, various issues.

—— (1986) *Fund-Supported Programs, Fiscal Policy, and Income Distribution*, Occasional Paper No. 46, Washington, DC: Fiscal Affairs Department, International Monetary Fund.

Jackson, R.H. (1990) *Quasi-States: Sovereignty, International Relations and the Third World*, Cambridge: Cambridge University Press.

Jackson, R.H. and Rosberg, C.G. (1982) "Why Africa's Weak States Persist: The Empirical and the Juridical in Statehood," *World Politics*, 35: 1–24.

James, W.E. (2002) "A Note on Pre-Shipment Inspection of Imports," Agency for International Development PPC/CDIE/DI, 28 January; available at: www.dec.org/pdf_docs/PNACQ680.pdf.

Jentleson, B.W. (2002) "The Need for Praxis: Bringing Policy Relevance Back In," *International Security*, 26: 169–83

Jepperson, R.L. (1987) "Conceptualizing Institutions, Institutionalization, and Institutional Effects," paper presented at Conference on Institutional Change, Center for Advanced Study in the Behavioral Sciences, Stanford, CA, May.

Jervis, R. (1982) "Security Regimes," *International Organization*, 36: 357–78. Reprinted in S.D. Krasner (ed.) *International Regimes* (1983), Ithaca, NY: Cornell University Press.

—— (1988) "Realism, Game Theory, and Cooperation," *World Politics*, 40: 317–49.

—— (1997) *System Effects: Complexity in Political and Social Life*, Princeton: Princeton University Press.

Johnson, H. (1965) "Optimal Trade Intervention in the Presence of Domestic Distortions," in R. Baldwin, J. Bhagwati, and R.E. Caves (eds) *Trade, Growth and the Balance of Payments: Essays in Honor of Gottfried Haberler*, Chicago: Rand McNally.

—— (1967a) "Optimum Tariffs and Retaliation," in H. Johnson (ed.) *International Trade and Economic Growth*, Cambridge, MA: Harvard University Press.

—— (1967b) *Economic Policies Toward Less Developed Countries*, New York: Praeger.

Jones, D. (1991) *Code of Peace: Ethics and Security in the World of the Warlord States*, Chicago: University of Chicago Press.

Jones, J.M. (1955) *The Fifteen Weeks*, New York: Harcourt, Brace, and World.

Kagan, R. (2006) *Dangerous Nation*, New York: Knopf.

Kant, I. (1795) *Perpetual Peace*, available at: www.mtholyoke.edu/acad/intrel/kant/kant1.htm.

Kaplan, M. (1957) *Systems and Process in International Politics*, New York: Wiley.
—— (1979) *Towards Professionalism in International Theory*, New York: Free Press.
Katzenstein, P.J. (1976) "International Relations and Domestic Structures: Foreign Economic Policies of Advanced Industrial States," *International Organization*, 30: 1–45.
—— (ed.) (1977) *Between Power and Plenty*, Madison: University of Wisconsin Press.
—— (1985) *Small States in World Markets*, Ithaca, NY: Cornell University Press.
—— (1987) *Policy and Politics in West Germany: The Growth of a Semisovereign State*, Philadelphia: Temple University Press.
—— (2005) *A World of Regions: Asia and Europe in the American Imperium*, Ithaca, NY: Cornell University Press.
Katznelson, I. (1986) "Rethinking the Silences of Social and Economic Policy," *Political Science Quarterly*, 101: 307–25.
Kaufmann, D., Kraay, A. and Mastruzzi, M. (2005) "Bottom Quintile of Aggregate Governance Rankings," *Governance Matters* IV, World Bank Policy Research Working Paper Series 3630, available at SSRN: http://ssrn.com/abstract=718081 or DOI: 10.2139/ssrn.10.2139/ssrn.718081.
Kavanaugh, A. (1986) "Star WARCs and the New System: An Analysis of U.S. International Satellite Policy Formation," *Telecommunications Policy*, 10: 93–106.
Kelly, J. (1975) "American Banks in London," PhD dissertation, Johns Hopkins University.
Kelly, Jr, W.B. (1963) "Antecedents of Present Commercial Policy, 1922–34," in W.B. Kelly, Jr (ed.) *Studies in United States Commercial Policy*, Chapel Hill: University of North Carolina Press.
Keohane, R.O. (1982) "The Demand for International Regimes," *International Organization*, 36: 325–55. Reprinted in S.D. Krasner (ed.) *International Regimes* (1983), Ithaca, NY: Cornell University Press.
—— (1984) *After Hegemony: Cooperation and Discord in the World Political Economy*, Princeton: Princeton University Press.
—— (1990) "Multilateralism: An Agenda for Research," *International Journal*, 45: 731–64.
—— (2003) "Political Authority after Intervention: Gradations in Sovereignty," in J.L. Holzgrefe and R.O. Keohane (eds) *Humanitarian Intervention: Ethical, Legal, and Political Dilemmas*, Cambridge: Cambridge University Press.
Keohane, R.O. and Nye, J.S. (1977) *Power and Interdependence*, Boston: Little, Brown.
Kim, K. (1980) *Korea, Japan, and the Chinese Empire, 1860–1882*, Berkeley: University of California Press.
Kindleberger, C.P. (1951) "Group Behavior and International Trade," *Journal of Political Economy*, 59: 30–46.
—— (1973) *The World in Depression*, Berkeley: University of California Press.
—— (1975) "The Rise of Free Trade in Western Europe 1820–75," *Journal of Economic History*, 35: 20–55.
—— (1977) "US Foreign Economic Policy, 1776–1976," *Foreign Affairs*, 55: 396–417.
—— (1978a) "Government and International Trade," *Princeton Essays in International Finance*, International Finance Section, Princeton University.
—— (1978b) *Manias, Panics, and Crashes: A History of Financial Crises*, New York: Basic Books.
—— (1986) *The World in Depression, 1929–1939*, Berkeley: University of California Press.

King, G. and Zeng, L. (2001) "Improving Forecasts of State Failure," *World Politics*, 53: 623–58.

Kingdon, J. (1995) *Agendas, Alternatives, and Public Policies*, 2nd edn, New York: Addison Wesley.

Knaus, G. and Martin, F. (2003) "Travails of the European Raj: Lessons from Bosnia and Herzegovina," *Journal of Democracy*, 14: 60–74.

Knorr, K. (1975) *The Power of Nations: The Political Economy of International Relations*, New York: Basic Books.

Krasner, S.D. (1972) "Are Bureaucracies Important?," *Foreign Policy*, 7: 159–79.

—— (1976) "State Power and the Structure of International Trade," *World Politics*, 28: 317–47.

—— (1978) *Defending the National Interest*, Princeton: Princeton University Press.

—— (1983) "Structural Causes and Regime Consequences: Regimes as Intervening Variables," in S.D. Krasner (ed.) *International Regimes*, Ithaca, NY: Cornell University Press.

—— (1984) "Approaches to the State: Alternative Conceptions and Historical Dynamics," *Comparative Politics*, 16: 223–46.

—— (1985) *Structural Conflict: The Third World against Global Liberalism*, Berkeley: University of California Press.

—— (1993) "Westphalia and All That," in J. Goldstein and R.O. Keohane (eds) *Ideas and Foreign Policy*, Ithaca, NY, Cornell University Press.

—— (1994) "International Political Economy: Abiding Discord," *Review of International Political Economy*, 1: 13–20.

—— (1995/96) "Compromising Westphalia," *International Security*, 20: 115–51.

—— (1999) *Sovereignty: Organized Hypocrisy*, Princeton, NJ: Princeton University Press.

Kratochwil, F. (1986) "Of Systems, Boundaries, and Territoriality: An Inquiry into the Formation of the State System," *World Politics*, 39: 27–52.

Kuhn, T. (1962) *The Structure of Scientific Revolutions*, Chicago: University of Chicago Press.

Kuznets, S. (1964) *Postwar Economic Growth*, Cambridge, MA: Harvard University Press.

—— (1966) *Modern Economic Growth: Rate, Structure, and Spread*, New Haven: Yale University Press.

—— (1967) "Quantitative Aspects of the Economic Growth of Nations: X. Level and Structure of Foreign Trade: Long-Term Trends," *Economic Development and Cultural Change*, 15: 1–140.

Laitin, D. (1978) "Religion, Political Culture, and the Weberian Tradition," *World Politics*, 30: 563–92.

Lake, D.A. (1999) *Entangling Relations: American Foreign Policy in its Century*, Princeton, NJ: Princeton University Press.

Lasswell, H. (1958) *Politics: Who Gets What, When, How*, Cleveland: World Publishing Company.

League of Nations (1945) *Industrialization and Foreign Trade, II.A. 10*, New York: League of Nations.

Lehmbruch, G. (1997) "From State Authority to Network State: The German State in Developmental Perspective," in M. Muramatsu and F. Naschold (eds) *State and Administration in Japan and Germany: A Comparative Perspective on Continuity and Change*, Berlin: Walter de Gruyter.

Lewis, B. (1995) *The Middle East: A Brief History of the Last 2,000 Years*, New York: Scribner.

Lewis, P. (1997) "Global Lenders Use Leverage to Combat Corruption," *New York Times*, late edn, 11 August 1997: 4.

Lijphart, A. (1974) "The Structure of the Theoretical Revolution in International Relations," *International Studies Quarterly*, 18: 41–74.

Lindblom, C. (1977) *Politics and Markets*, New York: Basic Books.

Lipset, S.M. (1983) "Radicalism or Reformism: The Sources of Working Class Politics," *American Political Science Review*, 77: 1–18.

Lipset, S.M. and Rokkan, S. (1968) "Cleavage Structures, Party Systems, and Voter Alignments: An Introduction," in S.M. Lipset and S. Rokkan (eds) *Party System and Voter Alignments: Cross National Perspectives*, New York: Free Press.

Lipson, C. (1982) "The Transformation of Trade: The Sources and Effects of Regime Change," *International Organization*, 36: 417–55. Reprinted in S.D. Krasner (ed.) *International Regimes* (1983), Ithaca, NY: Cornell University Press.

—— (1984) "International Cooperation in Economic and Security Affairs," *World Politics*, 37: 1–23.

Liu, K.C. (1980) "Foreword," in Key-Hiuk Kim, *Korea Japan, and the Chinese Empire, 1860–1882*, Berkeley: University of California Press.

Los Angeles Times, various issues.

Lowi, T. (1967) "The Public Philosophy: Interest-Group Liberalism," *American Political Science Review*, 61: 5–24.

—— (1969) *The End of Liberalism: Ideology, Policy and the Crisis of Public Authority*, New York: W.W. Norton.

—— (1972) "Four Systems of Policy, Politics and Choice," *Public Administration Review*, 32: 298–310.

Lumsdaine, D. (1993) *Moral Vision in International Politics: The Foreign Aid Regime, 1949–89*, Princeton, NJ: Princeton University Press.

Luther, S.F. (1988) *The United States and the Direct Broadcast Satellite: The Politics of International Broadcasting in Space*, New York: Oxford University Press.

Macartney, C.A. (1934) *National States and National Minorities*, Oxford: Oxford University Press.

McKinley Jr, J.C. (1998) "Kenyan Who Charged 4 Officials with Graft Is Suspended," *New York Times*, late edn, 31 July: 4.

Maizels, A. (1963) *Industrial Growth and World Trade*, Cambridge: Cambridge University Press.

Mancall, M. (1968) "The Qing Tribute System: An Interpretive Essay," in J.K. Fairbank (ed.) *The Chinese World Order: Traditional China's Foreign Relations*, Cambridge, MA: Harvard University Press.

Manley, J. (1983) "Neopluralism: A Class Analysis of Pluralism I and Pluralism II," *American Political Science Review*, 77: 368–83.

Mann, M. (1986) *The Sources of Social Power, Vol. 1: From the Beginning to 1760 AD*, Cambridge: Cambridge University Press.

March, J.G., with the assistance of Heath, C. (1994) *A Primer on Decision Making: How Decisions Happen*, New York: Free Press.

March, J.G. and Olsen, J.P. (1984) "The New Institutionalism: Organizational Factors in Political Life," *American Political Science Review*, 78: 734–49.

—— (1989) *Rediscovering Institutions: The Organizational Basis of Politics*, New York: Free Press.

—— (1998) "The Institutional Dynamics of International Political Orders," *International Organization*, 52: 943–69.

Marks, D. (1983) "Broadcasting across the Wall: The Free Flow of Information between East and West Germany," *Journal of Communication*, 33: 46–55.

Marks, M.J. and Malmgren, H.B. (1975) "Negotiating Nontariff Distortions to Trade," *Law and Policy in International Business*, 7: 327–411.

Martin, J.L. (1958) *International Propaganda: Its Legal and Diplomatic Control*, Minneapolis: University of Minnesota Press.

Maslow, A.H. (1954) *Motivation and Personality*, New York: Harper and Row.

Mathews, J.T. (1997) "Power Shift," *Foreign Affairs*, 76: 50–66.

Mearsheimer, J. (1990) "Back to the Future: Instability in Europe After the Cold War," *International Security*, 15: 5–57.

—— (2001) *The Tragedy of Great Power Politics*, New York: W.W. Norton.

—— (2005) "Better to Be Godzilla than Bambi," *Foreign Policy*, 146: 46–51.

Meyer, J.W. (1980) "The World Polity and the Authority of the Nation-State," in A. Bergesen (ed.) *Studies of the Modern World-System*, New York: Academic Press.

Meyer, J.W. and Rowan, B. (1977) "Institutionalized Organizations: Formal Structure as Myth and Ceremony," *American Journal of Sociology*, 83: 340–63.

Meyer, J.W., Boli, J., and Thomas, G.M. (1987) "Ontological Rationalization in the Western Cultural Account," in G.M. Thomas, J.W. Meyer, F.O. Ramirez, and J. Boli (eds) *Institutional Structure: Constituting State, Society, and the Individual*, Newbury Park, CA: Sage.

Meyer, J.W., Boli, J., Thomas, G.M. and Ramirez, F.O. (1997) "World Society and the Nation-state," *American Journal of Sociology*, 103: 144–81.

Millennium Challenge Account (2004) "The Millennium Challenge Corporation Names MCA Eligible Countries," press release, 6 May; available at: www.usaid. gov/mca/Documents/PR_Eligible.pdf.

Miller, J.E. (1986) *The United States and Italy, 1940–1950: The Politics and Diplomacy of Stabilization*, Chapel Hill: University of North Carolina Press.

Moe, T. (1984) "The New Economics of Organization," *American Journal of Political Science*, 28: 739–77.

—— (1987) "Interests, Institutions, and Positive Theory: The Politics of the NLRB," *Studies in American Political Development*, 2: 236–99.

—— (1990) "Political Institutions: The Neglected Side of the Story," paper presented at the Yale Law School *Journal of Law, Economics, and Organization* Conference on the Organization of Political Institutions, New Haven, April.

Moravcsik, A. (1994) "Lessons from the European Human Rights Regime," in Inter-American Dialogue (ed.) *Advancing Democracy and Human Rights in the Americas: What Role of the OAS?* Washington, DC: Inter-American Dialogue.

—— (1998) "Explaining the Emergence of Human Rights Regimes: Liberal Democracy and Political Uncertainty in Postwar Europe," working paper, Weatherhead Center for International Affairs, Harvard University, Cambridge, MA. Revised version published (2002) as "The Origins of Human Rights Regimes: Democratic Delegation in Postwar Europe," *International Organization*, 54: 217–52.

Mueller, J. (1989) *Retreat from Doomsday*, New York: Basic Books.

Murty, B.S. (1968) *Propaganda and World Public Order: The Legal Regulation of the Ideological Instrument of Coercion*, New Haven: Yale University Press.

National Journal Reports (1975) issues of 18 January; 10 May.

—— (1976).

Nelson, J. and Winter, S. (1982) *An Evolutionary Theory of Economic Change*, Cambridge, MA: Harvard University Press.

Neustadt, R. (1960) *Presidential Power: The Politics of Leadership*, New York: Wiley.

New York Times (1976) 12 June.

Nitze, P. (1954) " The Implications of Theory for Practice in the Conduct of Foreign Affairs," unpublished paper.

Nordlinger, E. (1981) *On the Autonomy of the Democratic State*, Cambridge, MA: Harvard University Press.

North, D.C. (1981) *Structure and Change in Economic History*, New York: W.W. Norton.

North, D.C. and Thomas, R.P. (1973) *The Rise of the Western World: A New Economic History*, Cambridge: Cambridge University Press.

North, D.C. and Weingast, B.R. (1989) "Constitutions and Commitment: The Evolution of Institutions Governing Public Choice in Seventeenth-Century England," *Journal of Economic History,* 49: 803–32.

North Atlantic Treaty Organization Security Council (1999) *Resolution 1244 (1000)*, available at: www.nato.int/kosovo/docu/u990610a.htm.

Obstfeld, M. and Taylor, A.M. (1997) *The Great Depressions as a Watershed: International Capital Mobility over the Long Run*, Working Paper No. 5960, Cambridge, MA: National Bureau of Economic Research.

Odell, J. (1976) "The United States in the International Monetary System: Sources of Foreign Policy Change," PhD dissertation, University of Wisconsin.

OECD, Partnership for Democratic Governance, Advisory Unit (n.d.) *Parternship for Democratic Governance*, available at: www.oecd.org/dataoecd/27/44/39408281.pdf.

Oksenberg, M. (2001) "The Issue of Sovereignty in the Asian Historical Context," in S.D. Krasner (ed.) *Problematic Sovereignty*, New York: Columbia University Press.

O'Neill, W. (2002) *Kosovo: An Unfinished Peace*, Boulder, CO: Lynne Rienner.

Onuf, N.G. (1991) "Sovereignty: Outline of a Conceptual History," *Alternatives*, 16: 425–46.

Onuma, Y. (2000) "When was the Law of International Society Born? An Inquiry of the History of International Law from an Intercivilizational Perspective," *Journal of the History of International Law*, 2: 1–66.

Oppenheim, L. (1992) *Oppenheim's International Law*, ed. R. Jennings and A. Watts, 9th edn, Harlow, Essex: Longman.

Owen, J. (2002) "The Foreign Imposition of Domestic Regimes," *International Organization*, 56: 375–409.

Owen, R. (1981) *The Middle East in the World Economy, 1800–1914*, Cambridge: Cambridge University Press.

Oye, K.A. (1985) "Explaining Cooperation under Anarchy: Hypotheses and Strategies," *World Politics*, 38: 1–24.

Packenham, R.A. (1973) *Liberal America and the Third World*, Princeton: Princeton University Press.

Paris, R. (2004) *At War's End? Building Peace after Civil Conflict*, Cambridge: Cambridge University Press.

Pastor, R.A. (1976) "Legislative-Executive Relations and US Foreign Trade Policy: The Case of the Trade Act of 1974," paper presented at the 1976 Annual Meeting of the American Political Science Association, Chicago, September.

Paz, O. (1987) "The Food of the Gods," *New York Review of Books*, 34: 3–7.

Pei, M., Amin, S. and Garz, S. (2006) "Building Nations: The American Experience," in F. Fukuyama (ed.) *Nation-Building: Beyond Afghanistan and Iraq*, Baltimore: Johns Hopkins University Press: 64–85.

Pelton, J.N. (1974) *Global Communications Satellite Policy: Intelsat, Politics and Functionalism*, Mt Airy, MD: Lomond Books.

Perrow, C. (1986) *Complex Organizations: A Critical Essay*, 3rd edn, New York: Random House.

Peterson, M.J. (1982) "Political Use of Recognition: The Influence of the International System," *World Politics*, 34: 324–52.

—— (1997) *Recognition of Governments: Legal Doctrine and State Practice*, New York: St Martin's Press.

Peterson, S., Tierney, J.M. and Maliniak, D. (2005) "Inside the Ivory Tower," *Foreign Policy*, 151: 58–64.

Peyrefitte, A. (1993) *The Collision of Two Civilisations: The British Expedition to China in 1792–4*, London: Harvill.

Pickering, J. and Peceny, M. (2006) "Forging Democracy at Gunpoint," *International Studies Quarterly*, 50: 539–59.

Piore, M. and Sabel, C.F. (1984) *The Second Industrial Divide: Possibilities for Prosperity*, New York: Basic Books.

Poggi, G. (1978) *The Development of the Modern State: A Sociological Introduction*, Stanford: Stanford University Press.

Pollard, S. (1974) *European Economic Integration 1815–1970*, London: Thames and Hudson.

Polsby, N. (1971) *Congress and the Presidency*, 2nd edn, Englewood Cliffs, NJ: Prentice-Hall.

Potter, D.M. (1954) *People of Plenty: Economic Abundance and the American Character*, Chicago: University of Chicago Press.

Preeg, E.H. (1970) *Traders and Diplomats: An Analysis of the Kennedy Round of Negotiations under the General Agreement on Tariffs and Trade*, Washington DC: Brookings Institution.

Quester, G. (1990) *The International Politics of Television*, Lexington, MA: Lexington Books.

Raeburn, P. (2000) "A Gusher for Everyone," *Business Week*, 6 November: 60.

Ramirez, F. and Boli-Bennett, J. (1982) "Global Patterns of Educational Institutionalization," in P. Altbach, R.F. Arnove, and C.A. Torres (eds) *Comparative Education*, New York: Macmillan.

Ray, J.L. (1989) "The Abolition of Slavery and the End of International War," *International Organization*, 43: 405–39.

Reno, W. (2003) "Sierra Leone: Warfare in a Post-State Society," in R.I. Rotberg (ed.) *State Failure and State Weakness in a Time of Terror*, Washington, DC: Brookings Institution.

"Revised NATO SOFA Supplementary Agreement" (n.d.) available at: www.oxc. army.mil/others/Gca/ᵃles%5Cgermany.doc.

Rhode, D. (2004) "Poppies Flood Afghanistan Opium Tide May Yet Turn," *New York Times*, 1 July.

Rice, C. (1984) *The Soviet Union and the Czechoslovak Army, 1948–1983: Uncertain Allegiance*, Princeton, NJ: Princeton University Press.

Rolfe, S.E. and Burtle, J.L. (1973) *The Great Wheel: The World Monetary System, A Reinterpretation*, New York: McGraw Hill.

Rosenau, J. (1990) *Turbulence in World Politics: A Theory of Change and Continuity*, Princeton, NJ: Princeton University Press.

Roskin, M. (1974) "From Pearl Harbor to Vietnam: Shifting Generation Paradigms and Foreign Policy," *Political Science Quarterly*, 89: 563–88.

Ross, M.L. (2001) "Does Oil Hinder Democracy?" *World Politics*, 53: 325–61.

Rotberg, R.I. (2003) "Failed States, Collapsed States, Weak States: Causes and Indicators," in R.I. Rotberg (ed.) *State Failure and State Weakness in a Time of Terror*, Washington, DC: Brookings Institution.

Ruggie, J.G. (1982) "International Regimes, Transactions, and Change: Embedded Liberalism in the Postwar Economic Order," *International Organization*, 36: 379–415. Reprinted in S.D. Krasner (ed.) *International Regimes* (1983), Ithaca, NY: Cornell University Press.

—— (1983) "Continuity and Transformation in the World Polity: Toward a Neorealist Synthesis," *World Politics*, 35: 261–85.

—— (1986) "Continuity and Transformation in the World Polity: Toward a Neorealist Synthesis," in R.O. Keohane (ed.) *Neorealism and Its Critics*, New York: Columbia University Press.

Ruggie, M. (1984) *The State and Working Women: A Comparative Study of Britain and Sweden*, Princeton: Princeton University Press.

Sabel, C.F. (1982) *Work and Politics: The Division of Labor in Industry*, New York: Cambridge University Press.

Sabel, C.F. and Zeitlin, J. (1985) "Historical Alternatives to Mass Production: Politics, Markets and Technology in Nineteenth-Century Industrialization," *Past and Present*, 108: 133–76.

Sakai, R.K. (1968) "The Ryukyu [Liu-Ch'iu] Islands as a Fief of Satsuma," in J.K. Fairbank (ed.) *The Chinese World Order: Traditional China's Foreign Relations*, Cambridge, MA: Harvard University Press.

Sartori, G. (1969) "Politics, Ideology, and Belief Systems," *American Political Science Review*, 63: 398–411.

Savage, R.I. and Deutsch, K.W. (1960) "A Statistical Model of the Gross Analysis of Transaction Flows," *Econometrica*, 28: 551–72.

Schattschneider, E.E. (1935) *Politics, Pressures and the Tariff: A Study of Free Enterprise in Pressure Politics as Shown in the 1929–1930 Revision of the Tariff*, New York: Prentice-Hall.

—— (1960) *The Semi-Sovereign People: A Realist's View of Democracy in America*, New York: Holt, Rinehart and Winston.

Schmitt, H.O. (1974) "International Monetary System: Three Options for Reform," *International Affairs*, 50: 193–210.

Schrader, E. (2003) "U.S. Looks at Organizing Global Peacekeeping Force," *Los Angeles Times*, 27 June: A1.

Schurmann, F. (1974) *The Logic of World Power*, New York: Pantheon.

Schwartz, B.I. (1968) "The Chinese Perception of World Order, Past and Present," in J.K. Fairbank (ed.) *The Chinese World Order: Traditional China's Foreign Relations*, Cambridge, MA: Harvard University Press.

Scott, W.R. (1995) *Institutions and organizations*, Thousand Oaks, CA: Sage.

Sen, A.K. (1977) "Rational Fools: A Critique of the Behavioral Foundations of Economic Theory," *Philosophy and Public Affairs*, 6: 317–44.

Sengupta, S. (2003) "Liberian Leader Sets Date, and New Terms, for Exit?" *New York Times*, 3 August.

Shepsle, K. (1986) "Institutional Equilibrium and Equilibrium Institutions," in H.F. Weisberg (ed.) *Political Science: The Science of Politics*, New York: Agathon.

Shue, H. (1997) "Eroding Sovereignty: The Advance of Principle," in R. McKim and J. McMahan (eds) *The Morality of Nationalism*, New York: Oxford University Press.

Silverstein, K. (2003) "With War, Africa Oil Beckons," *Los Angeles Times*, 21 March: 1.

Singer, P.W. (2003) *Corporate Warriors: The Rise of the Privatized Military Industry*, Ithaca, NY: Cornell University Press.

Skinner, Q. (1978) *The Foundations of Modern Political Thought, Vol. 2, The Age of Reformation*, Cambridge: Cambridge University Press.

Skocpol, T. (1979) *States and Social Revolutions*, New York: Cambridge University Press.

—— (1982) "Bringing the State Back In," paper presented at the Conference on States and Social Structures, Mount Kisco, NY, February.

Skowronek, S. (1982) *Building a New American State: The Expansion of National Administrative Capacities, 1877–1920*, New York: Cambridge University Press.

Smith, I.M. (2001) "One Sovereign, Two Legal Systems: China and the Problem of Commitment in Hong Kong," in S.D. Krasner (ed.) *Problematic Sovereignty*, New York: Columbia University Press.

Snidal, D. (1985a) "The Game Theory of International Politics," *World Politics*, 38: 25–57.

—— (1985b) "Coordination versus Prisoners' Dilemma: Implications for International Cooperation and Regimes," *American Political Science Review*, 79: 923–42.

Snyder, J.L. (2000) *From Voting to Violence: Democratization and Nationalist Conflict*. New York: W.W. Norton.

Soroos, M. (1986) *Beyond Sovereignty: The Challenge of Global Policy*, Columbia: University of South Carolina Press.

Stein, A. (1982) "Coordination and Collaboration: Regimes in an Anarchic World,": 299–324. Reprinted in S.D. Krasner (ed.) *International Regimes* (1983), Ithaca, NY: Cornell University Press.

—— (1990) *Why Nations Cooperate*, Ithaca, NY: Cornell University Press.

—— (2000) "Counselors, Kings, and International Relations: From Relevance to Reasons and Still No Policy Relevant Theory," in J. Lepgold and M. Nincic (eds) *Being Useful: Policy Relevance and International Relations Theory*, Ann Arbor: University of Michigan Press: 50–74.

Steinbrunner, J. (1974) *The Cybernetic Theory of Decision: A New Dimension of Political Analysis*, Princeton: Princeton University Press.

Stepan, A. (1978) *The State and Society: Peru in Comparative Perspective*, Princeton: Princeton University Press.

Stigler, G.J. and Becker, G.S. (1977) "De Gustibus Non Est Disputandum," *American Economonics Review*, 67: 76–90.

Stinchcombe, A. (1968) *Constructing Social Theories*, New York: Harcourt, Brace, and World.

Strang, D. (1996) "Contested Sovereignty: The Social Constuction of Colonial Imperialism," in T. Biersteker and C. Weber (eds) *State Sovereignty as a Social Construct*, Cambridge: Cambridge University Press.

Strange, S. (1982) "*Cave! Hic Dragones*: A Critique of Regime Analysis," *International Organization*, 36: 479–96. Reprinted in S.D. Krasner (ed.) *International Regimes* (1983), Ithaca, NY: Cornell University Press.

Strayer, J.R. (1970) *On the Medieval Origins of the Modern State*, Princeton: Princeton University Press.

Sugden, R. (1989) "Spontaneous Order," *Journal of Economic Perspectives*, 3: 85–97.

Suleiman, E. (1978) *Elites in French Society*, Princeton: Princeton University Press.

Suzuki, C. (1968) "China's Relations with Inner Asia: The Hsiung-nu, Tibet," in J.K. Fairbank (ed.) *The Chinese World Order: Traditional China's Foreign Relations*, Cambridge, MA: Harvard University Press.

Tetreault, M. (1991) "Autonomy, Necessity, and the Small State: Ruling Kuwait in the Twentieth Century," *International Organization*, 45: 565–91.

Thomas, A. and Thomas, A.J. (1956) *Non Intervention: The Law and Its Import in the Americas*, Dallas: Southern Methodist University Press.

Thomas, D.C. (2001) *The Power of International Norms: Human Rights, the Helsinki Accords and the Demise of Communism*, Princeton, NJ: Princeton University Press.

Thomas, H. (1971) *Cuba: The Pursuit of Freedom*, New York: Harper and Row.

Thomson, J.E. (1987) "International Institutions and the Rise and Decline of Mercenarism," paper presented at the Annual Meeting of the American Political Science Association, Chicago, IL, September.

—— (1990) "State Practices, International Norms, and the Decline of Mercenarism," *International Studies Quarterly*, 34: 23–48.

—— (1995) "State Sovereignty in International Relations: Bridging the Gap between Theory and Empirical Research," *International Studies Quarterly*, 39: 213–33.

Thomson, J.E. and Krasner, S.D. (1989) "Global Transactions and the Consolidation of Sovereignty," in E.O. Czempiel and J.N. Rosenau (eds) *Global Changes and Theoretical Challenges: Approaches to World Politics for the 1990s*, Lexington, MA: D.C. Heath.

Tilly, C. (1975) "Reflections on the History of European State-Building," in C. Tilly (ed.) *The Formation of National States in Western Europe*, Princeton: Princeton University Press.

Tocqueville, A. (1945) *Democracy in America*, New York: Vantage.

Toulmin, S. (1961) *Foresight and Understanding: An Enquiry into the Aims of Science*, New York: Harper Torchbooks.

Trakman, L.E. (1980) "The Evolution of the Law Merchant: Our Commercial Heritage, Part I," *Journal of Maritime Law and Commerce*, 12: 1–24.

—— (1981) "The Evolution of the Law Merchant: Our Commercial Heritage, Part II," *Journal of Maritime Law and Commerce*, 12: 153–82.

Treaty of Osnabrück (1648) in Clive Parry (ed.) *The Consolidated Treaty Series, Volume I, 1648–49*, Dobbs Ferry, NY: Oceana.

Triffin, R. (1964) *The Evolution of the International Monetary System*, Princeton Studies in International Finance No. 12, Princeton: Princeton University Press.

Trimberger, E.K. (1978) *Revolution from Above: Military Bureaucrats and Development in Japan, Turkey, Egypt, and Peru*, New Brunswick: Transaction Books.

Truman, D.B. (1971) *The Governmental Process: Political Interests and Public Opinion*, 2nd edn, New York: Knopf.

Tucker, R.W. (1972) *The New Isolationism: Threat or Promise?*, Washington, DC: Potomac Associates.

Tversky, A. and Kahneman, D. (1986) "Rational Choice and the Framing of Decisions," *Journal of Business*, 59: S251–S278.

United Kingdom, Department for International Development (2004) *Why We Need to Work More Effectively in Fragile States*, London: Department for International Development.

United Nations (2000) *Report of the Panel on United Nations Peace Operations*, New York: United Nations.

—— *Yearbook of International Trade Statistics*, various issues.

—— *Yearbook of National Account Statistics*, various issues.

United Nations, Office on Drugs and Crime (2001) "Afghanistan Ends Opium Poppy Cultivation," June, available at: www.unodc.org/unodc/en/news-letter_2001–6–30_1_page002.html.

United Nations Development Program, "UNDP Bill—It's Not Just What We Do, but Also How We Do It!" available at: www.undp.ba/osc.asp?idItem=2.

United Nations High Commissioner for Refugees, "History," available at: www.unhcr.ba/history/index.htm, and at Office of the High Representative, www.ohr.int.

United States, Congress (1979) *US Taiwan Relations Act Public Law 96–8*, 96th Congress, Washington, DC: Government Printing Office.

United States, Congress, Senate, Committee on Finance (1974) *United States International Trade Policy and the Trade Act of 1974*, Committee Print, 94th Congress, 2nd sess., Washington, DC: Government Printing Office.

United States, Department of Commerce, *Survey of Current Business*, various issues.

United States, Department of State, *Foreign Relations of the United States*, various issues, Washington: Government Printing Office.

—— (2004) *Trafficking in Persons Report*, Washington, DC: Government Printing Office; available at: www.state.gov/documents/organization/33614.pdf.

United States, Government Accountability Office (2004) *Telecommunications: Intelsat Privatization and the Implementation of the ORBIT Act*, Washington, DC: Government Printing Office; available at: www.gao.gov/new.items/d04891.pdf.

United States, National Commission on Supplies and Shortages (1976) *Government and the Nation's Resources*, Washington, DC: Government Printing Office.

United States, Office of the President (2002) *National Security Strategy of the United States of America*, Washington, DC: Government Printing Office.

—— (2006) *National Security Strategy of the United States of America*, Washington, DC: Government Printing Office.

United States, US Commission on International Trade and Investment Policy (1971) *United States International Economic Policy in an Interdependent World, Compendium of Papers: Vol. II*, Washington, DC: Government Printing Office.

Uriz, G.H. (2001) "To Lend or Not to Lend: Oil, Human Rights, and the World Bank's Internal Contradictions," *Harvard Human Rights Journal*, 14: 223.

Vattel, E. de (1852) *The Law of Nations; or, Principles of the Law of Nature, applied to the Conduct and Affairs of Nations and Sovereigns,* trans. J. Chitty, Philadelphia: T. and J.W. Johnson, Law Booksellers.

Verba, S. (1971) "Sequences and Development," in L. Binder, J.S. Coleman, J. LaPalombara, L.W. Pye, S. Verba, and M. Weiner (eds) *Crises and Sequences in Political Development*, Princeton: Princeton University Press.

Vernon, R. (1977) *Storm over the Multinationals: The Real Issues*, Cambridge, MA: Harvard University Press.

Vries, T. de (1976) "Jamaica, Or the Non-Reform of the International Monetary System," *Foreign Affairs*, 54: 577–605.

Wall Street Journal (1976) issues of 1 January; 12 March; 17 March; 5 May; 6 May; 6 July; 11 August; 16 December.

—— (1983) issue of 18 January.

Wallerstein, I. (1974a) *The Modern World System*, New York: Academic Press.

—— (1974b) "The Rise and Future Demise of the World Capitalist System," *Comparative Studies in Society and History*, 16: 387–415.

Walt, S. (2005) "The Relationship Between Theory and Policy in International Relations," *Annual Review of Political Science*, 8: 23–48.

Waltz, K. (1970) "The Myth of Interdependence," in C.P. Kindleberger (ed.) *The International Corporation*, Cambridge, MA: MIT Press.

—— (1979) *Theory of International Relations*, Reading, MA: Addison Wesley.

Walzer, M. (1980) "The New Masters," *New York Review of Books*, 27; available at: www.nybooks.com.

—— (1983) *Spheres of Justice: A Defense of Pluralism and Equality*, New York: Basic Books.

Wang, G. (1968) "Early Ming Relations with Southeast Asia: A Background Essay," in J.K. Fairbank (ed.) *The Chinese World Order: Traditional China's Foreign Relations*, Cambridge, MA: Harvard University Press.

Wang, Y. (1958) *Official Relations between China and Japan*, Cambridge, MA: Harvard University Press.

Weber, M. (1930) *The Protestant Ethic and the Spirit of Capitalism*, New York: HarperCollins.

Weil, G.L. (1975) *American Trade Policy: A New Round*, New York: Twentieth Century Fund.

Weiler, J.H.H. (1991) "The Transformation of Europe," *Yale Law Journal*, 100: 2403–83.

Weiner, M. (1985) "On Migration and International Relations," *Population and Development Review*, 11: 441–45.

Weingast, B.R. (1997) "The Political Foundations of Democracy and the Rule of Law," *American Political Science Review*, 91: 245–64.

Weinstein, J.M., Porter, J.E. and Eizenstadt, S.E. (2004) *On the Brink: Weak States and US National Security*, Washington, DC: Commission on Weak States and US National Security.

Wendt, A. (1987) "The Agent-Structure Problem in International Relations Theory," *International Organization*, 41: 335–70.

—— (1992) "Anarchy Is What States Make of It: The Social Construction of State Politics," *International Organization*, 46: 391–425.

—— (1999) *Social Theory of International Politics*, New York: Cambridge University Press.

Wendt, A. and Friedheim, D. (1996) "Hierarchy under Anarchy: Informal Empire and the East German State," in T.J. Biersteker and C. Weber (eds) *State Sovereignty as a Social Construct*, Cambridge: Cambridge University Press.

Wight, M. (1986) *Power Politics*, Harmondsworth: Penguin.

Wilkins, M. (1970) *The Emergence of Multinational Enterprise*, Cambridge, MA: Harvard University Press.

—— (1974) *The Maturing of Multinational Enterprise: American Business Abroad from 1914 to 1970*, Cambridge, MA: Harvard University Press.

Williamson, J. (1996) *Globalization and the Labor Market: Using History to Inform Policy*, Milan: Lezioni Raffaele Mattioli, Banca Commerciale Italiana, Unversita' Commerciale Luigi Bocconi.

Williamson, O. (1975) *Markets and Hierarchies, Analysis and Antitrust Implications*, New York: Free Press.

Wilson, E.O. (1975) *Sociobiology: The New Synthesis*, Cambridge, MA: Harvard University Press.

Windsor, P. (1984) "Superpower Intervention," in H. Bull (ed.) *Intervention in World Politics*, Oxford: Clarendon Press.

Wood, N. (2004) "60 Bosnian Serbs Dismissed for Aid to War Crimes Figure," *New York Times*, late edn, 1 July: 6.

World Bank (n.d.) "Chad–Cameroon Pipeline and Related Projects: International Advisory Group Terms of Reference." Available at: www.worldbank.org/afr/ccproj/project/iag_tor_en.pdf.

—— (1997) *World Development Report, 1997: The State in a Changing World*, Washington, DC: World Bank.

—— (1999) "Chad–Cameroon Petroleum Development and Pipeline Project," IBRD/IDA project information document, 23 June; available at: www.worldbank.org/afr/ccproj/project/td44305.pdf.

—— (2007) *International Advisory Group on Chad–Cameroon Petroleum Development and Pipeline Project*, available at http://web.worldbank.org/WBSITE/EXTERNAL/COUNTRIES/AFRICAEXT/EXTREGINI/EXTCHADCAMPIPELINE/0,content MDK:20560266~menuPK:1175824~pagePK:64168445~piPK:64168309~theSitePK:843238,00.html.

World Bank, Chad Cameroon Pipeline Project (2007) available at http://web.worldbank.org/WBSITE/EXTERNAL/COUNTRIES/AFRICAEXT/EXTREGINI/EXTCHADCAMPIPELINE/0,menuPK:843277~pagePK:64168427~piPK:64168435~theSitePK:843238,00.html.

Wriston, W. (1997) "Bits, Bytes, and Diplomacy," *Foreign Affairs*, 76: 172–82.

Yeager, L.B. (1976 [1966]) *International Monetary Relations: Theory, History and Policy*, 2nd edn, New York: Harper and Row.

Young, O. (1982) "Regime Dynamics: The Rise and Fall of International Regimes," *International Organization*, 36: 277–97. Reprinted in S.D. Krasner (ed.) *International Regimes* (1983), Ithaca, NY: Cornell University Press.

—— (1986) "International Regimes: Toward a New Theory of Institutions," *World Politics*, 39: 104–22.

Zahariadis, N. (2007) "The Multiple Streams Framework: Straucture, Limitations, Prospects," in P.A. Sabatier (ed.) *Theories of the Policy Process*, Boulder: Westview Press: 65–92.

Zakaria, F. (2003) *The Future of Freedom: Illiberal Democracy at Home and Abroad*, New York: W.W. Norton.

Zoellick, R. W. (2005) "Whither China: From Membership to Responsibility," remarks to the National Committee on US–China Relations, New York 21 September; available at: www.state.gov/s/d/former/zoellick/rem/53682.htm.

Index

Accountability Office (US) 170
Acheson, Dean 54, 56
Afghanistan 8, 18, 233, 236, 239, 245, 269
Africa 5, 87, 143–44, 180, 187, 237, 250; French Africa 139, 140; sub-Saharan Africa 237; West Africa 139, 237
After Hegemony (Keohane, R.O.) 171–72
Agendas, Alternatives and Public Policies (Kingdon, J.) 258, 259–60
AIDS 187
al-Qaeda 8, 239, 263–64
Albania 18, 207, 208
Albright, Madeline 256
Alford, R.A. and Friedland, R. 95
Allison, G. 44, 67
Almond, Gabriel 68, 73
American Journal of International Law 249
American States, International Conference (Havana, 1928) 195
Amin, Idi 206
Anand, S. and Krosnick, J. 240
Anand, Sowmya 240
Anderson, P. 101
Andorra 189
Annan, Kofi 239, 246
appropriateness, logics of 17
Aramco 26
"Are Bureaucracies Important?" (Krasner, S.D.) 44
Aron, Raymond 145
Aronson, J.D. and Cowhey, P.F. 167, 168, 170
Art, Robert J. 44, 150
Arthur, W. Brian 105
Ashdown, Paddy 244
Ashley, Richard 107

Asia 261, 270, 273; Central Asia 230; security in 269; *see also* East Asia
ASP (American Selling Price) 60
Athualpa, Inca Emperor 194
ATT (American Telephone and Telegraph) 165, 168
Augsburg, Peace of 15, 196
Australia 169; tariff levels 136
Austria 9, 208, 248; jamming of radio broadcasts by 159; South Tyrol 204; tariff levels of Austria-Hungary 135, 136
Austro-Hungarian Empire 18, 136, 174
On the Autonomy of the Democratic State (Nordlinger, E.) 66, 67, 74–75
Axelrod, R. and Keohane, R.O. 155
Axelrod, Robert 155

Bachrach, P. and Baratz, M. 77
Badie, B. and Birnbaum, P. 102
Bali 9, 74, 76–77, 93, 97
Baltic states 204, 208
Bangladesh 239
Bartsch, S. 208
Battle of the Sexes 153–54, 155, 164, 171, 173
Bauer, H. 167
Bauer, R.A. *et al.* 58, 63
Becker, Gary S. 90–91
behaviorism and state 73
Belassa, B. 134
Belgium: international trade, proportion of 138; tariff levels 135; US anti-dumping legislation against 64
Benjamin, R. and Duvall, R. 67, 70
Berlin, Treaty of 207, 208
Berman, H. and Kaufman, C. 125
Between Power and Plenty (Katzenstein, P.J., ed.) 66

Bhagwati, Jagdish 130
Bhushan, I. *et al.* 252
bin Laden, Osama 11
Binder, L. 92
Bishop Jr, J.W. 249
Blaisdell, D.C. 248
Blatherwick, D.E.S. 161, 162–63
Bodin, Jean 185, 186
Bosnia 20, 244, 245
Boyd, Douglas A. 159
Bracken, Paul 103
Bradford, E.D.S. 190
Brander, J.A. 154
Braudel, Fernand 86, 125
Brazil 5; emergent economy of 65
Bretton Woods system 125, 127, 145,
    204; breaking of 38, 48, 61;
    implementation of 52, 53, 55, 56
Bridging the Gap (George, A.) 255
Brierly, J.L. 186, 188, 191
Brimmer, A.F. and Dahl, F.R. 51
Britain 26, 33, 46, 206; British
    Commonwealth 210; British
    Dominions 189; broadcasting strength
    of 159; colonial preference 136;
    competitive telecoms environment,
    support for 167; Corn Laws 135, 143,
    144, 148; EEC and 59; free trade,
    Manchester School and 143;
    international trade, proportion of
    138; naval power of Britain 32, 45;
    postwar loan from US to 56; property
    rights, distribution of 86; religious
    wars in 185; slave trade, ending of
    206; social security system in 86; state
    power and international trade 130,
    142, 143–44, 144–45, 145–46, 149;
    tariff levels 135; US anti-dumping
    legislation against 64
Broad, Robin 241
Brownlee, J. 264
Brownlie, I. 200
Brunsson, Nils 17, 181, 184, 211
Building a New American State
    (Skowronek, S.) 66, 81–83
Bulgaria 18, 207, 208
Bull, Hedley 2, 11, 113, 118
Bumpus, B. and Skelt, B. 159
Burma 239
Burnham, W.D. 44
Bush, George W. 9, 65, 265, 266, 267;
    administration of 9, 256
Business Week 166
Byelorussia 189

Calleo, D.P. and Rowland, B. 132, 145
Calvinism 16, 203
Calvo, Carlos 194–95
Cambodia 189
Cameroon 250–51
Canada 169; tariff levels 136; US
    anti-dumping legislation against 64
capitalism: exploitative mechanisms of
    2, 10; opposition to 184, 269;
    preservation of 7; private property
    and 27–28, 101; rise of 86, 124
Caplan, Richard 243, 244, 246
Caribbean 32, 195, 206–7
Carothers, Thomas 242
Carroll, G.R. 94, 96
Central America 195, 206, 207, 245
Central Europe 18, 207–8
Cerny, P.G. 179
Chad 250–51
Chadwick, R. and Deutsch, K. 139
Chadwick, Richard 139
Chen, T. 215
Chesneaux, J.M. and Bastid, M.B. 217,
    218, 219, 222, 227, 235
Chesterman, Simon 244
Chicago School 90, 91, 92, 102
Chicken, game of 117, 154, 155, 171
Chile 271
China 4, 5, 188; British Empire and 19;
    broadcasting strength of 159; Central
    Asia and 220–22, 223; Chinese
    Empire 107; emergent economy of
    65; extra-territorial rights in,
    assertion of 107; Han dynasty 216,
    220; Hong Kong and 189–90;
    ideological bankruptcy of
    Communist party in 230; institutional
    behavior of 12; jamming of radio
    broadcasts by 159; Manchu dynasty
    225–26; Ming dynasty 220–21;
    Nationalists in 189; Nixon's visit to
    192; post-revolutionary strength of
    42; Qing dynasty 215–16, 222–23;
    remote sensing satellites of 162;
    Republic of (ROC) 192, 229, 230,
    234; as responsible stakeholder,
    conceptual framings and 268–71;
    rise of 263; Sinocentric system 11,
    19, 211, 213, 214–15, 217, 222–23,
    224–25, 226, 235; Taiping Rebellion
    218, 222; Taiwan and 20, 192;
    White Lotus Society 221; *see also*
    East Asia
Chirac, Jacques 192–93

Churchill, Winston S. 53
civil society: decision-making
  institutions and 76–77; political
  activities and 90
Claude Jr, I.L. 208
Cleveland, Robin 267
Clinton, William J., administration
  of 246
Coase, Ronald H. 174; theorem of 91
Cobden-Chevalier Treaty 135, 143, 144
Codding Jr, J.A. and Rutkowski, A.M.
  164, 166
cognitive evolutionism 126
Cohen, Benjamin J. 10, 114, 127
Cohen, M.D. *et al.* 255, 258, 262
Coleman, D.C. 132
Colino, R.R. 170
Collier, P. and Hoeffler, A. 239
Colombia 232, 239
Commerce, US Dept of 51
Communism 7, 29–30, 56, 183, 188,
  192, 202, 204–5, 208, 230, 249
Comparative Political Studies 2
"Compromising Westphalia" (Krasner,
  S.D.) 214
COMSAT (Communications Satellite
  Corporation) 169–70
Condliffe, J.B. 135, 136, 144, 147, 149
Conybeare, J.A.C. 61, 154, 174
Confucius (and Confucianism) 9, 214–15,
  222, 223, 225, 227
Congo, Democratic Republic of 232,
  236, 253
consequences, logics of 17
"Convention on Relations between the
  Three Powers and the Federal
  Republic of Germany (American
  Journal of International Law) 249
Conybeare, J.A.C. 61, 154, 174
Cooper, J. and Brady, D.W. 94
Cooper, Richard 89, 186–87
Cousens, E.M. 244
Cowhey, Peter 157, 165, 166, 167,
  169, 175
Crawford, B. 188
Crimean War 84
*Crises of Political Development in
  Europe and the United States*
  (Grew, R., ed.) 66, 69
Croatia 208
Crown Agents 252
Cuba 7, 207, 239; intervention by
  US in 32
Czechoslovakia 18, 160, 204, 207, 208;
  Sudetenland 205

Dahl, Robert 44, 45, 69, 70–72, 77, 186
Dai Bingguo 271
Dalai Lama 215
Darwin, Charles 4; Darwinian
  synthesis, criticism of 88, 99–100;
  gradualism, commitment to 99
Dawes, Charles G. 147
Dayton accords (1995) 208
DBS (direct-broadcasting satellite) 160
Deadlock, game of 161, 171, 173
decolonization 87
Defending the National Interest
  (Krasner, S.D.) 5, 6, 7, 10, 66
Denmark 204; international trade,
  proportion of 137, 138
Dervis, Kemal 271, 273
Deutsch, Karl 119, 139
*The Development of National States in
  Western Europe* (Tilly, C., ed.) 83
Diaz-Alejandro, C.F. 132
Diehl, Paul 260
DiMaggio, P.J. and Powell, W.W. 92, 106
Doha Round 65
domestic sovereignty 15, 16–17, 44, 179,
  180, 184, 185, 186, 208–9, 272;
  interdependence sovereignty and 187;
  international legal sovereignty and
  191, 192, 193; sharing sovereignty
  234–35, 238–39, 245, 247, 251, 252;
  Westphalian sovereignty and 186
Dominican Republic 7, 206–7;
  intervention by US in 32
Donnelly, Jack 201
Downs, G. and Stedman, S.J. 243, 245
Doyle, Michael 254
Doyle, M.W. and Sambanis, N. 243
Drago, Luis 194–95
Drake, William J. 165, 166, 167, 175
Drezner, Daniel W. 14
Le Droit de gens (Vattel, E. de) 188
Durant, R.F. and Diehl, P.F. 260
Durant, Robert 260
Durkheim, Emile 94
Dutch East Indies 32
Duus, Peter 218
Dyson, K.H.F. 107

East Asia 9, 11, 19, 187; appropriateness,
  logics of 212–13, 213–14; Central
  Asia, China and 220–22, 223; China
  and organized hypocrisy 216–19,
  219–23; Confucius (and Confucianism)
  9, 214–15, 222, 223, 225, 227;
  consequences, logics of 213–14;

contemporary Asia, organized
hypocrisy in 228–30; international
environments, organized hypocrisy
and 211; international relations, 19th
century, in 211–12; Japan 223–25;
Korea 225–28; military confrontation,
West with China 216–17; obeisance,
symbolic 215; Opium Wars 19, 217,
222; organized hypocrisy 213–14,
219–23, 228–30; Russia, China and
221; Ryukykus (Liu-Ch'iu Islands)
215–16, 217, 221, 224; Sino-Japanese
Treaty (1871) 224; Sino-Japanese War
(1894–95) 217, 225; Sinocentric
system 11, 19, 211, 213, 214–15, 217,
222–23, 224–25, 226, 235; sovereign
equality vs Confucian hierarchy 214;
treaty ports 217–19; tributary states
(and payments) 215–16, 217; Western
powers in 216–19; Westphalian
sovereignty 212, 217, 225, 228, 229, 230
East Timor 242
Easterly, William 266
Eastern Europe 109, 207–8
EC (European Community) 206, 208;
competitive telecoms environment,
support for 167; *see also* European
Union
Eckes Jr, A.E. 53, 54, 55, 57
Eckstein, Harry 73, 77
The Economics of Independence
(Cooper, R.) 186–87
Ecuador 239
Edelstein, D.M. 243
Eden, Lynn 274
Edson, Gary 254, 267
EEC (European Economic Community)
58–59, 145
EEZ (exclusive economic zone) 205
EFTA (European Free Trade Area) 59
Egypt 107; military bureaucracy in 84
Eldredge, N. and Gould, S.J. 87
Eldredge, Niles 4, 87, 99–101
Elisonas, J. 221, 225
Elster, John 156
The Elusive Quest for Growth
(Easterly, W.) 266
Emmanuel, A. 132
Equatorial Guinea 239
Europe 16, 60, 161; city states of 86;
direct-broadcasting satellites (DBS),
authorization of 161; economic
openness, commitment to 65;
Eurodollar market 61; European

Payments Union 57; feudal system in
87, 107; Huntington's comparison of
US with 45; party systems in,
development of 86; postwar recovery
in 50, 52–53; tariff levels in Danube
region 136; US capital market, access
to 60–61; *Zollverein* 135
European Central Bank 11
European Community (EC) 161, 167
European Convention on Human
Rights 108
European Court of Human Rights
200, 201
European Court of Justice 11, 108, 195
European Union (EU) 11, 20, 180, 195,
205, 210, 242, 244; coalition of the
willing? 246; Governance, Conference
on (Turin, 1996) 192–93;
international legal sovereignty 190,
193; supranational institution 17–18
Evans, G. and Sahnoun, M. 240
Evans, J.W. 47, 57, 59, 136, 147
EXIM (Export-Import Bank) 54, 55, 56
Exxon 27, 250
Eyal, J. 159

Fairbank, J.K. 215, 218, 220, 221, 222
FARC, Colombia 239
Fazal, T.M. 193
FCC (Federal Communications
Commission) 170
Fearon, James D. 236
Fearon, J.D. and Laitin, D.D. 232, 233,
236, 243, 256, 263
Feigenbaum, Evan 270–71
Feis, H. 248
Feldman, M. 166
Fenno Jr, R.F. 45
Ferdinand, Archduke Franz of
Austria 18
Ferejohn, John 91, 175
Fifteen Weeks (Jones, J.M.) 56
Final Settlement with Respect to
Germany, Treaty on the (1990) 249
Finance, US Committee on 47
Financial Times 161
Finer, S. 107
Firestone 26
First World War 42, 46, 146, 148, 158
Fletcher, J.F. 220, 223
Foday, Sankoh 237
Forced and Compulsory Order,
Convention on 200
Ford, Gerald R. 64

Fordism 86
Foreign Affairs 256–57
foreign policy 22; academic research, influence on 254–74; academic research and 254–74; *Agendas, Alternatives and Public Policies* (Kingdon, J.) 258, 259–61; bureaucratic politics and 25; China as responsible stakeholder, conceptual framings and 268–71; determination of 9–10; domestic authority structures and 18; domestic institutional structures and 21; function of 20–21; gap in relationship between academia and policy making 255–57; interpretations of 25–27; MCA, social science findings and foreign assistance 265–68; meta-theories 263; national interest and 25–35; organized anarchies 258; Partnership for Democratic Governance, academic idea to policy initiative 271–73; policy choice and political constraints 273–74; policy making and academia, gap in relationship between 255–57; policy research, intellectual challenge of 262–64; policy soup, academic work as ingredient 273–74; political constraints, policy choice 273–74; political cultures, effects on 30; political stream, policy makers in 264; politics, problems and policy alternatives 258; problem-oriented work in 263–64; rational decision-making (and alternative models) 257–62; sovereignty, institutional perspective on 89–110; state, historical dynamics and alternative conceptions of 66–88; systematic knowledge, deployment of 262–63; US commercial and monetary policy and 36–65
Foreign Policy (2007) 5
The Formation on National States in Western Europe (Tilly, C., ed.) 66, 83–84
Forsythe, D.P. 197, 201
Fowler, M.R. and Bunck, J.M. 188, 190
Fox, Vincente 267
Foxley, Alejandro 271
France 56, 143, 146, 189, 203, 248; international trade, proportion of 138; religious wars in 185; remote

sensing satellites of 162; tariff levels 135; US anti-dumping legislation against 64
Franco, Francisco 189
Frank, A.G. 132
Frankfurter Allgemeine Zeitung 193
FRG (Federal Republic of Germany) 249

G-8 267, 268
Gallagher, J. and Robinson, R. 144
Galtung, J. 132
Gardner, L. 145
Gardner, R.N. 39, 53, 54, 55
Garrett, G. 187
GATT (General Agreement on Tariffs and Trade) 6–7, 11, 14, 53, 54, 57, 115, 145, 167; Doha Round 65; Kennedy Round 38, 58–61, 64, 136, 147; Tokyo Round 115, 174
Geertz, Clifford 9, 34, 66, 67, 68, 73–74, 76–77, 78, 84, 88, 93, 97
George, Alexander 255, 256
Germany 18, 33, 83–84, 189, 204, 248; American loans to (1920s) 147; Bavaria 186; broadcasting strength of 159; international trade, proportion of 138; jamming of radio broadcasts by 159; Nazi Germany 39; radio propaganda, use of 158; religious tolerance in 203; tariff levels 135; television broadcasts, East and West 160, 161; trading bloc formed by 136; Treaty on the Final Settlement with Respect to Germany (1990) 249; US anti-dumping legislation against 64
Gerschenkron, A. 43
Ghana 159
Gillis, John R. 83–84
Gilpin, Robert 39, 136, 145, 149, 150
global communications, national power and 14, 151–75; Battle of the Sexes 153–54, 155, 164, 171, 173; Chicken, game of 154, 155, 171; classification of regimes 173; commitment, cleverness and 154; coordination problems, motivation and 151–52, 153, 172–73; Deadlock, game of 161, 171, 173; distributional consequences, conflict and 151–52, 154–55; electromagnetic spectrum 163–65; INTELSAT 13–14, 163–64, 166, 168–70, 173, 174; international communications 156–70, 172–73;

international regimes 152–56, 171; market failure, international relations and 151, 152, 155–56, 164, 168, 170, 171–72, 173–75; Prisoner's Dilemma 155, 156, 171, 173, 176; radio broadcasting 157–60, 173; remote sensing 161–63, 173; research programs, connotations and explicit logic of 171–72; satellite communications 168–70; Stag Hunt game 155, 171, 173; telecommunications 165–68; television broadcasting 160–61

"Global Communications and National Power" (Krasner, S.D.) 13

Golden Bull (founding document of Holy Roman Empire, 1356) 15

Goldstein, J.S. 89

Goldstone, J.A. *et al.* 236, 237

Gordon, Lincoln 27

Gorove, S. 161

Gould, S.J. and Eldredge, N. 87, 99–101

Gould, Stephen Jay 4, 87–88, 89, 99–101

Gourevitch, Peter A. 21, 135–36 150

Graebner, L.S. 62

Granovetter, Mark 95, 103–4

Greece 18, 56, 207, 208

Greif, A. 218

Grenada 264

Grew, Raymond 66, 69

Grieco, Joseph M. 152, 156, 174

Gross, Leo 15, 158

Grotius, Hugo: Grotian tradition 118–19; regimes, perspective on 116, 119–20, 127; worldview of 119

Gruber, Lloyd 14, 263

Gurria, Angel 271, 273

Guyana 239

Haas, Ernst 113, 119, 126

Haberler, Gottfried 132

Hagen, E. 130

Hailbronner, Kay 197

Haiti 207; intervention by US in 32

Hall, J.A. 89

Halperin, Morton 44, 254

Hamashita, T. 215, 221

Han dynasty 216, 220

Hannan, M.T. and Freeman, J. 96, 102, 104

Hapsburg Empire 203, 207, 208

Harsanyi, J.C. 90

Hart, Robert 222

Hartz, Louis 29, 39, 80, 83, 264

Harvard University Center for International Affairs 150

Hawtrey, R.G. 144

Hayek, Friedrich A. von 125

Heckscher, E.F. 132

Heclo, Hugh 86

Hehir, J. Brian 197

Helman, G.B. and Ratner, S.R. 236, 245–46

Helman, Gerald B. 245–46

Hinsley, F.H. 185

Hirsch, Fred 114, 124

Hirschleifer, J. 122

Hirschman, Albert O. 13, 40, 124, 125, 131

Hitler, Adolf 39, 264

Hobbes, Thomas 77, 96, 120, 185, 186; world of 30

Hoffman, Paul 56

Hogarth, R.M. and Reder, M.W. 91

Holland *see* Netherlands

Holy Alliance 18–19

Holy Roman Empire 15–16, 203

Hong Kong 20, 59, 189, 228–29; annexation of 217

Hook, S.W. 268

Hoover, Herbert C. 32, 147

Hopkins, R. and Puchala, D. 117–18, 119, 124, 125, 126–27

Hsu, I.C.Y. 215, 217, 223

Hufbauer, G.C. *et al.* 206

Hughes, Charles Evans 195

Huitt, R.K. 45

human rights: Copenhagen principles 18; Universal Declaration of 201; violations of 239–40

Hungary 18, 160, 204, 207, 208

Huntington, Samuel P. 44, 45, 80, 82, 83, 149–50

Hussein, Saddam 8, 11, 239

IBM 166, 167

IBRD (International Bank for Reconstruction and Development) 38, 54, 204

Ignatieff, Michael 238, 243, 246

ILO (International Labor Organization) 200

IMF (International Monetary Fund) 37–38, 53–55, 174, 184, 195, 204, 242, 265; Annual Report on Exchange Restrictions 60; Articles of Agreement, amendment of 62; Fiscal Affairs Department 241

India 5, 189, 219; emergent economy of 65; Indian Mutiny (1857) 217; remote sensing satellites of 162
Indyk, Martin 246
Inoguchi, T. (n.d.) 220
INTELSAT 13–14, 163–64, 166, 168–70, 173, 174
interdependence sovereignty 15, 179, 180, 184, 185, 186–88, 192, 208–9; Westphalian sovereignty and 187–88
International Crisis Group 244
International Development, Dept of (UK) 5
international legal sovereignty 11, 15, 16–18, 179, 180, 181, 182, 183, 184, 185, 188–93; cognitive perspective on 191; domestic sovereignty and 186, 191, 192, 193; interdependence sovereignty and 188; non-recognition under 191–92; recognition under 188–90; security of 190–91; sociological perspective on 191; territorial integrity and 193; Westphalian sovereignty and 180, 181, 182, 185, 192–93, 210; Westphalian sovereignty and, compromise under 192–93
"International Political Economy: Abiding Discord (Krasner, S.D.) 1–2
international politics 22; function of 21; global communications, national power and 151–75; international trade, state power and 129–50; national power and global communications 151–75; regimes and 113–28; state power and international trade 129–50
International Regimes (Krasner, S.D., ed.) 12
international relations 17; East Asia, 19th century 211–12; global communications, national power and market failure 151, 152, 155–56, 164, 168, 170, 171–72, 173–75; goals, hierarchy of, and 31; hierarchy of goals and 31; market failure and 2, 4, 12, 14, 121, 263; needs, hierarchy of, and 31; power distribution among states 30; realms of 22; state-centric model in 25
International Security 272
international system 10–14; anarchic nature of 18, 30; appropriateness, logics of 213–14; complexity of 20;

consequences, logics of 213–14; constructivism and international society 10–12; Marxism 10; norms and values, imperfect institutionalization of 12; state power and international regimes 12–14
International Trade and Investment Policy, US Commission on (1971) 47
International Trade Commission 47, 64
Intervention and State Sovereignty, International Commission on 239–40
Iran: institutional behaviour of 12; oil investment in 26, 27
Iraq 8, 9, 208, 269; al-Qaeda in 263–64; oil investment in 26, 27; shared sovereignty in 233, 235, 236, 239, 242, 245, 246, 253
Islam 9, 11, 213
Israel 109, 160
Italy 189, 204, 248; institutional behavior of 12; international trade, proportion of 138; Italian Peace Treaty 192; jamming of radio broadcasts by 159; tariff levels in Piedmont 135; US anti-dumping legislation against 64
ITO (International Trade Organization) 6, 38, 53, 54, 55
ITU (International Telecommunications Union) 13, 157, 163, 164, 165, 166, 167, 168, 169, 173

Jackson, R.H. and Rosberg, C.G. 109
Jackson, Robert H. 194
James, W.E. 252
Japan 9, 18, 29, 60, 107, 169, 223–25; Ashikaga shogunate 215; competitive telecoms environment, support for 167; domestic strength of 43, 45; economic openness, commitment to 65; import restrictions by 145; international trade, proportion of 137; Korea and 224–25; military bureaucracy in 84; postwar recovery in 50, 52–53; RCA in 62; remote sensing satellites of 162; trading bloc formed by 136; US anti-dumping legislation against 64; *see also* East Asia
Jena, Battle of 84
Jentleson, Bruce W. 257, 274
Jepperson, R.L. 98
Jervis, Robert 113, 117, 126, 127, 173, 174, 175, 257

Johns Hopkins School of Advanced
   International Studies 150
Johnson, Harry 130, 134
Johnson, Lyndon B. 9
Jones, D. 208
Jones, J.M. 39, 54, 56

Kagan, R. 264
Kanghwa, Treaty of 225
Kaplan, M. 114
Karadžic, Radovan 244
Katzenstein, Peter J. 12, 62–63, 66, 102,
   149, 249
Katznelson, I. 95
Kaufmann, D.t al. 5
Kavanaugh, A. 164, 170
Kelly, J. 149
Kelly Jr, W.B. 63
Kennan, George 254
Kennedy, John F. 30; administration
   of 59
Kennedy Round 38, 58–61, 64, 136, 147
Keohane, R.O. and Nye, J.S. 113, 119
Keohane, Robert O. 4, 13, 79, 93, 103,
   150, 188, 236, 247, 274; global
   communications 152, 155, 156, 171–72,
   175; regime consequences, structural
   causes and 113, 117, 120, 121, 127
Keynes, J. Maynard: Keynes Plan 55;
   Keynesian analysis 122
Kiakhta, Treaty of 221
Kim, Key-Hiuk 215, 217, 224, 225,
   226, 227
Kindleberger, Charles P. 13, 61, 122–23,
   135, 136, 144, 146, 147, 149
King, G. and Zeng, L. 236
Kingdon, John 255, 258, 259–60,
   261, 262
Kissinger, Henry 256
Korea 7, 8, 29, 215, 219, 225–28; Japan
   and 224–25; Korean War 50; military
   interventions in 217; Yi dynasty in
   227; *see also* East Asia
Kosovo 245
Kratochwil, Friedrich 107
Krosnick, Jon 240
Kurile Islands 228
Kuznets, Simon S. 132, 137

Laitin, David D. 124, 236
Lakatos, Imre, actor-oriented approach
   of 92
Lake, D. Anthony 216, 254, 256
Lamine Loum, Mamadou 250

LANDSAT 162
Larson, Al 267
Lasswell, Harold D. 67
Latin America 32, 107, 189, 204
The Law of Nations (Vattel, E. de) 16,
   214, 234
LDCs (Least-Developed Countries)
   115, 164, 169
League of Nations 142, 158, 189,
   200, 208
Lebanon 42
Lee, General John C.H. 192
Lee, Richard 70, 71
Lehmbruch, G. 16, 203
Lenin, Vladimir I. 207
Lewis, B. 248
Lewis, P. 241
Lewis, W. Arthur 125
Liberia 26, 27, 32, 236, 237, 253
Lijphart, A. 119
Lindblom, C. 69
Lipset, S.M. and Rokkan, S. 85
Lipson, Charles 127, 155–56
Liu, K.C. 216, 226
Locke, John 186; ideals and belief
   structure of 30, 39, 53; individualism
   of 264; liberalism of 29, 32, 33, 35,
   39; nature, state of 140
The Logic of World Power (Schurmann,
   F.) 28–29
Lon Nol 189
London Monetary Conference (1933)
   147
Lowery, Clay 267
Lowi, Theodore 42, 56, 69, 149
Luther, S.F. 166
Lutheranism 16, 203

Maastricht, Treaty of 205
Macao 217
Macartney, C.A. 196–97
Macartney, George 19
McConnell, Grant 69
McCormack, Sean 272
McCulloch, Rachel 150
McKinley, William 33, 241
MAD (Mutually Assured Destruction)
   126
Madison, James 44
Malaya 219
Malta, Order of Knights of 190, 209
Mancall, M. 215
Manchu dynasty 225–26
Mann, M. 89

Mao Tse Tung 207
March, James G. 90, 180–81, 213
March, J.G. and Olsen, J.P. 90, 92, 180–81, 213
Marks, D. 158
Marks, M.J. and Malmgren, H.B. 46, 60
Marshall, George 192
Marshall Plan 38, 52–53; opening a wedge (1950s) 55–58
Martin, J.L. 158, 159
Marx, Karl 186
Marxism 34–35, 42, 66, 67, 68; structural Marxism 7, 10, 26, 27–28; theoretical Marxism 25–26
Maslow, Abraham 31
Mathews, J.T. 186
MCA (Millennium Challenge Account) 265–68, 270
MCC (Millennium Challenge Corporation) 265, 268, 271
Mearsheimer, J. 263
Meiji Japan (and Meiji restoration) 4, 43, 223–24
Mexico 27, 29, 189; Aztec civilization of 93; Mexican Revolution 33
Meyer, John W. 17, 87
Meyer, J.W. and Rowan, B. 87
Meyer, J.W. *et al.* 95, 97, 212
MFN (Most-Favoured Nation) 14, 115
Middle East 8–9, 27, 32, 125; jamming of radio broadcasts in 159
Mill, John Stuart 186
Miller, J.E. 192
Min, Queen of Korea 227
Ming dynasty 220–21
Moe, Terry 90, 91, 171, 175
Molière 25
Mongols 212, 220
Monroe Doctrine 32
Montenegro 18, 207, 208
Moravcsik, A. 201–2
Mugabe, Robert 232
Münster, Treaty of 15
Murty, B.S. 158, 159

Nanking, Treaty of 217–18
Napoleon, Louis 144
Napoleon III 165
Nash equilibria 3, 151, 152, 153, 155, 171, 173, 175, 210
national interest: capitalism and 27–28; foreign policy and 25–35; historical evolution of US foreign policy in defense of 31–34; ideology and statist

paradigm in defense of 34–35; interest and ideology in US foreign policy 28–31; Marxist paradigm, societal interests and 27–28, 34–35; policy making by US and 26–27; state action and 26–27; statist paradigm, societal interests and 27–28, 34–35
National Journal Reports 47, 63
National Power and the Structure of Foreign Trade (Hirschman, A.) 13
National Security Strategy (US) 8
NATO (North Atlantic Treaty Organization) 249
Nazi Germany 39
Negara (Geertz, C.) 66, 67, 76–77, 84, 93, 97
Nelson, J. and Winter, S. 103, 104
Netherlands 248; Dutch in Indonesia 9, 27, 93; international trade, proportion of 138; religious tolerance in 203; tariff levels 135
Neustadt, Richard 44
New York Times 64, 161
NGOs (non-governmental organizations) 201, 243, 250, 252
Nicaragua 207; intervention by US in 32
9/11 attacks on US (and aftermath) 8, 18
Nitze, Paul 254, 264
Nixon, Richard M. 61
Nordlinger, Eric 66, 67, 68, 69–70, 73–75, 78
Noriega, Manuel 207
North, D.C. 89
North, D.C. and Thomas, R.P. 122
North Korea 238, 239; institutional behaviour of 12
Norway: international trade, proportion of 137, 138; tariff levels 135
NTT (Nippon Telephone and Telegraph) 167
Nye, Joseph 150, 255

OAS (Organization of American States) 195
Obstfeld, M. and Taylor, A.M. 187
Odell, J. 60
OECD (Organization for Economic Cooperation and Development) 247, 271–72
Oksenberg, M. 215
Olsen, Johan P. 90, 180–81, 213

O'Neill, W. 244
Onuf, N.G. 185
Onuma Yasuaki 215, 217, 218, 220, 221, 222, 227, 231
Opium Wars 19, 217, 222
Oppenheim, Lassa Francis Lawrence 186, 188, 190–91, 192, 195
ORBIT (Open-market Reorganization for the Betterment of International Telecommunications) Act 170
The Organization of Hypocrisy (Brunsson, N.) 17
"Organized Hypocrisy in 19th Century East Asia" (Krasner, S.D.) 9, 19
OSCE (Organization for Security and Economic Cooperation in Europe) 244
Osnabrück, Treaty of 15
Otho, King of Greece 207
Ottoman Empire 18, 107, 203, 207, 208, 248
Owen, John 19, 214
Owen, R. 248
Oye, K.A. 156, 171

Packenham, Robert 29
Panama 207, 264
Pareto, Vilfredo: equilibria of 13, 17; optimality of 117, 121, 130, 152, 153, 155, 172, 175; Pareto frontier 13, 17, 151–75; Pareto-improving agreements 198, 202; sub-optimality of 120–21, 151, 155, 171, 172, 174; terminology of 34
pariah groups, finance by 124–25
Paris, Roland 245
Pastor, R.A. 46, 59
Paz, Octavio 93
PBXS (private branch exchanges) 167
PDG (Partnership for Democratic Governance) 271–73
Peace of Augsburg 15, 196
Peace of Utrecht 203
Peace of Vienna 203
Peace of Westphalia 15–16, 193–94
Pei, M. *et al.* 264
Pelton, J.N. 170
Perrow, Charles 172
Persian Gulf 27, 107
Peru 27; military bureaucracy in 84
Peterson, M.J. 189, 192
Peterson, S. *et al.* 255
Peterson Commission (1971) 46
Peyrefitte, A. 19

Philippines 189
Pickering, J. and Peceny, M. 264
Pintner, Walter M. 83–84
Piore, M. and Sabel, C.F. 86
PLO (Palestine Liberation Organization) 189
pluralism 69, 70, 72, 73, 81, 88; group pluralism 6, 7, 92; neo-pluralism 69–70
PMCs (private military companies) 252
Poggi, G. 67, 103
Poland 9, 18, 207, 208; dismemberment of 93
Pollard, S. 135
Polsby, N. 44
Portugal 206, 217; tariff levels 135
Potter, David 46
Powell, Colin 270
power: British state power and international trade 130, 142, 143–44, 144–45, 145–46, 149; common good, power in service of 122–23; dispersion of power and authority in US 44–46; distribution among states 30; global communications, national power and 151–75; instrumental role of 122; international trade, state power and 129–50; naval power of Britain 32, 45; power asymmetries 179, 181, 182, 183, 184, 197, 199, 206, 209, 214, 223; special interests, power in service of 123–24; *see also* state power and international trade 132–35
Power, Samantha 240
Preeg, E.H. 59
President, Office of US 8
Prisoner's Dilemma 117, 120–21, 155–56, 171, 173, 175
A Problem from Hell: America and the Age of Genocide (Power, S.) 240
The Protestant Ethic and the Spirit of Capitalism (Weber, M.) 124
Prussia 9, 84
PTTS (post, telephone and telegraph agencies) 165, 166, 167

Qing dynasty 215–16, 222–23
Quester, G. 160, 161

RA (relative acceptance) indicator 139
Radelet, Steven 267
Radio Luxembourg 159
Radio Monte Carlo 159

Raeburn, P. 251
Ramirez, F. and Boli-Bennett, J. 87
RAMSI (Regional Assistance Mission for the Solomon Islands) 273
Ratner, Steven 245–46
Rawls, John 120
RCA in Japan 62
Reagan, Ronald W., administration of 82
Red Line Agreement 26
regimes: agreements and, distinction between 113–14; changes within 115–16; common good, power in service of 122–23; conventional structural perspective on 116–17; definition of 113–16; development of 120–27; egoistic self-interest and development of 120–21; friendship 114; Grotian perspective on 116, 117–20, 123–24, 125–26, 127; as intervening variables 113–28; knowledge and development of 126–27; modified structural perspective on 116, 117, 120–21, 123, 126; norms and principles of 114–15, 124–25; notion of, value of? 116–20; political power and development of 121–24; power, instrumental role of 122; realist perspective on 116–17, 120–21, 123, 126, 127–28; reciprocity 114; regime change 113–16; regime-governed behavior 114; rules and procedures, distinct from norms and principles 114–15; special interests, power in service of 123–24; usage and custom within 125–26
Reno, William 238
The Responsibility to Protect (International Commission on Intervention and State Sovereignty) 239–40
Review of International Political Economy 2
Revolution from Above (Trimberger, E.K.) 66, 84
Rhode, D. 239
Rice, Condoleezza 207, 254, 256, 270, 271, 272
Rogowski, Ronald 150
Rolfe, S.E. and Burtle, J.L. 57, 144, 146
Roman Empire 107
Romania 18, 207, 208
Rome, Treaty of 205

Roosevelt, Franklin D. 32, 53, 56, 147; administration of 55
Roosevelt, Theodore 33
Rosenau, James 187, 196
Ross, Dennis 254
Rostow, Walt 254
Rotberg, R.I. 238
Royal Dutch Shell 250
RUF (Revolutionary United Front), Sierra Leone 237–38
Ruggie, John G. 12, 107, 114–15, 118, 125, 127, 174, 254
Ruggie, M. 97
Russia 9, 33, 42, 83–84, 189, 223, 228; *see also* Soviet Union
Ryukyus (Liu-Ch'iu Islands) 215–16, 217, 221, 224

Sabel, C.F. and Zeitlin, J. 86
Sabel, Charles F. 86
Sakai, R.K. 221
Sardos, Andrzej 271
Saudi Arabia 27, 131; institutional behavior of 12
Savage, R.I. and Deutsch, K.W. 139
Schattschneider, E.E. 48, 149
Schelling, Thomas C. 125
Schmitt, H.O. 134
Schrader, E. 243
Schurmann, Franz 28–29, 39
Scott, W.R. 212
Scowcroft, Brent 256
SDRs (Special Drawing Rights) 60
Second World War 27, 33, 39, 40, 53, 264
Sen, A.K. 90
Serbia 18, 207, 208; Monopolies Commission in 203–4
SFOR (Stabilization Force), Bosnia 244
sharing sovereignty 232–53; alternatives to conventional sovereignty 234–36; conventional sovereignty 232, 233, 235, 236, 241, 242, 248, 252; crises, humanitarian 240; failed governance, consequence of 233, 236–37; failures of conventional sovereignty 236–38; governance assistance 240, 241–42, 251–52; historical examples of shared sovereignty 248–51; human rights, violations of 239–40; national authority structures, weakness of 232; protectorates 245–47, 252; shared sovereignty 245, 247–51; sovereignty failures, importance of 238–40,

252–53; State Failure Task Force 236; transitional administration 240, 242–45, 251–52; trusteeships, de facto 245–47, 252; US postwar arrangements 249

Shepsle, K. 93

Shimonoseki, Treaty of 217, 227

Shue, H. 185

Shultz, George 256

Sierra Leone 236, 237, 238, 239

Singer, P.W. 252

Sino-Japanese Treaty (1871) 224

Sino-Japanese War (1894–95) 217, 225

Sinocentric system 11, 19, 211, 213, 214–15, 217, 222–23, 224–25, 226, 235

SITC (Standard International Trade Classification) 49, 50, 51

Skinner, Q. 185

Skocpol, Theda 66, 75

Skowronek, Stephen 66, 68–69, 78–83

Slovenia 208

Smith, Adam 99, 122

Smith, I.M. 228

Snidal, Duncan 99, 152, 153, 154

socialization 12, 14, 17, 71, 95, 98, 103, 213

Sociobiology (Wilson, E.O.) 31

Solomon, Richard 254

Somalia 180

Soroos, M. 162

South Africa 5, 159, 206, 235, 245, 247

sovereignty 14–20; academic assumptions on 19; actors, definition of 96, 98; adaptationist arguments 99–100; allocation and 90, 91; alternative perspectives on 89–90; alternatives to 20; authority, assertion of 107–8; authority claims and 97–98; autonomy and 15; breadth of institutionalization 96, 97, 98; citizenship and 96; conventional approaches to 90–93; conventional sovereignty 17, 20, 229, 232; core elements 15, 16–17; customs, traditions and 91; depth of institutionalization 96, 97, 98, 103; derivative individualism and 95; dimensions of institutionalization 96–99; discontents and 179–210; East Asia, organized hypocrisy in 19th-century 211–31; endurance of 20; environmental alteration and institutional persistence 102–3; evolutionary analogy 99–101; firm, theory of, evolutionary theory

and 104; functional perspective 90, 92–93; gradualist-punctuationist debate 87, 100; individual identity and 96–97; individualism, actor orientation and 90, 91–92, 93; institutional inertia 102; institutional isomorphic change 106; institutional persistence 101–6; institutional perspective 14, 90, 93–96; internal resistance to organizational restructuring 104; juridical independence 15, 16–17; linkages of institutionalization 96, 97; nature of 94, 106–10; network externalities, path-dependency and 105–6; non-intervention in internal affairs, principle of 15–16; organized hypocrisy and principles of 19–20, 21–22; path-dependent development and institutional persistence 104–5; personal ties and institutional persistence 103–4; principles of 15, 16–17; problem mitigation and institutional persistence 103; punctuated equilibrium, idea of 99, 100, 101; routinized behavior and 95; sharing 232–53; social institutions and 94–95; sociology and 94–95; sovereign state system 89–90; state system, dominance of 109; state system, origins of 15–16; suboptimal institutional structures 89–90; time, persistence over 95–96; transborder control 108; utilitarian perspective 90, 91–92, 93; violations of 17–18; *see also* domestic sovereignty; interdependence sovereignty; international legal sovereignty; sharing sovereignty; Westphalian sovereignty

Sovereignty: Organized Hypocrisy (Krasner, S.D.) 15, 211

Soviet Union 7, 18, 33, 40, 65, 109, 169, 202, 248–49; broadcasting strength of 159; Cold War dictatorship of Eastern Europe 207–8; jamming of radio broadcasts by 159; post-revolutionary strength of 42; radio propaganda, use of 158

Spain 189, 203; jamming of radio broadcasts by 159; tariff levels 135

SSRC (Social Science Research Council) 83–84

Stag Hunt game 155, 171, 173

Stalin, Josef 202
state: as administrative apparatus 67; administrative incoherence 82–83; behaviorism and 73; branching tree in development of 85–86; characteristics of 79–80; city states of Europe 86; civil society, decision-making institutions and 76–77; constraints on public leadership 71–72; crisis, periods of 78; Dahl's theory of leadership 69–73; definition of 67; democratic values and 71; as exogenous variable 73–77; external threat, state capability and 84–4; fragmentation of 79–80; as government 67; ideology and 71–72, 80; individual liberalism and 70–71; industrialization and response to 80–81, 86; institutional characteristics and perpetuation of 86–87; institutional creation and perpetuation 85–86; institutional stasis 79, 81; intellectual approaches to idea of 66–67, 67–69; as intervening variable 78–85; leadership, pluralist theories of 72; localism and 82–83; military bureaucracy and social change 84; national capabilities, institutional structures acting against 81–83; neo-pluralism 69–70; as normative order 67, 77; pluralism 69, 70, 72, 73, 81, 88; political development 78–85; Political Development, SSRC studies in 83–84; political leadership, role of 70–71; political stratum and 72; preferences of 74–75; private dynamism, public stasis and 79–83; as public bureaucracy 67; public officials, role of 70–71; public policy 73–77; punctuated equilibrium, idea of 4, 14, 69, 85–88, 99–101; as ruling class 67; societal actors, influence on public policy and 69–70; societal resistance, state demands and 83–85; state autonomy 66–67, 73–77; state-building as patchwork 81; state harmony 66–67, 78–85; statist literature, characteristics of 67–69; symbols embodied in 77; *see also* regimes

The State and Society in Peru (Stepan, A.) 66
state-building 19, 22; external threat to, impact of 69; intervention and 21;

local sovereignty and 233; as patchwork 81; *see also* sovereignty
State Failure Task Force 236
state power and international trade 129–50; crisis and change in 148–49; economic power, distribution of potential for 141–48; external threat and change in 149–50; hegemony and openness in trading structures 133–34, 141–42, 142–48; institutional persistence 149; interdependence 129; interwar developments (1919–39) 141, 146–47; modest closure (1880–1900) 141, 144–45; non-tariff barriers to trade 136; open trading, hegemony and (1945–60) 141, 145; opening trade (1820–79) 141, 143–44; openness 129, 141–42, 142–48; patterns of trade and delayed reactions (1960–70) 141, 147–48; regional trading patterns 135, 139–41; relative costs of closure and 131; resource allocation and 132; social structures, state policy and 149; state interests, power and trading structures 130–41; state-power theory 129–30, 144, 146, 147, 148; state preferences 130–32; structural change in international trading 129–30, 148–50; tariff levels 134, 135–36; trade proportions 134–35, 137–39; trade proportions and regional patterns (1900–913) 141, 145–46; trading structures from state preferences 132–35
"State Power and the Structure of International Trade" (Krasner, S.D.) 13, 39, 40, 123
States and Social Revolution (Skocpol, T.) 66
Stein, Arthur 117, 120–21, 123, 126, 127, 152, 155, 256
Steinberg, James 254
Steinbrunner, John D. 103
Stepan, Alfred 66, 102
Stigler, G.J. and Becker, G.S. 91
Stinchcombe, Arthur 95, 101–2, 103
STR (Special Trade Representative), US Office of 46
Strang, David 181, 189
Strange, Susan 116, 128
Strayer, J.R. 107, 185
"Structural Causes and Regime Consequences" (Krasner, S.D., ed.) 93

Structural Conflict: The Third World Against Global Liberalism (Krasner, S.D.) 164
Sudan 12, 239, 269, 271
Sugden, Robert 185
Suleiman, Ezra N. 79
Survey of Current Business (US Commerce Dept) 51
Suzuki, C. 216, 221
Sweden: international trade, proportion of 138; social security system in 86; tariff levels 135; transnational learning in 86; US anti-dumping legislation against 64
Switzerland 201; tariff levels 135
Sylvania 62
symbolism and state 77
Syria 125
Taiping Rebellion 218, 222
Taiwan 210, 217, 229–30; China and 20, 192
Taliban 8, 18, 236, 239
Tamerlane 220
Tetreault, M. 235
Third World 29, 62, 64, 86; redistribution and order, calls for 115
Thomas, A. and Thomas, A.J. 194, 195
Thomas, D.C. 202
Thomson, J.E. 186, 188, 190
Thomson, J.E. Krasner, S.D. 187
Thucydides 21
Tientsin, Treaty of 217
Tilly, Charles 66, 69, 83–84
Timurid dynasty 220
Tocqueville, Alexis de 45, 71, 104–5
Tokyo Round 115, 174
Toulmin, Stephen 119
Trakman, L.E. 125
Treaty for Peace in Italy 192
Treaty of Berlin 207, 208
Treaty of Kanghwa 225
Treaty of Kiakhta 221
Treaty of Maastricht 205
Treaty of Münster 15
Treaty of Nanking 217–18
Treaty of Osnabrück 15
Treaty of Rome 205
Treaty of Shimonoseki 217, 227
Treaty of Tientsin 217
Treaty of Utrecht 203
Treaty on the Antarctic 108
Treaty on the Final Settlement with Respect to Germany (1990) 249

Treaty on the Law of the Seas (UN) 11, 108
Triffin, R. 144, 146, 147
Trimberger, Ellen Kay 66, 69, 84
Truman, David 44, 77
Truman, Harry S. 56
Truman Doctrine 55–56
Tucker, Robert W. 131, 150
Turbulence in World Politics (Rosenau, J.) 187
Turkestan 223
Turkey 8, 18, 206, 208; military bureaucracy in 84
Turkmenistan 12
Tversky, A. and Kahneman, D. 91

UAW (United Auto Workers) 64
Uganda 206
Ukraine 189
Underhill vs Hernandez (US Supreme Court) 190–91
United Kingdom *see* Britain
United Nations (UN) 189, 191, 206; Atlantic City Telecommunications Convention, endorsement of (1950) 158; Charter 195, 201; Drugs and Crime Office 239; General Assembly 246–47, 271; Helsinki Agreement (1975) 195, 202; High Representative for Bosnia, Office of 244; Law of the Seas Treaty 11, 108; Peaceful Uses of Outer Space, Committee on 169; remote sensing, rules for 162; Security Council 8, 11, 242, 243, 244, 246; *Statistical Yearbook* 41; transitional administrations 243; UNDP (UN Development Program) 244, 271, 273; UNHCR (UN High Commissioner for Refugees) 244; UNTAG (UN Transition Assistance Group) 245; *Yearbook of International Trade Statistics* 49–50; *Yearbook of National Account Statistics* 41, 138
United States 5–7, 18; abortion, public debate on 108; Agriculture Department 46; American Revolution 80; Anti-Dumping Act (1921) 46; apogee and decline (1962–71) in foreign economic policy 38, 58–61; broadcasting strength of 159; China, Taiwan and 20, 192; Civil War in 80, 136; Commerce Department 46; commercial and monetary policy 36–65; competitive telecoms

environment, support for 167; COMSAT (Communications Satellite Corporation) 169–70; Congress 46–47, 62, 192; constraints, internal and external, upon 36–37, 41–48; dispersion of power and authority 44–46; domestic challenges to decision-makers 37, 41–42, 42–48; domestic constraints on decision-makers 41–42; domestic interests, changing nature of 48–52; economic openness, commitment to 36, 65; economic power, potential for 40–41; economic strength of 33, 36, 40; expansionism of 29, 32, 33; external power, rise of 37; false start (1945–47) in foreign economic policy 37–38, 53–55; force, covert or overt, uses of 28, 29; force against Central America, use of 206–7; Fordney-McCumber Tariff Act (1922) 136, 146; foreign competition, exposure to 50–51; Foreign Direct Investment Program (1968) 61; foreign economic policy, postwar evolution 37–38, 52–64; foreign policy, historical evolution of 31–34; fragmentation of power and authority 44–46; FRUS 192; goals of central decision-makers 38–40; Great Depression 32, 33, 38–39, 147; historical evolution of US foreign economic policy 52–64; Huntington's comparison of Europe with 45; ideological goals 34, 35; ideology and decision making 39–40, 44; initiation of war by 9; institutional behavior of 12; institutional richness of 274; INTELSAT and 13–14; interest and ideology in foreign policy of 28–31; international monetary system 14; international structure, postwar 40–41; international trade, proportion of 137–38; Interstate Commerce Commission 81; intervention by, pattern of 7–8; judicial system 47; LANDSAT 162; liberal commitment in foreign policy 29, 30, 35; liberal trade regime, desire to construct 38–39; Long-Term Cotton Textiles Agreement (1962) 59; monetary policy, decision-making on 47–48, 60–61; national interest and policy making 26–27; National Security Strategy 266–67; neoliberalism of 10, 182, 187–88, 269; neorealism 182; 9/11 attacks on (and aftermath) 8, 18; NSC (National Security Council) 254, 255–56, 267–68; OMB (Office of Management and Budget) 267; opening wedge (1947–62) in foreign economic policy 38, 55–58; path-dependent developments in 104–5; policy goals, rank ordering of 26; political integrity of, protection of 29; political system, relative weakness of 42–48; property rights, distribution of 86; Protection of Diplomats Act (1971) 192; protectionism in 136; Reciprocal Trade Agreements Acts (various dates) 56, 57, 63, 136, 145, 147; Senate 47; shared sovereignty arrangements, postwar establishment of 249; Smoot-Hawley Tariff Act (1931) 136, 146; societal development and state structures in 79–80; society in, power of state relative to 42–44; State Department 37, 46, 239, 255–56; state power and international trade 130, 142, 143, 145, 146–47; *Statistical Abstract* (Census Bureau) 49; strains, external and internal (1970s) in foreign economic policy 38, 61–64; Tariff Act (1897) 46; Trade Act (1951) 47; Trade Act (1974) 38, 46, 47, 63, 64, 147; trade balances 49–52; Trade Expansion Act (1962) 38, 46, 52, 53, 58, 59, 61, 63, 147; Trade Negotiations Committee 47; trade policy of, institutional involvement in 46–47; USAID 258–59, 267, 272–73; Ways and Means Committees 47, 58; weakness of state, domestically 42–48

Uriz, G.H. 250–51
"US Commercial and Monetary Policy" (Krasner, S.D.) 5, 6
Utrecht, Peace of 203
Utrecht, Treaty of 203

Vatican City State 191–92
Vattel, Emmerich de 15, 16, 17, 188, 193–94, 214, 234
Venezuela 239; institutional behavior of 12; intervention by US in 32
Verba, Sidney 85, 95
Vienna, Peace of 203

Vietnam 7, 8, 28, 29, 34, 215, 217, 219
Vietnam War 61; Peace negotiations 192
Vries, T. de 62

Wall Street Journal 62, 64, 82–83
Wallerstein, Immanuel 89, 125
Walt, Stephen 257
Waltz, Kenneth 4, 92, 113–14, 131, 152
Walzer, Michael 96, 124
Wang, G. 216
Wang, Y. 224
WARC (World Administrative Radio
  Conference) 160, 163, 164
Washington, George 264
Washington Center of Foreign Policy
  Research 150
Weber, Max 94, 122, 124, 125
Weil, G.L. 47, 63
Weiler, J.H.H. 188
Weiner, Myron 108
Weinstein, J.M. *et al.* 5
Wendt, A. and Friedheim, D. 185, 196
Wendt, Alexander 2, 11, 95, 185
Westendorp, Carlos 244
Westphalia, Peace of 15–16
Westphalian sovereignty 15, 16–17, 17,
  179, 184, 193–97, 208–9, 210;
  coercion and imposition 205–6, 207;
  compromise under international
  legality 192–93; contracts, consistency
  with 202–3, 204; conventions related
  to 200, 201; domestic sovereignty and
  186; in East Asia 212, 217, 225, 228,
  229, 230; interdependence sovereignty
  and 187–88; international legal
  sovereignty and 180, 181, 182, 185,
  192–93, 210; modalities of compromise
  198–99, 200; sharing sovereignty 234,
  235, 241, 242, 245, 246, 247–48, 249,
  251, 252, 272; sovereign equality vs
  Confucian hierarchy 214; violation of
  183, 200, 204, 207, 209

White Lotus Society 221
Who Governs (Dahl, R.) 69, 70–72
Wilkins, Mira 39, 55, 142
Williamson, Jeffrey G. 187
Williamson, Oliver 103
Wilson, Edward O. 31
Wilson, T. Woodrow 28, 29, 30, 32, 33,
  39; Wilsonianism 38, 40, 55
Windsor, Philip 196
WMD (weapons of mass destruction)
  8, 233, 238–39, 251, 269
Wolff, Christian 194
Wolfowitz, Paul 254
Wood, Nicholas 244
World Bank 38, 53–55, 56, 204, 241,
  244, 265, 266, 268, 271, 273; Chad
  Cameroon Pipeline Project 251;
  International Advisory Group
  250–51; WDI (World Development
  Indicators) 237, 238
*World Development Report 1997: The
  State in a Changing World* (World
  Bank) 241
The World in Depression, 1929–1939
  (Kindleberger, C.) 13, 122–23
Wriston, Walter B. 186
WTO (World Trade Organization) 7,
  11, 14, 65, 189–90

Yeager, L.B. 57, 144, 146, 147, 149
Yi dynasty in Korea 227
Young, Oran 94–95, 117–18, 119,
  123–24, 125–26, 127
Young, Owen D. 147
Yugoslavia 18, 208

Zahariadis, Nikolaos 258–59, 260,
  261
Zegart, Amy 274
Zimbabwe: institutional behaviour
  of 12
Zoellick, Robert W. 268–71

For Product Safety Concerns and Information please contact our EU
representative GPSR@taylorandfrancis.com
Taylor & Francis Verlag GmbH, Kaufingerstraße 24, 80331 München, Germany

www.ingramcontent.com/pod-product-compliance
Lightning Source LLC
Chambersburg PA
CBHW060026030426
42334CB00019B/2200